Lapley

More Radical Hermeneutics

D1212461

Studies in Continental Thought

John Sallis, general editor

Consulting Editors

Robert Bernasconi	William L. McBride
Rudolph Bernet	J. N. Mohanty
John D. Caputo	Mary Rawlinson
David Carr	Tom Rockmore
Edward S. Casey	Calvin O. Schrag
Hubert Dreyfus	†Reiner Schürmann
Don Ihde	Charles E. Scott
David Farrell Krell	Thomas Sheehan
Lenore Langsdorf	Robert Sokolowski
Alphonso Lingis	Bruce W. Wilshire

David Wood

More Radical Hermeneutics

On Not Knowing Who We Are

John D. Caputo

INDIANA UNIVERSITY PRESS

Bloomington and Indianapolis

This book is a publication of

Indiana University Press
601 North Morton Street
Bloomington, IN 47404-3797 USA

http://www.indiana.edu/~iupress

Telephone orders   800-842-6796
Fax orders   812-855-7931
Orders by e-mail   iuporder@indiana.edu

© 2000 by John D. Caputo

All rights reserved

No part of this book may be reproduced or utilized in any
form or by any means, electronic or mechanical, including
photocopying and recording, or by any information storage
and retrieval system, without permission in writing from
the publisher. The Association of American University
Presses' Resolution on Permissions constitutes the only
exception to this prohibition.

The paper used in this publication meets the minimum
requirements of American National Standard for Information Sciences—Permanence of Paper for Printed Library
Materials, ANSI Z39.48-1984.

Manufactured in the United States of America

Library of Congress Cataloging-in-Publication Data

Caputo, John D.
    More radical hermeneutics : on not knowing who we
are / John D. Caputo.
        p.   cm. — (Studies in Continental thought)
    Includes bibliographical references and index.
    ISBN 0-253-33747-X (hardcover : alk. paper) — ISBN
0-253-21387-8 (pbk. : alk. paper)
    1. Hermeneutics. 2. Deconstruction. 3. Philosophy and
religion.   I. Title.   II. Series.

BD241 .C336 2000
121'.68—dc21   99-088428

1 2 3 4 5   05 04 03 02 01 00

To Tom,
For your friendship and your wisdom

Contents

Acknowledgments

In addition to containing previously unpublished studies, the present work makes use of thoroughly revised and expanded versions of some work that has appeared elsewhere. Permission to use the following previously published materials is gratefully acknowledged.

Chapter 1 is a lightly edited version of "On Not Knowing Who We Are: Madness, Hermeneutics, and the Night of Truth," in *Foucault and the Critique of Institutions,* ed. John D. Caputo and Mark Yount (University Park: Pennsylvania State University Press, 1993), pp. 233–262.

Portions of chapter 3 have appeared in "Who is Derrida's Zarathustra? Of Fraternity, Friendship, and a Democracy to Come," *Research in Phenomenology* 29 (1999): 184–199.

Most of the first half of chapter 4 first appeared as "In Search of the Quasi-Transcendental: The Case of Derrida and Rorty," in *Working through Derrida,* ed. Gary Madison (Evanston, Ill.: Northwestern University Press, 1993), pp. 147–169.

Most of chapter 5 first appeared as "Dreaming of the Innumerable: Derrida, Drucilla Cornell, and the Dance of Gender," in *Derrida and Feminism: Recasting the Question of Woman,* ed. Ellen Feder, Mary C. Rawlinson, and Emily Zakin (New York: Routledge, 1997), pp. 141–160.

About half of chapter 6 first appeared as "Heidegger's Philosophy of Science," in *Rationality, Relativism, and the Human Sciences,* ed. J. Margolis (The Hague: Nijhoff, 1986), pp. 43–60.

Most of chapter 7 first appeared as "The End of Ethics," in *Blackwell Studies in Ethics,* ed. Hugh Follette (Oxford: Blackwell Publishers, forthcoming).

Chapter 8 is an entirely revised and expanded version of a piece that first appeared as "Bedeviling the Tradition: Deconstruction and Catholicism," in *(Dis)continuity and (De)construction: Reflections on the Meaning of the Past in Crisis Situations,* ed. Josef Wissink (Kampen, The Netherlands: Pharos, 1995), pp. 12–35.

Chapter 9 is a thoroughly revised and expanded version of a piece that first appeared as "Radical Hermeneutics and Religious Truth: The Case of Sheehan and Schillebeeckx," in *Phenomenology of the Truth Proper to Religion,* ed. Daniel Guerrière (Albany: SUNY Press, 1990), pp. 146–172.

Chapter 10 is a completely revised and expanded version of a piece that first appeared as "Mysticism and Transgression: Derrida and Meister Eckhart," in *Continental Philosophy,* vol. 2, ed. Hugh Silverman (New York: Routledge, 1989), pp. 24–39.

Introduction

Hermeneutics and the Secret

"... writing in the passion of non-knowledge rather than of the secret."

"I am all for knowledge [laughter]. . . . So, this non-knowing . . . it is not
the limit . . . of a knowledge, the limit in the progression of a knowledge. It
is, in some way, a structural non-knowing, which is heterogeneous, foreign
to knowledge. It's not just the unknown that could be known and that I
give up trying to know. It is something in relation to which knowledge is
out of the question. And when I specify that it is a non-knowing and not a
secret, I mean that when a text appears to be crypted, it is not at all in
order to calculate or to intrigue or to bar access to something that I know
and that others must not know; it is a more ancient, more originary
experience, if you will, of the secret."

"It is perhaps there that we find the secret of secrecy, namely, that it is not
a matter of knowing and that it is there for no-one."

"[We] are *au secret,* as we say in French, and 'in the secret,' which does not
mean we know anything."

—Jacques Derrida[1]

The claim that circulates throughout this book, which is more of a confession than a claim, is that we are not (as far as we know) born into
this world hard-wired to Being Itself, or Truth Itself, or the Good Itself,
that we are not vessels of a Divine or World-Historical super-force that
has chosen us as its earthly instruments, and that, when we open our
mouths, it is we who speak, not something Bigger and Better than we.
We have not been given privileged access to The Secret, to some big capitalized know-it-all Secret, not as far we know. (If we have, it has been
kept secret from me.) The secret is, there is no Secret, no such access to
The Secret, which is what Jacques Derrida means by the *absolute* secret,
or a more originary experience of the secret. The absolute secret keeps
things safely secreted away, not passingly but in principle, due neither to
mischievousness on its part nor to a failure on our part to try hard enough
to crack it. It is just not anything we are going to get to know; it is not
even a matter of knowing.

The absolute secret is to be differentiated from the conditional, relative, garden-variety secrets that we all keep from one another and sometimes even from ourselves, and that could, in principle and under spec-
ified conditions, be revealed, like the secrets clients share with their
lawyers or that spies steal from the government.[2] For the absolute and

unconditional secret will never be cracked or disclosed, not under any conditions, not without shedding these mortal coils (and maybe not even then). The absolute secret means that there is no privileged access to what the philosophers call *die Sache selbst, la même chose,* the *rerum natura,* or the way things are *kath'auto.* There is no royal road that some philosopher's Method or divine Revelation will open to us, if only we obey its methodological strictures, or pray and fast, or learn how to run Windows 2000. The absolute secret means that we all pull on our pants one leg at a time, doing the best we can to make it through the day, without any Divine or Metaphysical Hooks to hoist us over the abyss. The absolute secret means we are not tuned into something "calling to us like a mystic voice from a better world: 'here is the truth,'" as Edmund Husserl puts it,[3] which means we must have the good sense to know our limits, not to inflate our conclusions, and not to put too high a polish on our principles.

But this is not all bad news and I am not complaining. For if by being in on The Secret one can lie and cheat and acquire an unfair power over others,[4] then that means the absolute secret can keep us safe. Whatever difficulty and discomfiture the absolute and more originary secret causes us, and that I do not deny, it is on the whole a saving and salutary thing to be "in the secret—which does not mean we know anything." It is this absolute secret that no one knows, and that is not a matter of knowing, that impassions hermeneutics and drives hermeneutics on. It is the absolute and unconditional secret, this structural blindness, that *radicalizes* hermeneutics, to pick up an argument I made a few years ago that I wish to continue in the present study.[5]

For Derrida, of course, hermeneutics is always a "mistake," the mistake of trying to "arrest the text in a certain position, thus settling on a thesis, meaning, or truth."[6] Derrida thinks that hermeneutics seeks to decode The Meaning, to break through the play of signs to the Meaning of the Author who gives meaning to the signs he uses, to find The Truth behind the surface of the sign. Derrida thinks hermeneutics is searching for The Secret that sits silently behind the text, like Husserl's pre-expressive *Sinn* silently awaiting a *Bedeutung* and an indicative sign to escort it into the world. But if Derrida can distinguish The Secret from a *more originary* experience of the secret, then it is only fair that I be allowed to distinguish hermeneutics from a more originary experience of hermeneutics, or what I like to call a "more radical hermeneutics," which signifies the situation we find ourselves in once we have given up the dream of pure *Sinn* and accepted our consignment to signs and the multiple play of meanings, in the plural. In displacing the rule of Meaning, I confess or affirm a multiplicity or profusion of meanings, of too many meanings, through which and among which we have to sort our way.

That is why I have always taken a devilish delight in trying to run together hermeneutics and deconstruction, letting deconstruction hound and harass hermeneutics (for its own good, you understand). The result is a child whom Derrida would never admit to fathering, a happy enough little prankster but quite a funny-looking little thing, which Derrida might at best call a hermeneutics *without* hermeneutics (but remember that the *sans* is never reducible to a simple negation). This more radical hermeneutics signs on to the idea of reading that Derrida has in mind when he says that "the readability of the text is structured by the unreadability of the secret, that is, by the inaccessibility of a certain intention, meaning, or of a wanting to say"[7] that lies beneath the surface of the text. Derrida rejects the idea that if we could just have fifteen minutes with the real William Shakespeare, in person, or better yet, with the real Prince Hamlet, we could find The Answer and spare legions of literary critics a lot of time and paper! "Literature" is the exemplary secret for Derrida, just because we are there deprived, absolutely and paradigmatically, of the luxury of laying aside the text and taking a peek around the curtain of signs to see what is really going on. In the hermeneutics that issues from confessing to the absolute or unconditional secret, things are always like that, not only in literature, but also, *mutatis mutandis,* in ethics, politics, science, or theology, where everything depends upon our skill in working out all the mutations and mutabilities in the *mutatis mutandis.*

In the present study, I call upon the "absolute secret" to serve as the hound of hermeneutics, somewhat the way I used "repetition" to harass hermeneutics in *Radical Hermeneutics.* If repetition or iterability gave us radical hermeneutics in the first place, let us say that the absolute secret issues in *more* radical hermeneutics, in more of it, *encore* or *noch einmal* (and there can never be enough!), as also in a *more radical* hermeneutics, in the comparative case. For me hermeneutics simply means the necessity of interpretation. Accordingly, hermeneutics properly hounded and harassed by deconstruction, a more radical hermeneutics, means that the necessity of interpretation is driven by the absolute secret. The structural non-knowing, "blindness," or unreadability by which we are beset in virtue of the absolute secret is what gives us passion. We are driven by the passion of non-knowing. Our readings and interpretations, our rereadings and conflicting interpretations, are like so many fingers clinging tenaciously to the edge of the cliff. Instead of arresting the play of meaning, a more radical or more originary experience of hermeneutics faces up to the inescapable play of interpretation, which is all we have to hang on to as our feet dangle dangerously over the rushing rapids below.

Think of radical hermeneutics as a kind of intellectual fire department that arrives on the scene to douse the flames of essentialism wherever they flare up and threaten to consume us. By "essentialism" I mean the various claims to be *in on* The Secret and thereby to have surpassed the limits of offering a mere mortal interpretation. Thus, against the metaphysicians and transcendentalists who claim to have made a deduction or reduction of or to The Secret, the radical hermeneutic comeback is that the dust of factical life clings fast to our feet. Against the mystics, who claim to have been Visited by The Secret, that whatever it is that has overtaken them and left them speechless (never fear!) still requires interpretation. In general, toward all comers who come proclaiming that they have found the way (The Way) around the difficulties of factical life, we radical hermeneuts assume the most dubious and disapproving countenance.

That is just a way of saying that radical hermeneutics is a coat cut to fit what Johannes Climacus calls "poor existing individuals," the folks who need to make their way through the ups and downs of factical life. There is surely something perverse about saying, as Husserl does, that "the particular fact is irrational."[8] Yet that is exactly what philosophers in general tend to think. The fact in all its "facticity," that is, in all its particularity as a fact, can be relieved of its irrationality only by being stripped of what is proper to it and lifted up into the heavens of *eidos*, essence or universality. But since the particular fact, the factical, is what actually exists, while the existence of the universal is a matter of considerable debate, this universality brings with it the disadvantage that philosophy tends thereby to set reason at odds with what exists and to take the side of something whose existence is debatable. That is why Climacus says that, given the choice between existence and philosophy, he would take his stand with existence, thank you very much. He would dedicate all his work as an author to serving the cause of the poor existing individual, even while speculative philosophy cuts ever higher and headier circles in the sky. Taking one's stand with such folks has always made more sense to me, and thus has always embodied a more sensible idea of reason, indeed, a way of bringing reason to its senses, constituting what we call in American English "horse sense," which may be a hitherto unnoticed and untapped paradigm for the *animal rationale*.

Knowing full well that the crown of philosophical knowledge tends to rest upon the head of what does not exist, I will, nonetheless, follow my hero Climacus and take my stand on the dense plain of existence, *hier stehe ich, ich kann nicht anders,* where the woods are lovely, dark, and deep. Accordingly, I take my point of departure in the present study from the following modest hypothesis (or open confession): if philosophical knowledge tends to soar high above the plains of existence, leaving the rest of us to face the worst,[9] then I hope to get the best results from confessing that we existing individuals here below do not know who we are, having been abandoned by philosophy up above. This should take the form, however, of a *common* confession, since the whole idea is to avoid setting up a hierarchy of those who know and those who do not, which would only serve to clear the way for someone who claims to know it all.

❈-❈-❈

Part 1: On Not Knowing Who We Are. I have taken my lead in this study from an essay on Michel Foucault that I wrote a few years ago, entitled

"On Not Knowing Who We Are," which is the lead essay of the present collection (chapter 1). There, following James Bernauer, I argue that there is a kind of negative or apophatic hermeneutics at work in Foucault, a hermeneutics of non-knowing that puts any claim to know the nature or determine the essence of human being into question. This non-knowing or *"anthropologia negativa"* explains Foucault's deep disquiet with any attempt to consolidate the way we are presently constituted, to canonize and institutionalize the present order. But it also feeds a certain hope—contra Richard Rorty, who thinks that there is no room for hope at all in Foucault—for something *else*, a certain passion for being *otherwise*, even if that other form of being or passion is not a positive or normative ideal. This apophatic hermeneutics links up with what I call in *The Prayers and Tears of Jacques Derrida* a "generalized apophatics," where I argue that mystical unknowing could serve a more general model, by putting us on guard whenever the eagle of philosophical knowledge hovers over us, its claws outstretched, claiming to grasp the Essence of this or that, of men or women, of nature or history, of God or world, of you or me.[10]

The perverse idea behind this prankster enterprise is to think of knowledge—which we are all for, understand—as building walls of identity around what happens, trying to set tolerances for the future, always trying to immure the future. If you think of knowledge as destiny or fate, then non-knowing starts to look better. Thus, the hypothesis, both impudent and timid, that wends its way through these studies is that we do not "Know" ourselves or one another, that we do not "Know" the world or God, in some Deep and Capitalized way that yields the capitalized Secret. *That,* if anything, is *who we are,* the ones who do not know who they are, and whose lives are impassioned by the passion of that non-knowing. We are, just as Parmenides complained, two-headed and errant (some days more than others). We lack a grasp on things that will really hold up, one that has teeth enough to cut through every "appearance" to some "Reality" behind appearances, which is what it would be like to know The Secret. What we know, as Socrates insisted, is that we do not know, and that is the beginning of wisdom. That Socratic, Kierkegaardian, and Derridean knowledge, that passion of non-knowledge, that structural blindness, I argue throughout, is the most salutary form knowledge can take. I do not deny that some days this non-knowing drives us hermeneuts into the ditch, but the idea is to climb back out, dust yourself off, and try again.

I insist that "I am all for knowledge [laughter]"—we can all hear the laughter—all for acquiring as much determinate knowledge as possible about our condition, about our multiple and varied conditions, all for the most searching and researching investigations, into anything and everything, where nothing is off-limits, nothing banned from discussion, or beyond question. Were it up to me everybody would be given an immediate sabbatical and full funding for three years of research! But my contention is that the more we learn about ourselves, about our several histories, traditions, languages, and cultures, about the multiple ways in which human lives are constituted, the more we will conclude that, in the face of such polymorphic, prolific, and positively dizzying diversity, our best bet is to put our shoulders to the cart of a kind of felicitous nominalism, a happy, anti-essentialist open-endedness. Our best bet is to say, yes, yes, and amen to the prudent wisdom of the absolute secret, to a happy minimalism about who we think we are, or who others are, or what history or nature or sexuality is, or who God is.

That minimalism will maximize the possibilities and keep the door open to results that have not come in yet; it will multiply the opportunities for what Derrida calls *l'inventions de l'autre,* the incomings of something we did not see coming.[11] Proceeding *"sans voir, sans avoir, sans savoir,"*[12] without seeing, savvy, or seizing hold of things (loosely translated), affirming a certain kind of structural blindness, will, contrary to what we might expect, keep us open to innumerable mutations and unforeseeable possibilities, to incalculable ways of being and knowing, doing and seeing, exposed to potentialities of which we cannot presently conceive, to things improbable and incomprehensible, unimaginable and unplannable. What better outcome for a minimalist then to find oneself, as Derrida says, "dreaming of the innumerable" and *the* impossible. So when I say I take my stand with poor existing individuals, I have no intention of cutting off our prayers and tears for *the* impossible, which *does not exist.* On the contrary, prayers and tears for what does not exist (yet) are what this non-knowing existence is all about.

Consider how blindness and non-knowledge are the condition of the future, for example. A real, robust future, one that brings about something truly different, depends precisely upon *not knowing* or being able to predict that it was coming. When something new, something utterly different, happens, that is precisely what none of us saw coming, something that was unforeseeable and unknowable. The future we can all more or less foresee and predict is thin and weak and timid, hardly a future at all, a plannable, programmable, predictable "future present" where it is mostly a matter of waiting for or maybe even working hard to make the future to roll around. If, on looking back, we see that our whole life has been made up of such future presents, we will conclude that, on the whole, life has passed us by.

But I insist that this non-essentialism is not bad news, and that I have come to pipe, not mourn. The absolute secret is something salutary and saving, a positively evangelical proclamation (which means good news) of the inescapability of interpretation, of the necessity to find our way as best we can, to invent and discover, to imagine and dream, to pray and weep for ways to be that are yet to come. The absolute secret is what sees to it that no word is ever Final, no Story ever all comprehensive, that we are all in this together, doing the best we can to make it through the day. This may make us sound more like the prisoners construing the shadows on the wall of the cave rather than those who get to ascend to the upper world, a little more like being stuck in the mud of the *khôra* than being bathed in the light of the *agathon,* except that that is too downbeat and dualistic a version of my non-essentialism to be the whole story. If the truth be told, we poor existing individuals pass our days reading between the lines, learning to make our way in this region of dissimilitude where no rule or method has yet trod or shown the way. We live for the most part in the in-between world that philosophy tends to leave behind, and learn to cope with shifting and elusive traces in the sand. But that is the condition of our inventiveness, for it keeps the police of The Secret off our back (the advocates of The Secret usually keep a fully staffed and well-armed Secret Police).

That is why the work of Rorty's pragmatic and upbeat, democratic and, as I call it, "Yankee" hermeneutics plays an important role in what follows. For Rorty has given up on the classical metaphysical idea of philosophy as a kind of super-science that cuts through the soft surface of appearances and hits the hard rock of Reality, even as he has given up on the modern and transcendental idea of philosophy as a science of science, a higher meta-scientific tribunal before which the several sciences present their disparate findings for adjudication. So Rorty is to be included in my catalogue of the masters of non-knowing, a friend of the "poor existing individuals," a hero for those of us who think that we get the best results by disavowing any claims to any secret *savoir absolue.*

I have found it particularly fruitful to bring Rorty's work together with that of Derrida, in whom Rorty—to the scandal of his Anglo-American colleagues and to my immense delight—has shown a great deal of respectful interest. The confrontation of Derrida and Rorty underlies two central issues that are important to this felicitous nominalism and minimalistic hermeneutics. First, it raises the problem of the uncircumventability of having *some account* of how or why we have given up on giving a *Final Account* of things, which is the problem of what Derrida calls the "quasi-transcendental"; this plays a crucial role for Derrida, while Rorty shrugs it off as just one more useless philosophical gimmick. Rorty is worried, and this is a good worry, that when all is said and done Derrida, too, thinks he has found The Secret and its name is the non-name of *différance.* Second, it introduces the problem of the commitment to democratic politics, which Rorty, Derrida, and most of us share: very much against the inclinations of Derrida, Rorty would say democracy is a matter of widening the scope of the "we" and of "achieving our country," while Derrida, who cannot quite bring himself to use the word "community," would resolutely resist such formulations (chapter 4).

The reason for Derrida's disagreement with Rorty on this second point, concerning the "we" and the "our country," has to do with the irreducible primacy of the "other" in Derrida, while Rorty thinks that the academic left has already worked this idea half to death and we need to get on with the business of organizing more labor unions. For Derrida, the other is the one who comes to us from on high, from a region to which we have no access, which is why Emmanuel Levinas speaks of the "wholly other," *tout autre:* the other sits in the spot we can never occupy, speaks from the point of view we cannot inhabit, presides over a secret we cannot share. For Rorty, the *tout autre* is a useless mystification. Consequently, rather than focusing on the "we," Derrida is more interested in the other who interrupts the "we," and rather than focusing on "our country" he is more interested in the immigrant and foreigner who requires admittance and *hospitality* in "our country." For Derrida, "we" are always the ones who cannot quite say "we" and who are never self-identically ourselves. For Derrida, the other "appears without appearing, without being submitted to the phenomenological law of the originary and intuitive given that governs all other appearances, all other phenomenality *as such.*"[13] That means that the absolute secret, the structural non-knowing, enters into and is the condition of the *other,* of the respect for the other who is always beyond our grasp, safe on a shore we will never reach. That is why I take up the *Politics of Friendship,* where Derrida, following Maurice Blanchot, pursues the paradoxical hypothesis that friendship is not a matter of the intimacy of shared secrets or the deep knowledge that friends have of each other, but that friendship too constitutes a relation that exceeds knowledge (chapter 3).

That is also why I return to the question of Derrida and Hans-Georg Gadamer, with whom, along with Paul Ricoeur, we most associate the word "hermeneutics." I am not interested in a wholesale critique of Gadamer, to whom I owe too much, but in pushing his hermeneutics a step further, into a more radical hermeneutic, and this by means of passing it through the passion for the impossible, the passion of the secret and of non-knowledge, that I take from Derrida. But I also see Gadamer and Derrida coming together on the issue of the hermeneutics of friendship—a point thoroughly obscured by their earlier exchange—which respects the alterity of the other. I will work this out by posing to Gadamer—whom I want to treat with a gentler hand in this volume than he received the first time around in *Radical Hermeneutics* (RH, 108ff.)—and to Derrida a similar aporia: how to prepare for the coming of the other? How to prepare for the one for whom one precisely cannot be prepared? (chapter 2)

Part 2: Passions of Non-Knowledge. In the second section of the book, I take up three specific and pointed instances—gender, science, and ethics—where the passion of non-knowledge is put to work so as to produce not confusion but an opening. If Derrida documents the centrality of the model of the "brother" in mainstream Western thinking on friendship, democracy, and religion—all of which turn on such models as "brotherly love," "sons of God," and "fellowship"—then where is the sister? What voice do women have in true friendship? In the polis? How do women count in a democracy, where counting is supposed to be important? That is why I open this section by studying the dance of gender, of "choreographies," by which Derrida means the invention of new steps of the dance, new "gender-bending" moves that open up hitherto unsuspected possibilities outside the prison walls of "masculine" and "feminine" by which we are all confined. I do this in connection with the thought of American feminist and legal theorist Drucilla Cornell, who has put deconstruction to work in a particularly felicitous way in feminist legal theory. Nowhere, I argue, does the claim to "know" The Secret of what is "natural" in human affairs exclude more possibilities, close off more openings, than in the area of gender (chapter 5).

However, the felicitous non-essentialist distance we maintain from some super essential Secret throughout this book seems to run up against its limit when we turn to the natural sciences and ethics. They mean business and are not content to look piously toward heaven and sigh that they do not know The Secret. For in the sciences, where they are hard at work on completing the human genome project and developing a theory of everything (The Secret of everything), we poor existing individuals do indeed seem to be getting some things right. In chapter 6, I argue that while it is a source of considerable intellectual embarrassment that continentalists have had so little of use to say about the natural sciences, easily the most astonishing intellectual achievement of our times, it would also be a mistake to let the success of scientific knowledge, the result of much hard work and acumen, stampede us out of hermeneutics into essentialism, which is what happened in modernity. The main thing of which to be wary, I am always claiming, is Capitalization, the assertion that we are so good at this or that, be it physics or theology, that we can cut through appearances to some sort of Capitalized Something or Other that makes the world we live in look like a veil of appearances. Alan Sokal has recently found a profitable new career in bashing French intellectuals— using the ploy of a "Transformative Hermeneutics" no less—for their mistreatment of science.[14] But I want to argue, instead, that science depends upon taking a hermeneutic turn, upon gaining an angle of entry onto the phenomena, adopting a revisable construction, which is at its most interesting just at that point where the rules begin to tremble and no method has yet shown the way, the point of taking a fresh cut into the things themselves, which is also and precisely the point of scientific invention or discovery.

By the same token, in ethics, what is required in a world overrun by violence is not a confession of ignorance, it would seem, but *direction*. Otherwise, the deluge. By "the end of ethics" (chapter 7) I mean the end (cessation) of overly prescriptive ethical accounts which claim to know The Secret of human behavior, which think it possible to program praxis, to erect guardrails around action, to draw maps, to write the manuals

that will keep us all safe and tell us all who to be. In its place, I would
speak of another end of ethics, in the sense of another *telos,* another point
or purpose of ethics, which is to maximize and optimize the possibilities
of human flourishing and minimize violence, by allowing for the invention of new forms and the coming of things we have not foreseen. This
essay was originally written as part of a "guide to ethical theory," and in
it I argue that such guides work best for the regularized and routinized
"decisions" which are hardly decisions at all, for choices that are programmable and decidable enough to serve as textbook "cases." Such decisions are so predictable that they actually make it into handbooks that
are supposed to guide the lives of poor existing individuals. But as soon
as something *new* or *different* happens in existence, ethical theory is left
speechless, at least until the ethics manual writers gather at their next
conference on ethical theory. There, after lengthy speeches, they conclude that our rules can in fact be made to cover this new turn of events,
heartily agreeing in the hotel bar that evening that they should all have
been able to see it coming, and that they should not all have panicked
and embarrassed themselves publicly.

Part 3: On the Road to Emmaus. In the final section of the book, this
prankster undertaking becomes downright devilish and I end up defending what I call a "devilish hermeneutics," that non-knowing and the absolute secret keep us safe even when it comes to God and religious faith,
whereas a holier hermeneutics, which thinks that God has whispered in
our ear, makes me nervous. This is another test case for me, because what
else does "divine revelation" mean than that something has dropped out
of the sky and revealed The Secret that we could not come up with on
our own? But my interest here is to keep faith safe from knowledge,
which also means to keep faith alive as *faith.* For faith is most truly faith
when it hits that point where it is *not* supported and sustained by knowledge, where we find ourselves pushing ahead mainly on faith, driven by
the passion of non-knowledge, with what St. Paul calls a "hope against
hope" (Romans 4:18). By the same token, what greater threat is there to
faith than to allow the passion of faith to be confused with the security of
knowledge, so that instead of seeing with the eyes of faith, the faithful
begin to see things period! Then they begin to believe that they know in
virtue of a higher knowledge. That is when the faithful become a danger
to everyone *else,* which is the problem of religious fundamentalism today,
which threatens the structure of democratic institutions in the United
States and makes life in the Middle East insufferably dangerous. Whence
the need for a devil's advocate, which is a venerable theological function.

The necessity for a devilish hermeneutics holds above all for the "religions of the Book," where everything turns on reading. In two essays on
scriptural hermeneutics (chapters 8, 9), I follow a hint provided by the
post-Easter story of Jesus meeting up with the two disciples on the road
to Emmaus, which is the one text in the New Testament to use the verb

hermeneuein. I argue that at this crucial juncture for the new "Jesus move-ment," which was forged and formed precisely in the face of an empty tomb, what was *required* was hermeneutics. The skies did not open up for the two disciples, the heavens did not announce that this was Jesus, the sun did not go dark. No pure given was lowered on a cloud. Instead, Jesus took up the Scriptures and offered the disciples a *hermeneutic* of how the coming of the Messiah can be found in the Book, if you know how to read. One has to have a certain amount of patience with the sluggishness of the disciples—read: "us"—for it is a complicated Book and an empty tomb is a polyvalent thing. Then, just when they finally got it, Jesus *dis-appeared* from their view, the assumption being that, given their new hermeneutic skills, they would be able to make it in his absence on faith and reading. They would know how to read the scriptures and the empty tomb, without his visible presence to sustain them.

In the final essay in this collection (chapter 10), I take up my beloved Meister Eckhart's famous prayer, "I pray God to rid me of God." I claim that in the end, this more radical hermeneutics is always a matter of pray-ing and weeping, which means, in my regard, praying like the devil and hanging on by a prayer. Mystical theology is always a paradigm for me, whose import is to raise our level of vigilance, to watch and pray, to be permanently on the alert against setting the effects of *différance* upon the altar of the things themselves (be they perceptual, scientific, or theologi-cal) and then falling down in worship. "I pray God that he may make me free of God" is Meister Eckhart's perpetual prayer to keep the discourse on God open and free of idols. That, I claim, has a felicitous generalizabi-lity: I pray God to rid me of these gods (read: science, religion, econom-ics, art, ethics, etc.). I am willing to say that this entire more radical her-meneutics is a long and weepy prayer to lead us not into closure lest we close off everybody else, lead us not into turning the latest effects of *dif-férance* into idols. Because we desire presence and to arrest the play, we can hardly resist building an altar to produced effects, to the golden calf of nominal and presumptive unities. So, with Meister Eckhart, I pray God to rid me of "God," that is, not in order to dance on the grave of the dead God, but to keep the future open, including the future of God with us. This will involve addressing the question of mystical silence, which is another way to lay claim to The Secret by passing itself off as an escape from language into a mystical *hors-texte.* But mystical silence, I will argue, is in fact an operation within language, of textuality and *écriture,* that is captured magnificently in Eckhart's beautiful prayer. Far from contra-dicting our devilish insistence upon *écriture* and *différance,* upon textuality and hermeneutical readings, mystical prayer speaks on their behalf and calls upon all their discursive resources. Far from leaving us speechless, this mystical experience of something I know not what leaves us scram-bling for words in which to say what is happening to us, interpretation being here as inescapable as ever.

Conclusion without Conclusion. Throughout this study, I cling steadfastly to Husserl's "principle of all principles," to stick to what is given just insofar as it is given, which has always meant for me a minimalistic injunction *not* to put a more sanguine gloss on things than they warrant. I have always been both braced and terrified by Friedrich Nietzsche's demand to take the truth straight up, forgoing the need to have it "attenuated, veiled, sweetened, blunted and falsified."[15] I readily confess that we have not been handpicked to be Being's or God's mouthpiece, that it is always necessary to get a reading, even if (and precisely because) the reading is there is no Reading, no final or game-ending Meaning, no decisive and sweeping Story that wraps things up. Even if the secret is, there is no Secret. We do not know who we are—that is who we are.

There is no more brilliant encapsulation of the radicality of the fix in which we poor existing individuals find ourselves, we who do not know who we are and are thereby driven to a prankster hermeneutics, than the magnificent objection voiced by "the young man" in Constantine Constantius's *Repetition*, who, upon finding himself already in the world, complained that he had not been consulted.[16]

> Where am I? What does it mean to say: the world? What is the meaning of that word? Who tricked me into this whole thing and leaves me standing here? Who am I? How did I get into the world? Why was I not asked about it, why was I not informed of the rules and the regulations but just thrust into the ranks? . . . And if I am compelled to be involved, where is the manager—I have something to say about this. Is there no manager? To whom shall I make my complaint?

That is a complaint that goes to the root of the radical hermeneutical situation, that says it all, and more. In it, the whole tragic-comic conundrum of life and death is encapsulated, a stunningly profound and unnerving joke, which leaves us laughing through our tears—and praying like mad.

A more radical hermeneutic does not mean some fanciful ability to make a clear, clean, or absolute start, to get back to some imaginary zero degree and to begin anew from there, which is the dream of idealists from Plato to G. W. F. Hegel, from René Descartes to Husserl, of philosophers from time immemorial. Rather, it confesses the necessity we are under to construe the traces, to follow tracks, to read signs. The hermeneutical situation means that we are up to our ears in historical, political, social, religious, sexual, and who knows what other sorts of structures and networks, saturated by them, radically saturated, which is, of course, another way of saying that we are all wet and not too sure that we know what is what. To employ one of Derrida's tropes—and it is the spirit and specter of Jacques Derrida that hovers over the hermeneutics that follow, feeding it lines from offstage—the more radical hermeneutical situation refers to the glue of *glas* that sticks to our fingers every time we start to make a fresh start.

Every time some astute-looking fellow rises to his feet to proclaim that he has surmounted the constraints of our condition and that he wishes, with all due modesty, to announce the discovery of The Secret—of an absolute starting point, an uninterpreted fact of the matter, a pure given, or any other kind of unconditional something or other—the solemnity of the occasion is invariably compromised. In this case, the audience notices to its horror that the chair from which the Herr Professor arose to address this august assembly is still sticking to his pants.

Part 1

On Not Knowing Who We Are

Toward a Felicitous Non-Essentialism

1

On Not Knowing Who We Are

*Madness, Hermeneutics, and the Night of
Truth in Foucault*

In this essay, which I take as the point of departure for the present study, from which indeed the whole has drawn its name, I argue that Michel Foucault's thought is best construed as a hermeneutics of *not knowing* who we are. I construe Foucault's work to operate according to what Jacques Derrida calls the logic of the *sans*. That means that we get the best results by proceeding *sans voir, sans avoir, sans savoir,* without sight, without savvy, and without seizing hold of what we love. This is a bit of a perversity, turning as it does, not on uncovering the truth or illuminating us, which is the standard hope philosophers hold out to us, but on living with the untruth, with what early on Foucault calls the "night of truth." The night of truth is the truth that there is no capitalized Truth, no "truth of truth." In the spirit of a certain Saint Augustine, I read Foucault as if he were engaged in a confessional practice, making a confession in writing, *confiteri in letteris,* that from the start, as Derrida says, the secret is there is no Secret. For there is no way around the beliefs and practices in which we are steeped, by which we are shaped from time out of mind. I see Foucault's work as very circum-fessional, confessing that we are all circumcised, cut off from the heart of unconcealed truth, but this without nostalgia, without concluding—as Richard Rorty attributes to him[1]—that we are thereby lost and have no grounds for hope at all.

So contrary to the received view of Hubert Dreyfus and Paul Rabinow,[2] according to whom Foucault's thought moves "beyond hermeneutics," I would rather say it moves beyond a certain "tragic" hermeneutics toward a more radical one, toward what I will call here a "hermeneutics of re-fusal." Foucault as I see him rejects a hermeneutics of "identity" in favor of a hermeneutics of "difference," negates an assured and positive hermeneutics in order to affirm joyously and positively a *hermeneutica negativa.* I will take my point of departure from Foucault's early writings on madness, although I am also clearly interested in confessions, and so in what he says later on about Christian "confessional techniques." At the end I will attempt to push out beyond Foucault, to a Foucault without Foucault, in keeping with this logic of the *sans,* by addressing the question of what I will call the "healing gestures" that should accompany all confession. Those who, like us, confess the humility of our condition should not be left to shiver through the night of truth all alone. I push forward in a direction that, while Foucault did not take it, is perhaps suggested by him, is one of the potencies of his thought, belonging to the wake of his passing ship, in which we push past a hermeneutics of refusal to one of response and redress.[3]

Tragic Hermeneutics: Madness and the Night of Truth

In his earliest writings on "mental illness" (*maladie*), Foucault drew a fascinating portrait of *déraison*—"unreason," the failing or giving way of reason—"before" it was interned and reduced to silence. By the nineteenth century, unreason had been constituted as "mental illness," an object for the "psychology of madness" (*folie*), which overwhelmed madness simultaneously with the external force of internment and the internal force of moralizing. The effect of this psychology was to foreshorten "the experience of Unreason," an experience in which, Foucault says, "[w]estern man encountered the night of his truth and its absolute challenge," which once was and still is "the mode of access to the natural truth of man."[4]

What Foucault had in mind at that time might be described as a "destruction of the history of psychology" that parallels Martin Heidegger's project of a "destruction of the history of ontology" in §6 of *Being and Time*.[5] Were psychology to reflect on itself, it would effect a kind of *Destruktion* that would constitute at the same time a *retrieval* of a more essential truth. It would suffer a kind of auto-deconstruction, coming under the scrutiny of its own eye. That is because psychology is the alienated truth of madness, the truth in a "derisory" or alienated form that precisely on that account harbors within itself and maintains contacts with something "essential." While deriding madness under the hypocritical veil of moralizing internment, psychology "cannot fail to move toward the essential," toward that originary point from which it itself arises as a science, namely, "those regions in which man has a relation with himself."

> If carried back to its roots, the psychology of madness would appear to be
> . . . the destruction of psychology itself and the discovery of that essential,
> non-psychological because non-moralizable relation that is the relation between Reason and Unreason. (MIP, 74)

Beneath its moralization by the humanist reformers—viewing madness as somehow a moral failing, an effect of ill will—lies its more essential truth. Psychology cannot master the truth of madness because the truth of madness is the soil from which psychology springs, the prior, anterior sphere of unconcealment of which it is itself the alienating, scientific derivative. Madness is the founding experience from which psychology derives, from the distortion of which it itself arises. Occasionally, Foucault points out, the founding, originary experiences of madness do find a voice—in such artists as Friedrich Hölderlin, Gerard de Nerval,

Raymond Roussel, and Antonin Artaud—and "that holds out the promise to man that one day, perhaps, he will be able to be free of all psychology and be ready for the great tragic confrontation with madness" (MIP, 75). Lying prior to the scientific truth of psychology, the poetic experience of the truth of madness represents a more radical unconcealment of madness.

"Mental illness" is "alienated madness," madness in an alienated form. The aim of Foucault's work at this point is to bring us "face to face" with madness in its unalienated truth, to let it speak in its own voice, which is not the voice of reason or science, to regain "madness freed and disalienated, restored in some sense to its original language" (MIP, 76). But what can this original experience be? What would unreason say were its voice restored? What is the truth of madness, the truth that madness knows but we have silenced? Madness is "difference," extreme, disturbing difference, inhabiting a "void." The Renaissance took the "risk" of exposing itself to this void. It let itself be put into question by madness, without shutting madness away. It allowed itself to be invaded by the "Other," the "insane." It allowed the familiar, the *heimlich*, to be invaded by the strange and *unheimlich*. It allowed reason to be tested by unreason: "it thought itself wise and it was mad; it thought it knew and it knew nothing" (MIP, 77). But in the seventeenth century there began what Foucault describes as "the negative appraisal of what had been originally apprehended as the Different, the Insane, Unreason" (MIP, 78).

So we have in the last two hundred years constituted *homo psychologicus*, the object of psychological science. Psychological man is a substitute that puts in the place of man's "relation to the truth" (MIP, 87) the assumption that psychological man is himself "the truth of the truth." By this Foucault means that the "real"—let us say "cold"—truth of our divided condition is explained away and forgotten by the "truth" of psychological science and its purportedly scientific explanations of an inner mental pathology. But the truth of truth, the truth of psychology arrives too late, only after madness in its truth has been closed off. Indeed, psychology itself is constituted as a science only on the basis of having closed off madness and turned it into a phantom of itself. Psychological truth is a way of forgetting the truth and reducing it to silence. Foucault refers to this truth that psychology allows us to forget, and that can be recognized in the modern world only in "lightning flashes" with names like "Friedrich Nietzsche," as a "tragic split" and "freedom" (MIP, 88).

Foucault thus pursues in these early writings an original approach to madness. He is not interested in its "physiological" basis, which he does not deny, or in its "cure," which he does not "oppose" (MIP, 86), but in the "truth of madness," in what the mad—shall we say—"know" or "experience." He is not addressing its physiology or its therapeutics but its "hermeneutics" and the way in which psychological science conceals, represses, forgets, and silences the truth of madness (rather the way that

Hans-Georg Gadamer thinks that "method" objectifies and alienates "truth"). In these early writings the mad "know" something that we want first to diagnose and then to treat (and in recent years simply to anaesthetize with powerful psychotherapeutic drugs), whereas Foucault wants to linger with it for a while, to listen and to learn from it, to hear what it has to say.

What do the mad know? What truth would they speak if we lend them an ear? A "tragic" truth, the truth of a "split," let us say, a tragic knowledge. This is the sort of truth that would kill you—or drive you mad—of which Nietzsche spoke. Was Nietzsche's madness a function of what he knew? Was his knowledge a function of his madness? Foucault suspends both alternatives because they are causal, etiological; he subjects both questions to a kind of *epoche* that puts physiological and therapeutic questions out of action. His interest is hermeneutic: he wants to hear what one says who has been driven *in extremis*. While Foucault does not cite it here, one is reminded of the passage in *Beyond Good and Evil* in which Nietzsche repudiates the need to have the truth "attenuated, veiled, sweetened, blunted, and falsified"—which is pretty much what Foucault thinks happens to madness in psychology. Foucault seems to have in mind what Nietzsche calls the "elect of knowledge," who are almost destroyed by their knowledge, which carries them off into "distant, terrible worlds."[6]

The mad, in these early writings, have experienced a terrible truth; they sail on dangerous seas, have been released from ordinary constraints; they are extreme points of sensitivity to the human condition. They are not truly "other" than "us." That is only the alienating gesture in which "we" constitute ourselves as sane and normal and constitute "them" as "other." The mad speak of a truth to us for which we have neither the nerve nor the ear, which is the truth of who we are. They instruct us about our hostility, meanness, aggressiveness, combativeness (MIP, 80–81). "Man has become for man the face of his own truth as well as the possibility of his death" (MIP, 82).

Foucault is not saying that the mad are the true philosophers but rather that they are precisely not philosophers at all, that they are the most forceful testimony to the breakdown of philosophy. They speak not with philosophical knowledge but with tragic knowledge. They have broken through the veil that philosophy lays over reality and that, in the form of psychology, philosophy tries to lay over them. The mad speak *de profundis*, from the depths of an experience in which both the reassuring structures of ordinary life and the comforting reassurances of scientific or philosophical knowledge have collapsed. They experience the radical groundlessness of the world, the contingency of its constructs, both social and epistemic; they speak of and from a kind of ineradicable terror. They speak to us from the abyss by which we are all inhabited; they are voices from an abyss.

This discussion, which Foucault inserted as the new part 2 of the 1962 revised edition of *Maladie mentale et Psychologie,* is an incisive summary of *Madness and Civilization*[7] published a year before, whose "Preface" and "Conclusion" it closely parallels. *Madness and Civilization* opens with a reference to the madness of not being mad, the dangerous and unhealthy (*in-sanum*) condition of failing to recognize that "we" too are a little mad, invaded also by unreason, and that it is mad to want to make reason a wholly insulated and pure region, a seamless sphere of the same insulated from its other. He speaks of the madness of sovereign reason, the madness of a reason that thinks it has purified itself of the madness that inhabits us all, whose exclusion constitutes us as "us," the madness that speaks in a "merciless" language of madlessness. The goal of *Madness and Civilization* is to arrive at a zero point, a point *before* madness is divided off from reason, before the lines of communication between the two are cut, before reason looks sovereignly—that is, without risk or threat—upon madness as its pure Other. This is a region in which "truth" and "science" do not obtain, which is prior to and older than science, which is older than the merciless "difference" between reason and madness, a region of an originary undifferentiatedness in which reason mingles with and is disturbed from within by its other. Such a return to the original scene of madness will isolate "the action that divides madness," the "originative . . . caesura" by means of which reason and science are made to stand on the side, or better to look on from above, while unreason spreads out beneath its gaze as its object" (MC, ix). Then unreason is constituted as madness, crime, or mental disease. That deprives madness of its voice— reduces it, in Jean-François Lyotard's words, to a *differend* in which it is impossible for madness to state its case—and establishes the monologue of reason with itself that we call psychology and psychiatry.[8]

The Greeks, by way of contrast, thought of *sophrosyne* and *hybris* as alternate possibilities—of moderation and excess—within *logos,* but they did not constitute some sphere of exile, of *a-logos,* outside *logos* (MC, ix). The discourse on madness Europeans conducted beginning in the Middle Ages gives a "depth" to Western reason that irrupts in some of its greatest artists and poets (Hieronymous Bosch, Nietzsche, Artaud) (MC, xi). Reason without unreason is a smooth surface, a superficial transparency; reason with unreason speaks from the depths, *de profundis.* Unreason reduced to its scientific "truth," constituted as a scientific object, is a surface event, a thin, transparent, placid object. If that depth is still apparent in the "dispute" conducted between reason and madness in the Middle Ages and Renaissance, the depth is gone and the dispute is hushed in the silent corridors of the mental institution. The task of *Madness and Civilization* thus is one of archeological restoration, a vertical plumbing of the dark sedimented depths from which *homo psychologicus* emerges, of which it still bears a faint trace, reminding us of these hidden depths even as it tries to make us forget them.

What is the "great motionless structure" (MC, xii) lying beneath the surface that is reducible neither to the drama of a dispute nor to an object of knowledge? Foucault's answer is again the tragic ("the tragic category"). By the tragic he means a radical breach or split within human being, a profound rupture that makes it impossible for reason to constitute itself as an identity, to close round about itself, to make itself reason and light through and through. Reason is always already unreason; the truth of man is this untruth.[9] The attempt to find the "truth of truth" is the attempt to expunge this untruth, to take leave of a more disturbing and disturbed region, to simplify and reduce human beings to pure reason by constituting the twin transparencies of reason on the one side and madness as the object of knowledge on the other.

In the "Conclusion" to *Madness and Civilization,* after tracing the story from the great confinement to the birth of the asylum, Foucault returns again to the theme of the tragic. At the end of the story, by way of a summation to his discussion of the asylum, he mentions the advent of Sigmund Freud. Freud, he says, reproduces in the person of the psychiatrist the confining structure of the institution of the asylum. For that reason, "psychoanalysis has not been able, will not be able, to hear the voices of unreason, nor to decipher in themselves the signs of the madman." Psychoanalysis can unravel some of the forms of madness; it is even able to let it speak (MIP, 69); but it remains a stranger to "the sovereign enterprise of unreason" (MC, 278). Were they freed from the fetters of moralizing internment, the voices of unreason would speak of "human truth" and "dark freedom," Foucault says. That is the role of the artists who lend unreason an ear, who give it a voice, or lend it a canvass.

Of Francisco José Goya's *The Madhouse,* Foucault remarks: "within this madman in a hat rises—by the inarticulate power of his muscular body, of his savage and marvelously unconstricted youth—a human presence already liberated and somehow free since the beginning of time, by his birthright" (MC, 279). In Goya's *Sleep of Reason,* "man communicates with what is deepest in himself" (MC, 280). In Goya we experience madness as "the birth of the first man and his first movement toward liberty" (MC, 281), the freedom to dissolve the world and even to dissolve man himself. The madman, Foucault suggests, lives *in extremis,* at the limits of the constitution of the world, where the world threatens to come undone, to deconstitute itself in a kind of pathological parallel to Edmund Husserl's famous hypothesis of the thought-experiment of the destruction of the world.[10] But whereas, in Husserl, such a deconstitution would leave sovereign consciousness still standing, Foucault suggests that, in Goya's work, the reduction of the world leads us back to naked unreason.

In Nietzsche unreason acquires a voice of "total contestation" of the world, contestations that restore "primitive savagery"!

In Marquis de Sade we discover the truth of nature, the savage truth that nature cannot act contrary to nature, that every desire arises from nature. As an "ironic Rousseau," Sade teaches the ethic of a more savage "fidelity to nature," "natural liberty." But Sade pushes beyond the truth of natural freedom to the "total liberty" of pure subjectivity that dashes even nature itself by its violence. Sade traverses the terrible path from "man's violent nature" to the "infinity of nonnature" (MC, 284), thus to a point where nature itself breaks up and reveals its own nature, its dissension and abolition. Sade dwells at that limit point where the world comes undone, where it is unmade, at "the limits of the world that wounds" the mad heart (MC, 285).

In Goya and Sade unreason finds a way to transcend reason in the path of violence and thus finds a way of "recovering tragic experience beyond the promises of dialectic" (MC, 285). The tragic always means the split, the rupture of human being—without the dream of dialectical rejoining and reconciliation—and here it means the unmaking and destruction of the world that reason builds around itself.

The final pages of *Madness and Civilization* are devoted to Nietzsche, who represents the tragic voice par excellence, the dominant voice from the abyss. Foucault's early writings are very much keyed to *The Birth of Tragedy* (and not, like the later writings, to *A Genealogy of Morals*), to which, Foucault says, all of Nietzsche's texts belong (MC, 285). Nietzsche is the philosopher of the tragic category, that is, of unreason and the undoing of philosophy. What interests Foucault about Nietzsche is that his writing fell silent under the blow of madness, that his final word to us after a lifetime of writing was the howl of madness followed by silence.

Foucault is not leading up to the conclusion that madness is, in Heidegger's language, the "origin of the work of art," but to an opposite conclusion, that it spells its death. "Pure" madness is not the origin of the work of art but its absence and abolition; there is no work where there is pure madness.[11] Madness is but the parting gesture of the artwork, its final word or nonword just as it subsides into chaos. The work of art springs not from pure madness but from the invasion of reason by madness, from the tension or confrontation between reason and unreason, Apollo and Dionysus. But it is rendered impossible if this tension is broken from the side either of pure reason or of pure unreason.

The work of art carries out a kind of *epoche* of the world, suspending its hold on us, which it does just to the extent that it is "interrupted" by madness, or exposed to it and held in communication with it. The work of art puts the rationality of the world in question, making the world, and not the madman, guilty, arraigning the world before the work of art. What is the world's fault? What has it done wrong? For what is it to be held responsible? For what does it owe reparation? The guilt of the world is that it has suppressed the world of unreason, and it is precisely the restoration of unreason that the work of art demands, or better, the "restoration of reason *from* that unreason and *to* that unreason" (MC, 288). So it is not exactly unreason that is restored to itself so much as it is reason that is restored to itself, to its originative belonging—together with unreason. Reason is itself only insofar as it also unreason; otherwise—and this is how *Madness and Civilization* begins—it is quite mad. Foucault has turned the tables—or the couch—on the doctor. Now, instead of the madman as patient silently observed by the figure of science, the world itself is put into question by the madman as artist, by a Dionysian artist.

These early works of Foucault are not only or even primarily histories of psychology and madness. As archeologies of the silence to which unreason is reduced in the asylum, they offer a positive view of being human, a view best expressed by the category of the "tragic." Human beings are inwardly divided, inhabited by an abyss, by both reason and unreason. We dwell in both the truth and the untruth. In such a view, neither "science" (the human sciences) nor "morals" can be what they are (or want to be) all the way through. They are at best limited, incomplete, or distortive, and hence in need of correction—the view that Foucault held in the 1954 edition of *Maladie mentale et personalité*. At worst, they are useless illusions and even hypocritical attempts to suppress the unreason by which they are inhabited and hence they are beyond correction—the view both of the 1962 revised edition of *Mental Illness and Psychology* and *Madness and Civilization*. The human sciences promote the illusion that unreason is a disturbance to be quelled, an abnormality to be normalized, a cry to be silenced. Ethics promotes the illusion that virtue is a unity, that the law is universalizable, that conscience is God's voice, suppressing the violence and confusion by which we are inhabited.

Against the illusions of science and morals, Foucault advocates a more originary tragic experience, an experience of reason's undoing and auto-deconstruction by unreason, which is the "truth" of the human condition. This truth is destroyed if it is allowed to evaporate into the "truth of truth." The truth is the night of truth, the midnight hour when reason allows itself to be interrupted and invaded by unreason. That happens in certain works of art that flash like lightning in the night of truth, illuminating for a moment a more originary and cragged human landscape.

Beyond Tragic Hermeneutics

Foucault's early writings came under fire both by his critics and by Foucault himself. In the first place, these texts are marked by a kind of phenomenological naivete. The goal of the early writings, which is to find an "undifferentiated" experience of unreason, before it is differentiated into reason and madness, before the lines of reason are drawn in its virginal sands, perfectly parallels the phenomenological goal of finding a realm of pure "prepredicative" experience, prior to its being carved up by the categories of logical grammar. To be sure, where Husserl thinks to find pure *Sinn* lying beneath the categories of logical *Bedeutung*, Foucault suggests that we will find a pure *Unsinn*, a kind of perfect, pure, free, natural, undistorted, prepredicative madness, beneath the categories of the prison or the asylum. It was with this in mind that Derrida says it is an impossible dream to think that one could write the history of madness from the standpoint of madness itself. Writing and history already represent the standpoint of reason and are already violent; they have already incised this virginal terrain with their cuts and divides.[12]

This point is well made and Foucault has clearly not avoided this objection. Still, we should recall that in the concluding pages of *Madness and Civilization* Foucault makes it plain that pure madness gives rise only to silence, that it leads to the end of the work of art. Now that surely implies that no work of history or archeology could ever enter the domain of pure madness. The voices of unreason issue in works of art, or works of any sort, only inasmuch as they interrupt, invade, intermingle with and confront reason. So Foucault is aware that there is no access to a "pure" madness or unreason, to a pure, ante-historical essence of madness, but only to the confrontation of reason and unreason in this or that concrete historical context.

Second, in a not unrelated way, Foucault criticized *Madness and Civilization* (he never spoke of the first book, in either edition, on mental illness and opposed its republication) on the grounds that it labored under the "repressive" hypothesis, that is, the notion that power works by excluding and repressing.[13]

> I think that I was positing [in *Madness and Civilization*] the existence of a sort of living, voluble and anxious madness which the mechanisms of power and psychiatry were supposed to have come to repress and reduce to silence. . . . In defining the effects of power as repression, one adopts a purely juridical conception of such power, one identifies power with a law which says no, power is taken above all as carrying the force of a prohibition.

It is certainly true that in *Madness and Civilization* Foucault thought that unreason is repressed, suppressed, excluded, silenced, denied, obstructed, and occulted by reason. On this point I think he was right and that virtually the whole power of his book rests precisely on his being right about this. Furthermore, I do not think he means to retract this point. In an interview he gave in 1977, he says that the repressive mechanisms of *Madness and Civilization* were "adequate" to his purposes in that book, that "madness is a special case—during the Classical age power over madness was, in its most important manifestations at least, exercised in the form of exclusion; thus one sees madness caught up in a great movement of rejection" (P/K, 183–184). Yet, Foucault was subsequently led by way of his investigations into the history of sexuality to see another mechanism of power, the productive one, which proceeds not by repressing and saying no but which "traverses and produces things . . . induces pleasure, forms knowledge, produces discourse" (P/K, 119). But this other form of power reflects not so much a change in Foucault's thinking as a discovery about a change that takes place in the later history of power and madness.

> However, in the nineteenth century, an absolutely fundamental phenomenon made its appearance: the interweaving, the intrication, of two great technologies of power: one which fabricated sexuality and the other which segregated madness. The technology of madness changed from negative to positive, from being binary to being complex and multiform. There came into being a vast technology of the psyche, which became a characteristic feature of the nineteenth and twentieth centuries. (P/K, 185)

One important result of this interweaving is that "sexuality" assumed the place—as the truth of madness—that Foucault would have earlier said belonged to the "tragic category." This is an important point to which I shall return below. The essential thing to see at the moment, however, is that at a certain juncture, instead of being repressed, unreason is forced to talk. At a certain point, one that Foucault ascribes to the rise of confessional practices in the Catholic Church in the seventeenth and eighteenth centuries, instead of being doused with water, berated with moral criticism, and subjected to a rigorous regimen, the mad are encouraged to say what they have on their minds, to associate freely, to dredge up their dreams, to tell us all about themselves and their parents (especially their parents) and childhoods, to reveal their innermost secrets, to bring them out in the public view of the world. In short, to talk, talk, talk, for in the talking is the cure.

Now it would be a mistake, I maintain, to think that the repressive hypothesis is somehow inconsistent with productive power. In fact, the two are quite compatible and, indeed, produce a similar effect. I would even say that the hypothesis of a productive power is a continuation of the repressive hypothesis by another means. The unreason by which reason is inhabited is again silenced, this time not by real, physical, institutionalized silence but, still more effectively, and rather more pleasurably, by talk. The notion that more and more talking is an effective way to silence what requires a voice was noticed early on in the nineteenth century by Søren Kierkegaard, who found that the idle chatter of the press addressed to the "millions," and the numerous compendia of Hegelianized Christian doctrine that were being turned out by the dozens were proving to be an exceptionally effective way to silence the quiet terror of authentic faith.[14] One of the most famous Kierkegaardian pseudonyms bore the name Johannes de Silentio because he was charged with the task of describing the indescribable "fear and trembling" of Abraham, who was unable to explain himself to others and whom everyone else took to be quite—well—mad. Kierkegaard played such silence against the foil of the sane and sensible "stockbrokers of the finite" with whom he draws a consistent contrast throughout *Fear and Trembling*.[15] In an age of top-down monarchical power, outright repression will do just fine but in the democratic age of the "millions," productive power does an even better job of silencing.

The fact of the matter is that unless power has a univocal essence, unless power means just one thing, it is impossible to sustain the idea that power is only or essentially or primarily "productive" and not also repressive. Power is only a descriptive category for Foucault and it means many things, in keeping with the plurality of historical situations in which it is deployed. There is no power as such; we can only describe the "how" of "power relations" (BSH, 217, 219). Power is now repressive, now productive, and now something else that Foucault had not noticed, and later on something else that perhaps has not yet come about. So there is nothing about Foucault's later adoption of the hypothesis of productive power to invalidate his notion that the work of reason is to silence and reject the voices of unreason by which it is inhabited, and hence to invalidate the early notion of the "tragic category." On the contrary, the two exist in a continual "interweaving" and "intrication."

The strongest challenge to the continued viability of "tragic hermeneutics" in Foucault's work is voiced by Dreyfus and Rabinow, who claim that after *Madness and Civilization* Foucault disavows any form of "hermeneutics," and, specifically, using Paul Ricoeur's term, the "hermeneutics of suspicion." By "hermeneutics" Dreyfus and Rabinow mean the unmasking and ferreting out of a repressed truth that tells the truth of man. In his "Foreword to the California Edition" of *Mental Illness and Psychology* (1987), Dreyfus says that even the 1962 revised edition remains under the spell of a Heideggerian conception of "'anxiety' in the face of madness" that is silenced by morality and science. Foucault is convinced that there has been a "repression of a deep, nonobjectifiable truth" (MIP, xxxii). So there is still a "conspiracy theory" at work in this book, a notion that something is being suppressed that, if we could just face up to it, would result in liberation (in the way that Heidegger talks about being ready for anxiety). In the first edition of the book, Foucault thought it was a matter of facing up to the alienation produced by social contradiction; in the second edition, he has succeeded only in replacing a Marxist conception of social alienation with a Heideggerian and existential conception of "strangeness" (*Unheimlichkeit*), but the overall (hermeneutic) scheme of reducing madness into its unalienated, liberating truth remains intact.

In the following years, Dreyfus argues, Foucault came to reject any such "hermeneutics" and with it the claim that there is some deep truth begging to be deciphered, some latent content that awaits "commentary,"[16] some meaning at once more hidden and more fundamental that demands a "hermeneutics,"[17] some interrogation of "the being of madness itself, its secret content, its silent, self-enclosed truth"[18] that would traverse what is said about madness at any particular historical time. There is no message from the depths. Madness is simply constituted in different ways at different times and nothing is being left out. There is no inexhaustible residue, no cover-up story, no buried saving truth (MIP, xxxiii). There is no ahistorical essential structure of madness (analogous to the ahistorical structure of *Dasein* yielded by the existential analytic), but only the changing, historical constitution of human beings. For Dreyfus and Rabinow, the critique made in volume 1 of *The History of Sexuality* of the search for a secret self—sexuality—as a "construction of modern thought," and hence as an important kind of modern power, is to be applied to *Madness and Civilization*. The latter sought to locate that secret, not in sexuality to be sure, but in "the sovereign enterprise of unreason" that is delivered over to us in flashes of lightning with names like Nietzsche and Hölderlin (MC, 11). But Foucault is led to give up this hermeneutic ontology that locates the transcendental being of unreason behind the play of the historical appearances of madness and *homo psychologicus*. He turns his attention instead to the patient description of the multiple historical forms in which modern man is constituted.

But if that is so, then what difference do the different historical constitutions of madness make? If madness is just produced in various ways, if nothing is repressed, lost, or silenced, why worry about what historical form the historical constitution of madness takes? If nothing is repressed, then nothing is to be liberated. If nothing is repressed, then there is nothing to offer resistance and no historical formation is better or worse than another. As Dreyfus and Rabinow query at the end of their book, "What is wrong with carceral society? Genealogy undermines a stance which opposes it on the grounds of natural law or human dignity. . . . What are the resources which enable us to sustain a critical stance?" (BSH, 206).

A good deal of what Foucault wrote in the years that followed *Madness and Civilization* raises these objections. In the remaining sections of this essay, I shall argue that an adequate answer turns on understanding what becomes of the hermeneutic impulse which is so clearly evident in the early writings, that it turns, in short, on seeing that Foucault has moved beyond a certain hermeneutics toward another hermeneutics more radically conceived.

The Hermeneutics of Refusal

In "The Subject and Power," the afterword to the Dreyfus and Rabinow book, Foucault speaks of the two "pathological forms" of power, two "diseases of power"—fascism and Stalinism—that the twentieth century has known (BSH, 209). Are we to think that these are "alienated power," power gone wrong, power that divests human beings of something unalienated or even inalienable? Foucault says they are marked by an "internal madness," but that such madness is merely the extension of contemporary "political rationality," of a kind of unlimited rationalization. Are we to think, then, that this is something like a political equivalent of the "other form of madness" that consists in not being mad, a political analogue of the "merciless language of nonmadness" (MC, ix)? Are we to think that something is lost, repressed, or occulted by fascism and Stalinism?

Foucault puts these expressions in scare quotes. They are normative expressions that seem to edge out beyond a felicitous positivism. He is perhaps concerned that he is drifting in the direction of the earlier writings that speak of a more originative sphere. He is worried that he is making himself look like the "doctor." In the next paragraph the metaphor switches to Immanuel Kant, to what Lyotard calls Kant's "critical watchman,"[19] and Foucault speaks of a need for a Kantian-like critique of the limits of political reason that keeps watch for "excesses" (BSH, 210). Still, although it is helpful—this is what the Frankfurt school has already done—it is not enough, Foucault says, to study the Enlightenment and the excesses to which it has led "if we want to understand how we have been trapped in our own history" (BSH, 210).

We are trapped in our history. But *who* is trapped? And how *trapped?* What is the opposite of being trapped? Does being trapped mean that something has been prohibited, occulted, blocked off, or repressed (P/K, 183), that is, trapped? What would it be like to be untrapped? Who would be untrapped? Who is the "we" who would be untrapped?

Instead of pursuing the strategy of the Frankfurt school, of analyzing the "internal rationality" of such excesses, Foucault says that he thinks it would be more instructive to approach such processes of subjection by way of a consideration of the "resistance" that is offered to them, of the "antagonisms" that they engender (BSH, 211). Insanity and illegality, for example, are (negative) indicators of what a society calls sanity and legality. Consider the "struggles" we witness nowadays against the power of men over women, of psychiatry over the mentally ill, of bureaucracy over people at large. Such struggles "assert the right to be different and they underline everything which makes individuals truly individual" and they fight against everything that "ties [the individual] to his own identity in a constraining way," which reduces the individual to the identity of "madman," "mentally retarded," "alcoholic," "handicapped," etc.

These struggles, Foucault says, "are not for or against the 'individual,' but rather they are struggles against the 'government of individualization'" (BSH, 212). It is not as though Foucault has a positive, affirmative normative idea of what an individual should be in the name of which he thinks these struggles should be waged. What the individual should be in some *determinate* way is none of Foucault's business. More important, the business of coming up with normative ideas of what the individual should be, and of developing administrative practices and professional competencies to see to it that such individuals are in fact produced, is precisely the problem, not the solution: it is exactly what these struggles are struggling *against.*

In sum, Foucault suggests, all such struggles "revolve around the question: 'Who are we?'" (BSH, 212). But Foucault's idea is not only *not* to answer this question in a determinate way but to see to it that no one else is allowed to answer it, or rather to answer it on behalf of anyone else and above all to enforce their answer. It is a question that each of us, in our singularity, requires the privacy to raise and answer for ourselves, without sweeping up everyone else in what we come up with, so that, contra Jean-Paul Sartre, we are not creating an essence for all humankind. It is like Derrida's adaptation of Augustine's question, "what do I love when I love my God?"[20] Foucault wants to keep this question open, and above all to block administrators, professionals, and managers of all sorts from answering this question on our behalf, thereby closing us in on some constituted identity or another that represents a strictly historical, that is, contingent constraint. While the tonality of hope and expectation is stronger in Derrida's slightly atheistic messianic expectation, in Derrida's *viens, oui, oui,* I think that the positions of Foucault and Derrida, their common desire to keep the future open, are close at this point. That goes some way to explaining what Foucault means by being "trapped by our history." There are too many theories out there of what Foucault earlier called "the truth of truth," of the scientific or therapeutic truth of who we are, too many ready responses to the question "who are we?" Foucault's program is to block off or delimit the truth of truth—and to leave us to what he named in the earlier writings our (simple) truth, to the truth that there is no truth of truth, which is not a statement of despair but a hope for the freedom to invent something new. Foucault wants to defend the impossibility of reducing us to truth, to shelter the irreducibility and uncontractability of being-human, its refusal of identity and identification, its refusal of an identifying truth, in order to open up the possibility of new modes of self-invention. Such refusal issues from a felicitous nominalism about the irrepressibility of being human, from its irrepressible capacity for being-different, for mutation and transformation.

Like Derrida, Foucault thus has a negative, nominalistic, and non-essentialistic idea of the individual. He struggles against any "positive" theory of the individual that takes itself seriously, that thinks it has the truth of truth, that thinks it can positively identify who we are. He opposes all "cataphatic" discourse about the individual, all discourse that tries to prescribe what the individual is or should be, and he does so in the name of a kind of "apophatic" discourse, of preserving a purely apophatic freedom. The gesture is actually classical, reminding us, as James Bernauer argues powerfully, of negative theology.[21] What you say God is, is not true, Meister Eckhart wrote; but what you do not say God is, that is true.[22] Foucault wants to keep open the negative space of what the individual is not, of what we cannot say the individual is, to preserve the space of a certain negativity that refuses all positivity, all identification, for that is always in the end a historical trap. To paraphrase the Meister, whenever the social sciences tell us who we are, that is not true; but what they do not say about who we are, that is true. Whatever lays claim to being the truth of truth, that is not true; but whatever concedes that we do not know the truth of truth, that is true. Whatever way the individual is historically constituted is not true; but whatever alternatives there are to the way we are constituted, that is true.

The modern exercise of power on Foucault's account represents a peculiar "'double bind'" (BSH, 216) that produces individuals (productive power) precisely in order to block off individuality (repressive power). Modern power combines the production of individuals ("individualization techniques") along with the repression of individuality and difference ("totalization procedures") (BSH, 213). Far from having abandoned the repressive hypothesis, the double bind depends upon the combined and simultaneous effect of both productive and repressive power, upon their "interweaving" and "intrication" (P/K, 185).

Productive power takes its rise from the spread of "pastoral power" over the social body (BSH, 215). In pastoral power the pastor gives himself over to the production of an individual soul (the "individual" is an invention of the Christian confessional). The pastor needs to know what is going on in individuals' hearts, to get inside their minds, to have them "confess" their innermost secrets, in order to give spiritual direction. Pastoral power depends upon producing the truth, the truth of truth, in order to produce good Christians. In the modern world pastoral techniques are multiplied everywhere: among the police, state investigative functions, and criminal justice and social work professionals; medical and health care professionals; clinical and counseling psychologists and psychiatrists; and educationists, demographers, etc. Wherever a "file" is kept, wherever an individual "case history" is to be written, the "individual" is the target of knowledge and power, of power/knowledge.

Against this totalizing, normalizing production of individuals, Foucault holds out for the "individual." This is the double bind. Not the individual in the sense of the individual case history, of the "subject" whose secret code we—psychiatrists, moralists, or educationists—know, but rather the individual who resists all secret codes, who has no identity, who is not reducible to one or another of the hermeneutic techniques of pastoral power, who is marked by the "right to be different" (BSH, 211). Against the positive production of individuals in keeping with some normative standard, Foucault holds out for the negative freedom of the individual to be different. Whatever the social engineers want the individual to be, that is what the individual wants not to be, what the individual refuses to be in this hermeneutics of refusal.

So what philosophers must do is ask not, like René Descartes, "what am I?"—as if there were a general answer—but, like Kant ("what is the Enlightenment?"), who are we *now*, at this particular moment of our historical constitution. Who are we high-tech, late capitalist, mobile, post-Enlightenment—shall we say—postmodernists? And how can we be otherwise? Or better still:

> Maybe the target nowadays is not to discover what we are but to refuse what we are. We have to imagine and to build up what we could be to get rid of this kind of "double bind" which is the simultaneous individualization and totalization of modern power structures. (BSH, 216)

The idea is to liberate us not only from the state but from the sort of individualization that the state produces. The idea is "to promote new forms of subjectivity through the refusal of this kind of individuality which has been imposed on us for several centuries" (BSH, 216).

Foucault's position is comparable to Lyotard's call for continual experimentalism, not only in art but in the artwork that we ourselves are, for the formation of new forms of subjectivity, for finding what Lyotard calls new idioms that provide a space for the right to be different. It corresponds, too, to Derrida's call for *l'invention de l'autre*, the coming, the incoming, of something other.

We are now in a position to address the question of what difference the different historical constitutions of madness make. If madness is just produced in various ways, if nothing is repressed, lost, or silenced, why worry about what historical form the historical constitution of madness takes? If nothing is repressed, then nothing is to be liberated, there is nothing to offer resistance, and no historical formation—including fascism and Stalinism—is better or worse than another. It is, I think, clear that Foucault does believe that something is repressed, and the cogency of speaking of a "double bind" depends upon it. The claim that every historical constitution is a contingency that threatens to become a historical "trap" means that something is being trapped. The idea that no particular historical constitution is exhaustive or totalizing means that there is always a residue, an irreducibility, a fragment that cannot be incorporated.[23] I do not mean a "transcendental residuum" like Husserl's pure consciousness, or a historical essence or nature of being human, but rather a purely negative, always historical capacity for being-otherwise, which is what Foucault means by freedom.

That is the answer to the objection that Foucault's writings provoke after *Madness and Civilization*, that he treats human beings as a kind of pure *hyle* capable of taking on indefinitely many forms, of being historically constituted in an indefinite multiplicity of forms, no one of which is any better or worse than another. Foucault clearly distinguishes the power that is exerted over material objects, for example, by means of instruments, from the power that individuals exert over other individuals, which is not power over things but power over freedom. Power is not a mere violence exerted on an object, like cutting wood or bending a piece of steel. Violence or force are effected on a "mere passivity" (BSH, 220). But the power in which Foucault is interested is exerted over "the other," over another person who acts and reacts. Power is a set of actions upon other actions. Nor is power *consensus,* a free renunciation of one's own freedom for the sake of a general arrangement. "Power relations" occur in the space between pure force and free consent, and they may or may not obtain in the presence of either. Power is a matter neither of pushing boulders about with great bulldozers nor of a pure dialogue between Platonic souls.

Power is a way of inducing, seducing, conducing (*conduire,* conduct [v.], conduct [n.]); power is conductive. It is stronger (more coercive) than what Husserl calls "motivation," which is pure intentional freedom, because it is a way we have of being led (*ducere*) around (con), but like motivation it belongs in a quasi-intentional sphere of human behavior and is not to be reduced to physical causality. Power is a way of "governing," shaping, forming—the seventeenth-century religious orders that Foucault discusses in *Discipline and Punish* called the time of apprenticeship in the order years of "formation." Power sets up (*stellen, auf-stellen*) or frames out (*Ge-stell*)²⁴ a preset range of possibilities within which action can take place, broad "ducts" through which actions are led; power "structures the field" of actions (BSH, 222). Thus "power is exercised only over free subjects, and only insofar as they are free" (BSH, 221). Slavery is not power but constraint because in slavery the range of possibilities has been "saturated," that is, determined to a specific outcome (*determinatio ad unum*). Power is exerted only over beings capable of being recalcitrant and intransigent. Power implies freedom since without freedom power is just constraint or force. Power and freedom belong together agonistically, in an ongoing "agonism," a struggle, in which there are winning and losing strategies, a victorious consolidation of power on the one hand or successful strategies against power on the other hand. If power is cunning and pervasive enough, it will coopt freedom; if freedom is resistant and persistent enough, it will cause power to tremble.

Power is not something that could be removed, the result being a perfectly free society. A society without power would not be a society but a physical aggregate; as soon as human beings come together (and when have they not?), in virtue of their coming together, power relations spring into being. A society is essentially a network of power relations that are more minute than its larger institutional structures. The idea for Foucault is not to abolish power relations—that would make no sense—but to alter them by means of winning strategies, to open up new possibilities, to restructure the field such that something else (being-otherwise) is possible (BSH, 223). Such an alteration is driven by the ongoing agonism between power and freedom that sees to it that any field of power is an unsteady state, an unstable and hence ultimately open, alterable system.

The idea is to keep open "the free play of antagonistic" relations, to refuse to let the social system harden into place with stable mechanisms that are overeffective in regulating conduct (BSH, 225).

So far from excluding or reducing freedom, power over freedom implies resistance. Freedom for Foucault is a kind of irrepressibility, a refusal to contract into an identity, a continually twisting loose from the historical forms of life by which it is always already shaped. Freedom is not a nature or essence but a lack of nature or essence, a capacity for novelty and innovation. Bernauer calls it "transcendence,"[25] the capacity to move beyond a particular historical constitution. That is in keeping with Bernauer's guiding motif of Foucault's "negative theology" (God transcends whatever we say about God), which I would say is rather a "high" theology for Foucault. I think Foucault has in mind a more modest freedom from below, a refusal, a resistance, a certain stepping back, not so much a transcendence, let us say, as a *rescendence*, which seeks to twist free from the trap of the present in order to find a variation.

We are now in a position to evaluate the claim of Dreyfus and Rabinow that, by turning himself over to detailed genealogies of the various ways in which bodies and minds are historically constituted, Foucault moved beyond all hermeneutics. This claim is tied up with the assertion that he dropped the idea of the repression of something deep and replaced it with the notion of describing the surface of productive relations of power.

I think this position is partly right. In the early writings Foucault clearly believed in "The Secret" and in finding the hermeneutic key to The Secret. The hermeneutics of suspicion he practiced at that point (suspecting psychology of repressing the tragic truth) turned on a positive idea of who we are, a particular—indeed, I would say a Dionysian—idea of a "tragic unreason." The authoritative account of who we are was to be found in *The Birth of Tragedy,* an account the human sciences would like to dismiss or forget. It is clear that by the time of the last works Foucault had given up the idea that there is some *positive* idea of "who we are" to be recovered, some *particular* identity that is being repressed which needs to be shaken loose ("destruction") and retrieved.

But if he has dropped the idea that there is some particular identity that is being repressed, he has not given up the idea that *something* is being repressed, something much looser, more unspecifiable and indefinite, something negative and unidentifiable. It is no longer an *identity* we need to recover (a secret tragic identity) but a *difference.* It is no longer a positive ideal that needs to be restored but simply a certain capacity to resist the identities that are imposed upon us just to set free our capacity to invent such new identities for ourselves as circumstances allow.[26] In short, the movement has not been beyond hermeneutics and repression but beyond a hermeneutics of identity (a positive tragic hermeneutics) to a hermeneutics of difference (a negative hermeneutics of refusal).

The later writings turn on the idea that there is always something other

than or different from the various historical constitutions of human beings, some "freedom" or resistance that is irreducible to the several en-
framing historical forms of life, some power-to-be-otherwise, some be-
ing-otherwise-than-the present that radically, irreducibly, irrepressibly
belongs to us, to what we are (not). We never are what we are; something different is always possible. As Derrida says in *The Other Heading,*
what is proper to the "identity" of a self or a culture[27]

> . . . *is not to be identical to itself.* Not to not have an identity, but not to be able
> to identify itself, to be able to say "I" or "we"; to be able to take the form of
> a subject only in the non-identity to itself or, if you prefer, only in the
> difference with itself (*avec soi*).

The "I" or the "we" is marked by its capacity to be otherwise. That is why
I think that Foucault has not dropped the hermeneutic project. He has
not abandoned a *certain* hermeneutics, a negative hermeneutics, a hermeneutics of refusal, of what we are not, which I like to call "radical hermeneutics."[28] In such a hermeneutics there is no question of deciphering a
"master name," of reapprehending through the "manifest meaning . . .
another meaning at once . . . more hidden but more fundamental."[29] On
the contrary, such a hermeneutics turns on the loss of fixed or determinate meaning, and on an understanding of being human as an abyss that
refuses identification, contraction, or reduction to a fixed meaning. If
Foucault has abandoned the hermeneutics of suspicion, that is because,
in my view, he has taken up a hermeneutics of refusal.

Foucault's more radical hermeneutics rejects the idea of the truth of
truth, of some nameable, masterable truth of being human. It rejects a
whole series of humanisms of truth—*homo psychologicus, homo economicus,
homo religiosus,* including his own earlier contribution to this theme, *homo
tragicus.* But he has done so, not in order to skim along the surface of
positivistic descriptions, but in order to open a hermeneutic dimension of
negativity: that we do not know who we are. He has abandoned the truth
of truth, the mastery of knowledge, in favor of the "cold truth," of the
truth that there is no truth of truth, of the truth that our being is always
already disturbed by untruth, which means an irreducibility to truth. This
I think is close to Derrida's notion of the *khôra,* that the things we come
up with when we describe our condition are written in the sand, a desert
sand that is vulnerable to the next storm. The essence of such Foucauldian freedom, were there such a thing, is its untruth, its irreducibility to
the truth of truth. Beneath the layers of *homo psychologicus* and all the
"idols" of the human sciences, of all the "graven images" of modernity
that we might collectively call *homo cyberneticus,* Foucault hears the mur-
mur of a capacity to be otherwise. His is a refusal of the idols of the
present, the idolatrous worship we are prone to offer the images that
present themselves to us today and threaten to hold us captive. That critique of idolatry, in my view, is linked to the critical power of the messi-

anic idea in Derrida. The later writings respond to a plea that quietly calls for something different, what Derrida and Levinas call "the call of the other." Conductive, productive power is *de*ductive: by leading us along (con) certain paths, it leads us away from (de) others, cutting off, closing off, the capacity to differ. Productive power is interwoven with repressive power. It wants to produce human beings of a certain sort because it is at the same time "anxious" about the human capacity for being-otherwise; it is not a little anxious about difference. Far from giving up on the idea of hermeneutic anxiety, pace Dreyfus, I think the power of Foucault's analyses, early or late, depends upon that anxiety.

We do not know who we are, not if we are honest about it. That is a hermeneutic point, albeit a negative one. It is the issue of a specific kind of ruthless facing up to the facts that neither ethics nor the human sciences can tell us who we are or what to do. It is, I would say, the issue of a certain "responsiveness" to the abyss that we are, to our endless ability to be otherwise. Dreyfus is mistaken to think that Foucault gave up on the hermeneutic idea of "facing up to the truth" (MIP, xxviii–xxx) if by that one means the "cold truth," the truth that there is no truth of truth, the truth that is invaded and fragmented by untruth. Whatever is called "Truth" and adorned with capital letters masks its own contingency and untruth, even as it masks the capacity for being-otherwise. For our being human spins off into an indefinite future about which we know little or nothing, which fills us with a little hope and not a little anxiety, a future to come for which there is no program, no preparation, no prognostication.

Beyond Foucault: Healing Gestures

I wish to close with a word about madmen and confessors, a word that Foucault does not utter but that belongs to the space he opens up, to the potentialities he awakens. Foucault's analysis of the normalization of the mad in psychology and psychiatry, and of the normalization of the faithful in the confessional, addresses the anxiety of modernity about difference and abnormality, and it does so in an incisive way. But it does not discuss another issue and concern, the issue of what *healing* means in such an analysis, since we can hardly think we are all okay. This would represent a final step, from hermeneutics to therapeutics.

Let us return to the question of madness. Madness is a "disturbance" but in a twofold sense both of what is "disturbing" and "disturbed." Foucault does a masterful job of showing what is "disturbing" about madness. To put it in the terms of Heidegger in *Being and Time,* Foucault treats madness as a particular way the world is "understood," not in a theoretical sense, of course, but in the sense of what Heidegger calls in *Being and Time* a certain *Weltverstehen,* a practical understanding that is heavily "mooded" or "tuned" (*bestimmt*). The disturbing thing about the mad is the nagging fear that they are "at-tuned" to something, to some deep-seated dissonance, from which the rest of "us" seek to be protected. We are apprehensive that, living at the margins of normal life, *in extremis,* the mad have been exposed to something the rest of us prefer to ignore. "We" are beset by an apprehensiveness that our sane, healed, whole lives mask a deeper rupture, that the settled tranquility of the sane is acquired only by repressing the "up-set" of the mad. We are disturbed that "the disturbed" are responding to a definite *turbatio* that is "there." "We" find the "disturbed" disturbing. Madness is a mirror of ourselves. It tells us who we are. If the mad exhibit "infantile regressions," it is only because childhood is infantilized to begin with, unrealistically insulated from real conflict. If madness takes on the form of "schizophrenia," it is because the mad reflect the contradictions of a world in which humans can no longer recognize themselves, because the social world itself is marked by struggle, hostility, and foreignness. It is the world that is mad, alienated, unfree, divided, and contradictory, and it is such madness that the mad take as their model and in which the world refuses to see itself (MIP, 80–81). That is what gives Foucault's analyses their bite.

But madness is also a being-disturbed, *patheia,* a way of suffering that causes *pain.* The mad *suffer from* their attunement, from what they experience/feel/undergo. Their ruptured lives are the site of a wound. It is not as though the lives of extreme manic depressives would be felicitous if we just left them alone or if the world would adjust to them. They live with terror; they wrestle with demons; their works are impaired, ruined, suicidal, brought to halt, reduced to inertia. Their lives are disrupted and destroyed, "disturbed." They have fallen prey to madness. They need healing. Their cry of pain is also a call for help. They lay claim to us, we who are whole (enough) to help, we who are perhaps not so much whole and sane as just a little less mad and better skilled at repressing our madness. There are, after all, only a few Nietzsches, Hölderlins, and Vincent Van Goghs among the mad. It was in the long run better to let Van Gogh and Nietzsche alone, to let mad genius run its course into the dark night of truth. But for the majority madness does not mean genius but pain, and they cry out for help, not for the immortality of the work of art.

I take it there is nothing in what Foucault says that opposes "a strategy of cure" (MIP, 76); it is simply not his subject. Indeed, I see in his work the makings of a certain therapeutic "direction," let us say, of a therapeutic of non-knowing. Such a therapeutic does not come from on high, does not proceed from the heights of science or episteme, and so does not suffer from the illusion that it knows what madness is (when madness is not clearly physiological). Such a therapy of non-knowing would take madness "seriously," that is, as an other from which we have something to learn. Indeed, it undergoes a change of direction by letting the mad come to us from "on high," in their extreme otherness. It does not look on the mad as "patients" in the sense of "objects" of medical knowledge, but as *patiens,* as ones who suffer greatly, who suffer from their knowledge, as Nietzsche says, and its look is not objectifying but *com-patiens,* compassionate. Such a patient would not be an object of knowledge but an author or subject of knowledge, one from whom we have something to learn. Such patients are not stretched out before the medical gaze as objects but come to us from on high, but rather lifted up by their suffering, in the manner of Levinas. We are not panoptical observers of madness, but we are put into question by the mad, seen and interrogated by them, above all, solicited by them. We have something to learn from the mad, above all that they are not "they" but who we ourselves are. We are instructed by them; they have set foot where the sane fear to tread. They tell us, unhappily, who we are; they tell us of our own unhappiness. The mad are not the subject of a medical observation but the source of a call that calls upon us and demands our response.

The mad do not ask for analysis and objectification by us but friendship, support, companionship, solace, joy. The healing gesture, the gesture meant to heal their suffering, is not intended to explain anything away or fill in the abyss but simply to affirm that they are not alone, that our common madness is a matter of degree, that we are all siblings in the same "night of truth." The healing gesture is not to explain madness, if that means to explain it away, but to recognize it as a common fate, to affirm our community and solidarity, and to divide their pain in two by taking on half of it in attentive compassion and counsel.

A comparable point can be made about the "confessional practices" of the seventeenth and eighteenth centuries that Foucault has adroitly analyzed. The meticulous ruminations of an Alphonse Liguori into the secret recesses of the soul are lurid exercises in a kind of confessional voyeurism, which are useful only as candidates for an inverted, perverted *ars erotica.* But they are also, and more importantly, from what I like to call a more authentically religious point of view, profoundly insufficient and, I would say, quite irreligious. The institutionalization, regularization, and methodologization of "confession" are religious perversity. The confessor (in the sense of *confiteor,* I confess) is a "sinner." "Sin" is like "madness": it is a larger-than-life term for life *in extremis,* at the limits, for life that has strayed beyond the safe and reassuring boundaries of everyday life, beyond the wide swaths of normalcy cut by our everyday practices. Sin is not reducible to wrongdoing—no more than madness is reducible to error. It is an expression, perhaps a mythic expression—that is arguably the status of "madness," too—that provides an idiom for a deeper breach, a profound rupture in the human heart. We are divided against ourselves. Like the madness by which we are all beset and upset, and from which we have something to learn, sin bears testimony to a deep divide. But, unlike madness, sin is not a disturbance in the sphere of reason and "truth," but in the sphere of justice and "good." "Sin" seeks to give words to profound self-diremption, a rupture, a radical unhappiness in our condition.

I believe that sin requires a healing gesture analogous to madness, a gesture of compassion and commonality. The sinner tells us who we are, tells us of our own unhappiness. Sin is not the object of a Liguorian gaze, not a secret to be ferreted out by confessional techniques, not an object of interrogation. Sin is not an object at all, but the Being of the being we ourselves are.[30] The language of sin provides an idiom for what Levinas calls the "murderousness" of freedom, the murderousness of our power. We who are free and well fed, we who are whole and hearty, fit and on the move, we who move easily within the relations of power, are murderous and we cause others to suffer. "Sin" likewise provides an idiom for our weakness, our infidelities to those to whom we owe loyalty. Sin is not the Other but who we are. Sin is the Other within, the serpent and the apple within our hearts. Sin comes to us from on high and gives us something to understand by telling us about ourselves, by telling us of the abyss within.

The healing gesture handed down to us by the great religious traditions is not analytic objectification, not minute, ruminating subjectification. The great healing gesture that sweeps down over us in Buddhism is called the "great compassion" and in the New Testament is called "forgiveness"! Jesus was the discoverer of forgiveness, Hannah Arendt says.[31] Forgiveness loosens the knots of the social network, slackens the ties in the relations of power, even as revenge draws them tighter and makes them more intractable and oppressive. Forgiveness opens the space of the social network; it makes the future possible and denies to the past its role as fate. Forgiveness makes new forms of subjectivity possible, even as revenge condemns us to repeat the past in endless cycles. Forgiveness releases and opens; revenge traps, incarcerates, and closes. Forgiveness is not given to minute interior rehearsing of the past and intensive subjectification, but is rather dismissive and forgetting. Go and sin no more! Forget it! Forgiving is active forgetting. Forgiveness does not ask questions, but understands that it has itself been put in question by sin. Forgiveness lets itself be interrogated; it does not interrogate. Forgiveness readily makes itself guilty for the sake of the other. Forgiveness asks who among us can cast the first stone; it looks lovingly on sinners, with whom it consistently consorts to the scandal of the Good and the Just. Forgiveness heals not by analyzing but by holding out a hand of compassion, by offering a forgiving word that affirms and confesses for its own part that we are all sinners, all siblings of the same dark night.

That is the "truth" of confession, the truth that there is no "truth of truth," no confessional techniques, no methodological examinations of conscience, no objectification by way of subjectification. That is also why Julia Kristeva thinks that Christian confessional practices have a notable, albeit mystified, healing power. (But then what is more mystifying than the creatures that psychoanalysis invents?) That is particularly true, she thinks, when confession centers on words of forgiveness and not on the rites of "penance," which is the view of Duns Scotus, whom Kristeva regards as the great theologian of confession.[32] Scotus of course lived before the age of subjectification/objectification, the age of the world reduced to a picture for the subject's gaze (*Weltbild*), as Heidegger says, and offered an antidote to the Tridentine confessional practices that Foucault has ruthlessly exposed.

The secret is, there is no Secret. The truth is that we cannot gain the high ground of a capitalized Truth, insulated from violence and unreason, destruction and self-destruction, "madness" and "sin." The truth is what Foucault calls—in a wonderfully unguarded moment—the "night of truth." His analyses constitute a remarkable hermeneutics of that night of truth, a cold and more merciless scrutiny of the human condition that is, at the same time, bent subtly in a direction not at all at odds with mercy.

2

How to Prepare for the Coming
of the Other

Gadamer and Derrida

How is one to prepare for the coming of the other? Is not the other, as other, the one for whom one is precisely not prepared? Does not preparation relieve the other of his or her or its alterity so that, if we are prepared, then what comes is not the other but the same, just what we were expecting? Would not extending true hospitality toward the other involve a certain unconditionality in which one is prepared for anything, which means that one is not prepared? Is the only adequate preparation for the coming of the other to confess that we cannot be prepared for what is coming? How then to be un/prepared, that is, prepared for the advance of one for whom we could never be prepared? This aporia of the other, the paralysis of this impossible situation or fix, provides us with an insight into the exchange between hermeneutics and deconstruction and opens up the way to radicalize hermeneutics, which turns on the secret.

The question of the "other" has been an especially important one in the hermeneutics of the secret, ever since Edmund Husserl's fifth *Cartesian Meditation,* in which he marked off with great precision the *structural* non-knowing, the *structural* secrecy of the other person. The alter ego, he said, is precisely someone whose mental life I will never know or occupy, not because of some contingent limitation on my part that I might overcome later, but because it is in principle inaccessible. The alterity of the other would be destroyed if I had access to it; the other whom I would know would not be other. The inaccessibility of the other's mental life thus is affirmative and nothing to lament, for it is exactly this non-knowability that constitutes the other as such. The other's appearing as other is constituted by non-appearing. It is the structural secrecy and non-knowability of the other that I am pursuing in this and the next chapter.

Let us agree that hermeneutics is what Hans-Georg Gadamer says it is, and beautifully, too, viz., a way of putting one's own horizon or standpoint "into play" (*ins Spiel*) and thereby putting it "at risk" (*aufs Spiel*) (WM, 366; TM, 388).[1] Then the difference between Gadamer's hermeneutical theory, to which I am deeply indebted, and deconstruction, to which I am still more indebted, turns specifically on the question of risk, of the high stakes game into which one enters, or into which one is entered, like it or not, by the approach of the other. Taking that risk, Gadamer goes on to say, is the only way to make what the other says one's own (*anzueignen*), which is what he calls the "fusion of horizons." For Jacques Derrida, taking that risk, putting one's own meaning and self at risk, indeed one's own home, is the only way to let the other come. But in so doing, Derrida would not say we make the other our own, but one would let the other break into what is our "own," which means that for Derrida the other would breach, not fuse with, our horizons. On such a construal, hermeneutics and deconstruction share a common commitment to hear the other, to make the other welcome, a common affirmation of what Derrida calls *l'inventions de l'autre*, the arrival, the in-comings, of the other, which is also part of the hermeneutics of friendship that I will discuss in the next chapter.[2] But hermeneutics and deconstruction have different ideas of what that means and how to go about it. On my telling, deconstruction is a more radical way of doing what hermeneutics sets out to do, providing a more radical version of what hermeneutics loves and desires, which is to let the other come.

The whole idea of post-Diltheyan hermeneutics goes back to the young Martin Heidegger's project of a "hermeneutics of facticity," the attempt to begin with the factical or hermeneutical situation in which we find ourselves, the concrete, pregiven world in which and by which we are formed, with all of its difficulties and impasses. These constraints, Heidegger showed, also constitute our angle of entry onto the world; like the Kantian dove, the resistance they provide is also what keeps us aloft. Under the influence of Plato and G. W. F. Hegel, Gadamer altered and corrected Heidegger's hermeneutics of facticity in a crucially important way by steering it in the direction of conversation or dialogue, the exchange between the self and the other, thereby bringing it into contact with Martin Buber, on the one hand, and with Emmanuel Levinas and his notion of living conversation, *le dire*, on the other hand, a relationship between friends, which is a contact Heidegger himself could not establish. For Gadamer, hermeneutics means a way to hear and welcome the coming of the other, both in person and living dialogue, and in the great texts and works of art of our tradition. Indeed, insofar as Derrida, very much under Levinas's influence, has come to regard faith as the medium in which we communicate—as soon as I open my mouth, I try to speak the truth—his work has come closer to Gadamer than to Heidegger.

Thus conceived, "hermeneutics," which is a word I do not want to lose, turns on an axis whose twin poles are "facticity" and the "other." I am still very attached to the word "hermeneutics" because I am quite attached to these poles. But, however much I am indebted to Gadamer, I remain a little suspicious of his version of hermeneutics. For under Gadamer's hand, hermeneutics is marked by Hegelian and Platonic metaphysics in such a way as to slacken its tensions and remove some of the bite of its openness to the other. I propose to show how this is so by way of an examination of Gadamer's notion of the "finitude" of hermeneutic understanding, for on the face of it finitude is a point on which hermeneutics and deconstruction seem to converge.[3] Gadamer's notion of finitude sets his work off from Hegel, situating his philosophical hermeneutics within the line of criticism that Kierkegaard made of Hegel (in terms of the existential situation) and that Heidegger made of Husserl in terms of the factical or hermeneutical situation. Seen from the point of view of Gadamer's hermeneutics, do not *écriture* and *différance,* supplement and trace, take their proper place within an analytic of hermeneutic finitude? Situated within the horizon of philosophical hermeneutics, what is deconstruction if not a patient, scrupulous, pitiless unfolding of the limitations and constraints under which human understanding labors, exposing in a bold and novel way the multiple illusions and traps to which we are subject *precisely* in virtue of the finitude of our understanding? To be bound up in the double bind, constantly to be buffeted by one aporia after another, concerning the gift, hospitality, the other—would that not be exactly what one would predict for a being bound up by its finitude? Does not deconstruction explore in ruthless detail the domain of finitude, a domain that has been marked out in advance by hermeneutics? Is deconstruction a special case of hermeneutics, a moment in the larger act of hermeneutic understanding and openness to the other which Gadamer describes?

About that I have my doubts. In my view Gadamerian hermeneutics needs to be pushed beyond itself, pushed in a direction it says it wants to go but about which it drags its feet, enticed to welcome an other for which its anticipatory forestructures cannot prepare or be prepared. That results in a more radical rendering of hermeneutics by deconstruction, one that holds the feet of hermeneutics more mercilessly to the fires of facticity and alterity. For Gadamer's notion of finitude functions in his work in a way that is decisively marked by Hegel and the metaphysical tradition generally, and indeed that communicates with a metaphysics of infinity of a classical sort. Gadamer's analytic of finitude cannot conceal a latent theory of essence, ideality, and infinity that softens the workings of facticity and narrows the range of alterity. The finitude of the understanding is not *différance,* and because of that there are limits on Gadamer's notion of alterity, and accordingly on any possible account of hospitality, of the aporia of hospitality, which turns on the impossible and paralyzing problem of how to prepare for one for whose coming we cannot be prepared.

Gadamer's Analytic of Finitude

Let us begin with Gadamer's critique of Wilhelm Dilthey, which is, in my view, where Gadamer's analytic of finitude does its best work. Dilthey's search for historical objectivity is essentially an effort at infinite understanding, according to Gadamer (WM, 218; TM, 232). Dilthey's infinitism takes the form of an objectivist historical consciousness which thinks it can cure itself of its finitude by means of methodological controls. The mind is finite but the historian can correct for that by exerting a rigorous, purifying reflection which strikes out the distorting contingencies of one's particular historical circumstances. As a being endowed with the capacity for reflection the historian can raise himself or herself above the fortuitous and ultimately prejudicial circumstances within which one is situated, thus successfully neutralizing the effects of finitude.

Gadamer rightly rejects this notion as a kind of Cartesian dream, an illusion of self-transparency which arises from an exaggerated notion of the power of reflection. Gadamer criticizes Dilthey by showing that Dilthey's historical objectivism is at odds with his own *Lebensphilosophie*. For the upshot of Dilthey's notion of life is so to bind the thinking subject to the conditions of life as precisely to disallow the kind of distantiation which his concept of historical consciousness demands, something which, as Gadamer shows, comes out in the famous correspondence between Dilthey and Count Paul Yorck von Wartenburg (WM, 229ff.; TM, 242ff.). Dilthey's notion of historical objectivity requires an abstract, disengaged, epistemological subject while his *Lebensphilosophie* commits him to a concrete, living, historical subject whose relationship to the past is not an objectifying one, but a living one, one which takes up, assimilates, and is nourished by the past.

By insisting as he does on the finitude of factical understanding, and hence on the impossibility of clearing away the encumbrances of historical situatedness, Gadamer remains loyal to the finitude or factical thrownness of *Dasein* in Heidegger's *Being and Time*. Finitude cannot be neutralized; prejudices cannot be annulled. Finitude is an ontological structure of *Dasein* and it can be laid aside only at the cost of the structure of understanding. *Dasein* studies history (*Historie*) because *Dasein* is in its very being historical (*geschichtlich*), and the past is the stuff of which *Dasein*'s existential projects are made. Understanding is a mode of self-understanding, a way that *Dasein* has of projecting its own possibilities (WM, 246–247; TM, 260). In short, the fact of *Dasein*'s factical finitude, its being bound and limited to its own existential projects, makes historical understanding possible. Finitude does not merely limit, but also enables historical understanding. That is the basis of Gadamer's rehabilitation of prejudice in the next section of *Truth and Method*, the net effect of which, he says, is to open the way toward the appropriation of our finitude (WM, 260; TM, 276).

There is, Gadamer confesses, a paradox attached to affirming the finitude of the understanding (WM, 324–329; TM, 341–346). For such an affirmation amounts to a self-limiting reflection, an understanding which declares itself to be limited, which knows that it knows only so much and knows that it knows no more. If consciousness can mark off its own limits, if it can draw a boundary line around itself, then it must at the same time know what lies on both sides of the limit. If that is so, then consciousness is not limited after all, for it has mediated its own limitation, moved beyond it, and taken another step forward in its own progressive self-possession. Thus, reflection is able to transform the effective reality of history (*Wirkung*) into scientific knowledge (*Wissen*). That of course is Hegel's critique of Kant, and it applies in advance to all of Hegel's later critics who want to hold speculative idealism to the fire of existential, historical, linguistic, or—in this case—hermeneutical finitude.

In response to this aporia Gadamer points out that such a merely formal consideration cannot settle the matter, which is why Plato used a myth to brush off the sophistic argument about the impossibility of learning anything. The issue is a substantive (*sachlich*) one and cannot be settled on solely formal grounds. In order to address the question substantively Gadamer takes up an analysis of our hermeneutical "experience"—our experience of the work of art, of the effective power of history, of the universal mediation of language—and he offers us an interesting, enlightening phenomenology of experience that shows the inherent limitation or negativity which is built into experience.[4]

Gadamer explicates the negativity of experience by shifting the concept of experience from the horizon of science—where experience carries the rather upbeat, positivistic sense of progressive accumulation, of the positive confirmation of a law—to the horizon of life in the *Lebenswelt*. In concrete, factical life, experience takes on a ring of negativity, a dialectical sense of "learning by" experience. In the realm of science, everything disconfirming and negative is to be gradually erased until a fully positive universal emerges. But in living experience things are different. Experience is acquired in the school of hard knocks, where to have acquired experience means to have learned one's lesson and to be wary of what is coming next. Thus in the life-world, the point is not to annul the negative but to be ready for it, to be ready for the unforeseeable, for what goes against our expectations (maybe even ready for anxiety, *Angstbereit*). Experience was described best of all by Aeschylus: *pathei mathos:* we learn by suffering, by running up against our limits, by the thunderstorm which is visited upon our plans and expectations (WM, 339; TM, 320). This notion of experience is in fact comparable to the one that Derrida advances when he speaks of having an experience of the impossible: experience worthy of the name does not involve the pedestrian matters of everyday experience, but only the "events" which shatter our horizon of expectation.[5] To experience the aporia, *the* impossible, which hospitality is, to go where you cannot go, this is what Derrida means by "experience."

Now the interesting thing is that Gadamer's idea of experience both is and is not Hegelian. It is certainly a dialectical idea of experience, inasmuch as experience is sharpened and strengthened by exposure to the negative, where the security of the positive must be tested, proved, and fired by the negative—putting it "at risk." But Gadamer rejects the Hegelian conception; it is not Gadamer's intention to supersede negativity once and for all by reaching a standpoint where the disruptiveness of the negative is simply transcended, put in its place, assigned a place by a reflection which has managed to slip past it. On the contrary, experience for Gadamer requires a continual openness to negativity, or readiness for it, *ad infinitum*. Experience means finitude *ad infinitum*. But a finitude which keeps revisiting itself upon us infinitely, which keeps deferring its completion, is a bad infinity, albeit a good finitude, indeed the very best.[6]

But, in my view, Gadamer has subtly shifted the ground from Heidegger's analytic of the finitude of *Dasein* to Hegelian infinitism, with the result that a more radically Heideggerian facticity has been subverted from within by a creeping Hegelianism. That is what I want to show now.

Finitude and the Metaphysics of Infinity

Gadamer is arguing for the limits of reflection, that is, for the irreducibility of being to thought, of the *Sache* to knowledge, of *Wirkung* to *Wissen*. In particular, he is asserting three more specific theses about our experience of the work of art, our historical experience, and our experience with language. First, he claims that the artwork never yields itself to conceptual thinking, that it is jealous of the meaning which it harbors, which indeed it selfishly keeps to itself—which is what Heidegger meant by its standing in itself.[7] Second, in historical experience we run up against the strangeness and alienness of the past which functions like the mysterious recess of another "thou," an inaccessible source of initiatives that we can neither predict nor control. Finally, we live and think and have our being in the fluid medium of language which is irreducible to the univocity of a pure grammar and fixed significations. Language is a play in which mobile and shifting assertions do their best to stay in play with the play of the *Sache selbst*. Yet it is precisely here that I press my point that Gadamer's infinity becomes a good infinity and his finitude is *aufgehoben* into a metaphysics of infinity.

Gadamer argues against assigning canonical validity to the intention of the author whose authority is delimited in a two-fold gesture that reflects the way the Heideggerian side of his hermeneutics is monitored and redirected by the Hegelian side. Gadamer wants to show both (1) that the act of understanding is always finite (the Heideggerian side); and (2) that what is understood—the artwork, the historical event, the work of language—has a certain infinity (the Hegelian side). The author no less than later interpreters must reckon with "the non-definitiveness (*Unabschliessbarkeit*) of the horizon of meaning within which his understanding moves" (WM, 355; TM, 373). There is thus a certain "noetic" finitude, a finitude which besets human understanding, which is unable to encompass or circumscribe its object because of its own factical, historical limitations. But corresponding to this, let us say on the "noematic" side, there lies a veritable infinity of both historical event and written text which likewise accounts for the impossibility of canonical interpretation. This correlativity of noetic finitude and noematic infinity is particularly clear in the following passage:

> Historical tradition can be understood only by being considered as something always in the process of being defined by the course of events. Similarly the philologist (*Philologe*) dealing with poetic or philosophical texts knows that they are inexhaustible (*Unauschöpfbarkeit*). In both cases it is the course of events that brings out new aspect of meaning in historical material. By being re-actualized (*Aktualisierung*) in understanding, texts are drawn into a genuine course of events (*Geschehen*) in exactly the same way as are the events (*Ereignisse*) themselves. This is what we described as the history of effect as an element in hermeneutical experience. Every actualization in understanding can be regarded as an historical potential (*Möglichkeit*) of what is understood. It is part of the historical finitude of our being that we are aware that others after us will understand in a different way. And yet it is equally indubitable that it remains the same work whose fullness of meaning (*Sinnfülle*) is realized in the changing process of understanding, just as it is the same history whose meaning is constantly in the process of being defined. (WM, 355; TM, 373)

To the noetic finitude of understanding (factical *Dasein*) there corresponds the noematic infinity of what is understood, a kind of infinite spirit. To the limited horizons within which the act of understanding must function there corresponds the inexhaustible depth of the historical material. There is a richness of meaning in historical events which just keeps unfolding, which is certainly not grasped by the original protagonists, which gradually unfolds over the course of time, and which is in principle never fully unfolded. By the same token literary and philosophical texts are inhabited by the same sort of inexhaustibility or infinity which can be mastered neither by the original authors nor by the succession of subsequent interpreters. The event or text is not an isolatable (finite) historical entity but a whole history—which is also a history of wholeness—a continuity of movement made up of both the original and the history of its effects which follow after it like a comet's tail. The fullness of meaning is never fully unfolded. It is an excess which keeps spilling over like a neoplatonic emanation. It cannot be contained by either author or interpreter, neither of whom is a match for or can contain the fullness which sweeps over them and holds them under its claim.

The subversiveness of Heideggerian facticity has been reinscribed within the reassuring framework of a classical, Aristotelico-Hegelian metaphysics of infinity. The text for Gadamer represents an infinite potential, a potentially good infinity, of which every new understanding is a new finite actualization, a new way in which what is understandable in potency becomes understood in act. But this Aristotelian process of actualization is carried out in a quasi-Hegelian process of historical unfolding. The essence (fullness, meaning) does not yield itself up at once, but rather its being is its becoming, its essence is to unfold its essence through an historical process. That is because of its inner infinity or intelligibility on the one hand and the finitude of the understanding on the other. Gadamer's position reminds us of the theological excess, the infinity of the divine being vis-à-vis the finitude of the human intellect.[8] The latter can do no more to compensate for its limitations than to multiply the names of God and to proclaim its own inability to exhaust the infinite riches of the godhead.

My point is supported in an interesting way by Gadamer's occasional essays on modern art, many of which have been translated under the title *The Relevance of the Beautiful and Other Essays*.[9] Here Gadamer is addressing artworks such as the "pure poetry" of Stéphane Mallarmé, "absolute" music, and contemporary non-representational painting (RB, 75). These art forms would seem on the face of it to resist traditional aesthetic categories like mimesis. They seem to represent a case not of the inexhaustibility of meaning but of a radical break with meaning and so to represent a rupture with the past history of art. But Gadamer's aim is to close this gap, to fuse these horizons, and to reconcile these differences. One might ask whether this is not a domesticative gesture, whether Gadamer is really ready to hear something new in modern art, something troubling and indigestible.

Gadamer insists that the modern artwork does not lack meaning or unity; rather it has decided to draw us more fully into its play by making us, the observers, toil harder to find meaning and unity. It leaves a certain leeway or space which needs to be filled in by an active construction or synthesis on the part of the observer. Thus cubism does not represent the loss of the object but the necessity for the observer to superimpose for oneself the different aspects in order to attain the unity of a perceptual object (RB, 27). It is as if Pablo Picasso and Georges Braque were Husserlians with a theory of intentional adumbration (*Abschattung*) up their sleeve, as if Marcel Duchamp's nude descending a staircase is an illustration of transcendental phenomenology. To perceive is to perceive an object—perception according to the reassuring German word is *wahrnehmen*, taking as true, taking in the solidity of a substantial unity—and what Picasso does is make this a bit harder to do. Again, the painting is a potentiality for meaning, and the observation or "reading" of the painting is its actualization.

It appears thus to be a fundamental metaphysical assumption on Gadamer's part that the modern artwork cannot be aimed at the disruption of perception itself, that it cannot mean to effect a deeper disturbance than merely to make perception more difficult. But what if the real difficulty posed by cubism or the more extreme forms of non-representational art were the way they set about disturbing the idea of a deeper substantial unity? What if they were trying to insist on the unmotivated, conventional character of experience, on the instability of our ideas of truth and reality? What if, in short, these were indeed Husserlians but Husserlians who had read Derrida's *Speech and Phenomena*,[10] or Husserlians who were more interested in the famous thesis of the annihilability of the world? That appears to be a horizon that Gadamer has no intention of fusing. On Gadamer's accounting, the modern artwork puts up a tougher fight—its deep potential is a lot more resistant to actualization that traditional art—but it remains within the horizon of the actualization of its inexhaustible potentiality.

Gadamer's view is at best "quasi-Hegelian" because Gadamer has modified Hegel, not only by rejecting Hegelian teleology, but also by departing from Hegel's understanding of art. Human being for Gadamer is finite and seeks fulfillment in the wholeness of the artwork. But this fulfilling meaning cannot be simply disengaged from the artwork like a message from its medium (RB, 36–37). It is important to see that Gadamer does not reject the idea that the artwork bears a message (RB, 142)—and to that extent he understands art very much in terms of a postal metaphysics[11]—but he does reject the idea that the message can be abstracted or distilled from the artwork in which it is embedded. He rejects the idea that art can be transcended by philosophy, that artworks can be thematically condensed into a conceptualizable meaning. Rather they represent a unique intensification or magnification of meaning—the mimesis does not diminish, it increases the being—which is uniquely embodied in this artwork, in this *hoc aliquid*. The horizon within which the artwork is considered is meaning, but meaning is realized with such sensuous immediacy as to be rendered non-transcendable by a desensualizing *nous*. The result of this is not to destroy the infinity and inexhaustibility of meaning but to let it sink even deeper into the artwork and to make the observer work even harder to actualize it. Gadamer speaks in terms almost of the stinginess of the modern art in its refusal to give up its meaning, to let itself be appropriated, to surrender a fixed sense (RB, 37). Its *Bedeutung* has become more and more *zweideutig*, its meaning more a riddle, its depths harder and harder to plumb.

All of this comes to a head when Gadamer speaks of the special "temporality" of the artwork, which is the temporality of making present again, of a sacramental repetition which Gadamer explicitly compares to the theology of the real (as opposed to the merely symbolic) presence of Christ in the Eucharist in Catholic theology. Indeed Gadamer's is a deeply "eucharistic hermeneutics," to borrow a phrase from Jean-Luc Marion,[12] a good gift really present and made present again and again over the ages, in works of art, historical events, and literary and philosophical texts. In the temporality of the artwork we become contemporaneous with a meaning and truth which transcends time, which is omni-temporal. Of this Gadamer writes—and here the Gadamerian cat leaps out the bag:

When we dwell upon the [art]work, there is no tedium involved, for the longer we allow ourselves, the more it displays its manifold riches to us. The essence of our temporal experience of art is in learning how to tarry in this way. And perhaps it is the only way that is granted to us finite beings to relate to what we call eternity. (RB, 45)

Différance *Is Other Than Finitude*

But just as, for Derrida, the notion of the "fragment" presupposes the idea of the whole,[13] so also does the idea of finitude presuppose the metaphysics of infinity. The "return to finitude," he says, "would not mean a single step out of metaphysics." Derrida continues:[14]

It is that conceptuality and that problematic that must be deconstructed. They belong to the onto-theology they fight against. *Différance* is also something other than finitude.

Finitude in Gadamer is not a scandal or rupture but part of an argument for infinity, a transcendental finitude, a kind of *felix culpa* which receives its reassuring complement from the infinity of what is understood. Human finitude is a broken symbolon which is made whole by the ideality and infinity of the artwork. The artwork is our other and better half with which we can be fitted together to form a whole. In virtue of its symbolic makeup, the artwork is according to Gadamer:

. . . that other fragment that has always been sought in order to complete and make whole our own fragmentary life . . . the experience of the beautiful in art is the invocation of a potentially whole and holy order of things, wherever it may be found. (RB, 32)

Consider the shock of juxtaposing the Gadamerian thematics of the fragment with the Derridean "remain(s)":[15]

what, after all, of the remain(s), today, for us, here, now, of a Hegel? (G, la)

"what remained of a Rembrandt torn into small, very regular squares and rammed down the shithole" is divided into two. (G, 1b)

The Gadamerian fragment is a symbolon which is to be fitted together with its missing half, which is a perfect match for it, a token by which we can recognize infinity, the whole, the holy. The remain(s) in deconstruction are the loose remnants that clog the Hegelian system, the loose ends in the texture of its garment which keep coming undone, the jammed gears which grind the Hegelian machine to a halt, the cut-up pieces which can be glued together this way or that, the scrambled messages that get all gummed up in the postal works, the *symbolon* which was shattered too badly ever to be fitted together, indeed which never was a whole.

That is why hermeneutic finitude does not translate or precontain *différance*. If hermeneutics is a philosophy of transcendental finitude—a fiitude which tends beyond itself and is stretched out into infinite full-ness—then deconstruction is addressing that bad infinity which just goes on and on, spread out of control in every direction. Deconstruction is greeting not Gadamer's finitude but the uncontrollable transfers, trans-missions, translations, and exchanges that go on and on *ad infinitum* in the postal play. Deconstructionist infinity is the mirror play *en abîme*, the endless transformation of phonic and graphic chains. As Derrida writes:[16]

> If polysemy is infinite, if it cannot be mastered as such, this is thus not because a finite reading or a finite writing remains incapable of exhausting a superabundance of meaning. Not, that is, unless one displaces the philo-sophical concept of finitude and reconstitutes it according to the law and structure of the text. . . . Finitude then becomes infinitude, according to a non-Hegelian identity.

We are not confronted with the infinite and eternal depths of the excess of meaning but with the endless play of grammatological superficiality.[17] Derrida is not thereby consigning us to senselessness and confusion, for the polysemy and dissemination of which he speaks is the setting within which his later messianic affirmation of the justice to come is to be situ-ated.

Gadamerian hermeneutics remains within the classical metaphysical distinction between essence (or ideality) and its concrete actualizations. Gadamer endorses Husserl's claim that the artwork performs a spontane-ous eidetic reduction, and he uses it to back up the Aristotelian claim that art is more philosophical than history. The artwork is not a less than real copy of an original but an intensification of reality which exceeds reali-ty as the universal exceeds the particular, as the essential exceeds the contingent, as the ideal exceeds the empirical. The historian merely re-cords individual events, but the poet brackets empirical contingencies and grasps the essence (RB, 133–134, 120, 129).

Consider in particular the difference between Gadamer and Derrida on writing (WM, 367 ff.; TM, 389 ff.). For Gadamer, writing (*Schriftlich-keit*, being written, writtenness, in proper written form) is the defining characteristic of the linguisticality (*Sprachlichkeit*) of the hermeneutic ob-ject (*Gegenstand*). He distinguishes it from the hermeneutic "act" (*Vollzug*) which is executed or carried out on the object, that is, the act of under-standing (*Verstehen*). Thus the distinction between what is understood and the act of understanding, between object and act, comes down to a distinction between object and actualization, between potentiality and actualization. An ideality is an ideal carrier of meaning which can be transformed into actuality by anyone with linguistic competence. Once again, we see the correlativity of noetic finitude and noematic infinity played out.

The key to Gadamer's notion of writing is that in writing language is detached (*abgelöst*, WM 367; TM, 390) from its actualization. That is both its advantage and its weakness. In writing, language is reduced to a diminished but ideal condition, to a linguistic concentrate, put in a sort of deep freeze which needs the thaw of speech or reading, the living act (*Vollzug*), to bring it back to life. Yet that is precisely what enables writing to survive, to live on, to acquire a deeper permanence than is granted to the finite, mortal readers and speakers before whose gaze it passes. Many living eyes have passed over these pages only then to pass away themselves, but this ideality, this permanent possibility of meaning, endures. It is precisely because writing has lowered the body temperature of language to near death, slowed down its living functions to a point of almost perfect immobility, that language can acquire the permanence which makes a tradition possible. It is just in virtue of this linguistic freeze that the ideality of meaning can go into dormancy, a deep linguistic sleep, from which it can be awakened again and again by the breath of the *Vollzug.* We see then the set of equivalences we are working with: writing: potentiality: ideality: meaning. And finally, which is not to be forgotten, alienation (*Selbstentfremdung,* WM, 368; TM, 390). For language is not at home, is still a stranger, is half dead, a ghostly shade, in writing, and it can be relieved of its exile in this land of shades only by the warmth of the living subject. A strange thing on earth is writing.

It is just this ideality, this ghostly *Geistigkeit,* which gives the tradition its real power to hand itself down, to endure, to make memory last (WM, 368; TM, 391), to become present (contemporaneous) again and again, in short to assume a certain infinity. The ghost returns. "I will speak of the *revenant.*"[18] Oddly enough, Gadamer here is never so close and never so far from Derrida—maybe here we are touching on a possible translation—especially when a few lines later he remarks that this ideality is not restricted to writing:

> But that language is capable of being written is by no means incidental to its nature. Rather this capacity for being written down is based on the fact that speech itself shares in the pure ideality of the meaning that communicates itself in it. . . . Writing is the abstract ideality of language. (WM, 370; TM, 392)

For, as Derrida, following Husserl, points out, the spoken word, "lion," for example, is also an ideal unity across time and space, one that is realized as many times as it is spoken by different speakers at different times and in different places.

If writing is the abstract ideality of language, then speech is its concrete or living ideality. Gadamer thus, if only momentarily, erases the distinction between writing and speech and identifies in both a common structure. But he characterizes this common structure as ideality or repeatability. He thus links ideality and repeatability in the classical metaphysical manner, for he makes repeatability a function of ideality, representation a function of presence. The defining characteristic of writing, and its great advantage, is that it provides a long term medium for passing on meaning; its disadvantage is, as Plato says in the *Philebus*, that it cannot fend for itself, that it is orphan who has lost its father. The defining characteristic of speech, and its great advantage, is that it can pass on meaning in a fluid and self-correcting, self-interpreting way which minimizes misunderstanding; but its disadvantage is its transiency, for it literally disappears into thin air. But both cases have to do with media which bear meaning, which have ideal content, which are carriers of ideality.

What Gadamer never allows is precisely the deconstructionist reversal which makes ideality a function of repeatability, presence an effect of representation, meaning the result of the trace.[19] It is true that Gadamer has bound meaning to language much more closely than the metaphysical tradition before him. He does not think that language is the expression of a pre-constituted meaning, but that language is the emergence, constitution, or coming into being of meaning (and indeed being itself). But it is the coming to be of *meaning*. Language is related to meaning as the explicit to the implicit, the emergent to the latent, the actual to the possible. Toward the end of *Truth and Method* he identifies the Neoplatonic theory of emanation as a good model for articulating the relationship between being (or meaning) and language: language is the way that being which is understood emanates forth, comes into presence (WM, 400; TM, 423; cf. WM, 134; TM, 140). All of the suppleness, play, and fluidity upon which he insists, which gives speech its advantage over writing, arises from the necessity which language is under to serve the needs of this emanation process, to be responsive to meaning, to let being and meaning emerge, to let it be.

What Gadamer refuses is exactly what Derrida calls the thought of the trace, not the trace which follows after and copies an original, but the trace which produces, which effects, which pre-delineates, precedes, and makes possible the multiple unities—of "meaning," "being" and even "language"—within which Gadamerian hermeneutics functions. That is why there is such a vast difference between Gadamer's treatment of Mallarmé, which seems intent as it were on containing the damage, on striking a balance between meaning and mark, sense and sound, and Derrida's approach, which finds in it all the energy of dissemination.[20] Gadamer hesitates before the abyss that opens up with such artists as Mallarmé or James Joyce, where what hermeneutics regards as the surface of language comes into play. Gadamer's play must always stay in bounds, within the bounds of sense. So too with modern, non-representational painting: Gadamer is reluctant to enter that abyss where the pure play of lines and color comes into play. Even though the modern painting has lost the frame which once contained it and centered it upon itself, it has not lost its unity (RB, 88–89). Gadamer will not say, as Derrida does, that there is painting, that's all; and the shoes are there for the painting, not to tell us about the dark mystery of the peasant woman's world, but for the painting, for multiple lacings and unlacings, to be tied and untied, cut up and glued together in multiple, unforeseeable ways.[21]

It is precisely the point of the Derridean stylus to stick us with the sharp cutting edges of the trace, to draw us into the land of the shades, of dormancy and the deep freeze, of the marks which can be made with pens and pencils, with a pulmonary organ forcing air out in measured and modulated ways, with paint brushes, with hands and feet, with arched eyebrows, with green phosphorous screens, with paws and tails, with who knows what. Derrida sticks our head back into the text whenever hermeneutics comes up for the air of living speech, its eyes bulging and a look of panic on its face. Derrida cuts and glues, pasting things together in the strangest ways, making things look and sound so odd, whenever hermeneutics tries to fit together the two exquisitely matched pieces of the symbolon. Derrida irreverently celebrates the gay First Communion whenever Gadamer bows his hermeneutic head at the Catholic theology of the Eucharist. Derrida hears the hissing of the disseminative "s," like air leaking from a tire, whenever Gadamer tries to strike a balance between sound and sense. Derrida shows the impossibility of the frame to maintain the distinction between inside and outside whenever Gadamer looks for the deeper unity which the frame once helped protect.

But can we not fuse these horizons? Is that not the finitude? All those scandalous things that scalawag Derrida does, are they not testimony to the finitude of human understanding and the difficulty which besets the search for meaning? Can we not translate deconstruction into hermeneutics?

Now for all the reasons that I have been developing in these pages I must insist that this is no translation, or a bad translation, a slight of hand, a way of copping out, a way that hermeneutics has found of not quite hearing something different, of reducing what is other to its own terms, of making its other into *its* other, which is what I am always worried Gadamerian translation attempts. One cannot translate *différance* with finitude if for no other reason than that *différance* is a lot more like a wild and formless infinity than a well-formed finitude. That is why Derrida insists that *différance* is not finitude. "*Différance* is also something other than finitude." Gadamerian finitude is transcendental finitude, a way of bearing testimony to the infinite, an edifying discourse which is meant to tell us that we float on a sea of infinite being, meaning, and truth, whose depths we can never fathom, whose bounty we can never consume.

So this finitude is an edifying finitude, a facticity with some of its bite gone. Nobody gets cut, castrated, guillotined, stuck in the behind (*Glas*). It is a pointer in the direction of infinity. It is a good finitude, which points us in the direction of an equally good infinity, albeit without the teleology of a final and fixed *telos* to aim at. When Gadamer tells us he is arguing for a bad infinity, I think he means a classical infinity without the teleology, which has given up the idea that we ever get the final canonical form, which has the good sense to recognize that the infinite keeps taking new forms. Where hermeneutics bows its head to our finite condition, deconstruction does a shocking, lewd dance of infinity which scandalizes the faithful and sends them heading for the doors. Deconstruction is bad and it makes no bones about it. It dines with sinners and thieves and it hangs around with Jean Genet's pimps and queens. It prefers the wild(er)ness of the *apeiron,* of infinity, to Greco-Germanic form and finitude, and the barrenness of the *khôra* to the sublime fertility of *agathon.*

Radical Hermeneutics

I am not arguing against hermeneutics, but for loosening the constraints that are imposed upon hermeneutics in its Gadamerian version in order to make possible a more radical hermeneutics. Gadamer says that in every hermeneutic act there is a moment of "self-recognition," a moment in which the text or work of art says to us "that is you" (RB, 64), just like when I hear a good sermon on Sunday and I am convinced that his reverence is speaking directly to me and that everyone in the church must know what I have done. I think that something like that is so, but with this difference, that sometimes what we hear is not the good news from the pastor but the bad news that there is no "you," that the I or the you is an effect, something constituted not constituting. There is no you—that is you! We do not know who we are—that is who we are. There is no Secret—that's the only secret.

That is the point at which I spoke in *Radical Hermeneutics* of the cold shiver (*phobe*), of the *ébranler,* of the *kinesis,* what I called cold or radical hermeneutics. The idea is that we get the best results if do not dodge the arrows of the trace, the displacement of the subject, the dissemination of meaning, the real difficulty in factical life. Now let us recall that back in 1921, after citing the *Nichomachean Ethics* to the effect that life is hard, which was itself a novel translation, Heidegger went on to say that pursuing that very thought is what he means by the "hermeneutics of facticity."[22] The aim is not to edify ourselves with the thought of transcendental finitude, which is the tendency of Gadamer's appropriation of Heideggerian facticity, but to face up to the infinite slippage, the grammatological infinity, which scrambles everything determinate, definite, and decidable. That is a big part of what it means to raise the question of being as presence, to make it questionable, and to hold it there, in question, hanging in suspense.

Still, why do have to call this "hermeneutics," even a radical hermeneutics? Why this nostalgia for this old word? For the two reasons with which I began, the twin poles of hermeneutics after Heidegger. (1) Hermeneutics means beginning where we are (Derrida),[23] in what Heidegger called the factical situation, the pregiven fix in which we find ourselves, the confusing web of our beliefs and practices, and proceeding from there as best we can; the hermeneutics of factical life means that we are under the necessity to think and act and hope, to press ahead, understanding full well the fix we are in. In this hermeneutic situation more radically conceived, the assumption is that no matter how bad things get, we always have our being to be, whoever or whatever "we," "being," and "be" may be. Deconstruction pushes facticity to its limits, radicalizing it, remaining rigorously loyal to our factical limits, ruthlessly, without pity, without appeal, without nostalgia, without a desire for presence, right on up to speaking of an experience of the impossible. (2) Hermeneutics has another dimension which Gadamer has happily brought out, which is not a side but a core, which lies in putting ourselves at risk, putting our own meanings, our own institutions, our own beliefs and practices, to the risk of the approach of the other, of the neighbor and the stranger. That means that "we" are the ones who cannot quite say "we," and, for Levinas, it means that the being that matters most is not mine but the other's, the being of the other who Levinas likes to say for reasons of his own is otherwise than being.

Now these twin poles of fidelity to our factical limits and of responsiveness to the other are powerfully at work in deconstruction. That is why it is necessary, in my view, to revisit the "Derrida-Gadamer" debate, or nondebate. The first and only exchange between Derrida and Gadamer was unsuccessful. Readers were left with the impression that deconstruction comes down to the ignoble and unrelieved suspicion that everywhere the will to power undermines the good will of people trying as best they can to communicate with one another, while hermeneutics, good fellow that it is, tries nobly to defend good wills. The Nietzschean side of Derrida was plainly in view in that exchange, but not his Levinasian or Jewish side. For Derrida has begun to speak of hospitality and friendship, of justice and the gift, of bearing witness and of doing the truth, of confession and forgiveness, and even of his "religion," which involves a certain messianic hope in the coming of the other, terms that are more congenial to Gadamer's notion of hermeneutic understanding. As I have insisted from the start, Gadamer and Derrida share a common commitment to the interchange between what Levinas calls in *Totality and Infinity* the "same" and the "other,"[24] between the sphere of my world, or ours, and the disruptive entrance into that world of one who knocks at our door, who does not know or share our assumptions.

Recall the question we have taken as our guide and test case: How to prepare for the coming of one for whom the only preparation is to be prepared for anything, for whom the only adequate preparation is to confess that we cannot be prepared for what is coming? How to address and respond to the "other," who by definition is a shore we cannot reach, a domain we cannot inhabit, a *terra incognita*, not only unexplored but unexplorable? That concern is a constant one in deconstruction which, however much it has been unfairly criticized on this point, has always had an ethical and political force centered precisely on this point. That force has become unmistakable in recent years as Derrida has more and more taken up the question of hospitality, the multiple questions surrounding the *aporia* of hospitality: how to welcome the other into my home, how to be a good "host," which means how both to make the other at home while still retaining the home as mine, since inviting others to stay in someone else's home is not what we mean by hospitality or the gift. Hospitality, as Penelope learned while Ulysses was off on his travels, means to put your home at risk, which simultaneously requires both having a home and risking it. Derrida's growing discourse on hospitality reflects the Jewish and Levinasian provenance of deconstruction, for hospitality is the most ancient biblical virtue of all. In a desert world, in a world of nomads, the primordial and life-giving virtue was to offer respite to the stranger, the traveler, the wanderer, the migrant, whose survival turned on the expectation of hospitality, who cannot so much as set out without anticipating hospitality, without *trusting* in hospitality. Today, Derrida is deeply concerned with the fate of the contemporary nomads, the immigrant, and displaced populations who are daily sent scurrying from their homes by the forces of greed, ethnic war, religious persecution, national hatreds, and oppression, and he pushes this paradox of hospitality to its limits by calling for the abolition of immigration laws, open borders, with all the Penelopean risks that such generosity entails.

That *trust* in the expectation of hospitality is the opposite of a cynical suspicion that everywhere the will to power makes playthings of our best intentions. It is a side of deconstruction that has tended to lie concealed not only from deconstruction's critics and but also from a few of its friends. Now my point is that all of this puts the anti-essentialism of Derrida in context, in an ethical and political context. His much vaunted critique of presence and *logos*, his suspicion of a hermeneutics of "meaning" and deep "truth," the wild antics of *Glas*, are not undertaken in the name of wanton play, of unbridled critique, of nihilistic suspicion, but in the name of the affirmation, the *"oui, oui,"* of the other, of the *tout autre*, in the name of hospitality, for he fears the barriers that essences build, be it the essence of truth or being, of art or language, of tradition or community. He fears the walls that "community" builds against those who are outside the walls, who are exiled, excommunicated, expelled, who seem to those inside to put the community at risk. For after all a "fort," a fortified dwelling, a structure that is walled on all sides from the approach of the other, is one of the most literal senses of community, which is a fortifying (*munire*) of ourselves all around (*com*). A community is precisely what does not want to *take any risks* when it comes to the other, *to minimize the risk of the coming of the other*. Derrida fears the walls of the deep essences "we" share in common, the essence of "our" tradition, "our country," which gets into the title of Richard Rorty's most recent book, which I will discuss in chapter 4, our gender, our religion, our culture, our family. The list goes on. So Gadamer's discourse on the deep "truth" of our "tradition," which is older than we can say, which has us before we can have it, can only worry Derrida, for Derrida's anti-essentialism springs from a desire for a softer sense of the sphere of same, one that maintains the porousness of the same, precisely in order to allow for the approach of the other. Now a *porous* fort is hardly a fort at all and would certainly not command a high price. For Derrida the tradition is through and through something "constituted," an effect, radically contingent, re-formable, reconstructible, not possessed of some deep identity, some essential truth or core that cuts off in advance the coming of the other:[25]

> . . . it is the idea itself of an identity or a self-interiority of every tradition (*the one* metaphysics, *the one* Christian revelation, *the one* history itself, *the one* history of being, *the one* epoch, *the one* tradition, self-identity in general, the one, etc.) that finds itself contested at its root.

The difference between Gadamer and Derrida, in my view, is that deconstruction, in virtue of its more radical anti-essentialism, provides for a more radical conception of friendship and hospitality, of putting oneself at risk, and if hermeneutics means putting one's own meanings at risk, as Gadamer has so beautifully written, then deconstruction also effects a more radical hermeneutics. Gadamer has a more Hegelian sense of equilibrium, of a balanced interplay between the same and the other, a dialectical equilibrium without a telos, a little like the balanced correlation, the *adequatio*, between noesis and noema in Husserl that Levinas criticized, that goes along with a sense of the inexhaustible depth of the tradition. In this way, Derrida differs from Gadamer the way Levinas differs from Buber. Derrida shares Levinas's suspicions of such dialectical balance and dialogical equilibrium, and he takes the Levinasian view that the advance or approach of the *tout autre* has an upsetting, overturning quality which leaves us a little scattered and lost for words, that the other is higher, as when I say "after you," putting you first. That is why Derrida would not embrace the rhetoric of a fusion of horizon, for it is only in the breach of the horizon that the other manages to gain a hearing.

That is also why, in Derrida and Levinas, the notion of infinity blocks the fusion of horizons, and sees to it that the Other always belongs to the step beyond, the step we cannot take, the other shore, the bridge we cannot build. Infinity is a part of Derrida's vocabulary—"we live in infinitude," he says, and that is what makes infinite responsibility possible[26]—but this infinity does not have to do with the infinite depths of a tradition which we endlessly plumb, but the infinite dissymmetry of the Other whom we cannot know or have, which is the point of departure for the hermeneutics of friendship to which we turn next, where the question might be taken to be, "how to prepare for the coming of the friend?"

On the more radical telling that deconstruction provides, the hermeneutical question is pushed to its limits. How then—to come back to our
test question—to prepare for the coming of one for whom the only preparation is to be prepared for anything? How to prepare for one for whom
the only adequate preparation is to confess that we cannot be prepared
for what is coming? How to be un/prepared? The idea for Derrida would
not be to try to answer or resolve this dilemma by some interesting theoretical move, but to experience all the difficulty of this *aporia*, all the
paralysis of that impossible situation, and then to begin where you are
and to go where you cannot go. The resolution for Derrida is not a matter
of knowing or of fusing horizons. The secret of the other, he says, is
caught up in "a structural non-knowing, which is heterogeneous, foreign
to knowledge. It's not just the unknown that could be known and that I
give up trying to know. It is something in relation to which knowledge is
out of the question."[27] The structural secrecy of the other is affirmed in
and by the "after you."

3

Who Is Derrida's Zarathustra?

Of Fraternity, Friendship, and a Democracy to Come

Appearing without Appearing

Would it be possible that friendship, too, would also belong to a herme-neutics of not knowing who we are, that friendship would indeed *depend* upon non-knowing, and that this non-knowing would alone keep it safe? Would it be possible that friendship, contrary to all our inherited intui-tions, would rest upon preserving the absoluteness of the secret of the other, rather than upon the intimacy of shared secrets, on a deep inti-mate knowledge that friends would have of each other? Might friend-ship, too, be a passion of non-knowing, a relation that in fact exceeds knowledge and truth, like an abyss calling to an abyss? *Abyssus abyssum invocat.*

That indeed is the view Maurice Blanchot advances when he writes:[1]

> We must give up trying to know those to whom we are linked by some-thing essential; by this I mean we must greet them in the relation with the unknown in which they greet us as well, in our estrangement.

From the depths of a "common strangeness" we concede that we do not know each other, and that, because of this, we can only speak *to* each other, not *about* each other. Words touching words across a distance that cannot be crossed, making contact across an interval that cannot be closed: "Words from one shore to the other shore, speech responding to someone who speaks from the other shore. . . ." The function of our words is rather to greet or welcome the friend—*Bonjour! Adieu*—to hail one who exceeds us, as a "who" to whom we speak, and not to make them the subject of our conversation, as a "what" about which we speak. The interval between us does not constitute the destruction of the rela-tion with the friend but its peculiar nature, its defining feature as a rela-tion without relation, a relation, as Emmanuel Levinas says, where the relata tend to withdraw from the relation. For it is the withdrawal of the friend that draws us out of ourselves toward the friend, in the happy futility of a pursuit that Blanchot calls *le pas au-delà*, the step (*pas*) be-yond I cannot (*pas*) take, the *"passage"* that is always being made and al-ways being blocked. This distance or interval does not confine us to soli-tude but summons up speech and communication, if only sometimes the speech of silent companionship. The non-knowing, then, is not a matter of withholding confidences from each other and keeping things to ourselves, but rather of safeguarding the alterity of the other. For even this sharing of confidences, reaching only imperfectly across the separation of our being, presupposes and confirms the "interruption of being" between us. The structural secrecy of the other, the non-knowing protects or saves the unfathomability of the friend, keeping the friend safe from the arrows of knowledge. I cannot call the friend "mine," like something I have, for this relation is always *sans avoir, sans savoir.*[2]

So deep and unbridgeable is this interval for Blanchot that we might be tempted to say that nothing essential is changed with death, that even, in a certain way, death might be thought to make this distance all the more secure and profound. But that would be an illusion, for the gross actuality and pressing presence of death—which Blanchot distinguishes from the air-light passivity of "dying," the exposure to the death which does not arrive—would in fact destroy the separation of the other, and undo the relation. With death, the withdrawal and distance of the other also dies away, and the non-relation which is essential to the relation with the other is "erased." With death, we lose not only the proximity but also the distance of the friend, not only the approach but also the withdrawal and the secrecy. When we settle all our differences with the dead friend—*de mortuis nihil nisi bonum*—that is a false and easy illusion, for the difference and disagreement have in fact been annulled. Speech "subsides," abyss no longer calls to abyss, authentic dialogue dies away, and we are left with imaginary dialogues and the memory of the friend, which Blanchot calls a "deceptive consolation." The memory of the friend is "thought's profound grief," which arises from thought's higher knowledge that memory does not in truth remember, that memory is lost in oblivion. Thought "must accompany friendship into oblivion," preserving the friend's absence as such, into a simpler and more painful separation, into separation *simpliciter,* which is not the living distance, and not the secrecy of the separation that draws us out of ourselves by means of the approach of the friend, upon which friendship depends.

It is the strange but friendly presence of Blanchot's discourse on the friend, and also of Levinas, Blanchot's lifelong friend, that accompanies Derrida throughout *Politics of Friendship.*[3] Like Blanchot and Levinas, who are Jewish friends, but contrary to the intuitions we have accumulated about friendship from Greek philosophy, Christianity, and the Enlightenment, Derrida seeks to show that the friend is to be thought of as the *other,* arriving in a night of un-knowing, to be described in the deeply unphenomenological discourse of appearing *without* appearing:

[T]he other appears *as such*—this is to say, the other appears as a being whose appearance appears without appearing, without being submitted to the phenomenological law of the originary and intuitive given that governs all other appearances, all other phenomenality *as such.* The altogether

other, and *every other (one) is every (bit) other* [*tout autre est tout autre*], comes
here to upset the order of phenomenology. (PF, 232)

There is a numbers game here. The friend is not another self (*allos
autos*), which is what Aristotle said (*Nicomachean Ethics*, Book IX, chapter
4), so that two make one. Nor is friend the better half of my soul (*di-
midium animae meae*), which is the line from Horace cited in "the flow and
the economy of tears on the death of the friend" in Saint Augustine's
"Christian infinitization of friendship" (*Confessions*, Book IV, chapter 6; PF,
186), so that I am not whole but only half. If friendship amounts to one
soul in two bodies, then to love the friend is to love my own reflection or
echo, or still more, to love myself all over again, my other, better half or
self. But suppose the friend to be a second, an other, even wholly other
(*tout autre*), another one, transcendent and separate in being from me, a
second one. As simple as $1 + 1 = 2$ (not 1)! If the friend is the other, then to
give to the other is genuine transcendence, passage beyond myself, expenditure without return, and the alterity of the friend is the condition of
the gift (PF, 178–179).

But would such a relationship still be friendship? Would it require another name? Would it belong to some friendship yet *to come,* a friendship
without friendship, a friendship *beyond* friendship? Indeed, might it be that
the mainstream Western canonical view of friendship has been *already*
invaded and disturbed from within by an understanding, or at least, a
haunting intimation, of this *other* friendship?

Cities of Brotherly Love, Societies of Friends, and the Democracy to Come

There is also a question of the gender of the friend. Toward the end of
the book, in the discussion of the important text from Blanchot that we
have just discussed, with which *Politics of Friendship* concludes, Derrida
speaks of the fundamental "disquiet" by which the book is inspired. He is
citing a letter in which Blanchot says that the Nazi persecution has taught
us that "the Jews were our brothers" and that Judaism, over and beyond
being a particular religion, is "the foundation of our relationships with
the other (*autrui*)." Derrida confesses that, as close as he feels to Blanchot,
this letter makes him uneasy on several counts. He is apprehensive about
its "exemplarism," about the exemplary role assigned to a *particular* religion—or language or nation—here to Judaism, which could have unfortunate political consequences for the others who are not exemplary (for
example, if the others are the Palestinians). Beyond that, Derrida asks:

Why would *autrui* be in the first place a brother? And especially why
"our brothers"? Whose brothers? Who, then, are *we*? Who is this "*we*"?
(PF, 304)

Derrida finds himself wondering:

... why could I never have written that [sentence] ... nor subscribed to it ... ? In the same vein, I was wondering why the word "community" (avowable or unavowable, inoperative or not)—why I have never been able to write it, on my own initiative, and in my name, as it were. Why? Why my reticence? And is it not fundamentally the essential part of the disquiet which inspires this book? (PF, 304–305)

He is, of course, not *against* brothers, or *against* fraternity, which are good names and good things, and he loves his own and only brother, with whom we know he has had a troubled relationship. He is instead asking the question of what a "brother" is and he worries when it becomes such a privileged figure:

... when the humanity of man, as much as the alterity of the other, is thus resumed and subsumed. And the infinite price of friendship. (PF, 305)

To be sure, it does no good to protest that one doesn't *mean* to restrict community, humanity, or friendship to brothers, *stricto sensu*, that is, to men. When the Society of Friends, the Quakers, named their polity "Philadelphia," the city of "brotherly love," their hearts were in the right place; they surely meant this only as a figure for loving *all* humanity, all our friends. But that is the very thing Derrida is questioning. What are the consequences, especially the political consequences, of making the "brother" the exemplary case of the friend and community? What are "the politics of this language," the political impact of the choice of this word, "especially—if the choice is not deliberate" (PF, 305)? Derrida is wondering, above all, about its implications for democracy, for which it is a constant metaphor, longing as he does for a politics that would remain attached to this old word "democracy," while dreaming of and desiring a democracy to come:

For democracy remains to come; this is its essence in so far as it remains ... even when there is democracy, it never exists, it is never present, it remains the theme of a non-presentable concept. (PF, 306)

The democracy to come will be marked by justice beyond the law, by equality and freedom beyond fraternity, by an infinite dissymmetry beyond equality, by a friendship beyond the fraternalism of the canonical concept of friendship that has contracted democracy to something less than it is, by a friendship which can only be measured by the measurelessness of its gift.

❦-❦-❦

"We today"—if these two, *we* and *today*, are not already two fictions of presence, of community and contemporaneity—"belong" to what Derrida calls in *Specters of Marx* a "disjointed" time.[4] A tremor shocks all "communal belonging and sharing: religion, family, ethnic groups, nations, homeland, country, state, even humanity, love and friendship, lovence [see below], be they public or private" (PF, 80). Disjointed and dislocated as we are, we can no longer say "we," not with assurance or self-identity. Today, when the value of "community" has been shaken, we are driven to what Derrida names a logic of the "without" (sans), of the "x without x," a locution by which he means that something is effaced without being annulled, put in question in the act in which it is asserted, much like the earlier use of sous rature. Derrida—a "little black and very Arab Jew," an Algerian pied noir who speaks "Christian Latin French," who is always being made welcome elsewhere—is troubled by the privilege of the natural community and the native place, of the nation-state, around which classical politics is organized.[5] Derrida is disquieted by the tendency of the community of friends to draw themselves into a circle (com) and forcibly exclude (munire) the other, and by the threat that communitarian values always pose of bringing the brother back (PF, 298), so that a democracy as a genuine "society of friends" would not be a community, much less a city of brotherly love. His work has always been a response to the importunate plea of the displaced and, today, of the immigrant, the countless people who lack the protection of "citizenship," which means that they do not belong "here," and perhaps that they do not belong anywhere. They have no native place, no place to rest their head. That is why the question of friendship is closely linked to that of hospitality.[6] For what does hospitality mean if not to make oneself the friend of the stranger, to treat the stranger and the wayfarer as a friend, to treat one who is not "one of us" the way we treat our "own," to take the other into our home. The man with an empty hand and a closed door, as Levinas would say, is hardly hospitable, is a friend to no one. Friendship and hospitality, the gift and forgiveness—these are themes of the Derrida of the 1990s, ethical themes inspired by Levinas that Derrida wants to press into the service of a politics, into an ethics-becoming-politics that pushes past the politics of Levinas, not to mention his rhetoric of the son, both of which contribute to Derrida's "disquiet."

Derrida's study of friendship has recourse, we have said, to the logic of the sans—of the "relation without relation" (Levinas), "community without community" (Blanchot), "appearing without appearing," and even of "religion without religion."[7] While Derrida cannot speak the word "community" in his own name, not straightforwardly, he does not mean simply to destroy or annul community.[8] Rather, he calls for communities that are pressed to a near breaking point, exposed to the danger of the non-communal, communities that are rendered porous and open-ended, without homogeneity and self-identity, putting their community and identity at risk, like the risk one would take, let us say the risk of Penelope, if one practiced an unconditional hospitality and issued an open-ended invitation to every wayfarer. These self-contesting expressions do not signify, for Derrida, that we are defeated and consigned to despair and solitude, to lives of private desperation, which is what the critics of deconstruction allege. They do not signify that we have lost our way and have no trace to follow, but rather that "we are on the track of an impossible axiomatic which remains to be thought" (PF, 81), in a time in which the value of these communal values, indeed the value of value itself, is in question, in which distance, separation, and non-knowing would be the conditions of a porous society beyond the self-enclosure of community.

It is with this logic of the *sans*, of the *x* without *x*, in mind that Derrida organizes *Politics of Friendship* around a saying first attributed to Aristotle by Diogenes Laertius in his *Lives and Opinions of Eminent Philosophers*,"'O my friends, there is no friend.'"[9] Derrida, who loves such enigmatic and overdetermined expressions, especially ones whose provenance is so obscure (PF, 176–177), proposes that one way (among numerous others) that this sentence may be understood is as follows. (a) *O my friends:* you who *today* have the requisite amicability to read these pages, for reading and writing well require friendship, require a certain congeniality and mutual understanding, a wanting to be understood (PF, 216). Now this is a hermeneutic point, a point about the "hermeneutics of friendship," a movement in the direction of Hans-Georg Gadamer that is completely obscured by Derrida's famous non-exchange with Gadamer, which left some thinking that Derrida defends ill-will.[10] As soon as we open our mouths, we assume, by an irresistible impulse, that we speak the truth and that we are trying to understand each other. Our entire conversation transpires in a field of friendship, a society of friends, which is a society of credit and belief, of an amicable trust. (b) *There is no friend:* O my friends, we today are at present without the friend *to come;* the friend who will not be weighed down by the baggage of the classical axiomatic of friendship is not yet present, is yet to come. So Derrida hears in this vocative an evocation or a *call* for *another* concept of friendship, without the canonical one, and by extension another, and a more porous concept of democracy, a more open-ended, hospitable democracy to come, a society of friends without the dominant concepts of national identity, citizenship, national borders, and immigration laws that now prevail. For Derrida, the idea is to set this sentence loose into its *destinerrance*, for like any sentence, it can always be recontextualized, in virtue of the structural iterability of the mark. It can always be addressed to new audiences and addressees, which means that it is always potentially addressed to more than one (*plus d'un*), "more than a" *plus qu'un*, for example, *à une autre*, to a feminine other. Nothing can stop this (PF, 216–217).

Like its sibling, *Specters of Marx*, the book on friendship is a contribution to politics "without" posing as a comprehensive political "theory." For a long time "reticent" about Marx, and always struggling to keep his distance from a "hegemonic" Communist Party, yet resolutely a man of the

Left, Derrida now, in the age of liberal euphoria and the hegemony of the Right, searches for a politics to come, the memory of which is still preserved in this old word "democracy."[11] This is a work of paleonymity, looking through the history of the old names of democracy and politics for signs of something new (PF, 104). The name "democracy" is contingent and may not last forever, only as long as it has to, but it is the best word at present because it signifies what is most open to what is to come, which is the "messianic" hope from which any deconstructive discourse on politics must set out.[12] So Derrida uses the word strategically, not anti-democratically, to be sure, but as a way to preserve the right to criticism and keep things open for the coming of the other and keep the polity from closing in upon itself. Deconstruction and democracy—and this is what he also says of literature—are indissociable, inasmuch as they each entail the right to criticize anything, which is also what he means by the "right to philosophy," which keeps things open. The auto-deconstruction at work in democracy and literature work themselves out, not in the name of a horizon of perfectibility and a foreseeable ideal, but in response to the urgency of justice, of friendship and democracy, in the here and now, which is not to be confused with a self-identical "present" (PF, 105–106).

What Derrida calls throughout this text the "canonical concept" of friendship is shaped by the cognate values, let us say the fraternal twin values, of *physis*—the natal, native, national, and natural—and the *fraternal*—in short, by the "natural born brother." Derrida is suspicious of the axiomatics of *physis* (PF, 155, 178), the privilege of the bonding tie of the natural (*nascor, nasci, natus sum*), the natural affinity, which allows the community to close in upon itself as a community of connaturality and of the "same." In the canonical view, the friend is defined in terms of native ties and natural bonds, and the political in terms of the friendly natural bonds of a nation, of native soil. Derrida's concerns are turned toward the natural outsider, the one who falls outside the natural bond, whose lack of birth cannot be repaired, toward the *"atopos,"* the one who lacks a natural place assigned by birth, who lacks autochthony, toward the "displaced" or exiled, the "other," who must be made welcome. Accordingly, this book on friendship is also a critique of the friendly overtures made by the later Martin Heidegger toward all those grandiloquent and capitalized Events—Being and History, Language and Thinking—which turn on the gathering power (*legein*) of *physis*, where *philia* is gathered to *physis* (PF, 242–244). That is also why the national and the native tongue, the homeland and rootedness, *Vaterland, Heimat,* and *Bodenständigkeit,* find a native soil in the Heideggerian thought of Being as *physis*.[13]

Now, to be precise, Derrida is concerned, not exactly with the dangers posed by the natural brother, *stricto sensu*—he is not against brothers or families—but with the *generalization* of that model, with the exemplarity of the figure of the brother, which Derrida calls "fraternization." For that is what dominates the canonical concept of friendship:

> [I]t is not the fraternity we call natural . . . that we are questioning and analyzing in its range and with its political risks . . . it is the brother figure in its renaturalizing rhetoric, its symbolics, its certified conjuration—in other words, the process of *fraternization*. (PF, 202)

It is not flawlessly natural brotherhood, in the strictest sense of consanguinity—which in any case is never entirely free from laws of legitimacy and family names, and hence is never a consolidated self-presence (PF, 149)—that Derrida puts into question, but the exemplarity of the "sworn" brotherhood, the circle of men who clasp their hands together and vow *fraternal* allegiance to one another, so that the bond of alliance always takes the form of the fraternal oath and virile associations. Natural brothers in the strictest sense form a family, not a political brotherhood, whereas Derrida's concern is with politics, which up to the present is supposed to imitate or resemble a natural brotherhood, which is the political model par excellence. The coming together of the community or the nation always take place under the "figure" of the brother, which serves as the exemplar for ethics, politics, and friendship, this exemplarity being of course the other side, or the son, of patriarchal politics. The interesting and dangerous thing is that the brother is consistently taken as the model for democracy, *especially* for democracy. As Aristotle says, the relation of father to child is monarchical, the relation of man to wife aristocratic, but the relation of brothers is the model for politics, the "democratic" model (PF, 197–198).

Democracy, like friendship, is a community of "equals," but that always means *equally excellent or superior* (*arete*), which is a property of men, which is why equality is always figured as brotherhood. The equality that obtains between free and autonomous beings settles regularly on men, whose equality then is fraternal, confreres in a *polis* taken as a city of brotherly love, the confraternity of all mankind under one father, be he God the father or the fatherland, Zeus or Yahweh. *Pro deo et patria.* Women may be lovers, slaves, or tyrants, Zarathustra said, but not friends, not with men (first exclusion), and not even with other women ("double exclusion") (PF, 278–279, 282). That does not mean, of course, that women never were actually friends, either with men or with one another, but only that their friendship was not credited and legitimized in the classical axiomatics. The fraternal model of friendship is ubiquitous: it prevails in both Athens and Jerusalem, in Christian Rome and Cicero's Rome, stretching with remarkable unity all the way from Plato and Aristotle through the Middle Ages and the Enlightenment, to Friedrich Nietzsche and Heidegger (PF, 188). The fraternal model is Greco-Roman, Judaeo-Islamo-Christian, philosophical and religious, part of the Roman Catholic monastic tradition of "religious brothers" but no less central to the eastern church and the Reformation, which on this point at least proposed no reform at all. Derrida tries patiently to explore "all the categories and all the axioms which have constituted the concept of friendship in its history" (PF, 294) and that have guided the Western canon of friendship to that doubly exclusionary conclusion, which is political and unfriendly to everyone who falls outside its fraternal scope.

The crucial problem for this book on friendship, Derrida says, is to explore the possibility of a friendship that frees itself from this figure of fraternal kinship, affinity, and analogy, which has not turned in upon itself in a circle of brothers seated around a hearth tended by women. The possibility of a friend who appears without appearing, who is kept safe by non-knowing, involves the possibility of

> a friendship without hearth, of a *philein* without *oikeios*. Ultimately, a friendship without presence, without resemblance, without affinity, without analogy. Along with presence, truth would start to tremble. Like this prayer which, as Aristotle reminds us, could be neither true nor false. Is an *aneconomic* friendship possible? Can there be any other friendship? Must there be another? Can one answer this question otherwise than with a "perhaps"—that is, by suspending in advance the very form of a "question" and the alliance of the "yes"—in order to think and to dream before them? (PF, 154–155)

Deconstruction would explore the "de-naturalization of fraternal authority," which would show that the "brother" is not a "natural, substantial, essential, untouchable given" (PF, 159), not the natural figure of the bond of allegiance.

Perhaps one day, by chance—Derrida is thinking out loud, hoping and longing for what may be, *peut être*, what is able to be, by chance or happenstance, perhaps—two people will love each other, a woman and a man, a woman and another woman, and the name for that love will be friendship, will also be friendship, since it will perhaps be sexual, too. Perhaps what will come one fine day will be radically new, or perhaps it will be a prolongation of love, a way that love becomes friendship, which Derrida calls *"aimance,"* "lovence" (like the English-language "romance"), love becoming friendship, the love that is in friendship, something beyond the classically determined figures of love and friendship (PF, 69). Perhaps, just this one time, this relationship could rightly, justly, be called friendship, unique and without concept, not with the ousiological constancy demanded by what Aristotle called *philia,* but in the flicker of a moment, in the blink of an *Augenblick* (PF, 66–67). The lines of demarcation, the conditions of possibility of such a chance, would not be staked out a priori by an ontology or a theology of friendship, but happen in a certain borderless experience of the *perhaps,* which is the experience of an impossible possibility, the experience of what is to all the world and its philosophy an impossible "event" taking place right before our eyes. But these eyes would be the eyes not of philosophy and its *theoria*, not the eyes of seeing at all but the eyes of faith, eyes blinded by praying and weeping for an impossible friendship to come. For friendship is such stuff as on dreams are made, a matter mingled with prayers and tears, with longing and desiring the impossible.

> Friendship is never a present given, it belongs to the experience of expecta-tion, promise, or engagement. Its discourse is that of prayer, it inaugurates, but reports nothing, it is not satisfied with what is, it moves out to this place where a responsibility opens up a future. (PF, 236; cf. 250)

The discourse of friendship is a prayer for an apparition, for the appearing of what does not appear.

A Hyperbolic Hypothesis

In order to counter the "resuming and subsuming" of friendship into fraternity, the drift or tendency of friendship to contract into fraternity, Derrida invokes the curved "space" and deferred "time" of a friendship to come. For Derrida, following Levinas and Blanchot, the friend is not a phenomenal appearance in the level space and regular time described in the philosophical tradition, with its steady, rhythmic beat of "presents" and the smooth surface of its homogeneous space. For the effect of such undistorted phenomenality is a peculiar distortion and injustice which fails to describe the force of the ethico-political relationship, of the re-lation without relation, the ruptured and interrupted relation. The lu-minous and even surface of equality levels off the alterity of the other and seems inevitably to slide down the slope of sameness and fraternity. Within the measured phenomenality of philosophical space and time, the *other* is contracted to the same, which always ends up meaning the *brother*, humanity is shrunk into fraternity, the society of friends into a com-munity of brotherly love. We can say in English—but Derrida cannot in French—that Derrida questions the tradition of the "(br)other," that he would deconstruct the brother on behalf of the other, break open the tradition of the brother in order to affirm the other. For Derrida space and time are bent by *différance*. The friend comes from on high, in the unfa-miliar proportions of infinite and measureless dissymmetry, even as the coming or in-coming (*invention*) of the friend is always essentially *to come*. The friend is what is to come, my friends, the one, he or she, for whom we pray and weep, long and dream. It would be the height of injustice—the most unfriendly thing imaginable—to say that the friend is present, here and now, in the flesh, instead of seeing the coming of the friend as demanding, here and now, what is to come, which keeps us open, here and now. Whatever calls itself the friend now is deconstructible, but the friend, if there is one, my friends, is not deconstructible.

Thus Derrida takes over the *hyperbolic* and unphenomenological model that Levinas uses to explain ethics and obligation—in which an invisible infinity comes over me and demands everything of me, the food out of my mouth—as a model for the friend and politics, which have always been understood in *egalitarian* terms. But this raises further questions: am I obliged and duty bound to be a friend? Would that be a friendly way to be a friend? Is everyone—*tout autre est tout autre*—my friend? If everyone is my friend, then does that mean that really I have *no* friends? "O my friends,"—if that is addressed to everyone—"there is no friend"—then I have none. The question of calculation and number: the friend is the other *one,* and tends to be just *one* other, so that friendship tends by its nature to the exclusion of others, to "particular friendships." Could we have more than one real friend? We must treat everyone as a friend but we cannot be friends with everyone. Are not real friendships rare? This is also a question for politics, which has never been insulated from the problem of number: how large can a democracy get? Could it accommodate a European super-state? What is the relationship of friendship and democracy on the question of number (PF, 101–102)? Do they both belong to the incalculable, to the sphere of something that we cannot count and cannot count on, both in the sense that they are not a matter of numbers—as long as one person suffers injustice, justice is still to come—and in the sense that we cannot by precise calculations foresee or program their coming? Do they not require that we set aside calculation in favor of the gift without return?

Derrida is not arguing *against* equality. He does not deny that the traditional axiom of equality should be universalized and extended to all, women included, and he clearly does not want to deny legal equality before the law. But equality would get no further than what Jürgen Habermas would call completing the Enlightenment project, shedding more light on the Enlightenment, so that the *Aufklärer* and *Aufklärerin* clearly see that it is not simply all *men* who are created equal and that friendship is not reducible to a polity of *brotherly love* and *fraternity.* That egalitarianism, as Habermas would argue, is something the philosophical lights of the Enlightenment should have been able to illuminate on their own. But Derrida presses for a more radical hyperbolic hypothesis, borrowed from Levinas and Blanchot, which invokes the dissymmetry of friendship and conceives the friend on the model of the infinity and dissymmetric heterogeneity of the *other* rather than of equality, intimacy, and sameness. Derrida pushes for a certain *hyperbolic* friendship, an overshooting of the mark of equality, which makes the friend more eminent. The question is for him, in what sense may one still speak of political equality and symmetry in the ethical dissymmetry of infinite alterity? How have the meaning of politics, law, and democracy been changed, and how can they be translated, on the hyperbolic hypothesis (PF, 233)?

It is as if merely aiming at equality or the mean state will inevitably fall back (*ellipsis*) into fraternity, for, contrary to Aristotle and the Pythagoreans and to the Greeks generally, the good for Derrida does not belong to the limited but to the unlimited. The friend for these friends—Levinas and Blanchot, and also Georges Bataille and Derrida—is not to be taken as the "other" of the "same," one who is of the same mind or heart, as in Aristotle's notion of *homonoia,* thus constituting a community (*koinonia*) of the same, which may perhaps even adhere to the modern senses of "friendship," "*Freundschaft,*" and "*amitié,*" in which case we need another word. The friend is my equal *and beyond, au-delà, hyperbole,* more than my equal, which means that friendship is caught up in the grip of the infinite disproportion of a gift without exchange, in which the "other," appearing without appearing, comes from a place of structural superiority and invisible eminence.[14] That is not best thought of as the completion of the *Aufklärung* for Derrida but as a re-imagining of it, the affirmation of "the Enlightenment of a certain *Aufklärung*" (PF, 306).

A History of Friendship

Derrida's argument is carried out in a series of analyses of canonical texts on friendship, all of which invoke the authority of the line Laertius attributes to Aristotle, beginning with Nietzsche, in which Derrida feels about for the inner disturbances and tremblings by which they are shaken, however slightly. Everything in Derrida's history of friendship depends upon the fact that this history, indeed any history or tradition, is not homogeneous. Instead, it is marked by dominant structures that have silenced and repressed others, and this deconstructive analysis, like any other, is aimed at finding the signs of tension, and feels about for the ruptures and heterogeneities in this tradition, for these are just so many openings for another friendship and another politics (PF, 234). The texts of Plato, Aristotle, and Nietzsche, for example, should not be taken as closed over and closed off, for there are already auto-deconstructive elements at work in them, under another name, which can be uncovered by patient analysis.

Who is Derrida's Nietzsche? Or, to paraphrase an essay by Heidegger, "Who is Derrida's Zarathustra?" Derrida takes his point of departure from Nietzsche's discourse on the "philosophers of the future" in *Beyond Good and Evil,* who represent a higher type to come that we long for and desire, philosophers who will transcend the limitations of the Christian-Platonic inversion of morals. Derrida reads this philosopher of the future in consonance with Zarathustra's prophetic sayings about a higher friendship and a gift-giving virtue, a friend who is able to give even to his enemy—which means this is not a Greek friend—who thus is generous to the other. Such a higher man will be generous beyond the present man, man up to now, who is incapable of such a "dissymmetrical gift" (PF, 283). But this friendly generosity is not to be confused with Christian gift-giving, where loving our enemies is a well-known counsel. For Christianity has a sharp eye for a good bargain and is always looking out for a heavenly return on what earthly investments it makes. "The logic of wages is everywhere in the gospel" (PF, 307 n. 21; Matt. 5:43). Zarathustra calls for a purer love of the *most distant* (*Fernsten-liebe*), beyond the economy of the Christian love of the *neighbor* or *enemy*. He calls for the "absolute gift," an "unrequited bestowal," which would not be afraid to love oneself, to love the earth, to love the "friend" who should be for us a "festival of the earth," not a means to a heavenly reward (PF, 286–287). This links up with the economy of salvation Nietzsche criticizes in the second essay of *A Genealogy of Morals,* with which Derrida concludes *The Gift of Death*.[15]

The signature "Nietzsche," by announcing that the value of what is called "value" is in question, by proclaiming an *Umwertung*, a transvaluation of all values, beyond the pusillanimity of these Christian-Platonic souls, describes a fundamental mutation that marks our disjointed time (PF, 79–81). For today values are being turned inside out, so that, by virtue of the slave revolt of morals, genuine friends—who would call us beyond ourselves—have become enemies even as the enemies of humanity—who resist self-overcoming and coddle our mediocrity—are treated as friends. That is why Nietzsche can make his own Aristotle's saying, while adding on a supplement: "O my enemies, there is no enemy." Derrida's Zarathustra calls for a new justice, beyond sheer equality and the eye-for-an-eye equivalences that lie at the basis of the squint-eyed equivalences of good and evil morality, a new spirit of gift-giving that does not keep a ghostly eye for after-worldly reward. This new friendship to come will be based on a shared rejoicing, not as at present a shared suffering and congregating of the weakest and worst. Such friends are *two* souls—not one—akin in their ability to keep their distance and resist fusion, able to laugh at evil, not to laugh it away, but to laugh magnanimously among friends at each other's faults (PF, 54–56). These new philosophers of the future seek an equality that does not calculate equivalences, that does not calculate at all, that moves in the sphere of disproportion and disappropriation. Their friendship is more loving than love, for love is tied up with property and possession. Love is *Habsucht*, the drive to possess and have new property. Christian love of the neighbor is but a new lust for possession. So Nietzsche contests both the Greek and Christian concepts of friendship. He contests the norm of proximity and the proper, of fusion and identification, equivalence and exchange. Nietzsche wants to preserve distance, whereas love would fuse and possess (PF, 64–65), and he wants a gift released from the economy of exchange.

Derrida is careful to point out that this is a "certain Nietzsche," a carefully culled and selected one, and only one—"one Nietzsche, in any case (for there is always more than one)" (PF, 297)—who is given a generous and friendly reading, "an active and hazardous" (PF, 70) interpretation. Derrida is compelled to "quickly inform the reader that we will not follow Nietzsche here. Not in any simple manner," that this will be at most a "following without following" (PF, 33). As usual, Derrida is here looking for a way to open up Nietzsche beyond Nietzsche. My hypothesis is Derrida invents/discovers another Nietzsche in *Politics of Friendship,* a Nietzsche beyond or without Nietzsche, a Nietzsche who has taken a step beyond (*pas au-delà*) Nietzsche. Derrida's Nietzsche takes a step not taken by Nietzsche's "followers," his "sons" and "brothers," but by Blanchot, which Blanchot calls *le pas au-delà,* the step/not beyond, as Derrida points out in an important note (PF, 46–48 n. 15). To Blanchot, of course, should be added Blanchot's friend, Levinas—a couple of Jewish brothers, both of whom Derrida follows, but also without following, inasmuch as both were a little too friendly to the fraternal figure (PF, 304–305). The result is that the Zarathustra who calls for a friendship to come, and for a prophetic of the love of the earth, starts to take on the tones of a Jewish prophet, of what we might impudently call a "*messianic,* quasi-Jewish or Jewgreek Zarathustra." In *Against Ethics,* in the course of arguing for the possibility of a certain ethics, or counter-ethics, in deconstruction, I describe a painting of a Dionysian rabbi, a kind of "Abraham of Paris," a heteromorphic figure of a Dionysus wrapped in a tallith unfurling a sacred scroll.[16] I would now wager that this Jewgreek sort of fellow I conjured up was working on a manuscript entitled "Politics of Friendship."

"Who is Derrida's Zarathustra?" A Zarathustra, if there is one, who flies in the face of the fraternalistic, elitist, oligarchical, anti-democratic— let us say the canonical—Nietzsche. For Derrida is *not following* the Nietzsche whose love of the *future* and joyous affirmation really have little to do with the love of the *other,* with the affirmation of the displaced, dispossessed, and disinherited, of whom Derrida is speaking and who would offend Nietzsche's aristocratic nose and fill him with nausea, he being the first philosopher to philosophize not only with a hammer but also with his *Nase.* The future figure of the friend of which Zarathustra speaks, on the one hand, is a figure of self-overcoming, in which humankind will assume a higher, undreamt of kind of *self-affirming excess,* which surpasses the present human as much as the present reactive human surpasses the beast. According to the canonical Nietzsche, the human to come, who comes over (*über*) what is at present called "man," represents an excess and an overflow, but this is an excess and an overflow that arises as a *discharge and release (ent-lassen) of energies* that can no longer be kept within and must be set free. This "gift-giving" generosity is really an *inability to contain and keep for oneself.* The figure of the friend to come that Derrida has taken from Blanchot and Levinas, on the other hand, which Derrida has grafted over Zarathustra's sayings, would give Zarathustra a rude shock, for this is excess of *response and responsibility* to the other, which *gives even what it needs for itself,* the food out of its mouth. That would be for the canonical Zarathustra the reactive pusillanimous virtue of the braying ass and the beast of burden, which puts the needs of others before itself. *Affirmation,* yes, yes, for Zarathustra must not be reactive, responsive, to something outside the life of the forces themselves, as if something could rule or provoke their response from without. Affirmation must arise from within, *ab intra*, from the sovereignty and magnanimity of the higher human's height. The one who comes from on high (emphasize comes!) in the canonical Zarathustra is the higher human, *über-kommen, übermensch*, not the *other;* he affirms not the other but himself; and he comes, he gives, not because the other solicits him—which would be an "ascetic ideal" and reactive virtue that would fill Zarathustra with nausea—but as a confirmation of his self-affirmation, as a further, confirming tribute to the greatness of his bountiful beauty and strength and his manly magnanimity.

So, if the Christian gospel is "repeated, doubled, parodied, perverted, and assumed" by Zarathustra (PF, 284), then, I argue, it is also "repeated, doubled, parodied, perverted, and assumed" *one more time* by Derrida's Zarathustra in a double parody, a second repetition in this game of numbers, producing still another Zarathustra put to work in the service of another friendship. Derrida's Zarathustra inverts the inversion and transvalues the transvaluation. The figure of the gift-giving virtue is transfigured into a figure of *responsibility*, of responding to the other, so that my responsibility is not mine but the other's, who provokes it in me, who elicits it from me. I decide with the decision of the other, with what Derrida calls—to the scandal of philosophy *and* I would add of Nietzsche—a "passive decision," the "decision of the other. Of the absolute other in me, the other than decides on me in me" (PF, 68), which alone "matches decision to the gift, if there is one, as other's gift" (PF, 69). That differs sharply, indeed it is a *Jewish inversion* of the "excess" for which the canonical Zarathustra calls, which is, I would say, a rather phallic and orgasmic discharge of uncontainable energy, not the food out of my mouth, not a response and a responsibility to what the other has wrought in me, which would reduce the forces to slavish, reactive powers, and would be beneath the dignity of the active forces.

The Zarathustra whom Derrida befriends in *Politics of Friendship* is a Jewgreek prophet, a quasi-Jewish "Zarathustra"—and we must respect this pseudonym and not simply substitute Nietzsche's name for his (PF, 288)—a kind of Dionysian rabbi, a messianic Nietzsche, calling us beyond Greek, Christian, and Enlightenment friendships, politics, and fraternalism. Certainly, it is in the course of a commentary on Nietzsche's philosophers of the future that Derrida retells the old rabbinic story of the Messiah who is to come that he learned from Blanchot's *The Writing of the Disaster* (PF, 37, 46 n.14). According to this story, which is quite central to Derrida's notion of the *à venir*, the Messiah is *always* and *structurally* "to come," so that even if he were actually to show up one day, the question we would put to him is, "when will you come?" That is because his coming is something that is both given and deferred, as also something we both long for and fear. Later on, Derrida comes back to the story and adds that "there is nothing fortuitous" in the fact that Nietzsche's discourse on the philosophers to come exhibits the same "teleiopoetic" and messianic structure as the line attributed to Aristotle—"O my friends, there is no friend." Both are addressed to someone, who must accordingly really be present, while also calling for them to come. Something is addressed to the other, but in such a way that "a chance is left for the future needed for the coming of the other, for the event in general" (PF, 173). There is both terror and hope in the messianic expectation, because we cannot count on exactly *who* is going to arrive, for the nature of this call is that I must leave the coming of the other to the other. Were I to determine or predetermine the coming in advance, that would represent more of the coming of the same. There is an inevitable intertwining of what is desired and resisted, of friend and enemy, so that this is not a self-assured, self-identical messianic hope but a hope against hope (PF, 173–174), a certain *dés-espoir,* a faith-filled despair that does not give up hope (PF, 220). I will come back to this Jewgreek point in my concluding remarks.

One of the lengthiest and most interesting discussions in the book is Derrida's analysis of Carl Schmitt, the conservative Catholic legal theorist, political philosopher, and National Socialist, whom Heidegger much admired. Derrida finds Schmitt a merciless figure, let us say, a "hostile" philosopher of the "absolute enemy" (PF, 157), of the same *against* the other. Schmitt defines friends as the ones who gather against the enemy, so that one needs one's enemies. Schmitt is driven by a virile madness into a philosophy of *Kampf* where *polemos* is the father of all, where everything turns on men of war, on warlike men whose fundamental *virtue,* whose precisely "political" virtue, is their readiness to kill. The effect of Schmitt's formal identification of the "concept of the political" is to isolate a sphere where men may kill one another with impunity, where killing, or at least the structural readiness to kill, is fair game, indeed the name of the game, and where bourgeois ethicists—Schmitt had his admirers on the Left as well as the Right—may not impose their effete injunctions against the manly virtue upon which "politics" depends.

For Schmitt, the concept of the political turns on the distinction between friend and enemy. Instead of a society of friends that turns on the affirmation of the other, he makes having a friend a function of having an enemy, friends being those who group together against a common enemy, producing a common defense (*com-munire*) against the other. Without an enemy I would go mad, my world would lose all stability and coherence (PF, 175–176). Were we to suffer the loss of our enemies, were we unable in the concrete to identify who the enemy is (PF, 118), the result would not be peace but confusion and a dangerous disorder, the emasculation of the whole political order and the depoliticization of the nation. The decision between friend and enemy is the critical difference that structures the political order. However, the political enemy, Schmitt insists, has to do with a formal structure, with public "hostilities" (*hostis*), not a personal hatred or private animosity (*inimicus*); the enemy is not anyone to whom we have taken a personal dislike. So the enemy might be our friend (*amicus*), might even be our blood brother (PF, 161), even as we might not personally like our political friend. Thus we encounter in Schmitt a Nietzschean reversal of values—we might indeed love our enemy whom we must kill.

Apart from pointing out the dubiousness of the Platonic provenance which Schmitt claims for the distinction between *inimicus* and *hostis,* Derrida regards this as an infinitely slippery and deconstructible distinction, in support of which one need only think of how much a "war effort" depends upon demonizing the enemy, racial stereotypes and slurs, and in general whipping up the most intense feelings of personal hatred. The distinction is Machiavellian, utterly divorcing the ethical and the political, instead of allowing the ethical to become political. It allows Schmitt the advantage of seeming to follow the evangelical counsel to love one's enemy—even as we slit his throat, which the enemy should not take as something personal. The New Testament counsel to love our enemies, Schmitt contends, was not counseling Christians not to defend Europe against the Saracens or Turks (PF, 89, 136 n. 19), and presumably, Derrida adds, would leave room for Christians today to love Muslims even while licensing all-out war on Islamic states.

The defining feature of the enemy is that we are prepared really and physically to kill him, which means, in this mad logic, that friendship depends structurally and in principle upon being prepared to kill the other, where killing is different from murder. That is also why Schmitt contested the Geneva conventions of 1949. The German generals were military men and as such not bound by civilian criminal law meant to protect the bourgeoisie and keep them safe from danger; killing the enemy should not be confused with the murder criminal law prohibited (PF, 143). It makes no difference if, empirically and contingently, war is not in fact waged and the threat posed to the enemy does not pass into act. The enemy must know we are serious, that we are prepared to shed blood to protect our sworn brothers, for that is what draws the lines of the political map. Indeed, it is the threat of war, the spectral logic of being haunted by the possibility of war, that preserves the peace, that keeps each side within its boundaries, which provides the "critical" power, the *discrimen* that draws political borders and prevents aggression. The loss of an identifiable enemy is what most threatens the political order. Schmitt theorized the structure of the inversion of values that more or less kept the "peace" for forty years during the "cold war" (PF, 76, 248). That famous bit of war without outright world war, or peace without peace, was anything but *shalom,* which is an *affirmation of the other.* It was rather the threat to *annihilate the other* if he crossed a certain line. The political order, according to Schmitt, turns on the man of war, on the military *virtus* of comrades in arms, brothers all, down to the last man. This merciless philosophy comes to a head, according to Derrida, in the war between brothers, in the story of Cain and Abel, although it is no less a Greek story, where the enemy is my own, my friend and brother, whose blood (consanguinity) I am sworn (the oath) to shed (PF, 163–164).

"And what about the sister?" Derrida asks, "Where has she gone?" (PF, 96). "Not a woman in sight," he says (PF, 155). Schmitt's landscape is an inhabited desert, devoid of women, but teeming with people, with men of war, colonels and generals, partisans, politicians, professors, and theologians, but "[i]n vain would you look for a figure of a woman, a feminine silhouette, and the slightest allusion to sexual difference" (PF, 156). The woman and the sister are massively evident by their absence in this philosophy of "merciless war" and "absolute hostility." They do not even manage an appearance in the form of a woman warrior—say, Joan of Arc—or women resistance fighters or partisans. But what if the woman were the "absolute enemy of this theory of the absolute enemy?" (PF, 157).

The response to Schmitt, for Derrida, is the "double gesture": we must recognize that this Machiavellian "logic of fraternization" is what "politics" has tended to mean while inventing something beyond this politics, something *other than* a concept of what Schmitt calls the "political," *and* we must also, at the same time, retain the old name "politics" and attempt to think it *otherwise*. That would come down to the hope and the dream, the prayer and the tear, for a politics to come, something that Schmitt—and Heidegger[17]—would regard as a feminized, effete *Kampflosigkeit*, a state and culture lacking political definition that would make a real man blush. Derrida dreams of a politics which affirms the impossibility of murder and is deeply troubled by the murderousness of the "same," which is a Levinasian way to put much of what is going on in Derrida's text. This formulation also opens Levinas up to a feminist rereading, which to a certain extent is adumbrated in *Politics of Friendship*. Democracy is the stuff of *another dream* or *another non-fraternal faith*. For remember that fraternity, too, is a faith, one that brothers put in each other when they lock arms. The brother is not a fact or a given but the effect of an oath and a faith, not nature but a crediting or promise, indeed, a construction of patriarchy, while the demand to denaturalize the untouchable givenness of the brother is "deconstruction at work" (PF, 159), the work of a deconstructive politics.

Having already seen the messianic openings Derrida finds in Nietzsche, let us turn back to Aristotle. Aristotle distinguishes three kinds of friendship, based on pleasure, utility, and virtue, of which the last is the highest, because it has to do with a relationship between two equally self-possessed men of excellence, men of equal merit and virtue. But there is a curious aporia in Aristotle, for the man of virtue must be "independent and self-sufficient, hence able to do without others, as much as possible: few friends, the fewest possible" (PF, 221). The idea of perfect friendship in Aristotle is at odds with itself. The virtuous man, the one man capable of the highest friendship, is least in need of friendship and is the most restrictive about the friendships he forms. His "autarky," self-rule, demands a "scarcity" of friendships, like the god, the *noesis noeseos*, who, occupying the summit of autarky, has no need of friends at all and does not even know us mortals here below. It is above all the god who can say "there is no friend." Only here below in the sublunary world, where there is no perfect autarky, where the other and the thought of the other are required, is friendship needed, and this just because we lack the autarky that perfect friendship requires. "Perfect friendship destroys itself," as Pierre Aubenque says (PF, 222).

Derrida is interested in displacing this autonomy and autarky and, to "translate" this Greek concept, wants to offer a "political" translation of it which is, he concedes, beset with "risks and difficulties." This he does by identifying a moment of dissymmetry and curved space in the Greek affection for equality and autonomy, a moment of infinite distance which the Greek concept finds intolerable *even as it calls for it*. So Aristotle *also* said that we can assist the slave, not as a slave, but inasmuch as the slave instantiates the human, viz., something infinite (PF, 196–197);[18] he said that by remaining loyal to the dead, we befriend those who cannot reciprocate our friendship; and he said that being a friend is found more in the activity of loving than in the passivity of being loved (PF, 8–11). So here and there we come upon openings in Aristotle's text where his "reciprocalist or *mutualist* schema of requited friendship" (PF, 10) is internally threatened by the stirrings of a more radical friendship "without hierarchical difference at the root of democracy" (PF, 232), of a democracy and a friendship to come, that it bears within itself "the power to become infinite and dissymmetrical" (PF, 290). Indeed, it is the structure of the *to come* that is unmistakable in the vocative form of the reputedly Aristotelian saying "O my friends, there is no friend," which has the form of a *call*, an appeal, a "prayer" for the future, a "messianic" prayer or "teleiopoesis" (aimed at bringing about a *telos*, an end):

> We know that there are no friends, but I pray you, my friends, act so that henceforth there are. You, my friends, be my friends. You already are, since that is what I am calling you. Moreover, how could I be your friend . . . if friendship were not still to come, to be desired, to be promised? . . . If I give you friendship, it is because there is friendship (perhaps); it does not exist, *presently.* (PF, 235)

It is in the name of the friendship to come that we say there is no friend at present. By the same token, in addressing you, "my friends," it calls upon the friends among whom we find ourselves, recalls the community to which we already belong, a sort of friendship that is already there, before contract and avowal, which provides the horizon for the prayer for a friendship to come.

Derrida next traces what we might label the Franco-Christian model of fraternal friendship that emerges in the call for "liberty, equality, fraternity" in the French Revolution. This model is Christian, because the French Enlightenment claims to be the *universalizing* and *infinitizing* of Christian brotherhood to the universal brotherhood of all humanity, delivering in this world, as Jules Michelet said, the brotherhood that Christianity deferred to the next (PF, 227). Of course women are not expected to understand these words, although women hear and understand what words are being spoken. That is also why Derrida rejects speaking of a "fraternity without fraternity," for in the logic of the without "one never renounces what one claims to renounce" (PF, 237). This model is French, because France is raised up as the exemplar for all mankind. Citing Michelet again, "'France is the necessary initiation to the homeland of all mankind. France is more than a nation; it is a living brotherhood'" (PF, 237–238). That is the sort of nationalist exemplarism, sans the brotherhood, that, as we will see in the next chapter, Richard Rorty tends to peddle these days about the United States, an exemplarism that is no less objectionable to Derrida when the Jews are made the exemplars of our relationship to the other in Blanchot and Levinas (PF, 304), which has disastrous implications for those others called Palestinians!

Derrida singles out the conception of a "sovereign" friendship in Michel de Montaigne, for whom, following Horace and Augustine, two friends amount to one, one soul in two bodies, which thereby constitutes a singular couple. The friend is the self all over again, *noch einmal*, each melted into or fused with the other, in what Derrida calls an "absolute community," as opposed to the more porous community without community he defends, which allows the friend to be a second, truly other. Such sovereign friendship is rare, being found only once every three centuries or so, Montaigne declares, which is why he can say with Aristotle, "O my friends, there is no friend." It is found only between two men, is deeper and more lasting than marriage which, being mainly a contract governing household arrangements and child-rearing, can also turn to hate (PF, 178–188). But suppose, Derrida suggests, this text suffered a graphic alteration, some chance error by a copyist, so that the initial omega in "O my friends" was actually aspirated (*hoi*), hence no longer a vocative but a dative, so that the expression, now transcribed into a constative assertion, can be translated: "he who has friends can have no true friend," that is, he has too many friends, perhaps even more than one, has no friends at all. *Cui amici, amicus nemo; viele Freunde, kein Freund.* That is actually how it is translated in the Loeb Classical Library and in several other modern editions (PF, 208–209). On this second, oligarchical, oligo-philial (PF, 3) rendering, the virtue of friendship is its rarity: too many friends means no friends. Friendship "recoils" into a few—whence Derrida calls this the "recoil" (*repli*) version—who are like brothers, which is a sentiment that would be close to Aristotle's heart, who wanted to restrict friendship to the best, who are rare.

But on either the standard or the recoil version, Derrida claims, the sentence is addressed to someone, to those who would understand me, and by whom I would be understood, hence "my friends." In that sense, every sentence begins "O my friends" and depends upon a hermeneutics of friendship. In either version my desire for a single friend, for a loving friend, for an "I love you" uttered once and for all eternity to my friend, will never cease. But at the same time, I will never stop pining after multiplication and repetition, and I grieve that I do not have several souls with which to be soul mates with many others. The incalculable indivisibility of the couple is divided and its singularity multiplied (PF, 215–216). Such internal divisibility affects even this sentence itself, which as a chain of iterable marks, can over a long history be repeated and recontextualized, addressed to others—nothing can stop this from happening —and eventually addressed to the feminine other, *une autre*. Then we might believe that Aristotle was dreaming of an "unusable friendship," one based neither on utility nor pleasure, yet not restricted to higher measures of masculine excellence, but of *another* friendship to come and hence another politics. Perhaps! Let us not be too assured, let us not exclude the possibility of failure, perjury, and evil. The future is not programmable, but must pass through the ordeal of undecidability, in which every free decision is made (PF, 218–219). We are dreaming and praying for an "I love you" which is "unilateral and dissymmetrical," an "infinite disproportion . . . which *gives* without return and without recognition," "whether or not the other answers." Friendship implies some reciprocity, which *aimance*, friendship becoming love, love becoming friendship, surmounts.

Derrida's analysis closes, rightly in my judgment, because it is so close to his point of departure, with a discussion of the text from Blanchot's *Friendship* with which I began the present chapter.

Conclusion: Thus Spake a Quasi-Jewish Zarathustra

I conclude by returning to my earlier suggestion that we read the *Politics of Friendship* as the work of a Dionysian rabbi, a Jewgreek prophet, a Zarathustra being fed some Jewish and messianic lines about expectation, desire, and longing for a friendship and a democracy to come. In my view, Zarathustra's doubling, parodying perversion of the gospel (PF, 284) is doubled and parodied again when the good news is given still one more twist in the mouth of Derrida's Zarathustra. Derrida associates himself with Zarathustra's critique of the more "sublime economy" of Christianity's heavenly mercantilism—which prefers wages that do not rust or wither away to ones that do—in the name of an "absolute gift" which is without return. But Derrida goes on from there to call for what he names

l'invention de l'autre, or the *tout autre,* which differs sharply from the deeply *self-affirming* higher type whom Zarathustra is calling for, who would
be a still higher type of auto-overflowing discharge. Derrida, as I have
argued, is following a path not followed by Nietzsche, whom Derrida is
not entirely following, by taking a somewhat more Jewish step, viz., the
passage, *le pas au-delà,* set by Blanchot and Levinas, which Derrida in turn
pushes in a political and post-Marxist direction.

The work on friendship, therefore, should be read in concert both with
the disjointed time of liberal euphoria criticized in *Specters of Marx* and the
concept of hospitality studied in *Adieu: à Emmanuel Levinas.*[19] In *Adieu,*
Derrida pursues the political thrust of Levinas's ethical appropriation of
the powerful and revolutionary command to recognize the trace of God
in the face of the neighbor and the stranger, of the friend and the enemy.
Derrida does this, I hasten to add, while rightly passing for an atheist,
albeit one who is interested in saving the name of God. The stranger is to
be treated as a friend, as a guest to whom we offer hospitality, like a
traveler who is displaced, expelled, or expatriated, who does not quite
belong here, who is "unsuitable" (*inconvenant*), lacking his or her own
place (*oideiotes*), lacking a bonding affinity with "us" (PF, 178). The friend
is above all the one who solicits us, who requires the food out of our
mouth (Levinas), a place in our home or native land or country (Derrida),
which is what the politics of being a "friend" outside the paradigm of
confraternity means for this other, slightly more Jewish Zarathustra.

Now this is to *invert* or *reverse the effect,* to transvalue the value of
the "divine" that dominates Greek philosophy, where the requirement of
equality meant there could be no question of being a friend of the god.
For the *noesis noeseos* is entirely and happily occupied with himself and
gives himself endless enjoyment as he trips an endless heavenly cycle of
the light fantastique. He neither knows us nor loves us; he has no friends
and needs no friends, and can say better than anyone, "O my friends"—
even this is an imaginary dialogue—that is, you changeable mortals down
below who come and go, if there are any down there, "there is no friend"
(PF, 223–224), not up here in the heavenly circles. But that effect is reversed in Christianity, as Søren Kierkegaard's Johannes de Silentio points
out, when the god, seeing that humanity cannot be elevated to the divine, decides to descend to the level of humanity.[20] Hence, the most deeply ethical, let us say, the most friendly, moment in Christianity is found in
the story in which the master says that whenever you befriended the
least of mine—whenever you fed them or visited them in prison—you
befriended me. For here the god is consolidated with humankind and
identified—to the scandal of the *noesis noeseos*—with those *most in need of
friendship.* The Greek effect is offset in Judaism not by the Incarnation but
by the notion that the trace of God is inscribed on the face of the neighbor, especially of those laid low by circumstance—the widow, the orphan,
the stranger—which is also why the Messiah appears dressed in rags on

the outskirts of the city. I take Levinas's ethics to be the Greco-philo-sophical elaboration of this biblical figure. In Levinas, the removal and eminence of the divine "orders" us to the neighbor, the face of the neighbor being the trace God leaves behind as God withdraws from the world.[21] For Levinas the eminence of God has an ethical force here below, whose political impact Derrida pursues in *Adieu*. So the effect of the divine trace is to level the aristocratic hierarchization of "equals," which means "superiors," which means men (brothers), around which Greek and Roman conceptions of friendship are organized.

To be sure, it is only too well known that this effect is all but effaced in the long history of Jewish, Christian, and Islamic patriarchy, fratriarchy, and militancy, on which, it is safe to say, the concrete messianisms have not cornered the market. That is in part why Derrida has a holy terror of religious exemplarism, and of allowing himself to be consolidated within a Jewish "community," and he is uneasy with Levinas's politics and patriarchy. The *last* thing Derrida is going to do is identify the figure of the friendship and the democracy to come as something specifically Judaic or to bring it to rest upon an "absolute theologization" or "theological-political authority" (PF, 302). His is at best a quasi-Judaic, quasi-atheistic desertified messianic, a religion *without* religion, which means an ethico-political messianic which tries to keep a distance between itself and the concrete messianisms, between itself and any specially chosen people.[22] For all these people of God have devoted an unholy amount of time to waging holy wars on one another and, whenever they are given the political power, on everyone else who disagrees with them. The history of the concrete messianisms is remarkable testimony to their capacity to betray the messianic call. But none of that gainsays the fact that the future figure of the friend that Derrida's Zarathustra is invoking, calling upon, and reinventing in *Politics of Friendship* is not the future of a still higher self-affirming, self-overflowing, self-discharging super-fellow, but one who solicits me beyond myself by his or her lowliness and alterity, a widowly, orphan-like stranger who would fill Zarathustra with nausea.

This figure, I have insisted, is drawn neither from Nietzsche nor from Aristotle, but from Blanchot and Levinas, who provide the starting point from which Derrida sets out to look for openings in the canonical texts of Aristotle and Nietzsche. For Aristotle and Nietzsche, friendship turns on what might be called the superior equality and measureless majesty of two souls made of the same virile stuff, equal in the sense of being equally superior in *Macht* and *arete*, each counting up to the same incalculable greatness and measureless overflow, to the same magnanimity as the other. True friends are men of surpassing excellence (*arete*), hyper-men (*über-menschen*) who are hyper-souled (*megalapsychos*). The excess and greatness of the friend—and also of my enemy, who should be a worthy enemy, one of whom I should also be proud, Nietzsche said—should "reflect" on my own greatness and pride. The friend should *re*affirm my self-affirmation, by sending back to me reaffirming reflections of the immeasurable measure and excess of my largess, of my self-affirming magnificence and gift-giving munificence. Excess and overflow in Nietzsche have the quality not of response to the other, which is the spirit of the camel and the beast of burden, but of a self-originating discharge or release (*entlassen*) which, as I have argued, has a somewhat phallo-orgasmic quality. Such hyper-friends and super-fellows, brothers, or megabrothers to the end, reflect each other in a reciprocal display of matching brilliance and phainaesthetic glory.[23]

But the friend for Derrida's Zarathustra, and for his Jewish friends, Levinas and Blanchot, is of another sort. This *other* more messianic Zarathustra, this *other* more Dionysian rabbi, calls for *another friendship*, one which will *not* be a matter of reciprocity and equality but of excess and expenditure without return, and will *not* be an excess of *discharge* but an excess of *responsibility.* The friend to come will not be marked by the "good sense" of "autarky and autonomy" (PF, 232), but by the madness and nonsense of heteronomy (PF, 68), by a longing for a democracy to come that will not only not resist dissymmetry and curved space but will in fact depend upon them, attempting as it does to think "an alterity without hierarchical difference lying at the root of democracy" (PF, 232).

Such a friendship requires not knowing who we are; it requires a confession of non-knowing and of the secret of non-appearing, of the appearing of what does not appear (PF, 232). It transpires unseen, in secret, without the lights of phenomenology, without all the hype of the play of reflections, without brilliant display, in the unseen scene of an incalculable and invisible gift, if there is one.

Thus spake (a slightly Franco-Jewish) Zarathustra. If there is one.

4

Parisian Hermeneutics and Yankee Hermeneutics

The Case of Derrida and Rorty

Yankee Hermeneutics

Richard Rorty belongs among the masters of those who do *not* know, who have renounced a privileged access to The Secret. He has even lately confessed outright to being, like Johannes Climacus, a "poor existing individual" with no head for the System (TP, 333).[1] Rorty is a leading figure among those who make no claim to knowing how to Lead the Way, who think that the way is a lot safer for us all when we confess that we do not know The Secret, and who think that it is more important to seek justice than to get a corner on The Truth. Rorty sides with Walt Whitman and John Dewey, who "tried to substitute hope for knowledge," "utopian dreams" for "knowledge of God's will, Moral Law, the Laws of History, the Facts of Science" (AOC, 107).[2]

I have long admired Rorty's work.[3] I relish his mastery of the idiom of American English, which succeeds in making philosophical sense without sounding like a bad translation from the German (or even a good one!). I admire the way he has defied the high priests of the American Church of Analytic Philosophers of the Strict Observance, and this from the pulpit of Princetonian orthodoxy. But I appreciate, too, the shock wave he sent through the American "continentalist" establishment when he stole some of their best lines by quoting their high priests, Friedrich Nietzsche, Martin Heidegger, and Jacques Derrida, and did so without hiding behind a layer of jargon that mostly serves the purpose of protecting continentalists from criticism. Unlike many continentalists, he takes the risk of making himself understood.

But most of all I admire Rorty because I think he is on to something, something which is deeply in accord with what I have been pursuing in my own groping quasi-continentalist way. What Rorty describes under the American name of "pragmatism" is very much in the spirit of what an American who has spent a lot of time and effort reading contemporary French and German philosophers might call a "more radical hermeneutics," or a hermeneutics of the secret, or of non-knowledge, or of facticity, all of which certainly sounds too French or German for its own good, but is nothing more than philosophy cut to fit a poor existing individual. Like Rorty, I want to try to make it without entertaining any illusions about big world-historical or Being-historical stories. Like Rorty, I do not think that philosophers have been sent into the world to give utterance to what Being would say were it given a tongue and vocal cords. Like Rorty, I am willing to concede that for the most part I am trying to make it through the day and will be delighted if I make it all the way to pay day. I am very much in agreement with Rorty's nominalist distrust of the idea that we can cut through appearances to seize hold of some essential core in things, a claim that I would advance on the basis of a more Derridean analysis of meaning as a contingent nominal unity, a constituted effect, which is really just a continentalist way to speak of nominalist non-essentialism. Like Rorty, I have renounced The Secret and all its pomps and works. I share, too, the upbeat and democratic passion for social justice for the least among us that animates Rorty, the anti-elitism of his anti-essentialism, which is the most felicitous ethico-political upshot of this way of thinking.

Rorty has given up on the classical dream of "Philosophical Knowledge," the (capitalized) idea that there is some sort of entity or realm, principle or condition which philosophers can come up with, so long as they argue carefully, which "explains" or "grounds" what the rest of us are doing. As a general rule of thumb, the way to see what Rorty and radical hermeneutics are both criticizing, to see their common targets, one needs only to capitalize it [It]. As soon as anything other than a proper name is capitalized, which is certainly the one thing that deserves capitalization, It acquires larger than life proportions, becomes too hypostatic, hyperbolic, and prestigious for its own good and begins to threaten everyone around it. Both Rorty's more Yankee hermeneutics and the Franco-American deconstructionist hermeneutics I advance are engaged in the de-capitalization, the decapitation of the most dangerous Capitals—geographic, philosophical, and economic. We both want to put a cap on this excess.

Rorty has given up the Kantian idea that there is a "philosophical tribunal" (CIS, 197), whose job it is to adjudicate conflicting claims about science or morals or art, in virtue of something that philosophers "Know" but nobody else "Knows," not unless they become philosophers, too. He rejects the idea that philosophers, in virtue of some method or capacity that they were apprenticed in during graduate school and mastered during the tenure process, can cut through the veil of appearances and get to what is "Really" going on, that they can penetrate beneath the surface or rise above the lower world the rest of us live in. He casts off the idea that it is the office of some "nonempirical super science" (CIS, 4) called philosophy to establish such entities as the Form of the Good, the *prima causa*, the monad, absolute Geist, the Will to Power, Being (as opposed to beings)—or generally anything we feel an irresistible urge to capitalize— whose role it would be to keep order either in the sciences or in the everyday world we live in. (He includes *différance* in this list; I do not, since it should *never* be capitalized.)

Rorty rejects every disguise that The Secret has been able to assume among philosophers. He discards the idea that philosophers can come up with an idea of human nature that would pick out something quintessentially human that would not be a function of socialization, that would see to it that socialization does not go all the way down (CIS, 185). He rejects the idea that philosophers have found a way to come up with anything quintessential, indeed with any essence at all, human or natural. He jettisons the idea that the physical sciences can come to the rescue, now that religion and philosophy have lost their reputation, and cut through the world of familiar objects, like Eddington's table, to the mathematical properties of Physical Reality. The urge to capitalize in the physical sciences is just as unjustified as it is in metaphysics and religion.[4] Rorty shows a steadfastly nominalist and historicist (CIS, xvi, 74) skepticism about essence, reality, overarching principles, ahistorical conditions of possibility, and whatever else is dreamt of in our philosophies.

Rorty has no knockdown arguments against these entities and principles; he does not think one can drive one's opponents up an argumentative wall (CIS, 53). He does not want to be drawn into the fray, get caught arguing the inverse side of metaphysics (which *is* philosophy, Heidegger says), which is metaphysics all the same. Rorty is incredulous toward such constructs: he greets them with a shrug and a smile. On this point, at least, Rorty fits François Lyotard's famous definition of postmodernism as "incredulity towards metanarratives,"[5] toward *grands récits,* big stories about Being or Truth, although he thinks the other side of the Enlightenment, the political side, is on the mark when it says that we are gradually making headway toward the goal of human emancipation. When it comes to big stories about Truth, Rorty is a big skeptic, although he is big on justice, which he does not regard as a Platonic Form, an Enlightenment Universal, or as a new Enlightenment Undeconstructible, and which he will not capitalize. He is incredulous about the sorts of things that philosophers have allowed themselves to believe, and he has set adroitly about finding a way of not letting himself be drawn into these beliefs. His idea is to back himself out of the vocabularies of the classical theories, to talk himself out of their language games, by simply "redescribing" the situations which the philosophers think are so troubled and aporetic as to drive them to the wall of coming up with a uniquely philosophical solution.

The effect of a good redescription on Rorty's terms will be therapeutic, to make the problem go away by seeing that, on this alternate description, there is no problem, that business can go on as usual without high-powered, second order supervening philosophical interventions. In Rorty's view, what Edmund Husserl calls the "natural attitude" can take care of itself, thank you very much, and nobody down here in the natural attitude is feeling the pain that the philosophers up there are trying to cure. All one really needs to see on Rorty's terms is that the vocabulary with which we describe the world or one another, when things get bad enough, can always be revised, that any person or object or event can always be recontextualized, that any description can be replaced by a redescription that will not suffer from the disadvantages of the prior description. Of course, the new vocabulary will generate new disadvantages of its own. But, as Nietzsche might have said, final vocabularies are something to be overcome. All this Nietzschean-Rortian insight requires is a certain ironic distance from our current "final" vocabulary which sees that it is not final at all but "contingent" (CIS, 73).

What lies behind the trouble that philosophers cause for themselves, Rorty thinks, is the philosophical cramp that language is a "medium," either of representation, as in the realist correspondence theory of truth, or of expression, as in the more romanticized idealist theories that language is the way Spirit, Thought, History, or Being comes into words and so comes to be a Spirit, Thought, History, or Being. Rorty's notion is to kick this habit of thinking that language is a medium, that it is anything at all, anything philosophical, that is, like a medium, and to realize that it is just a tool by means of which we make our way around the world.[6] Apart from the various natural languages which are the object of study in linguistics and in the sundry language departments, there simply is no philosophical thing called language (CIS, 14–15).

The skill and adroitness, the grace and good humor, the originality, insightfulness, and wide-ranging literateness with which Rorty has set about the delicate operation of articulating and defending this version of neo-pragmatism, which skillfully runs together the work of Ludwig Wittgenstein, Heidegger, and Dewey, is pretty much what we mean nowadays by "Rorty," which represents a Yankee hermeneutics with which I have a considerable sympathy. How shall we classify it—the problem of classification being a central question both Derrida and Rorty raise? What is its genre? Does "Rorty" stand for a "philosophy"? "If you like," he would say; "so long as you do not get in heat over that." So long as all one means by "philosophy" is a kind of writing, a frank and literate line of reflection which expresses itself about a wide range of human affairs, without pretense to expert knowledge (*episteme*).[7] Does this Yankee hermeneutics represent a *kind of philosophy*, philosophy *as it were*, a *quasi-philosophy*? That is the first question I ask. The second has to do with its politics. Let us take each in turn.

I. On Not Circumventing the Quasi-Transcendental

The first question is this: Must Rorty, too, like Derrida, having bid adieu to philosophy in the strong sense of supplying either metaphysical foundations or transcendental conditions, hang his hat on the more wobbly peg of the *quasi-transcendental?*

On Not Suspending the Natural Attitude

Let us begin by reconstituting Rorty's view. Put in Husserlian terms, Rorty sees absolutely no reason whatever to suspend the natural attitude which, as far as he is concerned, can take excellent care of itself and does not stand in need of transcendental intervention.[8] Some positions within the natural attitude are better than others, but it is the business of the natural attitude to put its own house in order, without any higher intervention or foreign aid, by letting the various views taken in the natural attitude compete with one another until one starts to look better than others in certain contexts, while other views look better in other contexts. There is no need to acquire, and no way to establish, the transcendental conditions of possibility which back up the empirical world, which ground and found it, which adjudicate its disputes and provide an overarching hook upon which the empirical ego can grasp whenever things get too stormy in the empirical world below. His eye is set on dissolving some of the muddles that philosophers, scientists, theologians, and artists have created for the rest of us, on untying a few such knots, and then letting the natural attitude take care of itself. The whole idea is to give the natural attitude some room to breathe and allow it to straighten out its own affairs. To call what he is doing "philosophy" at this point is for him mostly aimed at offering relief to desperate catalogue librarians, and it is based on little more than checking the footnotes to see what books are being cited. But it does not have much more punch, and it is not much more of an *episteme* or *strenge Wissenschaft* than that (CIS, 135–136).

Husserl would object that the "very idea" of the "natural attitude" is a philosophical idea. Nobody who actually lives in the natural attitude ever thought of it. The "very idea" of a natural attitude arises only from a transcendental standpoint, only by distinguishing the natural attitude from the transcendental attitude, so that the very identification of the natural attitude already presupposes the *epoche,* viz., that by thematizing the natural attitude as such one has already stepped outside of the grasp of the natural attitude.[9] That is why I think that Rorty has a delicate operation (cf. CIS 7–8) on his hands, which it seems to me must always involve two stages. First, he must defend the natural attitude against its metaphysical detractors and transcendental conquistadores, those who think the natural attitude cannot conduct its own affairs, that it requires transcendental monitoring and colonizing by a more "advanced," higher order consciousness. Second, he must eventually talk philosophers down off the ledge of making this distinction at all, so that eventually even talk about the "natural attitude" would disappear, even as Nietzsche hoped that the apparent world too would disappear, and even as Heidegger said we should leave metaphysics to itself and cease all overcoming of metaphysics.[10]

The idea is to just knock off philosophizing in the traditional way, to kick the traditional philosophical habit, to escape or walk away from philosophy (TP, 334–335), the way one would quit smoking or lay off fattening foods, or even merely "change the subject" until we forget about it. This of course drives "professional philosophers" mad, that is, people who get tenure and promotion, who give amazingly complicated papers at the

American Philosophical Association, who get sabbatical leaves and cushy grants to write more such papers (as if the world needed any more). These are the people who make a profitable living from "philosophy"—rather like the theologians about whom Søren Kierkegaard complained that they made a profitable living out of the Crucifixion. They do not want Rorty's line to get back to their academic deans or the wealthy alumni, to the National Endowment for the Humanities (NEH) or the Republican right wing. The delicious thing about Rorty's line is how nicely it cuts across the once (and future) well-entrenched divide between analytic and continental philosophy, how he overruns both camps, and leaves a lot of unhappy philosophical campers on both sides shaking their fists in anger at him. The analytic philosophers will not forgive him because he has, unforgivably, made philosophy interesting and significant to a larger public, which exposes the hollowness of what most analytic philosophers have to say; because he has broken ranks with a narrow in-group in the prestige universities who have made a career of patting each other on the back and recommending one another for prestige appointments while no one else reads or cares about their precious little papers on meaning and reference, which they have beaten mercilessly into the ground. (How many more articles can they write on meaning and reference? Aren't they finished yet?) The continental philosophers will not forgive him because he has invaded their turf, laid hands on their favorite thinkers, explained them in a way that can be understood, and stolen some of their best lines, like "the end of philosophy" or "overcoming metaphysics." And maybe he has even stolen some jobs in continental philosophy away from the continentalist doctoral programs. That's really serious and that is what is behind the continentalist critique of Rorty, in my opinion.

Professional politics aside, it is interesting how Rorty's line converges with the more radical developments in continental thought in the last twenty years. His work intersects in intriguing ways with Nietzsche and the late Heidegger; with the work of "postmodernists" such as Derrida, Lyotard, and Michel Foucault; it bears on the exchanges among Hans-Georg Gadamer, Lyotard, and Jürgen Habermas. Rorty's ability to spot this convergence and translate it into his own terms has made him, like it or not, the most widely read "philosopher" writing in English. Of course this point of convergence has been reached by tunneling toward the same center from entirely opposite directions: Rorty from a skeptical anti-metaphysical tradition which has been shaving down metaphysical pretensions ever since Ockham unsheathed his razor; the postmodernists from the high-flying speculations of Hegelian dialectics, Husserl's transcendental phenomenology, and Heidegger's History of Being. But they have joined rails in a middle which Rorty was the first to spot.

Rorty's "Derrida"

In open defiance of the Anglo-American analytic establishment, "the conservative know-nothings in the United States and Britain," who have tried to "excommunicate Derrida from the philosophical profession," Rorty shows a particular appreciation for the work of Derrida (DP, 13).[11] In Rorty's terms, Derrida is a master of "self-creation," a genius of "autonomy," that is, of creating idiosyncratic, virtually unclassifiable texts that hold our interest, that repay endless rereading, and that leave us wondering at how he does it. Derrida has succeeded in making himself different, has come to grips with the anxiety of influence with great aplomb by writing in a magnificently assimilative but creative manner, sounding now like Husserl, now like Jean-Jacques Rousseau, now like Heidegger—or Sigmund Freud, or James Joyce, or Maurice Blanchot, or G. W. F. Hegel, or Emmanuel Levinas (this could get to be a long list)—but always sounding different. Derrida has mastered the art of being idiosyncratic, of repeating the people he happens to have read but with a difference, a difference which is immensely creative, highly associative, ingeniously complicated (CIS, 126ff.; cf. xiv). In a manner that reminds us of Joyce (that is intentional), Derrida composes fantastic "texts," rich, lush, overfull texts that overlap with other texts, that allude to philosophers, psychoanalysts, poets, and novelists in a way that sends his readers scurrying to the library to track down the disseminative excess of allusion, citation, creative misrepresentation, miming, playing; texts full of multilingual puns and tremendously funny jokes. Derrida is not a master of "thought," which is the highest compliment humorless old Heidegger could pay anyone, but a master of writing, of texts, of invention, an impresario who stages breathtaking productions, a genius at being brilliant, a philosophical virtuoso the likes of which we have not seen since Nietzsche and Kierkegaard converted their personal demons into works of art.

Derrida, too, has made himself into a work of art, has created a text out of the unmasterable complex of people he has met (CIS, 100), books he has read, cities and even campuses he has visited, talks he has been invited to give. Derrida is utterly scandalous in this regard. He incorporates the most extraordinarily "contingent" things into his "philosophical" texts: the landscape at Cornell University, which is woven into a discussion of the philosophical problem of the "abyss," that is, of the ground without ground that Anglo-Americans call non-foundationalism; or the spelling of his name, which leads him to associate the "da" in Derrida with "*Da-sein*" (Heidegger) and Freud's *fort-da*. He writes a book—*The Post Card*—which is paradigmatic for Rorty of Derrida the writer—which consists of a series of love letters filled with private allusions, including an account of his visit to Oxford and a trip with Jonathan Culler to the Bodleian Library. The "book" includes a procession of fantastic, entertaining, outrageous, obscene speculations on a postcard which he found in the library bookstore—and which could still be found there as late as a visit I made to Oxford in 1988—in which a diminutive Plato appears to be standing behind (whence the obscenity) a much larger, seated Socrates, who is writing. Derrida's delight in this seeming reversal of the most honored filial relation in Western philosophy knows no limit, and the "book" he writes on the "subject" is only to be compared with the "aesthetic writings" of Kierkegaard for wit and imaginativeness.[12]

Unless one considers *Glas*,[13] which I would say is another masterpiece and is even more complex, more unreadably readable and idiosyncratic than *The Post Card*, and which is more germane for considering Rorty's relationship to Derrida, although Rorty tries to duck *Glas* (CIS, 126). *Glas* requires a companion volume entitled (what else?) *Glassary* in order to track down the allusions to Hegel, in the left column, and Jean Genet, in the right column. "Philosophically" (I can hear the analytic philosopher gasp), it turns on a series of interrelated philosophical problems.

The problem of the author: this Derrida addresses by means of a "theory" and practice of "auto-graphy," which means that a writer is always signing his or her own name. In the left column, Hegel is *aigle*, the soaring eagle of *sa, savoir absolue*, his/her, *s*(ignifi)*a*(nt*)*, *ça* (the unconscious), and later on, in *Circonfession*—a book Rorty also much appreciates (TP, 327ff.), it means Saint Augustine, and whatever else one can make work felicitously. *Sa*, the soaring eagle of speculative knowledge which swoops down on every unsuspecting particular, lifts it up (*relever*) into the universal and carries it back in its grasping (*begreifen*) conceptual claws to its cold mountaintop of absolute knowledge. On the right side, in a parallel column, Genet who cannot stop signing *genêt*, the mountain flower, who keeps spreading flowers all over the place, Genet whose queens wear flowers in the most embarrassing places. On the left, a column made stiff and hard by the rigor of the absolute *Begriff;* on the right, cut flowers, headcuts of criminals cut from newspapers hanging on the prison wall, guillotines, castrations, all of this cut and stitched together into the text of *Glas*, with the glue of *Glas*, which likes to slide these slippery (*glissant*) signifiers the one inside the other, maybe even *a tergo*, with the aid of a little Vaseline.

The problem of the family: on the left, the life of Jesus in *Hegel's Early Theological Writings*, that is, his *Jugend-Schriften*, the child-writings which are the father of the mature man/Hegel, according to any good teleological genealogy (for instance, Bernard Bourgeois's). Hegel is always telling the story of the "speculative family" in which the Father generates his Son who must be broken up and spread out as Spirit. That involves a holy family composed of a man with only an actual mother but a father that is being in itself; and the bourgeois family, a good Prussian patriarchal family, whose son leaves the inwardness of hearth and home for the outwardness of commercial life, in order finally to be reconciled by the *Staat;* and a number of improper homosexual families in the "other" column.

The problem of the woman: Antigone, the sister who defies the public law of the father, of the state, of the day, in name of the inwardness of the family, mourning, the night. While in the right column Genet is telling the story of transvestites, men/women, and of outlaw families, un-families of queens and homicidal rapists who make "unnatural" love and who bear the most delicately beautiful names, religious names like nuns who have left the world, such names as Our Lady of the Flowers, First Communion, etc.

The problem of the proper name: when they are arraigned before the judge, and called by their "proper," legal names, the names that have been attached to them by the law for the purpose of surveillance, their bourgeois names, then they know they are already dead men.

The problem of the system: a rich thematics of "fragments" and remnants which means to say, like Climacus, that the system can never close over, that there are always remainders and fragments, always outlaws, always the unassimilable, indigestible, ungraspable. *Individuum ineffabile est.* There is something always already incalculable in the infinite Hegelian calculus. And this "calculus" contains an almost perfectly private allusion, except that Derrida gives it away. In 1987, while lecturing on *Glas,* Derrida told his audience that the thematics of "calculus" in *glas* were also making allusion to his mother (the woman, who is daughter/mother/sister, is important in *Glas*) who was suffering from gallstones (calculs) at the time. That was a little joke, for Mom, who would appreciate being immortalized, or at least mentioned, in what would get to be a famous book, and who would later on become the subject of a beautiful and powerful analogy to Monica in *Circonfession.* A little like having a book dedicated to her, but inside the margins, and more important, privately, until Derrida let his joke out in public.

I could go on—which is of course the whole idea. One could always go on, enjoying more and more of this inexhaustibly complex text, more and more *jouissance,* so long as the audience gets the jokes. But you "get the idea." That, of course, is not the idea, just what Derrida does not want, that we would sum it up and "grasp" its logocentric "point" with our eagle claws, consume it, and then move on. The quasi-idea is to linger and languish in the gooey glue of *Glas.* Now that is the Derrida whom Rorty admires, Derrida on his best day, the Derrida who is making himself beautiful and different by one of the most fascinating exercises in what Rorty calls "autonomy" of this century, by weaving a rich full text out of his private life, even out of the contingencies of his name. Rorty is happy to join in this fun, so long as we do not turn serious in the middle of it and say "gotcha," as long as we do not ruin everything by saying that Derrida was only half kidding and that there is a deep and serious philosophical principle beneath it all which is writing straight with crooked lines. That is the sort of trap that Rodolphe Gasché and Christopher Norris try to spring, and it is a side of Derrida that Rorty does not admire, the side where Derrida's spirit of levity sags and he lapses into seriousness. That Derrida, no longer a comic writer, starts trotting out new metaphysical "ghosts" of his own, devising "quasi-transcendentals" whose hiddenness reminds us of the hidden God in negative theology, or other metaphysical specters, which remind us, alas, of The Secret, which purports to be the reality behind the appearance.[14] As one might expect, you can only get to know these quasi-entities if you are a philosopher and have the credentials to make the right arguments, have been properly trained —whether in Ferdinand de Saussure and transcendental phenomenology or the *Principia Mathematica*, it makes no difference. That is the side of Derrida Rorty dislikes, the side which shows a taste for such philosophical ideas as *différance, archi-écriture,* trace, supplement, undecidability, the impossible, etc., all of which sound just too philosophical. For a while, in his early writings, Derrida even adopted an unmistakably apocalyptic tone about these quasi-entities, announcing the end of the age of the book and the beginning of writing. While Derrida has shaken that particularly bad habit, he still talks like "metaphysics" is an inescapable, encompassing something or other which has a hold on us that is deeper than we can say. That makes Rorty squirm in his seat because Rorty thinks that deconstruction on its best day should help us "circumvent" metaphysics,[15] dodge the bullets of metaphysics, not mystify metaphysics all the more by making it an elusive and ghostly figure that stalks us when we least suspect its influence, which is what also happens to us when we are washed over by waves of Foucauldian "power" (AOC, 97).

The central claim that is made on behalf of *différance*, and the one that Rorty goes after, is that it is a transcendental "condition of possibility" for speech and writing in the empirical sense. That brings Derrida squarely back to a version of transcendental philosophy, a variation on Immanuel Kant and Husserl, which has an explanation for everything that is going on in the natural attitude. That puts Derrida and deconstruction in the superior position of knowing The Secret, of knowing, in virtue of a philosophical theory, what is going on in language and what sorts of traps those folks down there in the life world—for instance, literary critics— keep walking into. The clearest instance of this adaptation of Derrida is that of Paul de Man, who thinks that Derrida gives him the wherewithal to straighten out the "naive" literary critics who still think that language refers to the world.[16] According to de Man, naive literary critics "resist theory," that is, "literary theory," just because "theory"—that is, Derrida's theory of *différance*—problematizes this naive belief in the worldliness of literary language by discovering the purely literary quality of language whose virtue is that, unlike scientific language, it refers to nothing other than itself. That Diltheyan split (between natural and literary language) gives de Man his elegiac tone, always mourning the loss of the world, which picks up on the nostalgic, negative-theological, apocalyptic side of Derrida, which is the worst side of Derrida, the side in which he has forgotten that he is a comic writer. Derrida's job is to make fun of philosophy, to make it look bad by making it look funny, and this in order to have fun. The worst thing he can do is to get drawn into the game of which he makes such stupendous fun.

But that is simply not true, according to Norris and Gasché, whose readings of Derrida Rorty strongly opposes.[17] Norris says that it is a big mistake for Rorty and others to think that Derrida is just making fun of philosophy, that Derrida merely throws philosophy into confusion by showing that every time it thinks it has come upon reference all it really finds is difference, that philosophical arguments always get washed out by their literariness, that philosophy is only writing, that philosophers have no gifts or expertise of their own, that philosophy is always deluded to think that it has an argument over and beyond rhetorical force. Norris thinks that Derrida has rigor—he stands erect, like the left column of *Glas*. Derrida gives rigorous and close readings of philosophers, and his deconstructive analysis of Husserl is an exemplary piece of close argumentation, which displays how Husserl needs what he has excluded. What Derrida does, Norris says "amount[s] to a form of Kantian transcendental deduction. . . . [It] pose[s] the question: what must be the necessary presuppositions about language if language is to make any kind of coherent or intelligible sense?"[18] Derrida has "earned" his eagle's wings as a philosopher; he can soar with the best of them. He does deconstruction in a philosophical way which reminds us, as Norris says in *Derrida*, of the Enlightenment tradition of making arguments and doing critiques.[19] Derrida is not against philosophy but against a false idea of philosophy which is fed by logocentric delusions, like thinking that it has God's point of view. The Western philosophical tradition is all we have, and we have to work within it; we cannot go beyond philosophy any more than Foucault could write a history of madness from the standpoint of the mad.[20] One cannot have God's point of view, or the madman's; all one has is human reason. But Derrida's aim is to be relentlessly critical of what calls itself reason, particularly when the university starts building nuclear bombs in the name of reason, which would see to it there really is nothing rather than something. One works from within, including from within professional philosophical expertise, and tries to make a difference.

But Rorty thinks it actually would be odd for Derrida to end up like that, delivered over to the hands of Gasché and Norris. If *différance* picks out the transcendental conditions of possibility of speaking and writing in the empirical sense, then that

> would require us to envisage all such inventions before their occurrence. The idea that we do have such a metavocabulary at our disposal, one which gives us a "logical space" in which to "place" anything which anybody will ever say, seems just one more version of the dream of "presence" from which ironists since Hegel have been trying to wake us. (CIS, 125)

Rorty is right, in my view, not to challenge the "accuracy" (CIS, 123) of Norris's and Gasché's treatment of Derrida. Up to a point, their commentaries, in my view, play the strategically useful role of emphasizing Derrida's more serious transcendental side, since Derrida's wilder side is well known. However, I think they overemphasize this and that does generate an accuracy problem of its own.[21] Rorty's portrait merely shrugs off every serious moment in Derrida as a kind of philosophical hangover, and he reads works such as *The Post Card* too one-sidedly. But Rorty thinks that, if it is accurate, the Norris-Gasché line accurately portrays Derrida at his worst. Setting accuracy aside, the question is whether it is not just incoherent of Derrida to make a transcendental move, whether that is not simply one more unfortunate relapse into the metaphysical dream of presence, as Rorty says. How can Derrida possibly think that with his notion of *différance* he has attained some "logical space" within which he can place anything that anybody is ever going to say? How can one have a notion of *l'inventions de l'autre* if one has a theory in virtue of which every possible invention is precontained? But, if the surname of *différance* is *khôra*, is *khôra* a "logical space?"

Is Derrida a Quasi-Transcendental Philosopher?
(or, It Takes One to Know One)

Rorty's first complaints against Derrida were directed at his "transcendental" side, and it was soon pointed out to him that this is strictly speaking only a *quasi*-transcendental. That is, Derrida is not supplying conditions of possibility *simpliciter*, but rather showing that the conditions under which something, *x*, is made possible, also make *x* impossible, for instance, the gift. But that reply gave Rorty no comfort.

> [T]his is an unnecessarily high-faluting way of putting a point which could be put a lot more simply: viz., that you cannot use a word "A" [for example, gift] without being able to use the word "B" [for example, exchange], and vice versa, even though nothing can be both an A and a B. (DP, 16)

By talking about the *quasi*-transcendental Derrida is still trying to "sound transcendental," which is still being assigned the task of "unmasking" what is "really going on" down there in the naive natural attitude from the higher quasi-transcendental point of view, and that reenacts all the essentials of the reality/appearance distinction (DP, 14). It continues to make Derrida sound as if he is trying to steal The Secret. Derrida is coming up with one more philosophical theory about language which takes language to be something that *needs* a philosophical explanation to straighten out its affairs and put its house in order, instead of appreciating that language gets along fine without deconstruction or structuralism, expressionism or representationalism, or whatever else philosophers come up with in their competition for tenure, promotion, a NEH grant, or an endowed chair. The only thing that will give Rorty peace is if one admits with Donald Davidson, "There is no such thing as language" (DP, 43).

Let us examine this more closely, because it goes to the heart of the

difference between Rorty and Derrida and cuts to the heart of the hermeneutics of The Secret. Is *différance* a secret version, *in pectore,* of The
Secret? In my view, Derrida is indeed committed to something like what
Norris and Gasché attribute to him. Derrida does have a *certain* "philosophical idea" about language. One might even say he has a certain
"theory," or kind of theory, although that is a strong word implying mastery and a totalizing overview and Derrida avoids it, usually preferring to
speak of his "hypothesis," which is tentative, about which he is not sure,
which he hesitates to bring up before this intimidating audience, etc.
Derrida has at least a *quasi*-theory about what is going on in language and
not just language, but other sign-making or meaning-making or more
generally effect-producing quasi-systems, as he might call them (like
painting and architecture), which goes under the name of the quasi-transcendental.

Rorty is right to say that the quasi-theory of the quasi-transcendental
is still some kind of a second order account of language, no matter how
many "quasi-s" one inserts to qualify it or mollify the pragmatists. I agree.
To put things in too simple a way, I would say there are two phases to this
quasi-theory. (1) The first phase is the part that Derrida has borrowed
from Saussure. Derrida thinks these economies produce their effects by a
kind of "spacing," by producing marks or traces which make nominal
unities called "words" or concepts or meaning—or beauty, rhythm, symmetry or asymmetry, or whatever one needs—not merely and not primarily in virtue of the intrinsic "substance" of the "signifier" but in terms
of the "differential" relationship—the "space"—between the signifiers. It
does not matter whether one speaks or writes, whether one uses "give"
or *geben,* what does matter is that the "difference," the space between
"give" and "live," *geben* and *leben,* be discernible. Derrida calls this spacing
archi-écriture or *différance,* and he lately has been calling it *khôra,* which
are not quasi-entities but, to put it the way Rorty would prefer, just an
odd sort of vocabulary Derrida adopted as a contingent result of the books
he was told to read, or that he got interested in, when he went to school
in Paris. Specifically it was something he was getting from Saussure,
mediated through the Copenhagen school of structural linguistics, while
reading Joyce and Husserl.

(2) But it is with the second phase of Derrida's quasi-theory, the quasi-
transcendental phase, that the disingenuousness of what Rorty is trying
to pull off is exposed. I admit that Derrida does have an idea of what
language "must be" if it is, as Norris says, to make "any kind of coherent
or intelligible sense." What Derrida calls "iterability" is a feature of any
mark, and he is not bashful about that claim, no more than Rorty is bashful about saying things like "anything can be anything if you put in the
right context" (DP, 43). But is that not exactly what Derrida means by a
quasi-transcendental? Does Rorty not make a second order claim about
anything that anybody is going to say? Are we not clear that, *before any-*

one opens their mouth or turns on their word processor, we can recontextualize *whatever they are going to say,* any philosophical "candidates [that] sit there smugly (like Austin's frog at the bottom of the beer mug) thinking that they don't have and don't need a context" (DP, 43)? By having a theory of iterability (Derrida) or recontextuability (Rorty), Derrida and Rorty both explain how things get said and can always *and in principle* come unsaid, how the contexts that make linguistic strings meaningful, the mark or trace that makes them iterable, and thus allow them to succeed, *also* allow them to be recontextualized, falsified, doubted, or otherwise confounded. I do not see why Rorty thinks he is so much cleaner of the stain of philosophy than Derrida. Notice that when Rorty is confronted with an explanation of the quasi-transcendental his reply is *not* that this is non-sense or that he rejects the very idea, but rather that "this is an unnecessarily high-faluting way of putting a point which could be put a lot more simply" and that he does not like the way this "sounds." But whether we put it in a Parisian conundrum or in good old Yankee horse sense, the point is the same and Rorty, I think, must and does embrace it, which is why his Yankee horse sense also amounts to a Yankee hermeneutics. (Besides, Rorty of all people should not object if Derrida talks funny and does not sound like a Yankee.)

In other words, to put this in American English, if Rorty continues to complain even about Derrida's *quasi*-transcendental philosophy, I am replying to him by means of a technical and venerable philosophical argument known classically as "so's your mother," or "it takes one to know one," or, in common street talk, *tu quoque.*

Let us be deadly serious. Derrida is a transcendental philosopher—*almost.* He is close to the edge of transcendental philosophy; he hovers around its margins, is in between the columns of *Glas,* in their interplay, working the levers between the columns. Derrida is also supplying the presuppositions for thinking that whatever sense language does make will also be unmade, that the things we do with words will come undone. One of the things about "iterability" (Parisian version) is that it allows us to repeat and recontextualize (Yankee version) so that it is always possible to find some context in which an otherwise false statement is true, or an otherwise true statement is false, or an otherwise straight comment is funny, etc., and this tends therefore to undo the universalizability that we would want to attribute to a transcendental property. From Rorty's standpoint, Derrida is asserting that, and explaining why, final vocabularies are never final, that and why final vocabularies are always contingent and revisable, and that one needs different vocabularies for different things, such as praying and buying shoe polish. That point, which Rorty also requires (= "so's your mother"), is the point of calling the trace or iterability a *quasi*-transcendental, borrowing a (pretty funny) move in *Glas* (although the joke dies under Gasché's glass) in which Derrida, commenting on the analysis of Antigone in Hegel's *Phenomenology of Spirit,* addresses the question of something which a system cannot assimilate (a constant issue in *Glas*): "And what if what cannot be assimilated, the absolute indigestible, played a fundamental role in the system, an abyssal role, rather, playing. . . ." The text in the left column breaks here and is followed by twelve pages of inserted text drawn from Hegel's letters to and about his sister, and then continues: ". . . a quasi-transcendental role . . ." (G, 171–182a/151–62a).

The "quasi-transcendental" entity in this text is the sister, not just Antigone but the "figure" (*Gestalt*) of the sister in the *Phenomenology*, a fragment of this vast book to which no attention has been paid but which, for Derrida, is both necessary and impossible in the system. The fragment on the sister makes the system both possible and impossible, that is, it plays a "quasi-transcendental role." So the second step in Derrida's "quasi-theory" is to see to it that it is a theory which says that one cannot have a theory in a strong sense, without the "quasi-." Derrida is arguing that linguistic systems are differential; that they produce nominal and conceptual unities as effects of the differential play (or spacing) that is opened up between the marks or traces; that this differential spacing is, as Louis Hjelmslev shows, indifferent to the distinction between phonic and graphic marks; and finally that this notion of meaning as an effect of differential spacing displaces the primacy of intentional subjects expressing their thoughts by means of external signs.

But what Derrida adds to all this, the twist he puts on it—which is analogous to what Kurt Gödel does to mathematical systems—is to radicalize that argument, to push it further. He shows that Husserl's and Hjelmslev's attempts to enclose or regulate such a differential play by a purely formal system, to close the circle of its play, to formalize it, were misbegotten on the grounds of a differential play. For it belongs to the very idea of differential play that the play is self-differentiating, disseminating, and that any such formal rules as one could devise would be "effects" of the play not the "basis" of it, subsets of the play of signifiers, not rules which govern it.[22] In Rorty's terms, any rules one would devise about what future final vocabularies must look like would be contingent features of the final vocabulary one currently favors, without predictive power for what future vocabularies will look like. In Derrida's terms, it is always too late to assert our superiority over, our transcendental mastery of, language, for we are always already speaking and drawing on its resources. We have said yes to language before we say yes to anything else. Yes, yes.[23] That is another way of saying that we are caught up in the secret, but not *in on* The Secret.

But of course it is also true that anything Derrida would say, in the Parisian version, about the differential play would be in the same predicament, an effect of the play, not the play itself, in exactly the same way anything Rorty would say, in the Yankee version, about the contingency of final vocabularies would still be contingent. It is always already too late for Derrida too. That is why he devised the Parisian strategy of inventing such words as *différance,* with the purely graphic alteration, which is not a word or a concept—at least not the first three or four times he uses it, as Rorty rightly points out,[24] after which it is too late again. But at least the first couple of times he uses it we see what he is up to, what he is pointing to. Once it sediments, becomes part of the established vocabulary of "deconstruction," and starts getting into the journals and dictionaries of philosophy, he has to saddle up and ride on and try it another way. In his earlier works Derrida tended to spell all this out; in his later works he takes it for granted. In *Glas,* which is a major work, he is simply *doing* it, just putting it to work.

So what does that do to Derrida? Does that make deconstruction a practice with a philosophical theory behind it to back it up (which is what the title of one of Norris's first books suggests),[25] which is just what philosophy has always been doing and about which Rorty has well-known complaints? Well, yes and no. Almost. And remember, according to our ancient and venerable philosophical principle, the same goes for Yankee pragmatists such as Rorty.

Yes, inasmuch as Derrida did not merely drop out of a tree one day and start talking funny. He was led to what he has to say by Saussure, Husserl, Heidegger, Nietzsche, Freud, and Levinas (just for starters), and he works it out case by case with painful detail. That is, Derrida has "good reasons," something short of Transcendental Reason, for saying what he is saying (DP, 78), and every once in a while he will lay them out, as in his argument with John Searle, who, it seems to me (pace Rorty, CIS, 132–143), to this day does not get what Derrida is up to. If we make Derrida abandon this side, then the whole thing is crazy, and Derrida is just running off at the mouth, albeit in an entertaining way (if one has read the same books he has). Now that is what Rorty sometimes seem to want, that is, that Derrida would write in this entertaining way but for no good reason, or for his own amusement and that of those with a similar sense of humor. He is only having fun. He is just being brilliant, making himself beautiful, and carving out a sphere of autonomy for himself in a particularly brilliant way. So where is the problem? Derrida: that's not philosophy, that's entertainment.[26]

Now, in my view, not only is that not Derrida, it is also not Rorty.

Derrida is a philosopher who gives reasons if one disagrees with him or makes fun of him. It is also true that Derrida is not a transcendental philosopher. For what Derrida comes up with when he starts talking like a philosopher is that one cannot come up with anything like a hard philosophical theory, or with rigorous distinctions between theory and practice, or the *Geisteswissenschaften* and *Naturwissenschaften,* or analytic and synthetic, at least not for long. For sooner or later the differential play in what one's theory is trying to stick together will make it come undone. Sooner or later, someone will give us a close reading; they will descend upon us and disclose that our *arche/principium/*emperor-prince has no clothes, that the distinctions we are making have sprung a leak, that we need and use what we are excluding, that our metaphorics contradicts our thematics, that we cannot make the distinction between metaphorical and literal stick, and so on. That is, from Rorty's point of view, the Yankee version, somebody is going to come along, just when we are on a lunch break, and recontextualize what we thought we had definitively nailed in place. And that goes for deconstruction too were deconstruction ever to be so foolish as to state itself baldly as a theory in a strong sense.

The Parisian way to say this is to say that Derrida is both inside and outside philosophy, on the "margins" of philosophy, that he is a "certain kind" of philosopher. The Yankee way to say it is that he has reasons for thinking that what philosophy calls reason does not hold water, that is, is without reason or has become unreasonable. The reasons (plural) for not believing in Reason (capitalized, singular) are better than the reasons for believing in it. The reasons for believing that the secret is there is no Secret are better than the reasons for believing that such and such is The Secret. But Derrida is trying like mad to stay inside/outside philosophy and the university, to be adept at its games, to move with ease within its habits of thought and institutional corridors, and to disrupt its tendencies to start congratulating itself for being the home of Reason, the house of Being, the citadel of The Secret, the capital of everything that is Capitalized, including capital (money), or the place where the revolt against capital will be fomented, or the defender of bourgeois liberalism, or the guardian of truth, or any of the other unguarded things we say on behalf of academic learning or the university at commencement exercises. That is why Rorty is badly mistaken to think that "there is no moral to these fantasies, nor any public (pedagogic or political) use to be made of them" (CIS, 125, cf. 68, 83), a point which I will take up in more detail in the second part of this study. Derrida stays close to the philosophers and the university, moves with ease among their arguments, cultivates their language, reads them with a punishing closeness, gains their confidence, finds what is closest to their heart and then pulls the string, the loose thread in the text. After meeting all the standards of the philosophers, he breaks free and produces a scandalous writing which writes differently.

Now this marginality, this non-positionality of being inside/outside, which constitutes the "quasi-transcendental" motif in Derrida, is the moment of what he calls in *Glas* the quasi-transcendental ex-position (out of place). Antigone's place is both necessary and impossible. It is necessary because it provides the transition from natural to spiritual desire. That is, the relation of brother and sister in both sexual—they form a couple, a single pair of members of the opposite sex—and not sexual, without desire, and so it is the mediating *relève* between the two. Yet this is impossible, for it contradicts everything that Hegel says about the battle for recognition; this is a mediation and reconciliation of what has never done battle. The sister has transcendental status for Derrida because she is a possibility which the system must exclude even as she is needed as a stop or a station in the progress of absolute knowledge, an interruption to be assimilated, on the way to the reconciliation of divine and human law. We cannot have absolute knowledge without the sister, but once we do, we do not have the system any longer. It makes the system possible and impossible. The sister is inside and outside the system. The very thing that is excluded is what makes the system possible and must be included (G, 170a–71a/150a–51a).

That is what Derrida is always doing with philosophical texts, showing how the very thing that makes them possible also makes them impossible, that is, destabilizes them, which is something he can predict will happen inasmuch as any assembly of signifiers is always already set adrift by *différance* (Yankees: read recontextualizable). That is his almost transcendental, quasi-transcendental role, his broken or split transcendental. It is not a "logical space," exactly, but the space of *khôra,* of spacing itself, and it produces a lot more than logic. But notice that is not what Derrida does in the other column with Genet, a text which he just lets play. Genet is already set adrift, already in play: Hegel has to be reminded of the play; but Derrida, who is neither Hegel nor Genet, is the inter-play, is the space and the spacing between them, as their columnizer.

Rorty wants to push Derrida into the Genet column and keep him clear of Kant, and Norris and Gasché propel him into the Kant/Hegel column and barely acknowledge Genet, while Derrida is writing with both hands, doing a double writing. Rorty's "Derrida at his best" transgresses philosophy, strays outside its borders, drifts into a scandalous, comic, different discourse, which has dropped the pretense of being transcendental. Rorty's "Derrida at his worst" remains inside philosophy, has reasons for his distrust of Reason and sounds for all the world like a philosopher.

But, as I have argued, Derrida is not alone in this inter-columnal space. There is a sometime Princetonian Yankee in this Parisian court.

A Critique of Pure Autonomy

One other important thing about Derrida's quasi-transcendental is that it is a transcendental without a subject, a kind of anonymous transcendental, an impersonal field, populated by neither an empirical nor a transcendental subject, by no subject at all, but only by the play of differences. The standard transcendental is a subjective condition which makes the unity of objects possible, but the field of *différance* is a different transcendental, which makes any kind of unity, subjective or objective, things or subjects, possible and impossible (im/possible).

Rorty, in contrast, despite his account of the "contingency of the self"

(CIS, 23ff.) and its utter "socialization," and his rejection of the theory that language is the "expression" of the interior secrets of the subject, remains attached to the classical liberal subject and to individual, subjective *autonomy*. His redescription of Derrida in terms of "autonomy" falls wide of the mark. That redescription contradicts Derrida, where all the emphasis is on *heteronomy*. The whole point of Derrida's analysis of discourse in terms of *différance*, that is, of differentially related signifiers, is to underline the notion that language is not "invented" by "subjects" (and I would think that the same is true of any adequate conception of a "language game"). The very idea of thinking of language in terms of a language game or a play of signifiers is to get over the idea of a game invented and played by the players, which is the familiar, common-sensical, classical subjectivistic, and "metaphysical" model of language, one which in other respects Rorty seems intent on abandoning.[27] The idea is rather to think of language as a game which plays the players, which exceeds and overtakes, which precedes and antedates, the interiority of a private subjectivity. On both the Derridean and Wittgensteinian models, a language is not something a private, interior self devises in order to enter the world and communicate its inner thoughts. Rather it is a game into which one is entered from the start by being born into the world, a game which plays the "I," which brings the "I" about, and marks it forever with the contingencies of its birth and upbringing. Language is not a matter of an "I" which expresses its "inner thought" by outer marks. It is rather a behavior which is acquired by picking up the conventions of making marks in the ways adopted by those who "bring me up," by means of which "I" am slowly brought up or drawn into the higher order operations of thinking and imagining, and get to be a certain sort of "I." The "I" thus is not the interior, anterior inventor of the language, but one of the things produced by it, an "effect" of the game. So the extent to which I will be able to acquire these higher order operations is very much a contingent function of the subtlety, complexity, and nuances of the "vocabulary" (and the grammar) with which I am presented by my birth and education, of the degree to which the differential play to which I am exposed is differentiated enough, of the subtlety of the strategies that have been devised in the game I am taught to play.

On such a model it would be perverse to emphasize the "autonomy" of the subject, the "freedom" to engage in "self-creation." The point of this model is exactly the opposite, to stress the impersonal, structural, community-wide, historical, and even unconscious forces which rule over—but not with formalizable rules—or prevail in the language game to which I belong. Such quasi-structures prevent "self-creation" in any strong sense; indeed they make the "self" the "creation" (or effect) of the linguistic play. If anything enjoys "autonomy" here, it is not the self but the game which seems to carry the selves along by its own momentum, which is the "text" in the Derridean sense. For Derrida, if one had to speak of autonomy at all, that would be a more likely predicate of a text, of writing, that orphan which, having lost its voice and its father to speak on its behalf, is "on its own," cut off from its father/author to monitor its reference to the world.

That is why Derrida would never want to describe *Glas* or *The Post Card* in terms of a virtuoso performance of autonomy or self-creation, in terms of anything done by Jacques Derrida, the one who "signs" this text on the outside. He did not "invent" the linguistic chains which he strings together in *Glas,* the historical, etymological, graphic, and phonic associations with which he weaves. He did not make those puns, he fell upon them. This is not self-creation, and they are not "his" words. He is not responsible for the connection between *glas* and *classicus,* for its connection with bells and tolling, for the emblematic character of *glas* for language itself as a system of "classifying," for the Hegelian impulse to let the classifying universal assimilate the classified particular. He found them—and he confounds them; he points to them and he exploits them, in what he calls *l'invention de l'autre,* an invention/discovery which lets the other loose, lets the other come in (L. *in-venire*). He shows us how we are all a little lost in these concatenations, that no one can keep his or her head above water in the midst of them, that we are all always already swept up by them. That is why Derrida says we sign our names, not only on the outside of the text, outside the margins or on the covers—which would signify mastery, superiority, domination of the text, as if we really were the authors and knew what we are doing—but also, always and inevitably, inside the text. We cannot help ourselves, we too are drawn into the text, sucked up by its tendencies and metaphorics, caught in its complexities and web-like traps. Autography flatly contradicts autonomy.

Derrida does not "deconstruct" something by means of his facile and inventive capacity for redescription or recontextualization, as if a "deconstructor," if there is one, were a pure *pour soi,* or authentic *Dasein,* or an Overman of self-overcoming power. Rather the language games are consistently undoing themselves, "auto-deconstructing," not being deconstructed by an autonomous autocrat or master of the text. Derrida is like the first CNN reporter on the scene of an earthquake, sending field reports back from the scene, reporting on the fissures and gaps that are breaking out all around him, even as he reports new formations that are gathering before his eyes.

Far from providing a paradigmatic exercise in autonomy, the point of *Glas* is to confess the loss of autonomy, the displacement of the self, of the author, of the subject, of self-creation. Rorty objects to *Glas* because it is not "readable" (CIS, 126). That is only partly true. Derrida would never want something purely unreadable, fully Joycean (nor would Joyce). But it is true up to a point, true that it is unreadable, which is its point, the stylus tip that Derrida wants us to be pricked by: to experience unread-ability, undecipherability, the loss not only of authorial but also readerly authority, just the way Climacus does. Derrida wants us to get a little lost, to lose our autonomy and to let things auto-deconstruct. In *Glas,* that is not so much a theory he has but a performance he stages.

That is also why Derrida is insistently and consistently concerned, not with autonomy but with heteronomy, which, as we have seen in our discussion of *Politics of Friendship* and will see again below, is of decisive importance to his account of politics and ethics.[28] What strikes Derrida about language is not the ability of the subject to keep its head in the midst of the play—autonomy—but the dispersal of the subject into the play, the loss of the autonomy of the subject, and the loss of the identity of the object, in an anonymous transcendental field. That is in part an epistemological point which bears against Rorty's analysis. For, ironically, Rorty is still clinging to a modernist conception of the subject. His nomi-nalism turns on a freely inventive name-making subject, a virtuoso who invents "vocabularies," not an impersonal field whose quasi-structural laws, interrupted, ruptured, and breached as they are, allow certain tem-porary nominal unities called "words" and "concepts" to form ever so precariously. Rorty shows no interest in another nominalism, one which sees names as the effects of impersonal, structural forces, of an anony-mous quasi-transcendental field, which is "other" than the subject, and marks that subject indelibly with heteronomy.

Rorty's theory of the autonomous subject is too strong, which is why his suspicion of the "we" is too weak, whereas Derrida problematizes the "we," which he sees as the heart of the problem, and worries over the other, thereby strengthening the claim of the heteronomous.[29] That is bringing us to the political question. Derrida is less inclined to want to bring others into our conversation, to bring them up to North Atlantic speed, than to let them set their own terms for getting into the conversa-tion, so that maybe "we" will have to play the "them" to *their* "we." Der-rida is after a kind of praxis of the other, answering the call of the other, and that is why he says, in response to Rorty, that as long as one clings to the idea of an autonomous subject one will never have a responsible de-cision (DP, 84–85). His view is neither Marxism, whose twentieth-cen-tury manifestations have been a nightmare, nor bourgeois liberalism, be-cause it is more suspicious and less self-congratulatory than that. Derrida does not think one can "circumvent" metaphysics and change vocabular-ies at the drop of a hat. He thinks one is always already situated in the prevailing quasi-systems that one has inherited. He advocates not cir-cumvention but intervention, alterations here and there, wherever pos-sible, making some space, creating an opening just as the powers that be are about to grind someone up. That raises the question of politics, to which we shall return below.

The Uncircumventability of the Quasi-Transcendental

In a review of Gasché's *The Tain of the Mirror,* which Rorty entitled "Is Derrida a Transcendental Philosopher?," Rorty complained about the portrait of Derrida as a transcendental philosopher. Good nominalists, he said, only need to make empirical inquiries into the actual use of words, not transcendental inquiries into the conditions of possibility. When it was pointed out to Rorty, as we have just done, that the claim is that Derrida is a *quasi*-transcendental philosopher, Rorty responded in a piece he entitled "Is Derrida a Quasi-Transcendental Philosopher?," this time a review of *Jacques Derrida,* the collaborative work with Geoffrey Bennington which contains Derrida's beautiful, enigmatic, and highly autobiographical "Circumfession" at the bottom of the page.[30] Rorty is only slightly mollified by the weaker claim. He sees it to be largely an attempt to use an otherwise useless philosophical gizmo to identify the superiority of deconstruction over everything else, a crypto-claim to know The Secret, by situating it inside/outside philosophy, enough inside to be doing philosophy, enough outside not to be trapped by the metaphysics of presence (TP, 337). He takes the notion of quasi-transcendentality to be primarily a way of claiming that a deconstructive analysis uncovers the way every metaphysical view makes unexamined presuppositions that deconstruction alone can spot, while itself not falling prey to metaphysics. Rorty hates the idea that we are to set up Derrida the way most philosophers who claim to Know the Way like to set themselves up, as seeing what others have not seen, as avoiding traps that others stick their foot in, as questioning presuppositions that everybody else flat-footedly assumes (TP, 34). That for Rorty amounts to saying that, after all, Derrida knows The Secret and its name is *différance.* Rorty discards the classical view Derrida holds that if we reject philosophy and try to do without it, we will end up doing bad philosophy, viz., repeating an empiricism that is loaded with naive and naturalistic presuppositions. Trying to pull the rug out from one's opponent, Rorty says (TP, 341), by "spotting his unnoticed philosophical presuppositions" is as deeply Greek and as violently metaphysical as one can get, and it falsifies the Jewish side of Derrida exposed in "Circumfession," which I have elsewhere called "the prayers and tears of Jacques Derrida." It is the hermeneutics of The Secret all over again, with an added layer of sophistication. Rorty would rather think of Derrida on analogy with Climacus, with the portrait of the "poor existing individual" in Kierkegaard (an "honorary Jew," TP, 341), and hence of knowing nothing about the transcendental, even if it is softened, attenuated, and qualified as a quasi-transcendental.

As my whole idea has been to enlist Rorty and Derrida among the masters of those who do *not* know, who own up to owning no Secrets, among whom Kierkegaard is a leading light (if I may say such a thing about non-knowing), our honorary chairman, I agree with that whole-heartedly. Or, to be more precise, halfheartedly, because Derrida's idea is not to be a Jew, *simpliciter*, but a Jewgreek, not a transcendentalist but a quasi-transcendentalist, and so I think that Rorty is half right. He is right to complain about portraits of deconstruction as outsmarting, outflank-ing, and out-radicalizing everything, about having a critique of meta-physics which ends up being more smug and pretentious than the meta-physical views it sets out criticizing for their pretensions. But there is something else to the *quasi-transcendental* to which Rorty is not paying sufficient heed, which is that it provides a nice account of just why we cannot have a nice Account of everything, including smug metaphysical accounts. This is a feature of Rorty's thought that he shares with Derrida, which makes both of them highly provocative and important—what else can I say?—"philosophers," the explanation of which brings us back to the comparison of Rorty's notion of contextuality and Derrida's notion of iterability.

In my view, we need a *quasi-transcendental* Jewgreek point of view to defend the sort of non-foundational, ground without ground, approach both Derrida and Rorty take. Even though Rorty complains of the quasi-transcendental ghost or specter that disturbs the good fun that Derri-da otherwise provides, he ends up with a quasi-transcendental of pretty much the same stripe (well, red-white-and-blue) as the one he criticizes in Derrida. Rorty has such a theory even without wanting to have it. Despite his determined efforts to cling to good old Yankee horse sense, Rorty is a little bit haunted by a ghost of Yankee hermeneutics, even if, in a spirit of loyalty to his own *vouloir dire* and of loyalty to "our coun-try," we should say he is haunted by a distinctively American specter, let us say, by Edgar Allan Poe, who lived in Baltimore, not by any Parisian ghosts. Rorty wants to "sound" more like somebody from Baltimore, and to avoid sounding Franco-transcendental. He certainly wants to avoid any unnecessarily highfalutin way of putting a point which could be put a lot more simply, that is, he wants to produce Yankee noises. He wants to find a way of not sounding Greek while also not sounding Jewgreek, to forget both Levinas and *Seinsdenken* ("the thought of being"; TP, 342). But Rorty exhibits nonetheless, as I will summarize here, several unmistak-able symptoms of being spooked, quasi-transcendentally speaking. Let us revisit the two features of this ghost I discussed above—first, the "tran-scendental" rattle Rorty's specter makes, then the "quasi-"clanking in his work—in order to nail this down once and for all (until some rascal comes along and recontextualizes it).

(1) What is the "theoretical status" of Rorty's "theory"—of the noises he makes when he speaks—of the "contingency" of any "final vocabu-lary"? Where do these noises resonate? Rorty says that he does not see the utility of the notion of "theoretical status" (DP, 74) and that he is just getting his "romantic kicks out of metaphysics-bashing" (DP, 46). But is

that the end of it? Is that settled simply because Rorty has waived his hands at the question? My claim is that, whatever Yankee distemper such questions create for him, however much all this drives him to the end of his tether (TP, 337), however much this sounds like more metaphysics or religion to him, and whatever his own wishes (*vouloir dire*) might be in this matter, Rorty's noises occupy pretty much the same marginal place or khôral space as do Derridean noises. Rorty does not quite succeed in going cold turkey on philosophy at this point, in merely quitting the habit or walking away from philosophy, but rather, like a former believer who cannot entirely get God off his mind, Rorty, like Derrida, keeps moving inside/outside philosophy, even and *precisely* when the whole idea is to just leave metaphysics to itself and forget about it. Unlike Derrida, Rorty will not fess up: "I maintain that I am a philosopher and that I want to remain a philosopher" (DP, 81). But Rorty too has a philosophical account of final vocabularies; he has thematized them in a philosophical way. He just will not write his own *Confessions*.

I say this for the following reason. After denying that language and the world are separated by an abyss which philosophy must find a way to cross, after rejecting the idea that language is some sort of I-know-not-what medium which mediates between us and the world, either by representing the world accurately or bringing the world to expression, after insisting that we should cut out that sort of unnecessary quasi-entity-building, which simply reproduces all the old problems—Is the medium good or bad? faithful or distortive? transparent or opaque?—after all that, I say, Rorty does not simply change the subject, or drop the discussion, or walk off the field, or take up union organizing. Instead, he *goes on to say* that instead of all this theory-building, we should just content ourselves with the fact that vocabularies, as Davidson and Wittgenstein show, are "tools" we use which vary with our purposes and are either efficient or inefficient (CIS, 11–12), which is why anybody's final vocabulary is always revisable. But in so doing he restarts the argument and perpetuates the conversation by substituting an alternate and competing philosophical theory about language. Rorty uses Wittgenstein and Davidson, pretty much the way Derrida uses Saussure and Hjelmslev, to formulate a pragmatic, language-game theory, albeit one that flies along at a much lower altitude than those metaphysical theories about language that soar with the eagles or that treat the transcendental-empirical distinction as a major philosophical erection. But it remains a philosophical theory, not in the weak sense of a pacifier for overwrought librarians, but in a stronger sense, one which requires expertise of a distinctly philosophical sort, while not attaining to full philosophical "rigor" (*mortis*).

For Rorty is contesting ideas that have never crossed the mind of non-philosophers by introducing another idea that has never entered the head of people who spend their day in the natural attitude, trying not to be late for work, trying to get the shopping done, trying to get the grass cut on Saturday. After all, we have not walked away from philosophy just by throwing our hands up in the air and saying language is only a tool. Nobody "down there" in the natural attitude thinks that language is a "tool";[31] the folks in the natural attitude think that pens and lawnmowers are tools, but not language. And if they ever heard someone proclaim "there is no such thing as a language," they would roll their eyes, look at their watch, and wonder how much longer they have to endure such a pointless conversation. They think that some people are eloquent and others not, some things can be defined and others—one of their favorite examples is "love"—cannot. But above all people in the natural attitude have what Rorty calls "common sense" (CIS, 74). Common sense tells the folks in the natural attitude that their language tells it like it is, that other people may use "different words" but these others must mean the same things as "we" mean, because words pick out "chunks" (CIS, 5) of the world which are really there, even when we are fast asleep in bed at night, whether one dresses them up in English or French, Chinese or classical Greek. The world is sitting out there in itself begging to be named and there really is only one way to do that, even though some people are better at it than others, and even though there are many different languages in which it can be done.

In other words, people in the natural attitude do not appreciate the "contingency" of their vocabularies. They identify with their vocabulary and do not preserve the *ironic distance* which Rorty (and Derrida) require, the distance between ourselves and the vocabulary which we happen historically to have inherited, between our current vocabulary and any possible alternative. They lack a higher-order reflectiveness about language which disengages a speaker and user of a vocabulary from the vocabulary he or she uses. They are unable to make that much of an *epoche,* unable to effect that much of a distancing or disengaging from the contingent vocabulary they employ. After all, to recognize a contingent vocabulary as contingent is already to have risen "above" it or to have gotten "beneath" it, to have dislodged its grip on us just long enough that one no longer lives naively *in* it.

Rorty, in short, is reproducing several key features of the transcendental reduction: disengagement, reflective distancing, the breach of naivete, thematization of the natural attitude as such, exhibition of the contingency (merely presumptive unity) of the constituted effects. His ironic distancing is a bit of a specter, a ghoulish figure that sucks the blood out of the natural attitude, a bit of a quasi-transcendental spook or ghost. That is pretty much what Derrida means when he says that "this new form of transcendental questioning only mimics the phantom of classical transcendental seriousness without renouncing that which, within this phantom, constitutes an essential heritage" (DP, 82). It is in his *critique* of common sense that Rorty gets—understandably—a little bit transcendentally uppity (Yankee talk for *relever*), in a quasi-transcendental sort of way.

That is not a criticism; it is just part of the philosopher's trade, something I am arguing that Rorty needs because he is still implicated in a certain kind of philosophizing in a stronger sense than he is willing to concede.

(2) But then, by putting any final vocabulary into relief (*relève*), has not Rorty raised himself up a notch (*relever*) and flat out worked himself into a transcendental position? Does he not go sliding back down the slope landing right in the tent of classical philosophy? Almost. Not quite. For it is only a certain kind of weak transcendental, a quasi-transcendental, a broken or split transcendental, a transcendental ex-position. He certainly does not want, and has not embraced, "a meta-vocabulary" which "gives us a 'logical space' in which to 'place anything which anybody will ever say'" (CIS, 125). On the contrary Rorty has *given us reasons to give up the search* for such a space. His notion of the "contingency" of any "final vocabulary," which turns on the notion that language is a "tool," plays a distinctly quasi-transcendental role. It explains, in Wittgensteinian and Davidsonian terms, how we do things with words, even as it predicts that we will never have any final terms or unrevisable final vocabularies at our disposal. That is very much what Derrida thinks and what Derrida means when he speaks of "conditions of possibility and impossibility," viz., quasi-transcendental conditions. That is, Rorty and Derrida have reasons to believe that we will *never* (that is pretty *transcendental* talk) attain a meta-vocabulary within which we can place everything anybody will ever say, which will enable us to envisage what people are going to say before they say it, that will "program" the sorts of utterances that speakers will come up with. So that transcendental talk produces an *un*-transcendental result. Rorty has a theory about why we are not going to come up with a "theory" in the old hard metaphysical or transcendental senses, an account of why any account that is forthcoming of this, that or the other thing is going to be inherently revisable.[32]

"One can *always* recontextualize"—that emphasizes the *transcendental* move: it breaks the naivete of common sense and the natural attitude by calling upon the resources of a language-game theory (Yankee version) or a theory of *différance* (Parisian version). "One can always *recontextualize*"—that emphasizes the *un*-transcendental move, the broken transcendental, the one which shows the slipperiness of language, the unavailability of a final vocabulary, the sheer contingency and endless reconfigurability of the vocabularies we use and of the beliefs we entertain. That is the move with the historicist and nominalist drift, the one which preserves an ironic, quasi-transcendental distance. The claim is that the very thing that makes meaning possible, viz. contextuality, is the same thing that sees to it that it will not stay put (= impossible).

Rorty is now willing, "grudgingly" (TP, 342), to concede some of this, but only as a contingency of his autobiography, or Derrida's, poor existing individuals that they are, not as a necessary property of something called "philosophy," which floats above the empirical use of words like a ghost. It is true, Rorty will concede, that his end-of-philosophy talk, his delimitation of philosophical pretense, like Derrida's, sounds like still more philosophy. But that is purely a function of the books that he and Derrida happened to have been brought up on, books that have bled into their unconscious which they cannot just "forget," so that he does not think nowadays that it is such an easy thing to waive off an old vocabulary and come up with a new one. So, for truly autobiographical reasons, the therapy required to break the habit will tend to sound like the disease of which it should be the cure. Neither Rorty nor Derrida can simply "walk away" from their facticity, not without walking away from themselves; they cannot "circumvent the metaphysical *logos* without mutilating themselves" (TP, 343). While conceding that much, Rorty will not concede that this proves anything about "philosophy" or its "inescapability." There is nothing about philosophy that demands a specifically philosophical "remedy," nothing that decrees that every attempt to escape philosophy is philosophical. There is no reason to think that other people who were brought up differently, or future people, will have to bother their heads about philosophy, or consequently about overcoming philosophy (TP, 344). In the meantime we should savor the blood-stained and highly idiosyncratic things that Derrida writes in "Circumfession" even while not attaching too much importance to the bloodless ballet of concepts starring a quasi-person named "deconstruction" (TP, 348) that Bennington is staging up above. We should play up the idiosyncratic and autobiographical and try to keep a lid on the highly theoretical chatter. The most that can be said for speaking of Derrida as a "quasi-transcendental" philosopher, the most that Rorty is willing to concede, is that Derrida himself could not write his autobiography, could not write his Jewgreek confessions, without talking the talk of conditions of possibility and other philosophemes, not without losing touch with who he is, and Rorty is willing to concede that, for similarly autobiographical reasons, something similar would hold of himself, poor existing thing that he is.

But I think Rorty is in deeper than that, and that Rorty does not get to call this shot. He cannot, by a *fiat* issued straight from the *mens auctoris*, tell us what sort of discourse this is, that all he is doing is getting his kicks out of making jokes about sad, gray, humorless metaphysicians who serve as his straight men. I do not see what is so sad and gray about having a philosophical argument against doing philosophy in the old metaphysical way, that insists merrily that we make a now non-metaphysically-oriented philosophy stick to the facts of factical life and not fly off into the wild blue beyond of essentialism or transcendentalism. I for one am in search of a philosophy which is still philosophy but not metaphysics, a kind of hermeneutics of facticity which does not allow the little saplings of factical life to be crushed by the snows of metaphysical speculation. Speaking for myself, I find that a thoroughly uplifting but still philosophical prospect which cheers my heart. It is one thing to renounce trying to cut through appearances to hit the hard rock of Reality, to get past mere mortal *doxa* for timeless Truth, like deadly serious Greeks and other Metaphysicians of the Secret who seek the way things are *kath'auto,* but it is quite another to have good reasons for what one thinks about what is going on in factical life. That includes having reasons to think that we are not hardwired to Being in itself, that we do not Know the Truth of Being, have not been addressed directly from on high by the Most High, or been given privileged access to The Secret. That sort of cautious and trepidatious way of thinking is what is always being defended in one way or another by anyone who philosophizes in some non-foundational style—whether it is called hermeneutics (Parisian or Yankee, radical or more radical), deconstruction, pragmatism, or any other form of felicitous nominalism or quasi-transcendentalism. The truth of the matter is, at the risk of distressing and saddening an upbeat writer, that Rorty has a competing and appealing non-foundationalist, non-metaphysical but still philosophical line—as opposed to a pre- or post-or non-philosophical line—with which to outwit other philosophical lines, a line that is nicely situated in the locale of what Derrida calls the quasi-transcendental. Otherwise, Rorty and Derrida have just dropped from the sky and started to talk funny. Rorty is, furthermore, pretty good at selling this line. He shows us how, and gives us good reasons for thinking that, the sorts of things we say and think, however good they are for the moment, tend to come unstuck, not just because of our incompetence or bad luck, but structurally, and for a reason.

To fly around the NATO countries telling people again and again, "one can always recontextualize," to develop this line with all its nuances and implications, to defend it against all comers with Yankee clarity, lively wit, and insightful prose, is not only to maintain but to promote an energetic philosophical conversation, to keep it going. It is, in general, to make a lot of quasi-transcendental noise, regardless of what a person thinks he or she is doing. It is much more likely to perpetuate philosophy in America than if one just stayed at home and kept quiet, or devoted all one's time and talents to union organizing. If Rorty *really wanted* philosophy to die off, if he were *really serious* about wanting people to change the subject because they could not stand it anymore, or simply to walk away from the discussion, then he has made a serious strategic mistake. Instead of writing the lively and interesting books that he has produced, he should have stayed at Princeton, remained an Analytic Philosopher of the Strict Observance, and devoted himself to adding to the stock of articles about meaning and reference in *Mind* (which must be an ironic title). Nothing has been more effective in killing the conversation of philosophy in America than that!

So I would say, do not gently go into that dark night which Rorty describes, the one in which something like transcendental philosophy will have passed from the scene. If you do, do not expect to find either Rorty or Derrida there. They will be both back at the university (probably in California, where this Yankee and this Parisian have both ended up)—although you will have to check the Web to find out what department they are in—happily at work writing more books which the catalogue librarians, driven to the edge of despair, will finally, *faute de mieux,* classify (*classicus, glas*) as "philosophy."

Will they someday write a book so beset with genre-trouble that no one could classify it, a text for which no librarian or philosopher, encyclopedist or hermeneut, radical or more radical, speech-act theorist or communications expert, curriculum planner or computer programmer, realist or idealist, naturalist or romanticist, Yankee or Parisian, will find the *glas?* Is that not a Transcendental Ideal? Well, almost.

II. Why Deconstruction Is *Not* America

The second question has to do with the political upshot of all this, with Yankee politics and Parisian politics. Rorty appreciates that Derrida's work is driven by an ethical and also a political desire, by a prophetic and quasi-religious sense of justice, a hope in an "impossible" justice, or democracy, to come. Rorty approves of the tone of social *hope* and political aspiration in Derrida, which is what in his mind separates Derrida from Foucault.[33] Derrida's distinction between dreaming of a "democracy to come" and dealing with the democracies that exist at present corresponds up to a point with Rorty's distinction between democracy as a "counsel of perfection" and democracy as a matter of fact. "You have to be loyal to a dream country rather than to the one to which you wake up every morning" (AOC, 102). Rorty wants us to be loyal to the dream while coming to grips with the reality of the latter. But there are limits to Rorty's taste for this sort of thing (AOC, 102). It will not do to dream of being rescued by a coming God or by saving angels, or to worry about being preyed upon by devils, stalked by "Gothic" figures, dreaming of "inexplicable, magical, transformations" (AOC, 102) instead of working out doable and humanly proportioned "reforms."

When Derrida talks about deconstruction as prophetic of "the democracy to come," he also tends to sound uncomfortably preternatural or even *religious,* a category to which Rorty has an even greater allergy than "transcendental." Religion for Rorty—and on this point he is (like a lot of continentalists) an unreconstructed *Aufklärer*—is superstition, the surrendering of human interests and initiative to something more than human, which deprives us of the taste for squaring away human affairs as best we can on strictly human terms. Rorty approves of some sort of "civil religion," like that of Wiliam James and Dewey, which means a living faith in democracy, but he has no time for religion in any stronger sense, and it makes him downright nervous when Derrida starts sounding like a Jewish prophet—or like Levinas. For then, instead of furnishing determinate and usable analyses, Foucault and Derrida alike turn out "Gothic" tales full of spooks, such as Foucauldian "power," which is an elusive, diffuse, ubiquitous, ineradicable (and hence unfalsifiable) specter that can never be identified, like a preternatural force or original sin.[34] On this analogy, poststructural "theory" is the new theology, a "Gothic" world which offers a "quasi-religious form of spiritual pathos," instead of the upbeat optimism of Whitman or Dewey. Where Foucault spins out such Gothic figures as "power," Levinas and Derrida try to haunt us with "infinite alterity."[35]

Whitman and Dewey give us all the spiritual uplift we need and we have no need, according to Rorty, of Levinas's Other, which is no more "useful than Heidegger's Being—both strike me as gawky, awkward, and unenlightening" (DP, 40), and no need for what might be called by some the "prayers and tears of Jacques Derrida." We do not need a new round of latter-day prophets telling us that something is profoundly wrong and that it must be replaced with something wholly other, without giving us any idea whatsoever of what to do. We should give up spending all our time "thinking about otherness" and just get down to the nitty-gritty of what Dewey calls "the problems of men" (AOC, 97). (What to do about the problems of women Dewey does not mention here!) The problem with Derrida, then, is that he believes in ghosts, in non-naturalistic quasi-beings in the theoretical order, like the quasi-transcendental which we discussed above, and ghosts of a more practical order, too, like the *tout autre,* the infinitely other, and the democracy to come. Derrida should get rid of these Parisian ghosts, start reading Whitman instead of Edgar Allan Poe, and acquire a little Yankee horse sense. But is Derrida spooking us? Is "infinite responsibility" just a specter? Would Derrida object to the infinite haunting of which Rorty accuses him? Or would he take it as a compliment?

Private Ironist or Public Liberal. In *Contingency, Irony, and Solidarity,* Rorty argues that Derrida's work, like Nietzsche's and Heidegger's, is at best useless, and at worst dangerous if it is taken as a commentary on the structures that govern public life and institutions. It is, however, a source of great *jouissance* if it is understood as an exercise in self-creation which does not comment one way or the other on public institutions and practices. Reading Derrida's books cannot be beat as a way to occupy ourselves on weekends and evenings (DP, 44), but it is best to leave them home when the public structures of the workweek roll around. When Heidegger was suffering from the illusion that what he was saying had public and political bearing, the results could not have been worse, and readers of Derrida should learn from that disastrous trip to Syracuse.

Readers of Derrida will insist that while one might have (wrongly) drawn that impression from a selective reading of Derrida's earlier writings, Rorty's take on Derrida in *Contingency, Irony, and Solidarity* is out of date. For Derrida's work has more and more been taken up with the questions of politics, democracy, justice, law, friendship, and hospitality, even getting down to something as determinate as current immigration laws. Everything about Derrida's work—and his personal life, as well—goes to cross the lines between public and private, to show that "the distinction between the public and the private is rightly undecidable," as Derrida puts it (DP, 79). From the start, his work is implicated in giving an account of public institutions, of social and political practices. Derrida is a French intellectual and an activist, a man of the Left, a *post-Marxist* man of the Left, and while that caused some confusion, early on, about whether he was also *a*political, such confusion is no longer possible. Besides, he has been, if I may say so, quite right about Marxism. In the 1960s, he was a critic of the totalitarianism of Soviet communism and he kept his distance from the dogmatism of the French Communist Party. In the 1990s, he is a critic of the liberal euphoria of the New World Order and urges us to return to the spirit of a certain Marx, more directly at times even than Habermas. Right both times, I would say. Furthermore, Derrida has nothing to do with Heidegger's fascist celebration of the native land and native tongue, of *Bodenständigkeit* and *physis,* or with Nietzsche's sexist, elitist, anti-modern, anti-democratic celebration of the will to power of the best and the brightest. Derrida's is a philosophy of the displaced and outcast, the exile and the deportee, the immigrant and homeless, of those who have been deprived of their native tongue, where everything is organized around the in-coming of the other.

In his recent writings Rorty has updated his take on Derrida. He applauds Derrida's attitude toward Marxism in the 1960s but Rorty thinks that Derrida ought to kick the habit of dragging in the name of Marx, loyally but pretty honorifically ("a certain Marxism"), just to signal to everyone that he is a man of the Left and has a longing for justice, "the only thing we should not allow ourselves to be ironic about."[36] Notwithstanding Karl Marx's gifts as an analyst of political economy, Marxism in this century has been a nightmare and the best thing to do with it is to drop the subject. It also does no good to summon up the *specter* of Marx, as elusive and ghostly shade of justice to come, or to try to convince us that we are haunted by the spirit of infinite alterity, when what we need is concrete analyses of concrete human situations. Rorty applauds Derrida's faith in a democracy to come, but while a cheery and pragmatic faith in democracy is one thing, Derrida's Gothic tales of preternatural spirits are quite another. Rorty vastly prefers Walt Whitman, who issues in Dewey, to Edgar Allan Poe, who leads to Jacques Lacan, the *tout autre,* and other specters of contemporary Parisian theory that haunt Derrida and—since "deconstruction is America"—still haunt us.

Rorty's criticisms are frequently directed at Derrida's followers in the American academy, who are an important part of what Rorty calls the "cultural left" or "academic left," a "large number of admirers of Derrida who see writing in his manner as their contribution to the relief of human suffering" (DP, 45). These professors are a politically irrelevant and insular crowd more interested in taking over the English department, as Irving Howe said (DP, 15), than the real world, where the Christian Right runs everything and gets to impeach a centrist president whom they hate with a passion for his errant libido and silver tongue. Derrida does not think Rorty is necessarily wrong about this, and he regrets it if it is true, because Derrida's purpose is to bring the left (and the Left) into line with political reality, to politicize it with real, not merely academic, politics (DP, 85–86).

But if Derrida is *also* a social utopian, then he cannot be *simply* a private ironist, but must have something of a public face. Yet Rorty is dismayed that Derrida still wants to "sound *transcendental,*" that he continues to distrust naturalistic empiricism, and that Derrida remains "at his best" in *The Post Card* and still "fulfills *primarily* private purposes" (DP, 16; my emphasis). When Simon Critchley, Chantal Mouffe, and Ernesto Laclau press upon Rorty the ethico-political side of Derrida, and do so by going back to Levinas (and not merely Nietzsche and Heidegger) as predecessor figure for Derrida, Rorty shrugs his shoulders and complains that he just does not see a link up between "Levinas's pathos of the infinite" and ethics and politics, "real politics," not just grist for the mill of *Lingua Franca,* not simply battles over whether to hire or grant tenure to somebody in cultural studies, but politics in the sense of negotiating a contract that includes health benefits for part-time employees (AOC, 17).

I am all for wringing a decent contract out of people who are interested in amassing as much wealth for themselves and sharing as little of it with their employees as the law permits, people who have not the least qualms about shutting down their American factories to take advantage of lower labor costs in developing nations. But that is not exactly "political thought," although it requires a lot of brains, but a perfectly good example of a primarily political *praxis* that Derrida's *Politics of Friendship* would urge and encourage. That book seems to me close to the sentiment William James expressed and that Rorty cites in *Achieving Our Country:* "Democracy is a kind of religion, and we are bound not to admit its failure. Faiths and utopias are the noble exercise of human reason, and no one with a spark of reason in him will sit down fatalistically before the croaker's picture" (AOC, 9). It seems to me that a pragmatist like Rorty should approve of *Politics of Friendship,* not because it is a way to fashion one's inner self and makes for good reading on weekends, but because it provides a post-metaphysical way of thinking about politics. It proceeds without pretension to being a full-blown political *philosophy* with a "theory" of human nature or the state, or a comprehensive political program, but instead is content to make frequent albeit piecemeal inroads on the dominant masculinist and militarist culture within which the Western democracies have taken root. I think that Rorty should add to the list of things he likes about *Politics of Friendship* the fact that, even though it would not do as a handout that the AFL-CIO could distribute to union organizers, *Politics of Friendship* serves public purposes, concerns social and political structures, and addresses public issues. Beyond that, I think Rorty should throw away his rigid public/private distinction as a broken tool, at least as regards Derrida.

Achieving Our Country. As one might have guessed from its title, *Achieving Our Country* is a plea for national pride, but, as one might not have guessed, the title is taken from James Baldwin, in which Baldwin was referring to ending America's "racial nightmare." Rorty argues that, whatever America's shortcomings, disgust with what America has done wrong should not outweigh hope in what it stands for (AOC, 33). So "our country" stands for America's commitment to democratic ideals and it should form the center of a project of "forging a moral identity," which is fundamentally a public project (AOC, 13). Like Walt Whitman, for whom America is the vanguard of history, with the "fullest poetical nature," and the United States "the greatest poem,"[37] which means that the United States "will create the taste by which it will be judged" (AOC, 29), that the States are "the fulfillment of the human past" (AOC, 22), Rorty too applauds the use of "the words America and democracy as convertible terms" (AOC, 17). Thus Rorty articulates national pride, not in terms of right-wing militarist nationalism, but in terms of the ideals of the American Left—"the party of hope" (AOC, 14), a Left which "dreams" (AOC, 35) a secularized hope, not in God, but in social justice (AOC, 18), whereas the Right thinks we already have an identity and should keep it intact (AOC, 31). By social justice, Rorty means the minimization of useless suffering and humiliation and the maximal creation of diversity (AOC, 30). Unlike Europe, which is too burdened with metaphysical aspirations for *knowing* and a clear idea to guide human progress, Whitman said that America has opted for a non-normative diversity without a "template on which to model our future" (AOC, 24). America is the place where hope precedes knowledge (AOC, 36).

Achieving Our Country is a stinging rebuke of the cultural and academic left for spending all its time portraying America as a "violent, inhuman, corrupt country," deeply and intractably wrong (AOC, 66), which should be "replaced, as soon as possible, by something utterly different" (AOC, 7). The academic left has isolated leftist thought from the American labor movement, and thus from the political reality that daily oppresses the poor. Rorty wants us to give up the distinction between Left (= Marxism) and liberals and recognize that Marxism was a nightmare. The cause of the "reformist Left" (called by its critics the "old" Left) is to protect the weak against the strong (AOC, 43), a goal that was eclipsed in the 1960s by a student left that gave up on working within the system, to whom, nonetheless, we must be thankful for ending the Vietnam War (AOC, 68–69). The student left of the 1960s grew up to be the academic or cultural left of today, intellectuals who study Freud and French philosophy in literature departments but who know little or nothing about economics. They advocate the "politics of difference" that is, women's studies, gay studies, black or Hispanic-American studies—but *not* "unemployed studies" or "homeless studies" (AOC, 79–80). They are concerned with personal humiliation and they are not focused on poverty; they talk about stigma, not money. "It is as if the American Left could not handle more than one initiative at a time" (AOC, 83). Rorty suggests that the cultural left give up its preoccupation with esoteric theory, learn something about economics, reestablish contact with the trade unions, and revivify a sense of national pride. Hundreds of unintelligible academic books that "problematize" contemporary culture, readable only to a few members of the Modern Language Association, congratulate themselves on "serving human liberty" by means of the most "barren explanations imaginable" (AOC, 93), among which Rorty numbers the Gothic tales spun by Foucault and Derrida, whose discourse on "power" and the *"tout autre"* reproduce the operations of a theology of sin (AOC, 97). So far the main result of the attempts the cultural left has made to make Americans feel bad about being American has been to turn the country over to right-wing extremists from rural counties in Texas, Mississippi, and Louisiana who wage campaigns of hate against anything different from their life back home in the sticks.

The "justice" of which Derrida dreams and the "law" that has a real force will have next to nothing to do with each other if the academic left does not get out into the streets of America. It is one thing to take pride in being black as a way of countering the stigma that a racist society tries to attach to it, but it is another thing to allow that to block off our pride in America. The demons and angels fabricated by the cultural left contribute to a "politically useless unconscious." Just the way the "people" back in the 1960s wanted to know what we were to do once we got rid of the "system," they show no interest today in getting rid of capitalism and they want to know how a participatory democracy with hundreds of millions of people would actually work, what will happen when white patriarchs (devils) drop out and all the voting is done by victims (angels). The sensible alternative to this Franco-Gothic tale is "piecemeal reform within the framework of a market economy," which could well lead to worlds presently unforseen, to who knows what (AOC, 105).

Open-ended Interventionism versus Reformism. Rorty assumes that by calling for an unforeseeable democracy to come, Derrida is calling for a "revolution," not reform. Rorty makes Derrida sound like Foucault, waiting for a deep shift or reconfiguration in the order of things, or even like Heidegger, waiting for the god of the democracy (an expression that would have made Heidegger ill) to come save us by delivering a transforming, transfiguring fix that will cure everything and make all things new. Of course, if that is what the democracy to come amounted to, it would not amount to much. But because Derrida never was a Marxist, he never was a revolutionary either. Because he never much believed in totalizing schemata, he never had much faith in totalizing transformations. True, Derrida keeps his distance from Enlightenment liberalism, but not because liberalism is reformism, but because of the liberal theory of the autonomous subject, which he criticizes in the light of his more radical Levinasian theory of "infinite responsibility" (DP, 86–87). But just as Derrida does not subscribe to the wholesale periodization of "modern" and "postmodern," he also does not think that we are by hook or by crook, or by a Gothic *Geist*, somehow going to make a "revolutionary" flip from the present democratic order into some unforeseeable democracy to come. The very idea of the Messiah for Derrida is to keep the future open, to keep the future alive, to abide by the structure of the "promise," which is what "messianic" means for him. The democracy to come "does not mean that tomorrow democracy will be realized," and "does not refer to a future democracy," in which the world will be made over *in toto*, but is a way of keeping the future structurally open (DP, 83). Derrida's image of the ghost or specter is not a Gothic angel of deliverance but a figure—a Parisian one, it is true—meant to contest the self-presence of the present, to show that the present is always "inwardly disturbed," or "haunted," where the whole idea is to get a wedge into this rupture and open up the chance of something new.

But if Derrida is something of a piecemealist, rather than a revolutionary, he is also not a piecemeal "reformist" in the sense that Rorty advocates, but rather what might better be called an *interventionist*. For Derrida, we always begin where we are,[38] in the midst of existing frameworks, amidst the texts and traditions, institutions and structures that we have inherited, which have more or less constituted us to be the beings that we are, which constitute something of a maze in which we wander. The whole idea behind *différance*, Derrida says, is to put in question some absolute starting point and to consign us to a strategizing without a transcendental *telos* to guide the way, to consign us to "blind tactics, or empirical wandering."[39] But that is not the end of the story, but the beginning, for, beginning where we are, we then seek to *intervene* on these pregiven operations, try to inhabit their blind spots, to get a wedge in their cracks and crevices, in order to open possibilities that the prevailing system currently forecloses, to let many flowers bloom. Of all systems currently in place, Derrida can with the least discomfort associate himself with democracy, which is why he speaks of a *democracy* to come, and not of an oligarchy or a monarchy or a patriarchy to come. It is upon the democratic structures of the Western democracies in which he finds himself that he would intervene, and it is these democratic structures that he seeks to open up beyond their present limits, exposing them to the possibility of something presently unforeseeable within the settings of their current horizons. That means that, despite his talk of a purely formal and desertified messianic, Derrida's work has all the marks of the twentieth-century urbanized democracies of western Europe and the United States in which he is factically situated, and therefore it bears the marks of still *another* concrete democratic messianism.[40] Like the rest of us, like it or not, he begins where he is.

I would not describe Derrida's interventionism as "reformist" but as decidedly *open-ended*. He puts no constraints, or as few as possible, upon the democracy *to come*, and he certainly would not confine it to reforming the presently prevailing form of democracy, although that is where we begin. Derrida says that we proceed without a grand plan and a program of foreseeable results—"blind tactics"—and he is particularly fond of the role of chance in all this, of vagaries and unforeseeable consequences. He loves the idea that something might happen over and beyond the intentions of the agent that will produce the most wonderful results, like a gift from out of nowhere, which of course is risky business, because it also exposes us to unforeseen disasters. Derrida would embrace with enthusiasm Rorty's description of history as a "tissue of chances, mischances, and lost chances" (AOC, 123), which is just the direction in which he is led by his own deeply nominalistic, anti-totalizing instincts and by his famous notion of *différance*. The democracy to come, or the very idea of justice, or the messianic without the concrete messianisms, has, or even is identical with, the "formal structure of promise" (SOM, 59), which keeps things open. Far from being a revolutionary future that will sweep over us like a wave and make all things new, the democracy to come will never get here; it is not supposed to get here, its function is entirely *critical*, not *predictive*. It is prophetic not in the sense of telling the future but in the sense of denouncing the limits of the present, the way the Jewish prophets were famous for giving their contemporaries a hard time, which usually cost them their necks. The democracy to come will never get here, not because it is a regulative idea, an ideal schema or utopian program that we hope against hope will come and save us—which can then be criticized for its vacuity—but because it is *structurally* "to come." That does not mean it is empty or vacuous, a white ghost or phantom sublime, but rather that it functions like a kind of *white light* to hold against the flesh of the present which mercilessly exposes the blemishes of the current age.

Infinite Responsibility, Pointless Hype, and Politics. One way to see the functioning of the idea of the democracy to come, of the formal structure of expectation, and to see its political "use," is to observe how, in *Specters of Marx*, Derrida brings the democracy to come to bear against the right-wing millennialism of Francis Fukuyama's *The End of History and the Last Man*. The whole idea of the "logic of the ghost" is to intervene upon and even to contravene the logic of the ideal and the empirical of which Fukuyama makes use. *On the one hand*, Fukuyama tells us, the end of history has actually happened, here, now, already; it is the future already present, here and now, in the United States and the conquest of the evil empire. God Bless America (and the western European democracies, too).

On the other hand, since the empirical reality of drug-infested urban poverty zones, starvation, de facto racial apartheid, bought-and-paid-for elections, and multiple other evils are massively present all around America, evils which "contradict this advent of the perfect liberal democracy, one must at the same time pose this perfection as simply a regulating and trans-historical ideal" (SOM, 62). Thus Fukuyama can *also* argue that, in addition to having already arrived, in addition to having already flattened the evil empire, the ideal of liberal democracy is not yet here, not yet perfectly realized. Rather than a double bind, Fukuyama gets to have it both ways. Here and there a generation of urban youths is destroyed, lives are destroyed, families ruined by drugs, cigarette manufacturers are protected from their victims, special interest groups buy as many elected officials as they need to continue their evil ways, and bought-and-paid-for politicians sell the country to the highest bidder. Meanwhile, the stock portfolios of the upper twenty-five percent out in the suburbs (who have more shopping malls, doctors, and green space than they need, who read *The Wall Street Journal* as they ride suburban rail lines through the ghettoes to their center city offices) experience the benefits of an unprecedented bull market. Such things happen, alas. Nothing is perfect.

But Derrida, who takes a more radical view of democracy, is much more intolerant of this suffering than Fukuyama, intolerant with a prophetic intolerance for *anything* short of letting justice flow like water over the land. *As long as one of these least among us* is homeless or unfed, unjustly imprisoned or exiled, without a school to attend or a home to come home to, there is injustice, and that injustice is intolerable, "absolutely" or "infinitely" intolerable, and "we" are absolutely or "infinitely responsible," *here and now,* just in virtue of the justice or democracy to come. That is why Derrida insists that his ideas of singularity and the secret are anything but private, that they are meant to have public and political consequences, consequences for justice, by keeping the political field open, anti-totalitarian, and protective of the singular (DP, 80–81).

Our obligation to the singularity of the other is *infinite* and without limit simply because we can never, with good conscience, congratulate ourselves for having discharged our obligations. We can never say, it is over, I have done enough. The complacency, the unguardedness, of good conscience turns on taking responsibility to be *finite* and hence dischargeable. Finite responsibility, for Derrida, is something like finite love, something like answering someone who asks "do you love me?" by saying "well, up to a point, within certain limits, within reason," which means that you do not love them, not if love is love. We cannot rest with an easy conscience and say that on the whole we are doing well, and we have accomplished a lot, and that we should congratulate ourselves on all that we have managed to do up to now. There is too much that is unconscionable in good conscience. That is why Derrida says that "we cannot give up on the concept of infinite responsibility," as Rorty suggests, for "if you

give up the infinitude of responsibility, there is no responsibility. It is because we act and we live in infinitude that the responsibility with regard
to the other (*autrui*) is irreducible" (DP, 86).

That is also why Derrida is deeply distrustful of the "we" in Rorty. Up
to a point, Rorty's "we" functions in a salutary way, viz., to enjoin us
to widen the circle of the "we" to include as many "others" as possible,
and that is part of his Enlightenment affection for commonality and consensus. If the slave owners could have included their slaves in their
"we," they would have become abolitionists, and that is true enough. It
would correspond, as Mark Dooley argues, to Derrida's insistence, in "Violence and Metaphysics," on the symmetry that Levinas's notion of infinite dissymmetry requires, the symmetry that makes infinite dissymmetry both possible and impossible.[41] But having insisted on the qualification
of a certain symmetry, Derrida did not mean to simply disqualify the notion of infinite dissymmetry, or therefore of infinitude and infinite responsibility. Derrida does not frame this in terms of expanding the we,
because that sounds too assimilative of the other, too much like bringing
others into our conversation, like bringing them up to North Atlantic
speed, as I said above, rather than to let others set their own terms. Derrida regards the "we" with the greatest suspicion, because it smacks of the
assimilative commonality and community he distrusts. The only "we" he
will allow is the "we who cannot say we," and I think that he would
regard Rorty's "we" and "our country" with the same distrust.[42]

So the effect of "infinite dissymmetry" or the "pathos of the infinite" in
Derrida is to require decision and to put teeth into our responsibility here
and now, for justice cannot wait, because the demands of those who suffer press upon us without limit, infinitely, without compromise. That is
not a politically useless unconscious but an infinitely sensitive and un-
compromising political conscience. Rorty replies that it is "pointless hype
to dramatize our difficulties" like that (DP, 42), and that this hype has a
lot to do with "a traditional difference between European and American
intellectuals." Europeans think politics requires a special metalanguage
and an *Ideologiekritik* that penetrates to The Secret behind the veil of appearances (DP, 45), while Americans think ordinary language and Yankee horse sense will do just fine and that we should avoid "over-philos-
ophication" (DP, 69). The regions of first-order political decision making
and second-order philosophical "kibitzing" about politics never touch
(DP, 74), even when that philosophy is pragmatism.

But on this point I would say that Rorty is mistaken. The difference
between him and Derrida is not that his discourse is plain and simple
while Levinas's and Derrida's are unnecessarily inflated, but that Rorty's
tendencies are more protective of the existing frame of reference, more
attached to the American way, and hence they run the risk of being unguarded about the shortcomings of American democracy, whereas Derrida is more suspicious of all existing frameworks. The discourse on in-

finite responsibility cuts against the grain of "complacency" in Rorty,[43] against what Rorty calls the "danger" of "too much parochial all-Americanism" (DP, 75), about which I have complained in Rorty's liberalism, and it sensitizes us to those who are being ground under in the home of the brave and the land of the free. The problem is that the logic of ideal and actual allows for an *asymptotic gradualism*. Reforms made in the name of the infinite perfectibility of a regulative ideal raise the level of our tolerance for evil to a point of almost outright obscenity—as opposed to responding to the "singular urgency of the *here and now*" (PF, 105). So the *conservativism* that Rorty decries—which holds that we already have the basic schema in place and that it should be kept intact and protected from alteration, reform, or intervention (AOC, 31)—depends upon the logic of ideal and real that Rorty *also embraces*. That is why what Rorty says is constantly threatened with becoming, not conservative, but parochial, unguarded, and complacent about the Stars and the Stripes. But the logic of the ghost, or of the promise, the prophetic or messianic logic of expectation demands justice, here and now, and is absolutely intolerant of injustice, and so it wants *change,* here, there, wherever possible, and it wants it *now.*

That is also why Derrida would side with Lyotard on the differend and not with Rorty's and Habermas's predilection for consensus. There will always be a conflict of duty; indeed duty seems to arise precisely from a conflict (DP, 87). For the voices of dissent, speaking from their suffering, the voices of those who will always be *other,* and who will *always* be with us, can and must never be melted into some general voice.[44] *Tout autre est tout autre.* The "we" is never, structurally, going to include *everybody.* We can count on it, and we have to count their complaint in our accounting, and counting is what democracies always involve, as Derrida says in *Politics of Friendship.*

But in making piecemeal interventions on the structures in place, which is where Derrida *begins,* he puts no limits on where this will *end.* If Derrida has no truck with planning a totally transforming revolution, he also will not tie his hands by committing himself to the idea that we will just be "reforming" the "present structure." For Derrida, "[w]hat's important in 'democracy to come' is not 'democracy,' but 'to come.'"[45] The love of the democracy to come is an exercise in paleonymy, the love of an old name, the best name we have at present, strategically and polemically our best resource (PF, 104–105). But we can never *identify* the Messiah, never identify him with some person, gender, race, or country, lest we put everyone else at risk. It would be most unjust to say that justice is here, now, in this institution or contingent order. Democracy means the right to criticize, just as literature is a *public* institution implying that "anything can be said publicly" (DP, 80). Thus democracy must preserve the right and the duty to criticize itself, even as the Enlightenment needs to be enlightened about itself, right up to the point that the democracy to come might indeed, who knows, lead us toward something unforesee-able, for which democracy will have been but the predecessor form, but which will require the invention of another name, *l'inventions de l'autre*. That sounds more like Whitman's idea of living without a "template on which to model our future" (AOC, 24) than does Rorty's "reform."

O America, Adieu. Deconstruction and pragmatism join at the point where Derrida's felicitous and open-ended non-essentialism meets up with Rorty's upbeat "happy go lucky"[46] pragmatic contextualism, which is the point—Derrida calls it "pragrammatology" (DP, 78)—of their com-mon conviction that "anything can mean anything if you put it in the right context" (DP, 43). That contextualism should have led Rorty to be more suspicious of the contextual contingency—or what Derrida would call the contingent nominal unity—called "democracy." Let alone "Our Country" or "America." For his part, Derrida mightily resists calling this democracy to come "France." Or America. Or, in general, "Our Country." In this sense, deconstruction is decidedly *not* America! In *Achieving Our Country*, Rorty skirts dangerously close to what Derrida calls "exemplar-ism" in *Politics of Friendship*. Whitman told us that the United States is "the greatest poem" (AOC, 29) and "the fulfillment of the human past" (AOC, 22), and that prompts Rorty to approve of using "America and democracy as convertible terms" (AOC, 17), not unlike the way that Husserl said that "Europe" is not the name of a continent but of an idea, the very idea of reason. But at about the same time that Whitman was writing poems to New Jersey, Victor Hugo was writing of an *"extraordinary nation"* to come, whose capital will be Paris [Washington D.C.?], and will not be merely named "France" but "Europe" [NATO, the West], or "Humanity . . . *A people, which will be France sublimated, is in the process of hatching"* (PF, 264–265). "O France, adieu! You are too great to be only a country. One separates from one's mother who becomes a goddess . . . and you, France, become the world" (PF, 267).

In exemplarism, a proper name is sublimated and becomes, beyond a mere proper name, a common noun, nay, an uncommon noun, made to name something more and greater than its particular empirical self, such as a specific gender, race, or nation which does service for the whole of humanity. The histories of such national exemplars—Greece, Rome, Christianity, England, France, Germany—or gendered exemplars— "man," "brother"—are long and bloody, and not very exemplary, for they inevitably (this seems like an undeconstructible law!) put everybody *else* at risk. Heidegger must have somewhere said, I am sure he thought of it, that Germany is Being's finest poem. Today it is "our" turn, "we" liberals, "we" Americans, in the "American century" (just passed!), to make our-selves, "Our Country," the exemplars and the poems for all humanity, to bid *adieu* to the United States as a proper name and, by "achieving our country," graciously, generously, lovingly to surrender America to uni-versal humanity. Today it is "our" turn to put everybody else at risk.

I agree that this line of argument ought not to turn into outright contempt for the United States. But I am worried, and I am sure Derrida would be worried, that Rorty is just too *unguarded* about this name "United States of America," too "complacent" about "our country"—those are the spooks that scare Derrida—that Rorty ought to be a more ironic and cautious nominalist about this name and even about the older name democracy.[47] His love of "our country" ought to be paleonymical, the love of an old name which may or may not need to be replaced down the road, a road that Rorty should agree is unforeseeable. Achieving *our* country. *Whose* country? Must we block the translation of this book into foreign languages lest it provoke still more national strife? A world full of people out to achieve "our country"? Is that not pretty much what we already have?!

To be sure, Rorty's advocacy of "national pride" is centered on rallying us around the flag of the old and—I would like to think—timeless liberal idea of social justice, of using the arm of government to lift up the poorest and most defenseless people in our society, rather than throwing them upon the merciless mercy of the invisible hand. I agree that "we intellectuals" have to join hands with the unions and the labor movement to accomplish this. Rorty insists that this is just not going to happen as long as "we intellectuals" sit around at conferences on postmodernism thinking up meaner and meaner things to say about the "system." As the son of a blue-collar second-generation Italian American, nothing saddens me more than to see the working people I grew up with coopted by right-wing nationalists and populists, and the Church I grew up in stampeded to the right by the abortion issue. But perhaps such a project can be carried out in a more guarded way, one which identifies with the soaring rhetoric of Abraham Lincoln, to my mind the most powerful writer America has produced, and the lofty vision of the founding "fathers," while also singing songs to *today's immigrants,* since that is what we all were once, and reminding ourselves that the dangerous *imperial power* of England that first "settled" this country and then provoked "our revolution," has in the present century settled on the shores of "our country."

That is why I prefer the more open-ended interventionism in the name of the democracy *to come,* which is also the hospitality, the friendship, the gift, the justice, to come, that Derrida is promoting. But I am no less worried about the risk that Rorty describes of the growing gap between "us" and the workers, the working poor, and those who have no work, to whom Derrida says we are responsible without limit.

Part 2

Passions of Non-Knowledge

Gender, Science, Ethics

5

Dreaming of the Innumerable

Jacques Derrida, Drucilla Cornell, and the Dance of Gender

Provided that it is well understood that we are all for knowledge, for the most searching research, for the most vigorous and relentless investigations of anything and everything, let us now put what Jacques Derrida calls the "passion of non-knowledge" to work. Let us explore the positive and emancipatory effects of our humble confession of non-knowing, of our lack of access to The Secret, in three areas where it would seem that everything depends upon what we know, not on the limits of our non-knowing: gender (chapter 5), science (chapter 6), ethics (chapter 7). Can we still cling, even here, to our thesis about the absolute secret, here where ignorance is a curse, where knowledge is enlightenment, where we need a guide? Must we not abandon our love of the absolute secret and follow the lead of someone who Knows the Way? Has not the upshot of ignorance—but does the love of the absolute secret commit us to loving ignorance?—in these areas meant the flames for "witches" and Bruno, silence for Galileo, and persecution for all those who defy conventional mores? Are we here tossed about by waves of paradox too fierce for even the heartiest California surfer?

The Innumerable

> Of course, it is not impossible that desire for a sexuality without number
> can still protect us, like a dream, from an implacable destiny which
> immures everything for life in the number 2. And should this merciless
> closure arrest desire at the wall of opposition, we would struggle in vain:
> there will never be but two sexes, neither one more nor one less. Tragedy
> would leave this strange sense, a contingent one finally, that we must
> affirm and learn to love, instead of dreaming of the innumerable. (P, 108)[1]

I begin with gender, where I hope to show the clear advantages of confessing, with all the affirmative energy we can muster, with a great and sweeping amen, yes, yes, that we have no privileged access to The Secret and that we do not know who we are, that we are all a little blind, *sans voir, sans avoir, sans savoir.* For it is in matters of gender—when gender matters—that tempers flare and we are most likely to insist that we know exactly who we are and *especially* who we are *not.* It is when gender matters that we become the most insistent about the "natural order." In my view, the force of this discourse on the natural order is almost entirely negative, almost completely concentrated upon driving out what it declares as "unnatural," which is the special interest of this affirmation of nature. Our thesis is here more necessary than ever: by seeing to it that we can never "arrest the text in a certain position, thus settling on a thesis, meaning, or truth"—of woman, of the feminine, of nature, of anything (P, 96)—the absolute secret keeps us safe (but not without risks). In the present study of gender, this unfixable and unarrestable, this uncountable and unaccountable something or other, this *je ne sais quoi,* is called the "innumerable."

Derrida sometimes disconcerts feminists because he lets "woman" and even "feminism" disseminate or deconstruct, letting them slip into undecidability, letting it seem that he, or at least deconstruction, can do no good for feminism. But, for Derrida, dissemination and undecidability are the conditions, the "quasi-transcendental"[2] conditions, of justice—for women, for men (for animals, for everybody)—conditions of the dream of justice, which, when it comes to sexual difference, is called a dream of the innumerable.

Derrida's relationship to feminism has usually been examined in terms of his earlier, somewhat more Nietzschean writings, specifically, *Spurs.*[3] I am interested here in balancing this Nietzschean strain in Derrida with his later, more Levinasian preoccupations with "justice." Hence, after an initial look at the undecidability of "woman," I will take up the work of Drucilla Cornell, who puts deconstruction to work in the service of a feminist legal theory. Cornell employs a strikingly Levinasian and utopian reading of Derrida with which I am deeply sympathetic, and which I regard as crucially important for correcting an overly Nietzschean reading of Derrida, for understanding the ethico-political implications of deconstruction, and for understanding in particular what Cornell calls the "alliance" of feminism and deconstruction. From there I will turn to the "dance" of gender Derrida discusses in "Choreographies," by which he means the dissemination of the "opposing" genders. This I will interpret as not only a Nietzschean dance of differences (which seems to Derrida's critics to play lightly with the suffering of women), but also a dance of justice, as a utopic, or atopic, dream of a justice to come, and certainly a justice for women to come. I will argue that in "Choreographies" the dream of the innumerable is a dream of justice, which is, I hold, the final upshot of a Derridean approach to gender—and the good that deconstruction can do for feminism.

Living with Undecidability

Is "woman" a proper name? Does it have its own proper truth and identity, an identifiable property and a specific difference? If not, would that not constitute a loss of identity, a fracturing and breakdown of the sense of what or who a woman is, so that women would be disoriented, robbed of a sense of who they are and what they want, disappropriated? Drucilla Cornell writes:[4]

It is important to note first just how fundamentally misunderstood Derrida has been by his feminist critics. Derrida has been accused of advocating women's non-identity within patriarchal society. But was that not what patriarchy always rested on, women's non-identity? Deconstruction, in this reading, is just a disguise of the worst aspects of patriarchy. Who wants to fight for the non-identity we have had imposed upon us? Feminists, on the other hand, assert *our* identity at last. (BA, 101–102)[5]

Would that seeming disappropriation not represent a violence, an injustice against women? But if there is a truth of woman, if woman is a proper, identifiable name, would that not constitute another violence, the violence of classification, categorization, constriction, and even caricature, of typing and stereotyping, the violence of an essentialism that binds, not merely the feet but the being of women, that prevents movement and becoming and the step of the dance, precluding the possibility of becoming something different, something "sexual[ly] otherwise" (P, 108), otherwise than a feminine essence, otherwise than the essence of the feminine?

Who is authorized to speak or write, properly, of this name, in this name? Can a man write about women? Would that not make woman his "subject"?[6] Can a man write like a woman?[7] Would that not be more masculine mastery, one more masculine usurpation or co-optation of what is properly feminine, one more move men make against women? Were a man to adopt a feminine pseudonym and were he to write in a feminine voice, and even to do so quite well, would that amount, not to the invention of a new voice, but rather to stealing women's voice, and so once again to more injustice? But if a man could not write of or in the name of women, or like a woman, or if there were no room for men in feminism, or among women, or for a womanly side of man, if all that would be reducible to more injustice, then has not woman become something powerfully proprietary and appropriative, a way of silencing new voices, with all the exclusionary, excommunicative violence that appropriation implies?

These questions are not puzzles waiting to be solved or resolved, definitively, one way or the other, by a crucial piece of information or knowledge, by some skillful and clever theoretician, but they are more or less permanent aporias that block our way, that divert and detour us, that cost us time, even as they give us the time and space of sexual difference. These aporias are not temporary roadblocks to be cleared away but undecidables that hover over and constitute the time and space within which the question of woman takes place, the space of sexual difference, of the relationships of men and women, and of each among themselves. These aporias describe the aporetic or conflictual axiomatics of sexual difference, the basically permanent tensions within which gender theory and practice take place. It is not so much a question of settling these questions and then setting them aside, of deciding these undecidables, as it is of living with the permanent menace that they pose, of learning to operate within their lines of force. It is a question of acquiring a heightened sensitivity to the complexity and undecidability that haunt and disturb our reflections and choices, of maintaining a vigilance about the peculiar dangers that threaten us. That is pretty much what deconstruction is, by the way, in a nutshell.

For there are many women, too many to count or contain, in many places; advantaged and disadvantaged; educated and uneducated; Western and third world; women of wealth and women of color; powerful and powerless women; nameless women and women with old, honorable names; distinct women with different needs, in different situations, in different places. The more we know about the polymorphic diversity of what passes for the unity of "woman," the more the prudent wisdom of the absolute secret impresses us. The question of woman, of sexual difference, is really many questions about many women, about many differences.

In virtue of what Derrida calls iterability, and Rorty calls recontextualizability, we can say that nothing in itself, standing by itself, is sexist or non-sexist or anti-sexist, for or against women. Everything said of the name of woman, or in the name of woman, or like a woman belongs to a context, has a local purpose, serves a certain strategy, and can be turned around, turned against itself, can be made to work for or against women.[8] Identifying what is proper to women, separating women from men, defending a feminine difference, locating something distinctively feminine, something maternal or sisterly, establishing an identity and a place for women can be made to work for or against women, depending upon how it is used. "Making a place" for women can work for women, and just as easily be turned into identifying "a woman's place." For the signifier "woman," like every signifier, functions contextually, in a fluctuating, shifting environment, bent by the winds of undecidability.

For Derrida, "woman" even functions as the name of or for this undecidability, not indeed as a master name but as a name that undoes all mastery, as a certain quasi-transcendental name—like "hymen" or "invagination"—for the inside/outside, as a way to expose the shifting grounds upon which the powerful, masterful, dogmatic columns of phallogocentrism and *Identitätsphilosophie* are "erected." "Woman" is a name for "undecidability," but it is not, as Gayatri Chakravorty Spivak concludes, for "absence." "Woman" is the name not of a lack but of a "more" (*mère/mehr*), a yes, yes, always already more than any categorization can identify or more than any gender-role assigned her. So Derrida's anti-essentialism is a function not of skepticism or despair but of a respect for irrepressibility and excess. His anti-essentialism, or structural "blindness," always labors in the service of what is to come; his blindness always has a "messianic" twist, more like a critique of the idols of Aaron in the name of the *tout autre* than some sort of nihilistic attack on structure.[9]

What Derrida has written of and about, in the name of and on behalf of woman, is organized by the thought—if it is a thought—of undecidability. Does it still need to be said, now, after so many years of reading Derrida, that undecidability does not mean indecision or inaction, that undecidability is the condition that not only surrounds and besets decision, but also calls for decision, the condition that antedates, provokes, permeates, and follows upon decision?

The View from Cornell: Difference, Justice, and the Future

Perhaps it is my own autopoiesis as a woman that demands that I begin with difference, the future, and Justice, because the "present" of this social system and legal system is profoundly threatening to women. (PL, 144)[10]

Drucilla Cornell lays to rest in the most decisive way this misunderstanding about undecidability, the popular nonsense, repeated unfortunately by well-known philosophers, that deconstruction is some sort of enervating skepticism or even pernicious nihilism. For Cornell, Derrida is the author of a utopian ethics, an ethics of the "beyond," of unimagined possibilities, of "difference, the future, and Justice," and hence of the radical transformation of the present. Her "Derrida"—and his "undecidability"—do not witness to "paralysis" or leave us "helpless":

Instead, Derrida makes us think differently about the beyond. Iteration "is" as possibility because a system of representation given to us in language cannot be identical to itself and therefore truly a totality. This possibility is an "opening" to the beyond as a threshold we are invited to cross. As a "science" of the "threshold," deconstruction dares us to commit to "cross over" and perhaps, by doing so, to avoid the horror of having the door of the Law of Law finally shut in our faces. (PL, 110)

Because the word "deconstruction" has become too liable to this sort of misunderstanding, Cornell redescribes deconstruction as "a philosophy of the limit." By this she does not mean the philosophy of finitude that I criticized above (chapter 2) but a philosophy of de-limitation, of delimiting wholes which tend to close over, of showing relentlessly that systems—in particular, legal codes—do not reach closure without violence. This is also what Derrida means by "parergonality," locating the marginal, border-line phenomena that expose the main body of the work (*ergon*)—for Cornell, the body of law—to its other, to what it misses, erases, silences, excludes—for her, the parergonal bodies of women and homosexuals.

The unique effect of Cornell's formulations is to cast deconstruction as a philosophy of the "beyond," of the possible, of the threshold, of what is otherwise than the present—as an (important) dream. In this view of deconstruction, as Derrida says in a piece he wrote for the conference Cornell organized at Cardozo Law School on "deconstruction and the possibility of justice," nothing could be less old-fashioned than the classical project of emancipation (FL, 28).[11] That is also why Derrida is happy to describe deconstruction elsewhere as a "new enlightenment." Not the old Enlightenment, with its sclerotic eyes frozen open in unrelenting *Aufklärung*—that would be a monstrous beast, the monster[12] of a panoptical law—but an Enlightenment of the *Augenblick,* of a blink of the eye, a particular postmodern Enlightenment or enlightened postmodernity (PR, 19–20), one that goes along with a certain structural blindness.[13] Cornell's work instantiates this Enlightenment of the *Augenblick* in a theory of legal interpretation, an Enlightenment that is intent upon keeping the social and legal order open and loose, which looks—*blickt*—always for an opening, a crack or crevice in the system, through which the fragile shoots of freedom, novelty, and difference can make their way, something that is only possible if we deny that the System Knows it All. "Deconstruction"— not skepticism and nihilism, is but an openness to the beyond, a threshold of the possible, of the *mère/mehr,* of "the radical difference of the not yet" (PL, 110), a delimitation of the tendency of the present to close over and close off the future. The whole idea of deconstruction, in a nutshell, then, is contained in the uncontainable *"viens, oui, oui!"*[14]

Cornell's work, which is a badly needed counterpoint to the rash distortions and angry denunciations of deconstruction by which we are still being visited, is marked throughout by an acute appreciation of the proximity of Derrida to Emmanuel Levinas. She makes it clear that Derrida's notion of difference and alterity is driven by a Levinasian sense of the claim of the other, of the disruption of the same by the transcendence of the Other, and hence by a fundamentally ethical impulse, by a desire for or dream of justice. Thus for Cornell the energy of deconstruction is nothing less than the energy of the Good. Distinguishing the Good, or the Law of the Law, from the law as an empirical legal system, she rightly argues that the former prevents the closure of the latter. Every existing legal order is breached from within by the exigencies of Good, by the impossible demands laid upon it by the Good. In "Force of Law," Derrida claims that the law is always deconstructible just because Justice itself —the Good or the Law of the Law—"if there is such a thing," is not deconstructible (FL, 14–15).[15] The deconstruction of the law is not bad news. Deconstruction is good news, the good news of alterity, in virtue of which existing legal orders are exposed to continual correction, revision, and alteration in the light of the claim alterity lays upon them, that is, by what is beyond that code, by what is silenced or excluded by that code. Deconstruction demands the alteration of the law in virtue of the undeconstructibility of alterity. Deconstruction does not leave us with something missing but with an opening. Cornell writes:

The dissemination of convention as a self-enclosed legal system does not leave us with a fundamental lack, but with an opening. What I am suggesting is that the dissemination of convention, through *différance* as the non-full, nonsimple, and differentiating origin of differences, disrupts the claims of ontology to fill the universe, and more specifically the legal universe. (PL, 110)

To be precise, we should say that Cornell's philosophy of the limit is organized around Derrida's intervention upon Levinas in "Violence and Metaphysics" (PL, 83–85). There Derrida insists that the *tout autre* is not just wholly other, not just absolutely and utterly other, for in that case the Other would not be an other human being, an other self or subject or person. As such the Other would lack the only real transcendence that Levinas allows and, robbed of her transcendence, would be vulnerable to the worst violence. So, unless the Wholly Other is also just so far the same, the *tout autre* is not wholly other. Cornell calls this the principle of symmetry, and it plays a central ethical, political, and legal role throughout *The Philosophy of the Limit* where it is called upon to establish the symmetry of women and homosexuals—they are always treated together in *The Philosophy of the Limit*—before the laws of heterosexual men, the Monster which dresses itself up as Justice and "The Law."

Innumerable Goods; or, Too Good to Be True

Deconstruction: a philosophy of the Good. I love the impudence of that formulation, the scandalized look on the faces of the officials of anti-deconstruction, the shocked expressions of the self-appointed defenders of the Good and the True when they wake up in bed with the Great Deconstructor. I tried to produce the same shock and scandal by speaking of the prayers and tears of Jacques Derrida. Still, as much as I love the Good and savor this impudence, this is one point on which I would want to reformulate Cornell's use of Derrida, and this in the name of justice and in the name of Cornell's argument, in the name of the view from Cornell. The Good may be too Good to be true, too True to be of any good to deconstruction and deconstruction's dream of justice. This may be one award *honoris causa* that "the philosophy of the limit"—and hence, by extension, deconstruction which is at least its ancestor, predecessor, or *provocateur*—is forced to decline.

I understand the delicious justice of slipping this highly Levinasian expression into the pocket of the philosophy of limit. The Good is something Cornell wants in order to convince the officials of anti-deconstruction that deconstruction is not bad news for the law, that deconstruction is justice in itself, if there is such a thing, that deconstruction does not abandon lawyers and judges to the wolves of nihilism or paralysis. She introduces the notion in connection with two stories about postmodernism. The first, the received story, is that postmodernism has given up on the Good; there is not, there never has been, a Good because there is not, there never has been, an Origin or Presence of which the Good is but another name. Consequently, there is no "horizon of the Good, projected out of the principles embodied" in concrete legal systems, "to which one can appeal for guidance in evaluating competing legal interpretations." The result of this first story is legal nihilism, or legal positivism, which is helpless in distinguishing better and worse legal codes; the result is injustice.

The other story is the one Cornell is telling, a Levinasian-Derridean story of justice, that "the Good remains as the disruption of ontology that continually reopens the way beyond what 'is.'" Existing legal systems operate under the influence of a definite, albeit implicit, conception of a good life. But there is always a distance—a gap forming the site of deconstruction—between these concretely embodied goods and "the call of the Good." For the Good divests any existing system of its claim to finality, to being the final good, good once and for all; the Good pulls any legal code, however good it may be, beyond itself to a future that is undreamt of, or better, a future of which we all dream, which is what makes radical transformation possible (PL, 93–94).

As I love the Good and the use to which Drucilla Cornell puts it here, I also love this distinction between the two postmodernisms, which Edith Wyschogrod and I have also tried to defend.[16] Still, I worry about the strategy of using "the Good" to work out this distinction and hence to serve and save justice. Nothing is gained by pointing out that, as a textual matter, Derrida does not speak of the Good, at least not in his own name, since Cornell is making an interpretive, not a textual, claim, and she is redescribing deconstruction for the purposes of feminist legal theory. But I do not think that it is an accident that Derrida avoids this locution. That is because, contrary to Cornell, I take this expression to be trapped by its premodern provenance and unable to find a home in postmodernism. We do not count ourselves among those who claim to be hardwired to The Good. For The Good sounds much too much like The Secret, and those who claim to know The Good are out to punish those who disagree. Postmodernists have good reasons to keep a safe distance from the Good. The expression is too strong for Derrida. It is too Platonic, on the one hand, that is, too idealistic, too suggestive of a regulative ideal, of "projecting" a "horizon"—a locution that, following Derrida, Cornell elsewhere rejects but uses here—of a beyond that exceeds the present as the ideal exceeds the real, as the perfect exceeds the imperfect; and too Aristotelian, on the other hand, too suggestive of a communitarian unity, of a consensus about a shared paradigm, an agreement about the "good life" which "all men" desire with masculine desire. And if Derrida had any more hands, I would say it is also too neoplatonic—and finally, ultimately, too Levinasian for deconstruction's own good.

Cornell is sensitive to the notion that the Good is not a "horizon" or a "regulative ideal," and she offers numerous gracious and convincing accounts of why that is so. Justice in itself, if there is such a thing, is not a pure ideal that we can never reach but only hope to approximate, an "ought" with which "is" will never catch up. Rather, Cornell points out, for Derrida justice is an aporia, a perplexing and complex undecidability that brings us up short and forces us to choose, in this concrete and complex, knotted and undecidable situation (FL, 22–29). Justice compels us to decide what to do, to invent the law for the situation, which is always different. Justice is not an Ideal or a paragon but a parergon, and the law without parergonal justice is a monster. That is good Derrida, as good as it gets, but Cornell's recurrent talk of the Good creates a tension with this good Derrideanism. For I think that all Cornell's arguments against the "ideal horizon" of Justice tell equally against projecting the horizon of "the Good" and that the needs of Derridean justice are better served by giving up on the Good (and by not capitalizing "justice").[17]

Historically it is worth noting that, for its contemporary advocates, the "Good" is the antidote to the modern malaise of "value theory," to the subjectivism of valuing that is decried by anti-modernists as different as Martin Heidegger, Alasdair MacIntyre, and Allan Bloom. The Good, says its defenders, is not the flimsy effect of the will willing but something substantive "out there" that brings me up short. Not "my values" but *the* Good, capitalized, like a worthy German noun. The term has made its way into Cornell's work by way of Levinas, for whom the Good means the Other (*autrui*), the Infinite One (*l'infini*), the Other over and beyond all being-other, beyond all being (*epekeina tes ousias*), and, more deeply still, the "other than Other" (*autre qu'autrui*), God Himself [*sic*], who is the other infinite one. In Levinas, the other is a positive infinity, like the Cartesian God, or like a neoplatonic excess that wells up from an infinite source and flows toward me. Within this classical discourse a "philosophy of the limit" would be atheism, the denial of the infinite, of positive infinity. In Levinas, too, the Good is a way to displace modern subjectivism and value theory—it is the truth of modern anti-humanism, Levinas says —by a radical substitution by which the subject is handed over to the Other before all consciousness and freedom.

Now while Derrida agrees that the Other comes to me with the shock of transcendence, that the alterity of the other is no subjectivistic value posited by the ego, still he does not speak of "the Good," if only because, in his radically post-classical view, the Good has been disseminated. There are "innumerable" goods, too many to count, too many ways to be and not-be, to be otherwise and different. I would say that, at most, at best, the Good, "if there is any" (*s'il y en a*), for Derrida is a radically negative and deeply pluralistic notion that bears almost no resemblance to its classical ancestors. On the point of the Good, Derrida is more like the Enlightenment, albeit a new Enlightenment, an *augenblickliche* neo-*Aufklä-rung,* which also rejects a substantive or strong conception of the Good. That is part of the reason that, while he does not speak of the Good, he is not averse to speaking of the "right"—to philosophy, to literature, to say anything.[18] To be sure, Derrida does not defend a pure autonomous Subject whose Rights flow like water from its pure rational Subjectivity. A little, perhaps a lot like the Enlightenment, Derrida rejects the Good and sides with a justice that differs over the Good. He cannot avoid thinking that the Good, like every *arche,* suffers dissemination, that it has been irretrievably pluralized, localized, and multiplied. The Good is something to which we have no access. On this point, Derrida is a little more modern than classical, and if this is postmodernity, then this postmodernity is a continuation of modernity by another means. By reason of its distinctive notion of alterity, deconstruction emphasizes not my rights but the right of the Other One to be different, the right to be left alone, as the late Supreme Court Justice Harry A. Blackmun said (PL, 162; 208 n. 39.), even as it is moved by the plight of the one who is left out, ground under, excluded, erased, or silenced, and hence by that Other's right to be heard, to be addressed, to be given standing "before the law." And to that claim of the Other corresponds the responsibility of deconstruction.

If we pressed Derrida about what the Good is, he would be a little nonplused, at least as much as Socrates, but instead of telling us the allegory of the Sun, he could give us an allegory of the simulacrum, of the lowest of the low on the line. Like Socrates, Derrida would tell us what the Good is not, not because the Good is so surpassingly beyond Being, *epekeina tes ousias,* but because the Good is so entirely negative, more like the *khôra* than the *agathon.*[19] The Good, if there is any, is *in principle,* if it has a principle, something negative. Deconstruction does indeed disturb all existing legal systems by posing an alternative to the present order— that is the central point of *The Philosophy of the Limit.* This it does not in virtue of "the Good" but in virtue of a parergonal analysis of what the present order is leaving out, excluding, erasing, or silencing. The Good, if there is any, is at best something parergonal, nothing else, nothing more.

Furthermore, if we pressed Cornell about what the Good is, her answer too will always be something negative; that is, she is much more likely to tell us what is evil than what is Good. She does not, in truth, defend the Good, but keeps telling us to avoid the evil of enforcing the Good on the bodies of women and homosexuals. For Cornell, too, justice demands that we give up on the Good. For it is the defenders of heterosexuality who claim to know the Good, to know that heterosexuality is *the Good,* a good gift given to us by God or nature which obliges us to be good (heterosexuals) in return, in accord with the binding logic of the gift.[20] Cornell is clearly making a weaker, "alternistic"[21] claim, not that homosexuality is the Good, for that would be very homogenizing, but that homosexuality is a difference that should be protected, one of many alternative goods, in the plural, among a vast and unheard of panorama of "innumerable" goods. Homosexuality belongs among the parergonal, polymorphic possibilities that the Other (than the heterosexual), the "sexual otherwise," has the right to embrace. Homosexuality is at best *a* good, and this because it is not evil, and it is in the end nobody else's business if someone considers it good, and certainly not the business of the state of Georgia (PL, 159–160). It is precisely because there is no such thing as "the Good" that the state of Georgia should stay out of the bedroom of "[t]wo men peacefully making love"—or even two men noisily and stormily making love, for that matter—which is one among many innumerable goods (PL, 159). (The advocates of The Secret always keep a fully staffed Secret Police.)

By the same token, it is the opponents of abortion who hold that the preservation of life under all circumstances is *the Good,* that life is a good given us by God and that it flies in the face of God or nature to take life away, even embryonic or fetal life. But Cornell's argument is that the law must be loosened and deconstructed, that it must lift women out of the prelegal silence and invisibility to which women have been historically consigned by the law, that it must treat women as fully constituted, symmetrical legal agents. And after that the law must let women make their own considered choice—for better or worse, but not for the Good. Justice—not the Good—demands that women be let alone to decide, symmetrically with the law, what they think is good, to decide for themselves whether it would be good for them to have an abortion or not to have one (PL, 162).

So even Cornell's theory of the Good is entirely negative: avoid evil, avoid violence, where evil arises precisely when someone—the Same—tries to inscribe his—and it usually is "his"—conception of the Good on the bodies of the Other—above all, for Cornell at least, on the bodies of homosexuals and women. As Robert Cover says, the law is "a field of pain and death," that is, of evil, and it is the minimization or reduction of evil that concerns us, while leaving people the space to decide what they think is good. That indeed is why Cornell begins with evil, not the Good, that is, with a remarkable account of the ethics of sympathy in Arthur Schopenhauer and Theodor Adorno, of an ethical materialism which is organized around carnal violence to the bodies of the Other.[22]

One way to see the significance of my stand against the Good is to see that Levinas would have no sympathy at all for Cornell's Derridean stand for homosexual rights, given his portrait of the modest wife who bustles quietly about the house preparing His dinner. Levinas would have still less sympathy for Cornell's Derridean stand on abortion rights—in fact he might be angry with her—given that for Levinas the offspring of the Good is offspring, the child, indeed the Man-Child born of this loving couple.[23] When Cornell writes "Of course, the fetus can itself be recognized as Other, with infinite right" (PL, 152), she reproduces the position that Levinas would take on this issue, which for Levinas would be absolute and non-negotiable. As she says in the next sentence, that would allow "the rights of women"—their symmetry with the fetus and with the law —"to go unnoticed."

My concern is this: homosexual and abortion rights are not protected by "the Good," but only by disseminating the Good in the name of nameless and innumerable goods, of polymorphic, polysexual possibilities that the monster of the law wants to close off. The Good is another version of The Secret. Only such a Derridean pluralism of goods will provide the approach to law upon which Cornell insists and that renders these rights intelligible. In deconstruction, it is necessary to disseminate the Good to make room for justice. Insisting on "the Good" is at least confusing and possibly dangerous to these rights—although I do love the consternation it causes to the officials of anti-deconstruction.

What I find in Cornell is a good account of why there are too many goods, too many to enumerate, classify (*glas*), or legislate, and of why there is no Good. If Derrida were of a more apocalyptic frame of mind, he would claim that the age of the Good is over, that it is necessary to deny the Good in the name of the dissemination of many goods, to negate or disseminate the Good so that the Good no longer has any identity. For at that point at which "the Good" congeals into something identifiable, at which it acquires a positive identity, it becomes, like the law, a monster, a terror which terrorizes difference. The Good is the Monster's claw, the teeth with which it chews the morsels of difference. Derrida would say of the "pure Good" what he says of the "pure Gift": the pure good, if there is one, is something utterly disseminated, devoid of all identity, so that at just the moment it is recognized or identified as the Good it goes bad, and the gift turns to poison. As soon as someone says "here is the Good," it has gone bad and turned into a monster.

Cornell is at her Derridean best when she talks about monsters, not about the Good, when she stops talking about the Good and instead calls Derrida a ragpicker (*chiffonier*). Ragpicking does not sound very good. On this account, deconstruction keeps its neo-Enlightenment eyes peeled for the fragments, the leftovers, the leftouts, the remains, the morsels, the outsiders. Deconstruction is the scavenger of the Other. The disreputability of this image, its slightly shocking incongruity, is what makes it good Derrida and good deconstruction. The Good is much too respectable, too powerful, too prestigious, too Ideal, too good for deconstruction. Deconstruction is bad, not good; it is disruptive, trouble-making, Socratically disturbing, possessed of a negative *daimon* not a positive *eu-daimonia*. Deconstructive vigilance, as Cornell shows again and again, keeps a lookout for a break, a crack, or a crevice through which something different can break out, for a small spark that might be given off by the system, a spark that will perhaps, if we are lucky, ignite a bigger blaze.

Justice, if such a thing exists, has to do with these bits and fragments that have escaped the Look of the Monster, with the least among us, the outsiders and the excluded. If justice is "beyond" the law, that is not because justice is too big for the law but too little, because it has to do with the fragments and remains, the *me onta* who are before the law, beneath the law, too trivial or worthless or insignificant for the law to notice, with rags and litter, the nobodies, the outsiders.

With the "shit." Deconstruction deals with shit. I hasten to say that this is a scholarly reference, an erudite mention, not a rude use. I am citing Derrida citing a text from Jean Genet, not trying to be vulgar, in proof of which I supply the scholarly reference.[24] Deconstruction deals with what Saint Paul calls *ta me onta* (1 Cor.1), or, in a less edifying reference, with the ones that the law treats like shit, in both cases referring to the excluded and the excremental. And it is Cornell's constant contention, if I may say so, that the law is a monster that treats women and homosexuals like shit. That is much better than the rhetoric of the Good, which is far too edifying, too sanitary, a little misleading and idealizing, neoplatonizing, and even vaguely patriarchal—since the Good is the Father of us all. Even if young Socrates could persuade old father Parmenides that there is an *eidos* for dirt and maybe even one for shit, he would never dare to argue before the old man that the Good is shit. And for good reason. The Good suggests an ideal that we cannot instantiate, realize, or actualize; a "horizon" of infinity that nothing finite can replicate. But the "justice" Drucilla Cornell has in mind, if there is any, is the singularity that is too small, too finite, to be lifted up into the grandeur and universality of the law, too powerless and impotent when it is brought "before the law."

The Feminine Imaginary and Messianic Feminism

For Cornell, the "feminist alliance with deconstruction" takes the form of an "ethical feminism" (T, 59), which is a utopic remetaphorizing of women "to come," and that, if it is linked with Derrida's most recent work, might be described as a certain messianic feminism. Like deconstruction itself, this feminist alliance with deconstruction, turns on a utopic, even messianic call—epitomized in Derrida's *viens, oui, oui*—and an irrepressible aspiration which continually works against the fabric of closure and exclusion, a "faith in justice" (ID, xii). This alliance has several features I will sketch here.

Central to Cornell's work is her elaboration of Derrida's deconstruction of Jacques Lacan. Lacan, Cornell says, "cuts off the revolutionary implications of his own statement, 'Woman does not exist'" (T, 86). Lacan means to say that woman is essentially the truth of castration or of the hole, essentially the place of the lack, essentially the substitution for the hole in the real. Lacking the penis, the little girl is deprived of the masculine fantasy which can identify with the Father and so she cannot compensate for the primary narcissistic wound by imaginary identification with the phallus; hence her being is reduced to a "masquerade of 'being'" without really being (DF, 170). Derrida turns Lacan's statement around into a statement of non-essentialism. Woman does not exist if existence is given the sense of fixed identity and permanent presence. She does not exist, not out of lack or defect but excess, for the feminine disrupts the proper place, including and especially the proper place to which she is assigned by Lacan as lack. Woman is not the "place of the lack" or even the lack of a proper place, but rather the disruption of propriety and assigned place, and thus—on Lacan's terms—something radically other, *tout autre*, to any enclosing, binary system of gender and gender hierarchy.

Derrida, according to Cornell, takes more seriously than Lacan the claim that Lacan advances that the real is radical alterity, radically beyond the symbolic, the beyond of the real. If we cannot know the real, then we cannot know its *truth*, including the supposed truth of the logic of castration. If the real is what we cannot know, then the real is what cannot be contained in any logic, and so the real is precisely uncontainable, unsystematizable, exactly *without* the "destination" which Lacan assigns men and women. Then the feminine becomes—on Lacan's terms—the "allegory" of ethical alterity, that is, of what Cornell calls "the endless transformative possibility that attempts to eradicate injustice demands. In this sense the end of conceptual knowledge in the strong sense is forever the beginning of hope" (DF, 164). Ethical feminism is then not only the ethics of feminism, but the feminism of ethics, the turn of the ethical toward radical alterity, toward the *tout autre*, which is also toward the justice to come—something that emerges most clearly in Derrida's work in "Force of Law." In "Choreographies," the justice to come takes the form of the innumerable genders to come.

Thus for Cornell the aim of deconstruction is to interrupt the "structure of rigid gender identity which has imprisoned women and made the dance of the maverick feminist so difficult to keep up" (T, 88). Its aim, she offers, is to "affirm the power to dance differently" (T, 88). This is to embrace the call by Emma Goldman, who said, "If I can't dance, I don't want to be part of your revolution" (P, 89), which Christie V. McDonald refers to as the "maverick feminist" in the opening remarks of "Choreographies." Feminist analysis and practice would always involve—this is invariably true of what deconstruction does—the invention of the other (*l'invention de l'autre*), which would mean here, as Derrida says in "Choreographies," "a completely other history . . . of absolutely heterogeneous pockets, irreducible particularities, of unheard of and incalculable sexual differences; a history of women . . . who are today inventing sexual idioms at a distance from the main forum of feminist activity"—which does not, however, prevent or excuse them "from becoming militant for it" (P, 93). The dance, the invention of something fresh, the new step, the turn toward *l'àvenir,* must keep in step with the present, with the confrontation of present injustice and the ongoing, present revolution. While there is nothing powerless about a dance, nothing can "serve as an alibi for deserting organized, patient, laborious 'feminist' struggles" (P, 95). The feminist alliance with deconstruction proceeds by inhabiting the stereotypes by which women are confined and then turning them on their head in order finally to displace them. In Derrida's "allegory" of gender, the hard, upright, canonical Knight of Truth is spun around—this is the well-known argument of *Spurs*—to mean a rigid, dogmatic, phallogocentric essentialist and philosopher of identity, while the beguiling, deceptive temptress woman becomes an allegory of *différance,* of the historically inventable and reinventable, self-correcting, self-interrupting history of invention, of *l'invention de l'autre,* and, specifically in "Choreographies," of "inventing sexual idioms." Woman thus becomes the *mère/mehr,* the excess, *au de-là* imprisoning stereotypes and confining gender identities. Hence Cornell writes:

> In *Spurs* Woman is the very figure of the constitutive power of the not yet, the beyond to Lacan's Symbolic. The play of difference does exactly the opposite of what it is thought to do; it does not make utopian thinking impossible, it makes it absolutely necessary, because the meaning of Woman, and of sexual difference, is displaced into the future. (T, 93)

The unknowable of the essence of the Woman is the figure not of a lack but an excess and an opening to the future. The upshot of the play of differences is not relativism but an ethics and a politics of difference, a choral dance of the right to be different which does not move within the binary oppositions of male/female, but which responds, is responsible to, the call for something to come.

Cornell also explores the implications for Derrida as a man writing about women, which is a problem for men, because they risk preempting the voice of women, and for women, who may find themselves dealing with someone who has heard their complaints and taken them seriously. Derrida rejects the status or the standing of gender-neutrality. For gender goes all the way down and exposes the pretense of a neutralizing, transcendental reflection which pretends to disengage itself from the factical situation of men and women and always ends up sounding just like a man. But neither does Derrida want to be trapped by his gender. Consequently, Cornell argues, he often has recourse to a multiplicity of voices, a polymorphic chorus in which we are not sure of the number or the gender of the speakers. The ethical for Derrida is not a neutral, asexual universal, applying without exception to every particular, but on the contrary always something singular, and in the case of feminist analysis, something deeply marked by sexuality, always settling into the concreteness of a sexualized situation, always on the lookout for the invention of sexual idioms to come. By confining ourselves to only *two* possibilities, men and women, masculine and feminine, we "engender" if I may say so the risk of hierarchy and domination.

That is why the feminist alliance with deconstruction always has two "phases," one of reversing and overturning the logic of sexual difference, of the binary opposition of masculine/feminine, which is the basis of affirmative action programs, and then of displacement, which disseminates this binarity into the polymorphic multiplicity of the invention of innumerable sexual idioms. However, Cornell hastens to point out that this is not a disguised way of supporting the Texas or California Board of Regents' decision to drop affirmative action, as if affirmative action has run its course and we may now move on to displacement. As Cornell writes,

> [Reversal] is not a phase that one simply surpasses, because the oppositions continually reassert themselves. The phase is structural, not temporal. We never just get "over it." We cannot settle down once and for all. In this sense, deconstruction is interminable and there cannot be a clear line between "phase one" and "phase two." (T, 97)

Indeed, Cornell concedes that there is a "tension" in Derrida's texts on this point, between overturning oppositions and his hesitancy—inspired by his dislike of essentialism—to speak of a new metaphorizing of women. The result, Cornell maintains, is "the danger . . . that Derrida jumps too quickly to the new 'choreography of sexual difference'" in spite of his great care to recognize the phallocentric nature of metaphysics.

It goes to the heart of Derrida's position to delimit "identification," to resist reducing things to something "rigorously or properly identifiable," to hesitate placing or locating someone or something in its proper place. That is why Derrida says that it is not so much a question of finding a new concept of woman as of questioning the very concept of "concept," of the whole order or operation of fixing and locating, defining and confining, which can only serve to repress and suppress the *mère/mehr* (P, 100). In *Beyond Accommodation,* commenting on this text, Cornell rejoins that, if it is not a question of a new concept of woman, there can at least be a new "metaphorizing" of woman, which corresponds to Luce Irigaray's call for a "feminine imaginary."[25] Derrida's "hesitancy" about this, Cornell says, "may be my central disagreement with him" (BA, 110, 118).

> If we do not allow for the broad intervention of the power of refiguration through metaphor and, indeed, fantasy and fable, we can potentially participate in the repudiation of the feminine.

As I have argued elsewhere, any demythologizing must be replaced by *new* mythologies, and feminism in particular is better served not merely by "demythologizing patriarchal myths, but [also] by inventing a new, empowering mythology of the maternal and feminine. . . ."[26] That of course runs the risk of reinstating, not displacing, oppositional schemata, but that is a risk worth running, part of the aporetic or risky axiomatics of the question of sexual difference. Who ever said that things could happen without risk or anxiety? Indeed, I would say that Derrida's dream of justice, his dream of the innumerable—along with Levinas's dream of the justice due *"l'infini"* and with Jean-François Lyotard's dream of a "sublime" justice—are all just such new, more salutary, empowering myths, postmodern myths, if that is not too paradoxical, myths of justice that inspire *another* postmodernism.

On Cornell's telling, the feminist alliance with deconstruction involves, if not a new "concept" of woman, certainly a fresh metaphorizing and symbolizing, a new imaginary of woman, one which opens up the psychic space of women to imagine themselves differently and to twist free of the imaginary imposed upon them by men. Cornell has recently defended this view against Catharine A. MacKinnon, for whom any such effort is an attempt to find consolation in the place and role women have been assigned by men and hence complicity with the oppression of women.[27] MacKinnon's view holds only if one accepts the masculine view that openness to the other, that giving oneself to the other, is a way, indeed the very structure of "getting fucked." But is that not to pay too high a price, Cornell asks, one which makes affectivity and sexual intimacy impossible, instead of celebrating the figure of openness to the other and disseminating these roles across innumerable genders? The power of sexuality is not—for men or women—supposed to be "empowerment" but intimacy (T, 105) and the feminine imaginary must be cultivated, much in the manner that Irigaray has shown.

I do not think that there ever is a way out of the imaginary and myth or that we should be looking for one, which would be the height of modernism. I think that the line to be drawn is not between the imaginary and the non-imaginary, but rather between good and bad imaginaries, between myths of freedom and myths of nature, imaginative constructions that emancipate and those that enslave. I believe that the undeconstructibility of justice in Derrida, the sublimity of justice beyond representation in Lyotard, the positive infinity and invisibility of the Other in Levinas, the sublimity of the divine in Irigaray, and the imaginative faith in justice in Cornell all belong to a postmodern imaginary. As Cornell writes:

> [T]he best weapon against myth is to signify it in turn, and to produce an artificial myth; and this reconstituted myth will in fact be mythology. I am suggesting that even an allegory of woman that protects the beyond as beyond can only express itself through an interchange with a mythology of the feminine. There can always be other mythologies. (T, 107–108)

This need not turn the figure of Woman into a religion, unless of course religion is reinterpreted as a desire for intimacy, and that I think conforms nicely to what Irigaray means by the divine and to what Derrida has recently called a "religion without religion" (GD, 49). Myth is *her*-story, a cultivation of feminine imagination, a constellation of "symbols, images, and metaphors which give us an inspirational and shared environment" (T, 109). Like any religion, this religion too would turn on an impossibility. The myth of Woman is not a way of reducing women to nature and this because it is a myth of justice, that is to say, a way of affirming her impossibility, affirming her as *the* impossible, to come, who always already exceeds her Truth and any reduction of her to her Truth. That would make the religion of intimacy a slightly messianic religion. That is why I suggest we could, in the spirit of Derrida's citation of the story of the coming of the Messiah in Maurice Blanchot's *The Writing of the Disaster*, reimagine this tale as *her*story, as the story of a "messianic Woman."[28] Once, when the messianic woman was to be found disguised, dressed in rags, among the wretched of the earth, someone approached her and, identifying her as the Messiah, said, "when will you come?" The point of this story, Blanchot comments, is that we not confuse the *coming* (*venue*) of the Messiah with his—we rewrite—*her* presence. For the Messianic Woman is always to come, structurally to come, so that she cannot be identified or reduced to her presence, and indeed is meant to confound the present, to disturb and disrupt the present. Thus, in a way that Lacan never dreamed, it is true to say that the Messianic Woman does not exist. She can never exist, and this because she is always to come.

Fathers and Sons

Drucilla Cornell's work, I think, effectively counters Kelly Oliver's critique both of Derrida and of Cornell's feminist alliance with deconstruction. Oliver argues that the "mother" for Derrida is always a figure of nature, mother earth, mute and without language or writing, the phallic mother. Oliver rejects Cornell's defense of Derrida, and Cornell's repeated argument that deconstruction represents an intervention on Lacan's phallocentrism in which woman is a figure of non-essentialism, not of nature.[29] This is not the place to take up the careful analyses of *Glas* and *Circonfession* required by Oliver's criticisms of Cornell and Derrida. Accordingly, in order to defend the force and cogency of Cornell's argument, I will restrict myself to a recent piece in *Diacritics*,[30] in which Oliver criticizes Derrida's argument in *The Gift of Death*.[31]

The Gift of Death is a deconstructive reading of Søren Kierkegaard's *Fear and Trembling*—which itself turns on a telling of the story of Abraham—that is meant to inch Levinas and Kierkegaard closer together. Derrida is arguing that it is not possible to keep the religious and the ethical as cleanly apart as do Kierkegaard, who would suspend ethics for the sake of religious faith, and Levinas, who would suspend religious ritual and dogma for the sake of ethics. Derrida carries this out by a deconstructive allegorizing of the story which shows how the religious and the ethical tend to converge around an infinite obligation, and unconditional "gift" to a *tout autre*. In his allegorizing, deconstructive account, the three figures in the story, (a) Abraham, (b) God, and (c) Isaac take the place or stand in for, respectively: (a) the self, the one called upon to say *me voici* (= Abraham); (b) the *tout autre*, the wholly other, the other one who calls upon me in his/her singularity (= God); (c) all the other others, the ethical universal, both *oikos* and state, both *Moralität*, a purely formal law, and *Sittlichkeit*, the concrete ethical community, of family, nation, and state (= Isaac).

But on Oliver's account, which flies in the face of everything that Cornell has written about deconstruction, Derrida is telling us the story of and associating himself with a tale of "the sacrifice of mothers and their daughters," so the "gift of death" for him means "the father's gift of the death of the mother that promises life to the son," which is about what deconstruction seems to mean for Kelly Oliver.[32] This astonishing result is achieved by allowing Oliver her hypothesis that *The Gift of Death* is a story of two sets of fathers and sons: God/Abraham, Abraham/Isaac. That, of course, is what it literally is in Genesis and in *Fear and Trembling*, and exactly what it is *not* in *The Gift of Death*, where it has been, to adopt the categories of Cornell, allegorized or remetaphorized or remythicized. Oliver's approach is to disarm the deconstructive re-reading so that, if Derrida is here commenting on a story steeped in biblical patriarchy, he is therefore to be identified with the patriarchy rather than with the deconstruction of it.

Once we allow Derrida his premise, that the story is or can be taken to be an allegory of the tensions inherent in all ethical responsibility, then it is clear that the position of woman on the Derridean telling, and this is what "the feminist alliance with deconstruction" in the work of Cornell makes unmistakably clear, is not that of Isaac but of the *tout autre*. As Cornell's work makes plain in numerous places, on the one hand, in what she calls Derrida's "intervention" on Lacan, the father belongs on the side of the "law" and of the patriarchal legal structures that bind women to hearth and home. Women, on the other hand, are precisely the ones who are ground under by what Cornell terms the "monster" of the law, who call for such interventions, who call for a respect beyond the law, who call for civil disobedience to unjust laws,[33] and then, ultimately—since we need good laws—who call for laws that respect women. In Derrida, and in Cornell's use of Derrida in constructing her ethical feminism, the *tout autre* is not the father because the *tout autre* comes from "on high" just because she is laid low (the *tout autre*, if I may dare say so, and I do so with great fear and trembling, is exactly the one who is "getting fucked," to use the category of MacKinnon; or the widow, the orphan, the stranger, to use the more edifying categories of Levinas), her height being ethical, not legal, the moral height of justice, not the legal force of the law. Thus the three positions allegorized in the story are for Derrida and Cornell the positions of (a) the ethical subject (Abraham); (b) the call of justice, which is supple and subtle (the voice of God); and (c) the law (Isaac), which is what Cornell would call the law of the father, where the law is necessary even as its patriarchy must be interrupted for the sake of justice.

On Derrida's telling of the story, Sarah is drawn out of her silence, so that the mother here, far from being a figure of mute silence and nature without culture, speaks the most eloquently of all, calling for justice. If Sarah does not get a word in Genesis, 22, or in *Fear and Trembling*, it is precisely the woman/*tout autre* who calls, who addresses us by her absence, from beyond the law and beyond the letter of the story and bids for justice. Derrida remarks that one cannot but be "struck by the absence of woman" in this story of "father and son, of masculine figures, of hierarchies among men," and Derrida asks if everything would be changed "if a woman were to intervene in some consequential manner" (GD, 76). For the story as it is portrayed by Saint Paul and Kierkegaard is a high stakes poker game, a confrontation of divine and human testosterone, a phallic test or ordeal to see if Abraham has the guts to spill the blood of the one he loves so much. Levinas follows an honorable rabbinic tradition when he reads the story as a story of the *end* of human sacrifice, in which the sacred writer has God call the whole thing off and lead us back to the ethical plane by staying the hand of the patriarch. Derrida allegorizes the story, totally recasting it as a story of justice due the singular one beyond the "monster" of the law.

What Derrida identifies with in the story is the tension between respect for the law, which wants to treat each individual uniformly and remain deaf to proper names, and justice, which wants to draw a line of absolute respect around the singularity of the individual and suspend the law. Cornell has shown that among the clearest results of such deconstructive analyses of this tension as it affects women and the law are: (1) civil disobedience to laws that deny women's rights (FID, 149ff.); and (2) affirmative action laws that call for a justice beyond equal treatment, since if one has been disadvantaged from the start, then equal treatment is a disadvantage and the law ought affirmatively to intervene in order to lift one up or cut the person a break. As Cornell makes plain, nothing better illustrates the affirmation in deconstruction, the *"viens, oui, oui"* of deconstruction, than the "affirmation" in "affirmative action," which is precisely to affirm those who are the other of the law. Thus the "family" that gets "sacrificed" on Derrida's telling of this story is the family enshrined in legal structures that confine women to the home and assign them irremissibly to the role of childbearing and rearing, the family of right-wing "family values" which deny women the rights enjoyed by the father whose name the entire family bears, which thus become "his" family.

Cornell and Derrida are not denying that there should be laws, but pleading for better, less monstrous laws, laws that allow themselves to be interrupted by the other of race, gender, and national origin, laws that practice an absolute "hospitality" to the other. Even as he has recently said that the import of deconstruction on the question of national identity is to advocate an absolutely "open admissions" policy on immigration, so Derrida would advocate a corresponding openness of the law on matters of race and gender. In her most recent work, Cornell has put these deconstructive analyses to work in dialogue with John Rawls on the thorniest questions of abortion, pornography, and sexual harassment.

The feminist alliance with deconstruction as it emerges in the work of Drucilla Cornell turns on the notion that the laws governing women's lives and bodies are something to be deconstructed, and justice, if there is such a thing, is not deconstructible. In Cornell's feminine imaginary, justice and woman are essentially *to come, à venir*, so that were the Messianic Woman to make an appearance, our first question to her would be, "when will you come?" The first words of deconstruction, *viens, oui, oui*, are already second, in response to her call from afar, her call from the future, her call for the future—for difference, justice, and the future.

Dreaming of the Innumerable

Cornell's interpretation of Derrida shows in a convincing way the affirmative character of deconstruction, indeed that it is doubly affirmative, *oui, oui*.[34] Deconstruction is the affirmation of innumerability, of innumerable goods, of alternity and all the alternatives, all the polymorphic, pluralistic possibilities (so long as they are good, that is, not evil) that are left out by the monster of the law. But deconstruction is affirmative without being positive, without identifying positively and definitively what it wants, without wanting the Good, without claiming to Know the Secret. Deconstruction is the affirmation of justice; indeed Derrida says it *is* justice. Derrida does not think that only a God or *the* Good can save us; on the contrary, he thinks that our only hope is that they never show up. If the Messiah never comes. As Cornell shows so convincingly, deconstruction settles into the intricacies of the situation—legal, political, social, artistic, academic, etc.—in which it always already finds itself, and looks around, parergonally, alternistically, for the possibility of something different. It does not know what it wants, even and especially when it wants something else, when it affirms something different. Deconstruction cultivates the possible as the possible, as *the* impossible.

Derrida's strategy is radically utopic, as Cornell insists, or perhaps better atopic, inasmuch as this utopia is thoroughly negative, completely free of any positive—and hence of any positional, positionalizing, thetic—Ideal. His strategy is invariably to insist on the possibility of being otherwise, on a possibility to come, on a "beyond," by which he means not a paragon but a parergon, not a transcendent ideal but rather a little chance for something different or new, a new "dance," a new step—*pas*, which is also a new "not."

It is important to see that this step (*pas*) is not only a step in a Nietzschean dance,[35] but let us say a dance around the absolute secret which
sits in the middle and does not know. It dances in response to a quasi-
Levinasian call of the other, the call for something different, here, for the
"sexual otherwise," of fresh possibilities for gender and sexual difference.
It is a call for the invention of the other, of new possibilities that will open
up alternatives within the present gender-traps, the lures that draw into
repeating again and again well-worn sexual roles and sexual stereotypes,
that form and conform us to regularized patterns and expectations. It is a
call for justice from and for the sexually otherwise, and a call to find ways
to be otherwise than the present tolerances permit.

That is why making a place for women in structures or institutions
that hitherto had no room for women—the workplace, the academy, the
professions, etc.—represents an important but incomplete feminism for
Derrida, a reversal, however urgent, of the desire to confine women to
the home, that as such remains within a binary scheme. It is a gesture,
however necessary, that still belongs (as its other side) to the most classical topo-eco-nomy of man versus woman which identified the *oikos* as a
woman's place. The more radically Derridean gesture, beyond all reversal
and replacing, is to dis-place or disseminate or dislocate this topographi-
cal desire, this "law of the proper place" (P, 94), to thwart it—with a
dance:

> The most innocent of dances would thwart the *assignation à résidence*, es-
> cape those residences under surveillance; the dance changes place and
> above all changes *places*. (P, 94)

None of this is to be construed, Derrida hastens to add—and this point
is directed at his critics—as an excuse for skipping the urgent, difficult,
laborious work of reversal, for "deserting organized, patient, laborious
'feminist' struggles," the "incessant, daily negotiation" (P, 95).[36] The *"real*
conditions in which women's struggles develop on all fronts (economic,
ideological, political) . . . often require the preservation . . . of metaphysical presuppositions that one must . . . question in a later phase—or another place . . ." (P, 97; BA, 96).

It is never a question of having to choose *between* reversal and displacement, both of which are integral, even simultaneous, phases of the movement of deconstruction. The "feminist alliance with deconstruction," I
think, is rather a matter of adjusting deconstruction's velocities: insofar
as it advocates displacement, deconstruction needs to be slowed down;
insofar as it advocates reversal, deconstruction needs to be given a push.
So granting Cornell's precaution about these texts, which is also Derrida's
precaution, that there is a danger of moving too quickly here, of jumping
too quickly into this new choreography, we should not lose sight of the
"ultimate" "theoretical"—if this is a theory and if it is ultimate—tendencies of deconstruction, which means we should not lose sight of its dream.

Deconstruction is deeply anti-essentialist, deeply resistant to the "essentializing fetishes" of "woman" or "feminine sexuality." Deconstruction refuses to let sexuality or gender, or anything else—masculine or feminine, or both, or neither, or both and neither—contract into an identity and settle into a proper place. Deconstruction loves the *mère/mehr*.

This displacement of sexual difference is not intended to make its way back to a neutral terrain, prior to sexuality, to a neutered, generalized, presexual or asexual human essence, devoid of sexual markings, the upshot of which, ironically, is always to assure a masculine victory. This victorious masculinity is visible in both Heidegger and Levinas, in the crypto-masculinity of a supposedly neuter *"Dasein"* or "spirit" (P, 102–104). The displacement of sexual difference in deconstruction is rather a displacement of the *binarity* of the two sexes, of the figure 2, of the oppositional polarity, of the male/female opposition, which is the form of the "war between the sexes," regardless of the victor's identity, regardless of whether the spoils go to phallocentrism or gynocentrism. The dream of justice for and among the genders is not a dream of a neutral presexuality but of a sexuality that goes all the way down, a sexuality that, to use Heidegger's vocabulary, is ontological and not merely ontic. That is why Derrida can have recourse to terms like "hymen" and "invagination," not in their "widely recognized sense" (P, 105), which means their strictly localized, anatomical sense, which would make them reductionistic and masculine images of women, but in a quasi-transcendental sense. As quasi-transcendentals, hymen and invagination are intended to sexualize or resexualize the hitherto strictly "neutral" territory of the transcendental, while not collapsing into a binary scheme. But Derrida "dreams" of a sexuality free from the start of the classical oppositions, which is how he reads Heidegger's originary *Geschlectlosigkeit* (P, 104), a sexuality, let us say, not of sexual "difference," but of the strewing of sexual "differences," not a binary but a polymorphic sexuality, a disseminated "choreographic text with polysexual signatures" (P, 107).

Derrida "dreams"—this is the "desire" of deconstruction—or "thinks" —that is its utopic or atopic thought or aspiration—of justice as something impossible, something "innumerable." In terms of the question of sexual difference, this is a dream of a "sexuality without number," not marked by opposite sexes or identifiable opposites, not stamped with two opposing "classifications," man and woman, submissive to the classificatory law of genre and gender. That dream is meant to protect us from a tragic fate that would assign us like an "implacable destiny" to the straits of one gender: to each "man" or "woman" one gender only, and there are only two to choose from. But instead of loving this fate (*amor fati*), Derrida speaks of "dreaming of the innumerable," a dream which, by a certain theory of intentionality, is self-validating, for where there is a dream "something dreamt of must be there in order for it to provide the dream" (P, 108). He dreams of a "dance," of a "choreography" to replace and displace the reigning "topography," a choreography that is not merely a matter of "exchanging" places, but a choreography that improvises, that creates new steps, new moves, new dances, new styles, that invents new and unheard-of combinations and mutations. He dreams of "incalculable choreographies" meant to enact innumerable possibilities, unheard of, more than are dreamt of in our philosophies, impossible and innumerable genders, born of a quasi-transcendental desire and quasi-transcendental dream of an innumerable *mère/mehr*.

That is why Derrida's "thought" and "desire" culminate in what is "to come," in a future, *à venir*, and in a "come," a *viens*. That is why he speaks of a democracy to come, or a Europe to come, of a friendship to come that is beyond fraternalism and brotherhood, of a woman or a man to come —without being able to say who or what is coming. Joining hands with Cornell, as many hands as possible, not merely two. I would say—Derrida would say, Cornell would say—it is neither a man nor a woman who is coming, but something new, some odd kind of a new being, a new step, an effect yet to be produced, some new sort of s/he or wo/man, something innumerable and unclassifiable. Maybe what is coming is nothing as simple and unambiguous as an hermaphrodite or an androgyne, but something undecidably miscegenated, something that has not happened yet, something singular, something possible, something impossible, something unimaginable and innumerable.[37]

The cutting edge in Derrida's work, as Cornell's work shows, the thought that does not contradict but reorients his Nietzschean side, is the "thought" of the "beyond," of justice as the "impossible" something that will create an alternative and free us all from the straits of identity. The thought of the beyond delimits the knowledge of our identity, which opens the future. Derrida's feminism, then, takes the form of the delimitation of gender, a philosophy of the limits of the two genders and of the law of gender, of the limits "on the proliferation of sexual voices, each with its own unique notes" (BA, 98). That, in my view, is where gender theory is led by Derrida and that is the good Derrida can do for feminism.

The two genders, masculine and feminine, not one more, not one less, to which each of us, one by one, is implacably destined: Are they not walls by which we are all confined, men and women, by which we are all "imprisoned" (BA, 84–85), "trapped,"[38] and straitened? Do they not dominate and manipulate us all, narrow us and confine us, making us all less than we can be, blocking off the "beyond"?

What is coming? Who knows? Who can count? Maybe what is coming will be good (almost). Maybe we are about to be visited by the most marvelous and innumerable goods, by the most amazing transformations of gender, in the blink of an eye, by a dance of innumerable steps. *Viens! Oui, oui.*

6

Hermeneutics and the Natural Sciences

Heidegger, Science, and Essentialism

The steadfastly nominalistic skepticism about overarching ahistorical principles, about touching fingers with the Essential Reality behind the veil of appearances, about hitting a rock-hard Secret beneath the soft surface of semblance, this salutary skepticism about our own world-historical importance, this felicitous non-essentialism, as we like to think of it, that I have advocated throughout this book seems to run up against its limit when we turn to the natural sciences. For there we really do seem to know what we are about and to be getting things right in a sustained and serious way. Is science, after all, the Way? The natural sciences, as I say in *Radical Hermeneutics* (RH, 214), and as Robert P. Crease elaborates, are the hard case.[1]

The model of a *docta ignorantia hermeneutica,* which keeps alive a multiplicity of interpretive possibilities while humbly confessing the humility of our condition, is admittedly drawn primarily from what are called in the Anglo-American world the "humanities" and "social sciences." But we seem to run up against the stone wall of hard knowledge when it comes to the natural sciences where relentless progress is made daily against *ignorantia,* learned or unlearned, hermeneutical or straight up. Regardless of what the philosophers are saying about them, the scientists go about their daily business—completing the human genome project, exploring new reaches of outer space, achieving astonishing new successes in medical technology, and maybe, just maybe, turning the corner on Albert Einstein's dream of coming up with a single unified field theory, the so-called theory of everything. If, as Edmund Husserl said, the sciences pay little attention to transcendental philosophers who tried to help them out by providing them with absolute foundations, they pay even less attention to philosophers who seem to deny them their absolute grip on things.[2]

Indeed, philosophers who try to delimit scientific objectivity call down upon themselves the most merciless and unfriendly fire. Alan Sokal has recently found a new career in exposing to ridicule what the "cultural studies" movement is saying about science.[3] Sokal thinks that the meanest and most satirical thing he could possibly say, the cruelest cut of all, would be to cloak his hoax under the name "hermeneutics." Meanwhile, Nobel laureate Steven Weinberg began helping *The New York Review of Books* sell subscriptions to *Aufklärer* and *Aufklärerinnen* by joining the war on this movement which he took to be relativizing the natural sciences. In his most recent sally, Weinberg criticizes Thomas Kuhn's *The Structure of Scientific Revolutions* for offering no revolution at all but mostly just driving under the influence of an intoxicating word ("paradigm").[4]

I have no wish to be drawn into these polemics, in which *The New York Review of Books* (*NYRB*) manages, as usual, to implicate Jacques Derrida. But I do want to argue at least this much, that a hermeneutic approach to the natural sciences offers a sensible and persuasive account of what is happening in the natural sciences, and it does this without embracing either a scientific realism, which seems to me simply another, albeit scientific, version of essentialism, on the one hand, or throwing it to the wolves of "anything goes" relativism, on the other hand. It is important to show that the reach of hermeneutics extends across all the *Wissenschaften*, both *Natur-* and *Geisteswissenschaften*. For in the absence of having anything sensible to say about the most powerful achievements of intellectual life in the last four centuries, hermeneutics can only be an embarrassment to itself and can merely leave itself defenseless against the scorn of the *NYRB* and other venerable Western institutions outside New York City, *s'il y en a*. The triumph of scientific knowledge, the result of much hard work and acumen, need not stampede us out of hermeneutics into essentialism. As I said in my discussion of Rorty, the main thing of which I am wary is Capitalization, the claim that we are so successful at this or that, be it physics or theology, that we can cut through appearances to some sort of Capitalized Something or Other, some super-essential Secret that makes the world we live in look like a veil of appearances. With Rorty, I think that this is the case even if the contender to the crown of Capitalization enjoys the endorsement of a winner of the Nobel Prize in physics. We are back to the argument about Eddington's table, the one at which we eat, and the one at which we would all starve to death.

To this end, I take up the case of Martin Heidegger. In *Being and Time* Heidegger was neither pronouncing Jeremiads on modern science and technology—as in his later writings—nor declaring science an arbitrary construction, but sketching the outlines of an evocative and constructive view of scientific work. This hermeneutic view bears suggestive similarities with the work of Thomas Kuhn, Paul K. Feyerabend, Michael Polanyi, N. R. Hanson, Mary Hesse, and other post-positivist theories of science, and, although that will give no comfort to realists of the Sokal-Weinbergian persuasion, who want to leave no room for hermeneutic play at all, it illuminates scientific practice without at all throwing it to the wolves of irrationalism or decisionism. To be sure, in his later writings, Heidegger turned away from this sensible hermeneutic account of science and became a strident and radical critic of the epoch of technological thinking.[5] He saw the present as the age in which Being bends before human control and exploitation, an "atomic" age which defines our times in terms of natural forces and threatens to overrun our lives with "cybernetic" manipulation.

So Heidegger is the author both of an important "hermeneutics" of science in *Being and Time,* which does not at all deserve the scorn that Sokal and Weinberg direct at the cultural studies movement, and of what I regard as an essentialist, indeed a higher, hyper-essentialist critique of the "atomic age," an explication that I believe becomes as objectionable in its own way as other forms of essentialism—from the natural sciences to metaphysics to mysticism. Heidegger dropped the patient hermeneutical suggestions about science found in *Being and Time* in order to undertake a critical analysis of technology or, more precisely, of the "essence" (*Wesen*) of technology, where *Wesen* had the Middle High German verbal sense of coming to be, coming to pass, coming about.[6] He was concerned, not exactly with technological instruments themselves—personal computers, for example, and e-mail (had there been any in the 1950s)—but with what is coming to pass in and through a world saturated by these instruments. What mattered for Heidegger is the understanding of Being, that is, what is made of the world and of our place in the world, in an age governed by the paradigm of technological control. He offered an important critique of the totalizing tendencies of contemporary culture, the culture of "virtual reality," a phrase that, I imagine, would have greatly interested and tantalized him and about which, we can count on it, he would have written several difficult but delicious essays. These technological tendencies Heidegger gathered together under the word *Gestell,* which means the way the world and the way we with it are gathered into and framed about by technological thinking.

I have no wish to deny that Heidegger issued a significant, prophetic, and salutary advance warning to a world in which computers have worked their way into every last corner of our lives and in which we have become correspondingly vulnerable to and dependent upon the way our microchips work.[7] My complaint is rather that, on the one hand, the later Heidegger neglected his own earlier more sensible hermeneutical reflections on science and drifted, ironically, into a positivistic conception of science,[8] while, on the other hand, he moved steadily toward situating science within a deeply essentialist, "*Seins*-essentialist" view of History (capitalized). The alarm he was sounding about the real dangers the technological age poses would have been better served had he continued to argue, as he did in *Being and Time,* against a misunderstanding of what science is in the first place and avoided all the hype about the History of Being. The misunderstanding of what scientists do in their workshops is corrected by a hermeneutical approach to scientific work along the lines suggested in *Being and Time* in images that evoke Kuhn three decades before *The Structure of Scientific Revolutions.* Instead, driven no doubt by a lifelong sense of "crisis," that things are teetering on the brink and only a god or something just as large can save us now, Heidegger shifted his attention away from the hermeneutics of science sketched in *Being and Time* toward warnings about the dangers of totalization and normalization by which science, civilization, and humankind threaten to be engulfed.

So in the present chapter my aim is twofold. (1) I want to explore Heidegger's early hermeneutics of science which takes the form of an "existential genealogy" of the birth of science in the historical life of the scientific investigator, which is to be distinguished from an alleged "pure logic" of science. I want to show that this hermeneutic genealogy throws considerable light on scientific practice, offering as it does a view of science that is sensible without being relativistic, in accord with a sagacious idea of reason, not as Reason, but as "good reasons." In *Being and Time* Heidegger avoids reducing science to some sort of capricious human invention while dodging the bullet of unqualified scientific realism. Science does not descend from the sky like a god to save us, but neither are we just making it up as we go along. (2) Next, I want to show that in his later essentialistic (*wesentlich*) investigations, where the natural sciences are located within the "history of Being" (*Seinsgeschichte*) and entered into the historical sweep of an entire understanding of being-human, of being-true, of Being and truth, Heidegger tends to lose sight of his achievement in *Being and Time*. He chooses to do battle with the God, or Idol, of the *Gestell* by means of a new and true God who would save us, a fresh sending of Being's shining splendor. While salutary up to a point in offsetting an unbridled scientism, Heidegger's analysis of the *Gestell* is implicated in problems of its own, problems that arise from his "essentialism" or "hyper-essentialism," in which the critique of technological culture overwhelms certain ethical and political considerations which belong to a genuinely hermeneutical approach to science. The problem with essentialism is that it is too overwhelming, that the concerns of concrete, factical life tend to be swept aside in favor of broader, deeper issues which present themselves as, shall we say, more essential, which is basically why I argue for "demythologizing" Heidegger.

The problem, I am always arguing, lies in laying claim to some privileged access to the Secret in any of its versions, whether as Scientific Truth or Pure Reason, as the Truth of Being or the Word of God, and not settling for such truths as we have the good fortune to come upon, as come our way, in the course of the day. The more radical hermeneutical claim is that we are on our own, devising such constructs as we can to make sense out of our lives and our experience, without Direct Assistance from On High. For even when we do believe in assistance from on high, it is not direct but indirect, and it does not provide an escape from the hermeneutical situation for it, too, requires faith and interpretation. It is always, as a famous believer and well-known Apostle said, through a glass darkly.

Thus, recovering the "genealogy" of science adumbrated in *Being and Time* offers us latter-day more radical hermeneuts two advantages. On the one hand, it provides a non-relativistic account of scientific practice that undoes the shrill cries of science bashing raised by such critics of hermeneutical reflection as Sokal and Weinberg, indeed by realists everywhere. On the other hand, it corrects the excesses of Heidegger's later critique of *Gestell*, his "mythologizing" tendencies, to make room for an ethico-political critique of totalization of the sort one finds in French philosophy of the last two decades. This is an ethics and a politics for which, I hasten to add, Heidegger would have had no taste and which his own elitism blocked. By taking science as one more thing done by human beings who have not dropped from the sky, who have not been born into this world hardwired either to Scientific Truth or to the Truth of Being, we can restore to science its human proportions as an inherently revisable way to understand the world, while keeping an eye out for the well-being of human beings who live in tangible time and a concrete human history, not Being's own fabulous history, who dine at concrete, tangible tables, who too often count themselves lucky to eat at all.

The Hermeneutics of "Normal" Science

In §3 of *Being and Time* Heidegger speaks of a "productive logic" which leaps ahead of the concrete work which the positive sciences do and breaks new ground, as opposed to the standard logic "which limps along after, investigating the status of some science as it chances to find it, in order to discover its 'method'" (SZ, 10/30).[9] This productive logic differs in principle from a merely reproductive one, which can do nothing better than describe the work of science in its creative past, vainly attempting to fashion and formulate that past into an epistemology by which scientific practice should presumably be guided in the future (SZ, 10/30). Such logics and methodologies are always written at dusk, to borrow G. W. F. Hegel's image, just when they have become obsolete. Methodologists are constantly being disrupted by the unorthodox turn of events awaiting them around the next historical bend.

We learn more about this new logic in §69b, where Heidegger discusses what he calls an "existential conception of science" (which we might gloss as the sort of science done by poor existing individuals):

> This must be distinguished from the "logical" conception which understands science with regard to its results and defines it as "something established on an interconnection of true propositions—that is, propositions counted as valid." The existential conception understands science as a way of existence and thus as a mode of Being-in-the-world, which discovers or discloses either entities or Being. (SZ, 357/408)

There is thus a difference between the standard logics of science, which treat science as a constituted result, attempting only to display the logical

chain of connections among its propositions, and the existential genealogy of the origin of science from prescientific life.[10] It is the latter that
interests Heidegger, and it is this shift in perspective that gives rise to a
fundamentally different conception of science in *Being and Time*. The attempt to treat science as if it were a pure logic, as if it dropped from the
sky, is an illusion, indeed a transcendental illusion, that vainly tries to
endow science with a pure transcendental status. Science derives from
the concrete historical life of the scientific investigator.

It is this new logic of science that Heidegger describes as "hermeneutic." But Heidegger's hermeneutic conception of science differs consider-
ably from Wilhelm Dilthey's. In the first place, Heidegger rejects Dilthey's
"objectivism," which regards science as somehow or other able to seize
upon a thing in itself, whether that be nature in itself, as in the natural
sciences, or indeed some cultural object in itself, as in the *Geisteswissenschaften*. Second, Heidegger discards Dilthey's division of the sciences into
two qualitatively different sorts, natural and human, which confines hermeneutics to but one side of the distinction. Heidegger insists that the
sciences constitute a unity, albeit a hermeneutic and not a positivistic
one.[11] In *Being and Time*, hermeneutics is a universal, ontological structure determining the understanding itself and it includes all the sciences
in its sweep. "Hermeneutics" is not the name of a method of the human
sciences, but of the ontology of the understanding itself. Heidegger takes
hermeneutics out of the domain of the purely methodological or epistemological and shows that it ultimately has an ontological sense. We
understand as we do because we are as we are. Understanding follows
Being; *intelligere sequitur esse*. There is no field of pure epistemology for
Heidegger but only of the ontology of knowing or understanding.

According to Heidegger in *Being and Time*, every science is a way the
historical investigator has of "casting" things, of framing them out, within
a certain conceptual framework. Far from attempting to leave one's interpretive framework behind, as in Dilthey's naive objectivism, scientific understanding is not possible without it. Hence, instead of differentiating
the natural sciences from hermeneutics, Heidegger is interested in showing how all science, natural and human, is made possible by an anticipatory, hermeneutic fore-structure. The fundamental feature of the understanding, and thus of the hermeneutic theory of science Heidegger
defends in *Being and Time*, is its "projective" character (*entwerfendes Verstehen*). For Heidegger, to understand it is to contextualize, to situate a
thing within the contextual arrangement in which it belongs. And that is
what Heidegger means by "projecting" a thing "upon its horizon," or
"projecting a being in its Being": to set it forth in or on the horizonal
backdrop which it requires to be manifest as the thing that it is, to "cast"
it in the appropriate terms. Indeed the English word "cast" captures a
good deal of what Heidegger means by "projection." It operates within
the rule of the same metaphor (*werfen* means to hurl or cast): to cast a

thing in a certain light, to thrust it into a particular framework. To understand a hammer is to situate it within the chain of equipment, the equipmental context, to which it belongs, just as in the foreground-background analysis of perception in *Gestalt* psychology.[12] Correspondingly, scientific or theoretical thinking consists in projecting an adequate conceptual horizon, one that allows not tools or everyday things but scientific objects to appear.

Hermeneutic understanding proceeds from a network of presuppositions that must always be adequate for the matter to be interpreted. In *Being and Time* it is never a question of getting free from presuppositions but, on the contrary, of securing an adequate presuppositional frame, of seeing to it that the complex of presuppositions one brings to bear upon the object is wide enough and sharp enough to give an adequate rendering of the object. It is never a question of assuming too much, but of assuming too little. The "hermeneutic situation," or complex of hermeneutic conditions under which understanding is possible, must accordingly meet three conditions. In the first place, the projective fore-structure must cover the whole range of entities to be understood, which is what Heidegger calls the "fore-having" (*Vorhabe*). That is to say, any projective or horizonal framework that we employ must be ample enough to provide for all the phenomena which can appear within its range. Second, the projective understanding must be guided by a certain conception of the kind of being, or categorial type, of the phenomena included within its range; this Heidegger calls the "fore-sight" (*Vorsicht*). Finally, the pre-understanding requires an articulate table of categories that unfold, delineate, and provide for an adequate analysis of the mode of being caught sight of in the fore-sight, which Heidegger calls the "fore-grasping" (*Vorgriff*) (see SZ, 150–151/191–192, 231–233/274–275).

Together these conditions supply the hermeneutic fore-structures, the anticipatory conditions of possibility, the required presuppositions that constitute the pre-understanding under which explicit understanding is possible. *Being and Time* clearly defends a holistic, horizonal interpretation of understanding according to which the character of an individual act of understanding is set by the constellation of presuppositions that condition it and make it possible. These presuppositions hang together in a system so that there are neither isolated, atomic acts of understanding, on the one hand, nor non-contextualized objects on the other. It is just this projective, horizonal theory of understanding that we need to characterize more carefully in order to grasp Heidegger's hermeneutical theory of science in *Being and Time*.

In the first place, the hermeneutic fore-structuring of human understanding is an ontological condition rooted ultimately, according to Heidegger, in the temporality of human existence as a being pointed toward the future. That is why talk about "escaping" this fore-structuring, which is what "freedom from presuppositions" would mean, makes no sense.

On the one hand such "escape" would be ontologically impossible; one would have to walk away from one's condition as a temporal being and it is always too late for that. On the other hand, such talk of escape misunderstands the very nature of understanding, which proceeds, not by means of a presuppositionless blank stare, but by projecting the horizonal pre-understanding that befits a given category of entities (SZ, 153/194–195) to disclose the entity before us.

Therefore, the hermeneutic makeup of the sciences is but a particular instance of the universal hermeneutic structure of all understanding. The Diltheyan opposition of explanatory-causal natural sciences and clarifying-hermeneutic human sciences makes no sense in *Being and Time*. Both explaining and clarifying, both natural and human sciences, are possible only on the basis of a prior hermeneutic projection which constitutes the field of objects that discipline carves out. Heidegger shows little interest in, and puts little emphasis on, the distinction between the natural and the human sciences in *Being and Time*. Indeed, he takes all the sciences to have the same ontological weight. All science, as science, is a projective determination of beings in terms of some categorial framework or another, be it natural, social, or humanistic. What does interest Heidegger, however, is a different and, for him, far more important distinction, between science itself and prescientific life. It is that distinction that his existential genealogy seeks to establish and clarify; it is upon that distinction that he thinks everything depends.

Let us examine this genealogy more carefully. In *Being and Time* Heidegger emphasizes the primacy of our concrete involvement in "factical" existence, that is, the sphere of historical and cultural practices in which we find ourselves "always and already," and the secondary or derivative status of abstract, theoretical investigations. The concrete historical world is first of all the world of "instruments" whose primary character is their "being ready to hand" (*Zuhandensein*), that is, their availability for use. *Zuhandensein* is to be differentiated from the complementary concept, *Vorhandensein*, which refers to the world in its "objective presence,"[13] its sheer reality apart from our use, which is the way it is considered in the natural sciences. However, we must resist the temptation to give the theoretical-scientific relationship to the world a purely negative genealogy, as if it arises as the simple privation of our primary practical engagement with the world ("circumspective concern"):

> . . . it would be easy to suggest that merely looking at entities is something which emerges when concern *holds back* from any kind of manipulation. What is decisive in the "emergence" of the theoretical attitude would then lie in the *disappearance* of *praxis*. (SZ, 357/409)

That would flatly contradict the universally projective nature of understanding, suggesting that, while our concrete involvement with the world is hermeneutic and presupposition-bound, the natural sciences treat the world in a neutralized, presuppositionless way.

Consider the famous case of Heidegger's hammer. The hammer which is used *as* a hammer is grasped only in the using; one cannot explain in theoretical terms its "feel," its balance, its aptness as an instrument, its place in the instrumental system. One knows how to use a hammer only by trying one's hand at hammering with it. But one can step back from using the hammer and describe its "properties" in a series of "assertions," indicating for example that "the hammer is heavy." In that case the hammer shows itself in a new light, but not merely because we no longer use it.

> Not because we are simply keeping our distance from manipulation, nor because we are just looking *away (absehen)* from the equipmental character of this entity, but rather because we are looking *at (ansehen)* the ready-to-hand thing which we encounter, and looking at it "in a new way," as something objectively present. The *understanding of Being* by which our concernful dealings with entities within-the-world have been guided *has changed over.* (SZ, 361/412)

As an object of the theoretical attitude, the hammer ceases to be a hammer-in-use and is *recast* as a thing-with-properties, obedient to the laws of gravity, measurable in mathematical space, etc. It is projected positively and anew, literally re-cast, re-projected, now no longer on the horizon of its readiness-at-hand, but rather of objective presence (*Vorhandensein*). One can imagine a graded series of such assertions, from the after-hours talk of two carpenters comparing the relative advantages of various sorts of hammers, all the way up (or down) to the considerations of a physicist who would treat it purely in terms of its mass and velocity.

Hence it is a mistake to think that in the scientific attitude things lose their interpreted character, their character *as* something (which Heidegger calls their "as-structure"). It is a mistake to think that the ready-at-hand is treated *as* a tool while the present-at-hand has to do with things *in themselves,* free of any "as." On the contrary, we have simply shifted projective frameworks, hermeneutic fore-structures. We have ceased to regard the hammer as a tool and now regard it as an entity with mass, shape, gravity, etc. In other words, "objective presence" is a positive projection of the Being of entities, a hermeneutic-interpretive act. It should also be clear from this passage that there is nothing mystical or mystifying about the word "Being" as Heidegger uses it in *Being and Time;* it simply refers, in continentalese, to the conceptual framework, the horizon, in terms of which a thing is grasped (= "projected").

Furthermore, one ought not to treat the genesis of the scientific attitude from our concrete involvement with the world as a passage from practice to theory. For that presupposes a hard and fast distinction between practice and theory—as if theory did not have a praxis of its own, and practice did not have a "sighting" of its own—a distinction which Heidegger thinks cannot be defended. On the contrary, scientific work is a complex praxis which requires skilled investigators, and this is no passing or incidental feature of science, but of the utmost importance to it. In a text that might have been written by Michael Polanyi, Heidegger says:

> Reading off the measurements which result from an experiment often requires a complicated "technical" set-up for the experimental design. Observation with a microscope is dependent upon the production of "preparations." Archaeological excavation, which precedes any interpretation of the "findings," demands manipulations of the grossest kind. But even in the "most abstract" way of working out problems and establishing what has been obtained, one manipulates equipment for writing, for example. However "uninteresting" and "obvious" such components of scientific research may be, they are by no means a matter of indifference ontologically. The explicit suggestion that scientific behavior as a way of Being-in-the-world, is not just a "purely intellectual activity," may seem petty and superfluous. If only it were not plain from this triviality that it is by no means patent where the ontological boundary between "theoretical" and "atheoretical" really runs! (SZ, 358/409)

It is also important to see that Heidegger does not think that science is exhausted by, or restricted to, the change-over in conceptual frameworks from readiness-to-hand to objective presence. For that change-over explains the possibility of the natural sciences, but not of the social and humanistic sciences. Science is constituted, not only when cultural objects (tools) are treated as physical objects, but also when tools are grasped *in their tool-ness* and made objects of scientific inquiry: "The ready-to-hand can become the 'Object' of science without having to lose its character as equipment"(SZ, 361/413). Hence economics is a science of the goods that humans make, and the laws of supply and demand by which they are regulated, which preserves the character of the tool as a tool. Economics is a science of the ready-to-hand *as* ready-to-hand. The same would be true of architecture, interior design, and product design.

The genealogy of the scientific attitude in *Being and Time* therefore involves two things: (1) the change-over from the attitude of immediate involvement ("concernful dealing") to a certain distancing objectivity; (2) the positive projection of a kind of Being which befits the beings under investigation, which will supply a horizonal or hermeneutic framework within which they can be investigated. In the natural sciences, that means the projection of things in terms of their objective presence, but in the social and human sciences it obviously does not. Economics, politics, and literary and historical science would cast things in their objective presence only at the cost of their existence as matters of meaningful inquiry. The natural and human sciences arise from another sort of projective horizon, with different conceptions of time, space, law, and meaning. These differences amount, however, to "ontic" differences in *Being and Time,* inter-disciplinary differences about their presuppositions (their fore-having, fore-sight, and fore-grasping). They do not affect the ontological makeup of science as science, but the intra-scientific differentiation of the sciences among themselves.[14]

Heidegger's concern in *Being and Time* is to see to it that the natural, social, and human sciences, which together are characterized as "positive" or "ontic" sciences, for they have to do with entities, with posited, existing things, do not get mixed in, indiscriminately, with the ontological science that he is conducting in this work. His ultimate interest in *Being and Time* is in Being, not beings, that is, in the ontological framework which renders possible every human practice, both scientific and prescientific, or, as he puts it, every ontic comportment with beings (*Verhalten zu Seiendem,* SZ, 4/23). Heidegger's aim in *Being and Time* is to reach a determination of Being as the horizon, not of any particular region, but of all horizons, and this he will argue is "time." It was thus of the utmost importance that the inquiry into *"Dasein,"* which serves as the point of departure in this ontological investigation, not be taken in ontic terms, as if it were an anthropological, psychological, or sociological science. And while he wished to keep this purely ontological interest in human being in *Being and Time* distinct from the positive-ontic human sciences, it was not his intention to question the validity of the latter. He wanted neither to demean the natural sciences in the light of the human sciences, not to demean the particular, positive sciences in the light of fundamental ontology. On the contrary, Heidegger meant to offer a hermeneutic account of the possibility of science, and to offer an ontology of human being as a hermeneutic being.

The genesis of science is to be traced back not to its objects but to the *projective attitude* with which it carves out and constitutes a field of objects and defines a formal approach to them. When an historian trains her students to look for certain patterns, to value individual documents, to be on the alert for specific clues, she is engaged in establishing the projective standpoint that constitutes and defines a scientific inquiry into history. The same thing holds true of the literary critic teaching students to thematize poetic imagery or the construction of English novels in the nineteenth century, or of a physicist working with a team of assistants in the laboratory.

Scientific thinking is objectification. Objectification, which is the constitution of any sort of scientific object, whether natural, social, or human, is effected by the change-over (*Umschlagen*), a new way of projecting beings in their Being. The piece of equipment is released from its place within the equipmental totality and treated as a detachable thing, isolated from its equipmental context. But if it is decontextualized as equipment it is recontextualized as an object within a new theoretical framework and made the object of a new and more sophisticated praxis. It makes its appearance as a scientific object only by assuming its place within a fresh horizonal setting.[15]

It is also clear from this hermeneutic or projective theory of science, that Heidegger is committed to denying "bare" or uninterpreted facts of the matter. Indeed, for Heidegger, the selection of facts in any science is a function of its capacity to discover a way to project things; a scientist can pick out facts only in virtue of a prior frame that the scientist "has in advance." Take the case of physics, which is for Heidegger a "paradigmatic" or exemplary case of scientific projection. Mathematical physics proceeds by projecting a strictly quantitative nature, a nature cast or projected in terms of mass, location, velocity, etc., which thereby enables it to discover facts.

> The "grounding" of "factual science" was possible only because the researchers understood that in principle there are no "bare facts." In the mathematical projection of nature, moreover, what is decisive is not primarily the mathematics as such; what is decisive is that this projection *discloses something that is a priori*. Thus the paradigmatic character of mathematical natural science does not lie in its exactitude or in the fact that is binding for "Everyman." It consists rather in the fact that the entities which it takes as its theme are discovered in it in the only way in which entities can be discovered—by the prior projection of their state of Being. (SZ, 363/ 414)

This is one of the most significant points of contact between Heidegger and the post-positivist rereading of the history and philosophy of science. There are no "bare facts," no "uninterpreted facts of the matter." Facts are facts within the frame that picks them out, only within the pregiven horizon that enables them to appear in the first place.

However, one ought not to conclude from Heidegger's denial of "bare facts" that he regards all projective horizons as arbitrary or pragmatic fictions, which is what Alan Sokal and Steven Weinberg think hermeneutical and poststructuralist theories do. On the contrary, projection has for Heidegger a "disclosive" power. Understanding discloses the world as the sort of world it is; it renders it manifest in a certain way. And disclosure, manifestness, is what "truth" means in *Being and Time* (SZ, §44c). Projections are not arbitrary; we must involve just the right kind of framework to free beings up for the kind of Being which befits them. The sciences do not traffic in "free-floating constructions" (SZ, 28/50) but seize upon something in the things themselves. Thus Heidegger holds *both* that it is impossible to gain access to bare and uninterpreted facts, which is to reject any notion of objectivism or absolutism, as if we could jump out of our skins and make some absolute contact with things, *and* that our hermeneutic constructions, when they are well formed, do capture something about the world, which is to provide for the objectivity of knowledge. Thus in one stroke Heidegger provides for the possibility of science while delimiting the claims of objectivism. He has no reason to think that science does not seize something about the world, even while he thinks it nonsense to suggest that this constitutes a break in the hermeneutic circle to some Secret in the center that had hitherto eluded us.

Scientific Crises

Up to this point we have treated Heidegger's views on what Kuhn would call "normal" science. Heidegger has given us a good account of how a certain framework of scientific understanding is established and the work of the several researchers in the field produces more and more confirmation of the framework, extending its results to the next decimal point. However, there is also a clear picture of "revolutionary" science in *Being and Time,* in §3, where Heidegger treats the "crises" and "radical revisions" of "fundamental concepts" that periodically shake the sciences.[16] The sciences, as we have seen, are guided in advance by certain basic concepts (*Grundbegriffe*), the interpretive fore-structures that constitute or project the field of objects that belong to that science:

> Basic concepts determine the way in which we get an understanding beforehand of the area of subject-matter underlying all the objects a science takes as its theme, and all positive investigation is guided by this understanding. (SZ,10/30)

"Basic concepts" are a good deal like Kuhnian paradigms, viz., guiding fore-structures that guide a whole scientific practice. The difference is that speaking of "concepts" tends to obscure Kuhn's emphasis on the practical character of the paradigm, an emphasis, however, that Heidegger clearly would share (SZ, 358/409). Now just as the transition from everyday concern to science is effected by a fundamental change-over (*Umschlagen*), which is a shift from a prescientific to a scientific projection, so *within* each science fundamental shifts of projective understanding are possible which result in revolutionary changes internal to that science.

> The real "movement" of the sciences takes place when their basic concepts undergo a more or less radical revision which is transparent to itself. The level which a science has reached is determined by how far it is *capable* of a crisis in its basic concepts. (SZ, 9/29)

At the time he was writing *Being and Time,* Heidegger thought that any number of such fundamental revolutionary movements were under way. He speaks of a crisis in mathematics, in the dispute between formalists and intuitionists; in physics, as a result of relativity theory; in biology, because of the dispute between vitalism and mechanism; and in theology, because of Martin Luther's fundamental insights about the nature of faith. So the work of a Galileo, Newton, or Einstein; of an Augustine, Aquinas, or Luther; of a Smith or a Keynes; or any of the founding or revolutionary geniuses of the respective disciplines, consists not so much in making new factual discoveries, or generating new information, as in effecting particular fundamental conceptual breakthroughs, in revising radically the fundamental terms in which the practitioners of a discipline think about a field of objects, in thoroughly "re-casting" them.

Inasmuch as Heidegger holds to a "horizonal" or holistic theory of understanding, he regards progress in a science as possible on two levels. In the first place, the scientist can continue to fill in the existing horizon, building up in a continuous way the known body of information (confirming predictions, refining calculations, etc.). This is what Husserl calls the "fulfillment" (*Erfüllung*) of a predelineated horizonal scheme. And it is also, of course, the everyday business of what Kuhn calls normal science. But it is possible, and sometimes necessary, that the horizon undergo revision, and that can occur only by a discontinuous revision or shift of horizons. Certain fundamental thinkers in a discipline, working at its boundaries, force a reorganization of the whole field of disciplinary activity. In the language of phenomenology, their work is carried out on the level of "regional ontology," that is, of the ontologically guiding and horizonal concepts within which all the work in their field is conducted.[17] The great creative geniuses work on and at the horizons within which their more pedestrian colleagues labor unquestioningly. The phenomenology of horizons explains the phenomenon of scientific revolutions.

The history of science is punctuated by these horizonal shifts which reorganize the data contained within the horizon. How, then, are we to think of scientific "progress"? Heidegger wrote in 1938, over two decades before Kuhn:[18]

> When we use the word "science" today, it means something essentially different from the *doctrina* and *scientia* of the Middle Ages, and also from the Greek *episteme*. Greek science was never exact, precisely because, in keeping with its essence, it could not be exact and did not need to be exact. Hence it makes no sense whatever to suppose that modern science is more exact than that of antiquity. Neither can we say that the Galilean doctrine of freely falling bodies is true and that Aristotle's teaching, that light bodies strive upwards, is false; for the Greek understanding of the essence of body and place and of the relation between the two rests upon different interpretations of beings and hence conditions a correspondingly different kind of seeing and questioning of natural events. No one would presume to maintain that Shakespeare's poetry is more advanced than that of Aeschylus. It is still more impossible to say that the modern understanding of whatever is, is more correct than that of the Greeks. Therefore, if we want to grasp the essence of modern science, we must first free ourselves from the habit of comparing the new science with the old solely in terms of degree, from the point of view of progress.

The individual scientist works within a projective horizon that sets forth its own standards of what is reasonable and scientific. Scientific theories belonging to different projective structures, operating within different constellations of basic concepts, may be compared and contrasted as to their presuppositions, and they may be compared in a general, holistic way, but they cannot be compared one on one, they cannot be submitted to a common measure (commensurated), in such a way that one can be labeled more rational or progressive than the other as a whole.

On a horizonal theory of the understanding, therefore, scientific development is not uniform and continuous, but at certain times must be shocked by more or less radical revisions of the existing horizons. But what in particular occasions such crises? What are the reasons that lead scientists to abandon the old horizon and adopt a new one? What place can the data gained under the old horizon assume within the new horizonal framework? Heidegger does not answer, or even ask, these questions in *Being and Time*. That is why I think that Kuhn's conception of scientific revolutions is not only congenial to the standpoint of *Being and Time*, but elucidates, works out, and corrects what is only a seminal suggestion in Heidegger. Indeed, Kuhn's approach is so preeminently in keeping with the hermeneutic conception of science which we are defending here that he himself has been led to describe his view as "hermeneutic."[19]

If Heidegger failed to investigate the character of the decision that the scientist makes at the point of crisis, when the old horizon wavers in instability and a basic shift is about to be made, Kuhn's account of this moment created a storm of criticism, including Imre Lakatos's famous observation that Kuhn reduced scientific decision making to mob psychology.[20] Kuhn might have avoided this criticism had he at his disposal the hermeneutic conception of *phronesis* that Hans-Georg Gadamer developed by listening to the young Heidegger's lectures on the *Nichomachean Ethics* and whose counterpart in *Being and Time* is the theory of *Verstehen*.[21] Heidegger and Gadamer were using the model of ethical intelligence (*phronesis*) to cast the general structure of understanding, while Kuhn was using a political one ("revolution"), which was more vulnerable to the mob psychology complaint. The Aristotelian model shows that the understanding does not always have explicit rules to fall back upon, that at certain critical points it is left to its own devices to grasp what the situation demands. This does not mean that for Aristotle we are sometimes driven to act wildly and irrationally. On the contrary, the understanding is never more faithful to its nature than it is in these moments where it is, so to speak, on its own. For it is precisely the work of understanding to make the first cut into the complexity of the concrete world, to find the nerve of intelligibility which runs through it. It is exactly at these moments, when it lacks rules to fall back upon, that intelligence must be what it most essentially is: insightful, capable of grasping what is

demanded in a concrete setting. It is to Gadamer's credit to have elaborated the notion of *phronesis* in an admirable discussion in *Truth and Method*,[22] and in so doing to have set forth an essential implication, not only of
Aristotle, but of *Being and Time*, for the theory of the sciences.

We should not fail to notice, moreover, that Heidegger's examples of
crises in fundamental concepts in the sciences cut across the spectrum of
natural, social, and human sciences, including in one sweep: physics, economics, and theology. Such revolutions affect *Wissenschaft* itself, in the
wide sense that this term has in German,[23] so that Heidegger means any
disciplined investigation, in which a particular region or field or object
has been staked off and thematized (objectified) in terms of a certain projection or conceptual organization. That happens both in theology and
physics, whose respective histories are punctuated by basic upheavals in
their fore-structures. Accordingly, one requires *phronesis*, hermeneutic
insight and understanding, a feel for what one is about, which Polanyi
calls "personal knowledge," across the board, in the natural, social, and
human sciences.

It is clearly a myth to think that there is a hostility or denigration of the
sciences in *Being and Time*. On the contrary, Heidegger brings to fruition in
this book the work he began as a student of Heinrich Rickert who, as a
leading Neo-Kantian of the day, had written extensively on the theory of
the sciences, a point clearly reflected in Heidegger's *Antrittsrede* at Freiburg
in 1915.[24] Heidegger is interested, not in undermining the sciences, but in
providing them with a hermeneutic accounting. In particular, he wants
to show that scientific activity, of whatever disciplinary type—natural,
social, or human—is nourished by a prescientific, historical life which is
its matrix and point of departure. He wants to explain how science is
"derived" from historical life (= "Being-in-the-world"), how it is ontologically generated from our concrete entanglement with the world, viz., by
a horizonal change-over from our primary and inescapable "concern"
with the world to a relatively disengaged projection of the world as a field
of objects. He wants to show that, while legitimate in its own sphere, any
such scientific projection is limited. Scientific projections are theoretical
constructions aimed at explicating a world from which we cannot finally
or wholly extricate ourselves and to which we belong more primordially
than science can say. It is always that prescientific belonging to the world
which has primacy for Heidegger. It is that world that Heidegger ultimately wants to elucidate. In so doing he does not intend to hold science
in contempt, but only in check. He delimits its claims by subordinating
science to the world in which we live, which has a prior claim upon us. If
science is made possible by a hermeneutic projection of a sphere of objects, it is also limited by the hermeneutic horizon of the scientist. A *pure*
scientific standpoint is thus an illusion; science is always a projective undertaking of Being-in-the-world or, as Johannes Climacus would say, of
poor existing individuals.

The "Essence of Technology" in the Later Heidegger

Heidegger's later writings on science and technology are marked by a dramatic change of tone.[25] The sober hermeneutic analyses, suffused with the technical vocabulary of phenomenology, give way to a voice of alarm and protest. The existential-hermeneutic genealogy of science is displaced by a critique of the *Wesen* of technology as a moment in the "history of Being," of what is coming to pass in the present age conceived now as an age granted by the movement of Being. There is a tone of urgency and shrillness as if responding to a danger taken to be imminent, even as there is a strange mystifying of the age as the movement of some force that is larger than human life and even larger than a merely human history. Heidegger is no longer concerned with a logic of science, not even an existential or hermeneutic logic, a genea-logic, but with the place of technology in the history of Being. Science belongs together with technology as inseparable forms of Being, as the will-to-power, the will-to-know, the will to dominate and manipulate, somewhat like what Michel Foucault calls "power/knowledge" except that now power/knowledge is taken to be a moment of Being's own story, not a film of micropractices covering the surface of our bodies. The "History of Being," like the history of "power," is one of those Gothic tales we have seen Richard Rorty complaining about. A useful point is about to be buried alive in a Big Story. Heidegger does not take technology to be applied science, but he thinks scientific understanding to be caught up in a logic of technological control that he calls the *Gestell,* the all-encompassing momentum of the times, the gathering power (*ge-*) which gathers all things, human and otherwise, within the sway of technical control and positing (*stellen*). The *Gestell* as the metaphysics of the will-to-power stamps our age, marks our epoch, dominating all the phenomena of our time, political and social, scientific and artistic. We are in danger of being swept away by an enormous totalitarian and totalizing movement which aims to bring every individual, every institution, every human practice under its influence.

Heidegger's protest, thus, is not directed precisely against science and technology, but against *Gestell,* which is their "essence," which means, what is coming to pass in a world in which science and technological thinking have acquired exclusive and exemplary status. He is not concerned with science and technology, but with the way being, human being, and truth are understood in this age, with the way they have all succumbed to the enormous success and growing prestige of mathematical natural science and the control, manipulation, and power over nature and ourselves that such science provides. The metaphysics that articulates the guiding conceptions of modern technological civilization is to be found in Friedrich Nietzsche's conception of the will-to-power. A dangerous momentum has been set loose in the modern world, one that conceives nature, and human being itself, as the raw material of a manipulative technology, that conceives all problems, political, social, and personal, as technological problems for which an appropriate technology of behavior is required. The world has become the raw material for the various technologies of power: political technologies that manipulate and control public opinion and policy; social technologies that manipulate and control personal mores and standards of conduct; educational technologies that insure the normalization and regulation of educational practices. It is not only nature that must submit to our control, but education, sexuality, the political process, the work of art, in short, the whole sphere of human practices. If children have easy online access to the *Encyclopedia Britannica* on the relatively inexpensive personal computers they have at home in order to look up the entry on Greek tragedy, whatever the children learn will be threatened by the mode in which they learn it. The felicitous ease of access sucks them into an understanding of how things work which is at odds with the experience of uncanny dis-ease the Greek tragedy teaches. The danger lies in what is coming to pass (*Wesen*) in science and technology, not in the sense of what is explicitly taught by science, but in the sense of frame of mind of a culture dominated by the success and ease of cybernetic control.

Heidegger's later work is a protest against the totalizing tendencies of late capitalism that has, up to a point, an intriguing kinship with the work of Emmanuel Levinas, Lyotard, Derrida, and Foucault in France; with Theodor Adorno's negative dialectics—despite the latter's well-known diatribes against Heidegger—in German social theory; and in the United States, perhaps with Paul Feyerabend. It is an oddly eloquent protest against normalization, regulation, manipulation, against the rule of the police. As a thought of *Gelassenheit*, it is a philosophy of freedom and letting be, of letting be the world and human being, and even letting the gods be. Unfortunately, in the course of lodging this otherwise salutary protest, two things go seriously wrong.

(1) Heidegger loses sight of his earlier, more careful, more perspicuous, hermeneutic suggestions about scientific practice. Thus, in his later writings, Heidegger speaks of science as if it were an unbending method which knows only how to apply fixed rules to unchanging circumstances, as if it were, by its nature, part and parcel of the disciplinary society, and even as if there are no human beings at work in science but some sort of overwhelming, irresistible force. Unhappily, he seems to forget what he said in *Being and Time* about understanding as *phronesis*, about the concrete historicity of the scientific investigator, about horizonal shifts and breakthroughs, crises and groundbreaking discoveries. And that is a regrettable development. For Heidegger's argument is with the totalizing forces which exploit science and which sweep it up in a vast political and economic armature, a complex of forces and power which knows no bounds. That argument would have been strengthened, not weakened, had he continued to insist, as he did in *Being and Time*, that science, in its

real practice and practical reality, as a hermeneutic work, is not the rigorously rule-governed, inflexible apparatus it is made out to be. That is why we need to hold the later Heidegger together with the early Heidegger, and among contemporary post-Heideggerian figures, to hold him together with both Gadamer and Derrida. We need an affirmative hermeneutic rendering of science that would make use of Gadamerian hermeneutics, and a vigorous protest against standardization, normalization, and ideological imperialism, such as we find in Derrida and in Foucault, and in recent French philosophy generally.

Heidegger's best side has always been to feel around for the world that precedes science, that funds it, that has its grip upon us long before science arrives on the scene, to which science always returns, and from which scientists are never granted leave. In *Being and Time* Heidegger characterizes this prescientific sphere in terms of the "factical world," which is the historical, cultural "life-world" Husserl describes in his phenomenology. In the later writings, Heidegger speaks of it in terms of a more poetically conceived life of "mortals," "under the skies," "before the gods," "upon the earth," a picture inspired ultimately by his readings of the poetry of Friedrich Hölderlin. In the movement from the earlier to the later writings, a more soaring vision, a more powerful mythology, than could be provided by the sober analytics of Husserlian phenomenology took the place of the more patient work of hermeneutics.

(2) The displacement of hermeneutics by mythology was bound to spell trouble. Heidegger's critique of the *Gestell,* as the essence of technology, was so massive, so monumental, so essentializing—so "Being-historical," as he put it—that it was not to be taken as the doing of any individual human being, or even of collective humanity, of *human* history, but the doing, the history, of Being itself. That massive essentialism began to overwhelm human considerations, began to inundate the fate of concrete human beings, of what he started out calling in the early 1920s "factical life," which was the starting point, the best point, of his entire philosophical work. This became painfully and embarrassingly clear when Heidegger began to offer pronouncements from the standpoint of the history of Being upon the condition of post–World War II Europe. To a continent brought to its knees by war, in which hundreds of thousands of people were displaced and homeless, Heidegger offered the advice that the "essence" of a housing shortage (*Wohnungsnot*) is not to be starving and out in the cold but to have lost one's relation to the poetic essence of dwelling, something that we might get over by giving thought to the essence of dwelling, whence it becomes a misery no longer![26] To a world which had just witnessed the explosion of the first atomic device on a civilian population, that contemplated the prospect of the destruction of all human life on the planet, he said that the real destruction and the "greater danger" really is to be found in the ruining of our poetic relation to things.[27] Finally, and most scandalously of all, Heidegger said

that the *Wesen* of modern agriculture and the *Wesen* of the gas chambers were essentially the same, inasmuch as both were implicated in the same darkening of the poetic nature of dwelling.[28] The utter bankruptcy of this *Seinsgeschicklich* way of thinking speaks for itself. It allows itself to adopt a standpoint—the "history of Being" or of the "essence of Being"—in which the distinction between agriculture and murder, or between Stalinism and the Western liberal democracies, is neutralized. Essentialization is always dangerous, but in Heidegger it acquires monumental proportions. The one thing that insulates us from and greatly minimizes the dangers posed by Heidegger's thought is that he writes in a way that only a few academic specialists can understand and they in turn write in a way that no one can understand.

Conclusion

Heidegger would have been better served by holding on to his earlier hermeneutical rendering of the natural sciences as the work of concretely situated investigators projecting nature in testable ways and to have laid off the mythology and the essentializing history of Being. The essentialism served the interests of his right-wing and elitist politics, his love of the German soil and language, which left everyone else unloved, unwelcome, and off to the side in the History of Being. The essentialism made it possible, almost inevitable, that he would lose sight of the factical fate of concrete human beings. The hermeneutic version of science was a refreshingly non-essentialist, projective, or constructionist account of scientific work, which explained how scientists get things right without embracing relativism, on the one hand, and without leading us to believe that scientists have dropped from the skies like avatars of the contemporary world, on the other hand, and—if I had a third hand—without implying that they signed a pact with the devil, and were his messengers, sent here to punish us for our sin of no longer speaking Greek.

We are better served by leaving Reality, Great Greeks, God, and the Devil out of the argument and taking natural science for what it is, an astonishingly successful and insightful way to conceptualize natural processes and to get a handle on them, one that unquestionably gets at things in a more disciplined and incisive way than do common sense or uncommon philosophical explanations like matter and form or a priori forms of intuition. But science need not, for all its success, be elevated to the status of some sort of Secret seizing upon the essence of Reality, and it need not suffer the fatal inflation of capitalization. Science is one more thing we do, and with some considerable success, we who are not sure what we are doing or who we are. It can improve our longevity, accelerate our prosperity, facilitate international communication and cooperation, and illuminate the history of the universe—Weinberg's *The First Three Minutes*[29] is a good case in point of that side of physics—which is its philosophically most suggestive side. It can and should also promote the interests of democracy, provided we have the sense to see that it belongs to the context of human life as a whole, that it is not outside the text of politics, social structures, gender, art, ethics, religion. We should, for example, on the one hand, have the good sense and the good will to be worried by the fact that computerization tends to leave the poorest people behind and to reduce society's need for the unskilled labor that the poor traditionally provide in order to earn a living. On the other hand, trying to situate science and technology in terms of some overarching or deeper essence like *Gestell* runs the opposite risk of demonizing it and of sending us all scurrying back to Greece or southern Italy to sit wistfully at the foot of the ruins of a Greek temple, weeping over the "The Origin of the Work of Art" and waiting for a god to save us. While the rest of the world, which has electricity, is on e-mail.

7

The End of Ethics

A Non-Guide for the Perplexed

Suppose we confess that we do not know who we are? Would that not mean the end of ethics, for, lacking the knowledge by which action is to be guided, how could we do anything other than wander about, two headed, without a trace to follow or a law to keep us safe? If no one claims to know The Way, which way are we supposed to go? If everybody is perplexed, there will be no one around to write a *Guide*. Would not this hermeneutics of not knowing who we are mean that all hell has broken loose? Would it not mean that the philosophers, having nothing to say about Good and Evil, can do aught but lend their voice to the general anarchy, to unchecked greed, the free flow of drugs, and widespread violence? Would it not mean that "anything goes," which can now be taken to be official, because even the philosophers concur?

In what follows, which pursues a particular ethics of not knowing who we are, I will defend the "end of ethics," which I take to mean that for certain philosophers—for this is a philosophical position, with all the usual complexities and perplexities that accompany such thinking—the business as usual of ethics has given out and the ethical verities that we all like to think are true, the beliefs and practices we all cherish, are now seen to be in a more difficult spot than we liked to think. The end of ethics is thus a moment of unvarnished honesty in which we are forced to concede that in ethics we are more likely to begin with the conclusions, with the "ends" or triumphant ethical finales we had in mind all along, and worry about the premises later. Waiting for firm theoretical premises to bolster and back up our ethical beliefs is a little like waiting for a proof of the veracity of perception to come in before getting out of the way of a tornado barreling down the highway right in our direction.

The end of ethics means that the premises invoked in ethical theory always come too late, after the fact. To this way of thinking, ethicians appear rather like the crowd that gathers around the scene of an accident to see what has just happened. An accident, of course, is something that no one saw (*theorein*) coming, although afterward everyone has something to say about it, up to and including insisting that the proper authorities should have seen that this would happen. So if there are "cases" in the end of ethics, the cases are casualties, "falls" (*casus*), stumbling over unforeseen difficulties and obstacles, the "accidents" that strike at us in daily life, that sometimes strike us down.

If anyone were courageous or foolish enough to produce a "guide to ethical theory" and wanted to give this view a place in an ethics book, then we might want to call it "accidentalism." An accident is something that happens to us beyond our control and outside the horizon of foreseeability, part of what Jacques Derrida calls the "coming of the other," for which, as we have seen above, we cannot really be prepared. Our theories and principles, whose whole aim and purpose is to prepare us for and help us foresee what is coming, were still fast asleep at this early hour of the day. The singular situations of daily life fly too close to the ground to be detected by the radar of ethical theory. Ethical life is a series of such accidents and casualties, against which ethical theory can provide little insurance. At least not when life gets interesting. Guides to ethical theory work best, if they work at all, for the more routinized, everyday, foreseeable decisions that do not demand much of us, decisions that are more or less programmable and decidable, decisions that so much resemble the past and are so stale that they have actually made it into the ethics handbooks, the "manuals." But as soon as something *new* or *different* happens ethical theory is struck dumb, the crowd gathers around the scene, and everyone starts buzzing, until finally it is agreed that we should all have seen this coming.

It is thus arguable that the discourse on the end of ethics has no place whatever in a "guide to ethical theory." For in such a discourse all our efforts are concentrated on what Johannes Climacus liked to call the "poor existing individual." Now one might think that Climacus's expression was redundant, that the adjective "existing" is unnecessary, but Climacus realized that in doing "theory" existence is the first thing to go. So the only guide for ethical life that thinking at the end of ethics can give to the existing individual is to shout "heads up," rather like the shout of "incoming" in the trenches, for one never knows what is coming. The end of ethics does not mean the end of concrete, "factical" life, as Martin Heidegger liked to call it, of making ethical decisions. On the contrary, it is trying to recall us precisely to the difficulty of such choices—but the end of "ethical theory," of "guides to ethical theory," in any strong, hard, virile sense, which pretends to show the way to the perplexed. For at the end of ethics, we always proceed in the blind, divested of the sure guidance theoretical seeing feigns to lend in advance as we negotiate the ups and downs of existence. In short, the end of ethics would have to be a bit of a black sheep in any guide to ethical theory, given its reluctance to be a guide, its recalcitrance about ethics, and its resistance to theory.

In the end of ethics, ethical judgments, decisions about what to do in concrete or "factical" life, are buffeted and beset by two difficulties. (1) They are not derived from a theoretical premise upon which they depend for their "justification." It is not as if, were the theoretical premise challenged or refuted, the existing individual would have to be sent home, thoroughly disheartened and disillusioned, knowing now that the ethical life and practice is over, refuted, shown to be a sham. Among other things, that would leave the existing individual with the further or intensified embarrassment of still having to live. (2) Ethical judgments occur in the singular, in the unprecedented and unrepeatable situations of individual lives. That means that we can never say a law or a principle is just, for that would be too sweeping and pretentious, the manifestations of its injustice being right around the corner, and certainly not that a human being at large is just—the more just the individual the less likely he or she is to make such a claim. At most, we might say, with fear and trembling, that a singular event was carried out with justice. But we would want to underline the "fear and trembling," lest an ethician who might by chance be standing in the crowd watching the proceedings rush out and phone his editor with the latest "principle," which will soon enough prove to be too sweeping. Such a principle will make good copy for the next guide to ethical theory, which will be published any day now, revised and updated, taking into account everything that has happened recently. It will of course fail to note what has not happened yet, which will be treated in the next revised and updated edition. That at least makes for a profitable business for the authors and publishers of such guides.

The Wholly Other

But why then does all hell *not* break loose? Have we not been painted into a corner, forced into the most erratic decisionism, compelled to lurch from decision to decision with no idea of what we are doing, or why, or what to do next? How are we to proceed if no one knows The Secret, if there is no one to show The Way or serve as The Guide? The way out of this seeming impasse is to stress what is positive or affirmative about what we are calling, not without a certain devilishness and a radically hermeneutical love of giving scandal, "the end of ethics." For thinking at the end of ethics is "affirmative" but without being "positive." That is to say, such thinking is through and through the affirmation of something it dearly loves, yet without setting out a positive position, a positive, rule-governed program about what to do and what not to do, about which such position takers are all too positive. The end of ethics means that the business of ethics is to be conducted with a little more fear and trembling than philosophers have been wont to show. To a certain extent, the end of ethics is a little bit like the death of God for people who still believe in God: it clears away the idols and allows a more divine God to break out. In the same way, the end of ethics clears the way for a more ethical ethics, allowing the ethicalness of ethics to break out, while insisting that most of what passes itself off as ethics is an idol. The end of ethics is also like the end of metaphysics for those of us who still believe in philosophy: it clears away the speculative brush in order to let the little sprouts and saplings of concrete factical life get some sun.

On the view that I am defending here,[1] everything turns on a specific affirmation, beyond any positivity or positionality, of the "other," the affirmation of—to borrow the language of Kierkegaard and Emmanuel Levinas,[2] which was later on taken up by Derrida[3]—the "wholly other," *tout autre*. As an affirmation of the wholly other, this view originates not in a no but a yes, not in a refusal but a welcome—*viens* and *bienvenue*—to the wholly other, opening our home to the stranger who knocks at our door like Elijah. Strictly speaking, the expression "wholly other" would mean something absolutely unthinkable, something so utterly alien to us that we would have no relationship to it at all, not something that we love and affirm. Something absolute and truly wholly other would just pass us by like a ship in the night. That would reduce the "wholly other" to a simple irrelevancy or even to a logical impossibility or contradiction in terms. So the expression "wholly other" obviously is a term of art for thinking at the end of ethics, and it can have several senses.

In one sense, which is futural, the wholly other means something that takes us by surprise in a radical way, something that in some important way we did not see coming. The wholly other refers to something importantly unforeseen, unanticipated, unexpected, for which we are unprepared, something that exceeds our horizon of expectation. Seen from the point of view of a classical ethics of virtue, this sort of thinking at the end of ethics cultivates the virtue, the excellence and *arete,* of openness to the other, the slightly paradoxical frame of mind of a radical hospitality in which one is ready to be surprised, ready to be overtaken by that for which one cannot prepare or be ready, a point that we explored above (chapter 2) in connection with Derrida and Hans-Georg Gadamer.

The way to think about the wholly other is to differentiate it from the relatively other, something that is, we might say, "merely new," which is what François Lyotard calls a new move in an old game.[4] In the merely new there is nothing really or radically new going on, but only some sort of new example or new instance of a form that is already familiar or in place, a new maneuver or strategy within an already agreed upon and familiar set of rules. A college basketball coach may design a new defense that completely confounds the opponents while abiding by all the current NCAA rules. An artist might make a new contribution, produce a new work of art, that remains within an existing art form while representing a new piece, a new example of the genre that exemplifies everything that the existing form stands for, or even takes it to a new height. Suppose, for example, that we found hidden away in some library basement archives the manuscript of a hitherto unpublished and unknown novel by Anthony Trollope, which was truly wonderful, and which included all the usual Trollopian gestures, the conflicts that arise when a member of one class wants to marry another, the unfair position in which young women are placed who are forced to secure their futures by way of marriage, the tensions between the partisans of high and low Anglicanism, etc. Or suppose we find a hitherto unknown Rogers and Hammerstein musical. Or an old Beatles recording that was lost and utterly forgotten. We would then encounter one more twist, one more novel innovation within the form or genre, which would deepen our understanding of the genre but would not force us to imagine some wholly different genre in order to understand it. Or suppose that in her dissertation, a young Ph.D. student in astrophysics supplied data and argumentation that demonstrated still one more implication of the big bang theory, in which she would show with some finesse and elegance that she certainly understands the workings of this theory, which her dissertation director happens to hold, but without changing basic assumptions about the theory as a whole.

But things get really interesting when something radically new, or absolutely new, happens, which is what we mean by the wholly other. For that would represent, to use Lyotard's formulation, not a new move in an old game, but the invention of a new game altogether. Then we are sent back to the drawing boards, forced to reexamine basic assumptions, a little bit stunned, shocked, amazed, and confused. When Marcel Duchamp takes a urinal, signs it, and places it solemnly upon a pedestal, and by so doing declares it a work of art, the critics are confounded and, rocked by the oddity and novelty of it all, they wander out of the gallery asking, "but is it art?" It is only when we are driven to the extreme of asking if it is art, or literature, or physics, that something wholly other is happening. For then the horizon of expectation and foreseeability is shattered and the basic assumptions that are shared by everyone who understood the old form have been shaken to their roots. When an artistic genre or a scientific paradigm is in place, that means that a "community" of practitioners has formed around it, a group bound together by their common understanding of the rules that the existing form obeys and the criteria by which new productions within the genre are to be judged. The works that are produced in the old form already have a preexisting audience and standards of judgment. But when something wholly new happens, the shared assumptions and the agreements about criteria are broken up, the preexisting audience is dispersed and this work is on its own. Then the new production will simply die of its oddity, perish of its own strangeness, or "catch on," which means that a *new* community and a *new* audience will form around it, and begin to conceptualize and formulate what has happened. By the time *that* has happened, the new work or production will have been imitated and assimilated, *new* criteria will have been formulated, the crowd of critics and commentators who have gathered around the scene to see what just happened, will have regained their composure. The owl of Minerva, as G. W. F. Hegel said, that is, the newfound wisdom and composure of the critics, commentators, and dissertation directors, manages to spread its wings only at the dusk of this long day. Only then can the critics explain to us what this is and why, really, given the rules of art, science, or basketball, it was inevitable that such a thing would happen, and indeed, though this is strictly between us, they themselves, privately, knew all along that it was bound to happen. Just about then something *else* happens, which utterly confounds them.

The end of ethics is very much oriented toward these surprises, these anomalous, unexpected, horizon-breaking events that leave us asking, "what is this?" What is going on? What is happening to us? What is going to happen next? Is this ethical? Is this humane? The affirmation that moves and inspires thinking at the end of ethics is the affirmation of something to come, something deeply futural, that we cannot foresee.[5] It does not merely brace for it but desires it, welcomes and affirms what is to come, because it always thinks the present is an enclosure that needs to be shaken loose and opened up so as to permit the emergence of the new and novel. It treats the rules that define the present situation with a certain provisionalness, as regulations temporarily in place, a temporary shelter taken before something else comes along that takes us by surprise.

The unforeseeability of the wholly other represents a kind of nemesis to the present that keeps the present off balance and prevents it from acquiring too much prestige. The affirmation of the wholly other is the affirmation that justice—since we are talking about ethics, justice is the issue—is always to come, that the present order can never be called just. Or that *democracy,* since politics should always be ethical, is not to be found in the empirical democracies all around us, but belongs more deeply to a democracy to come. The most unjust and undemocratic thing we can say today is that justice or democracy, at least in principle and in broad outline, is here, today, now, and we need only fill in the dots, while not getting too impatient about all the injustice and undemocratic oppression that surrounds us. This distancing of ourselves from the present is not only an empirical decision, not just a factual conclusion drawn from the observation of the many injustices around us, although it is also that.[6] Injustice, like the poor, we always have with us, and we can always count on the fact there will be more than enough examples of injustice to assure us that the present cannot lay claim to justice. The notion of the wholly other is the affirmation that justice is always to come, is always *structurally* to come, so that there will forever be a structural gap between the present and justice. The alternative is to say that justice is an idea that we more or less understand, the ideal end of inquiry, as in pragmatism, an ideal that we have made much progress in implementing, and that the present is an imperfect approximation of justice. The danger of that way of thinking is that it tends to promote "good conscience" about the progress we have made in reaching this ideal against which we measure the present, leading us to conclude that, despite the poor and wretched people all around us, we are not doing badly at all and it is time to go out and have a drink to toast our success. For thinkers at the end of ethics, that sort of thinking leads to a complacency with the present, a high level of tolerance for injustice, which can always be written off as a certain empirical shortfall, a temporary setback, over and against the ideal which is being implemented here and now, among us, we the chosen ones of historical progress. It is not much consolation to anyone to be told that the broken lives, ruined futures, children disabled from the womb, the ones being left out from these ideal visions, are so much empirical shortfall on the way to the ideal.

To be sure, the ever present press of injustice might produce despair and dejection, for the poor will be with us no matter what we do. That is why we insist on taking an affirmative tone, on an affirmation that proceeds from a love and desire for justice, from the affirmation of the least among us, of their needs and wants. Hence by insisting that justice is always to come, our aim is to expose the present to the white light of an absolute scrutiny which has zero tolerance for injustice, for injustice is all around us. What is to come is urgently needed now. On this telling, we can never have a "good conscience," which would be a complacent state of mind, but rather we have installed bad conscience as a kind of structural feature of ethical life. Citing a story from Maurice Blanchot, Derrida speaks of the notion of a Messiah who is never actually going to show up, a Messiah whose meaning or structure is never to be here, now, in the present, so that the Messiah is always, structurally, *to come*. In this story, when someone identifies the Messiah one day, dressed in rags, on the outskirts of the city, he approaches the Messiah and asks, "when will you come?" For the meaning of the Messiah is always that, to be the horizon of hope and expectation, and we should never confuse the coming of the Messiah, his *venue*, with actual *presence*. If the Messiah ever appeared in the flesh, that would ruin everything, for what have we left to hope for and expect? How could we ever have time and a future? In Christianity, where the faithful believe the Messiah did come and take flesh, they concluded that the world was over, that it was ending any day now, and that there was no more future. When it did not end, and they realized that the future was still open, they set about asking and praying, "when will you come *again?*" For this "when will you come?" is the key to having a future. The Messiah, or justice, or democracy—something—must always be to come, and the present is always to be pried open with hope and expectation, for the present is certainly not the messianic time, except as regards the past. That is Walter Benjamin's point: *we* today are the ones who were expected, to make right the wrongs suffered in the past.[7] To live in time is to hope in what is to come. Always.

I am not saying that we have no idea at all of justice, in which case we would not recognize injustice when we saw it. Justice always has to do with the wholly other, with the affirmation of the coming of the wholly other, with the promotion of the life of the wholly other, above all of those who suffer from their alterity, who are the victims of the "same."

But the singularity of the situations in which justice is to be realized, in which the wholly other is found, makes the prospects for justice, the prospective forms that justice will assume, unforeseeable, and forces us to stay open to the multiplicity of its possible forms. The multiplicity of justice, remarks Lyotard, is the justice of multiplicity.[8] If we put it in Kantian terms, Lyotard says, then the "concept" of justice is less like a category and more like an unrepresentable sublime.

The unforeseeable, unforegraspable character of the wholly other keeps us on our toes about the unfathomable difficulty that the future poses to ethical judgment. I have in mind the difficulties that arise from rapidly advancing medical technologies that make it possible, to choose among many examples, for infertile couples and lesbian women to have children, technologies that force us to distinguish between birth mothers and other sorts of motherhood and throw us into confusion about who or what a mother is. The classical patriarchal anxiety used to lie in finding ways for men to make sure that they were the fathers of the children of their wives, there being no question at all as to who the mothers are. Even if with some sanguinity we say that those patriarchal days are numbered now, still each day greets us with some new surprise about what is technologically possible, which raises the question of how to open to the future, to affirm what is to come, without doing more harm than good, while knowing that we cannot just resort to rules, for the rules were made for the old game, and that medical technologies change with such swiftness that the old games grow obsolete almost daily. Today, the latest challenge is the prospect of human cloning, something one does not see discussed in the ethics books of even a decade ago, which raises difficulties of unexplored complexity. Gregor Mendel, carefully working his little pea-garden, would not have been able to imagine the human genome project. Thinking at the end of ethics means that the most serious reflection is conducted at the frontiers, in the passage beyond the present borders, limits, or ends, where we are forced to think anew, to confront what we did not see coming, to cross over into foreign lands, to rethink what we thought we knew in the light of what now imposes itself upon us and impresses upon us how little we really did know.

Singularities

The wholly other takes still another twist that is captured in a famous phrase by Derrida which is trickier in French than English, *tout autre est tout autre*, "every other is wholly other."[9] That is a way of signaling the unfathomableness of the singular, of singularities, if we may pluralize the singular. The singular, we recall, is not a specimen of a species, a case that falls under a general rule, a particular subsumed under a universal, an individual member of a class. It is rather marked by its idiosyncrasy, its idiomaticity, its uniqueness, its anomaly, its unclassifiability, its unrepeatability. It is unprecedented, which is why it poses a problem for Anglo-

Saxon law, which loves precedents, and it is unrepeatable, so it will not give rise to general rules which the theoreticians and authors of manuals can rush to record and organize into a general system. The singular is something for which one cannot make a substitution: I can pay you to do a lot of things for me, to mow my lawn or plough the snow off my driveway, and I can get a machine to substitute for my labor. But I cannot ask someone else to bear my responsibility to you (not "ethically," anyway, although we get away with that sort of thing all the time). Or to die for me, which would only temporarily defer my own death, which I am not in the end going to outrun. The idiosyncrasy of the singular is resistant to all the resources we have to get hold of things, to get them within our grasp, to "conceptualize" them, if that means to grip them round about, to seize hold of them, to get them within our sights, to clutch them, know them, master them. When I am in a singular situation, faced with something singular, I do not have it, but rather it has me.

Of course, in some sense, we need concepts, as I have been conceptualizing all along in these pages. So we need to make our way by means of special "concepts," ones that do not grasp or pretend to dominate or totalize, which is why Lyotard prefers the "sublime" to "categories." The best sort of concepts are those which are internally structured to point to their own inadequacy, concepts whose meaning is to say that what we are here signifying exceeds our grasp. The most famous such idea was Saint Anselm's idea of God as that than which no greater (*majus*) or better (*melius*) can be conceived, or, as that which is greater and better than anything that can be conceived at all. That is a concept which says that whatever conceptual understanding one may reach of God, God is greater or better than that: God is in-finite by de-finition. The "concepts" of singularity or of the wholly other are also like that: they point to the excess of difference beyond the concept of what they signify. (Indeed, perhaps, if one is resourceful enough with evolutionary theory, one could even make the "concept" of the human "species" and human "specimens" dance.)

In the ethical situation, it is the singularity of the other which I encounter here, the utter singularity, the wholly other character of what faces me here and now, that I must settle into. The singularity of this situation makes demands upon me to which I must respond, elicits a choice from me for which I do not have the comforting recourse of universal rules. I must respond, be responsible, in a deep and radical way. If all I had to do would be to invoke a rule, pull the lever of a universal principle, it would be much easier—it would not take much agonizing, much fear and trembling—and it would be far less "responsible." If things turned out badly I could always blame the rule, the universal. "I would like to help you," injustice says, "but rules are rules." "I understand your situation," injustice declares, "but it is the principle of the thing that prevents me." "Don't blame me, I do not make the rules. I just work here. I am just doing my job." Seen thus, the singular is always the exception, the excess, that which exceeds and excepts itself from the sweep of universality, from the horizon of predictability and foreseeability.

Among the ancient Greeks Aristotle was the most sensitive to singularity, at least in his ethics, since as a biologist and a metaphysician he loved species and substantial form and unchanging being as much as the next Greek. At the beginning of his ethics Aristotle warned that if one loves precision one will hate ethics and should try mathematics, because in ethics we have to do with singular situations that defy precise prescriptions. The best we can offer, he said, is a general schema, one that it will be up to us to put into practice, to learn how to put it into practice, which is what he called *phronesis*.[10] *Phronesis* means having the wit to cope with the shifting circumstances of singularity that call for different things at different times. It is usually translated as practical wisdom, the wisdom to make practical judgments, and in the Middle Ages it was translated as *prudentia*. *Phronesis* is not just a matter of "application," of taking a universal and applying it, of accommodating an ideal to the imperfect circumstances in which it is to be realized, which is not *phronesis* but *techne*. In a technical judgment or application, I start with a perfect model or exemplar and try to realize it in imperfect materials. No existing circular object, try as hard as we might, can be made absolutely, perfectly, mathematically circular. No engineer ever succeeds in erecting a building as perfect as the one in the architect's blueprints. So in *techne* the passage from the ideal to the real, the universal to the singular, is a movement of loss of formal perfection, although we are glad enough to have the real material building and we cannot live in blueprints. The builder does the best he can and then he throws his tools on the truck and heads home.

But in *phronesis* the movement into the concrete represents an improvement, for the universal with which we begin in ethics is just a schema, a vague and general outline, and the movement into concrete practice (*praxis*) is an enhancement, a filling out, giving flesh and blood and detail to what was in the beginning only a vague or general idea. So Aristotle would tell us that courage as a schema is a matter of dealing with an approaching danger in a manner that is not too rash and not too timid. On the one hand, courage is practical wisdom not practical stupidity: it is not courage but foolishness to stand in front of a bus that is out of control in order to prevent it from crashing into a crowd of people. Nor is it courage to take off and head for shelter without taking a certain measured risk in warning others of the danger and helping them seek safety. But just how much is enough and not too much? Well, that is where the *phronesis* comes in; that is where one will have to use one's judgment, which one should have been practicing or exercising before now, in order to know how to decide what to do here and now, which depends upon the circumstances. Aristotle cannot decide that for us in advance. He cannot stand in our shoes, make our decisions. We are the ones who are responsible, not Aristotle. Aristotle has his own responsibilities. When one makes a decision, if it is a wise one, one will have taken a more or less empty schema and made it dance, rather than to have taken some perfect ideal and adapted it to limiting circumstances.

But even Aristotle, who is a sage commentator on these matters standing at the beginning of ethics and an antecedent figure for the thinkers at the end of ethics, is not enough. That is because Aristotle has a more settled view of things than they do. Aristotle thought the main problem facing ethical judgment lay in the movement from the general schema to the concrete situation, but he did not think there was a crisis in the schemata. The general schemata are the beliefs and practices we have grown up with, that we have grown up in, that have shaped and formed and nourished us and made us to be what we are. So the main thing we have to do is to assimilate them, to make them our own, so that we can keep them going, and keep ourselves going, in a living and innovative way, so that we will be able to judge wisely in the shifting sands of singular reality. Aristotle was looking for new moves in traditional games.

Furthermore, his *polis* tended to be a homogeneous, top down, aristocratic, rigidly closed little world in which barbarians took their orders from Greeks, slaves from free men, women from men, and craftsmen from the best and the brightest. The latter, Aristotle's *phronemoi,* are the well-bred, well-educated, proud and noble, good-looking men of practical wit and wisdom who get all the girls (or boys). They are the leisured set who get into the best schools and set the standards for everyone else, something like an honorable English "gentleman," over whom a munificent nature beams with pride, and upon whom everyone else was to keep their eye, with an eye to imitating them. ("Upstairs, Downstairs," the BBC *Masterpiece Theater* series, gives us a nice little glimpse of the sort of stratifications and gentlemanly ideal of the Greek *polis.*)

That is a bit too much for thinkers at the end of ethics, who would point to widespread and radical disagreement about the schemata, who affirm a radical plurivocity and heterogeneity of ways to live, who are radically egalitarian about matters involving men and women, rich and poor, upstairs and downstairs, etc. For them, the problem the singularity of judgment poses is not just a matter of moving from the universal to the particular but of assessing radically singular situations where the general schemata are in doubt. In the multi-cultural, multi-racial, multi-lingual world that is sometimes called "postmodern," where immigrants legal and illegal move freely about, where gay and lesbian rights are regularly defended, where medical advances throw us into confusion about who is the parent of whom, where human cloning is foreseeable, things are not so simple. Even Aristotle, smart as he was, would have a tough time telling us who the *phronimos* is today whom we are supposed to follow, for there are many prudent men, and quite a few prudent women too, straight and gay, white and black and in between, well-to-do and indigent, and they do not all agree. What we require now is a kind of *meta-phronesis*, the wit to move about in a world where there is no agreement about *the* good life, where there are many competing good lives, too many to count and tabulate, a world where there is no agreement about *the* person of practical wisdom, or *the* schemata. We must be more radically fixed upon the demands made upon us by the singular situation which is filled with surprises that upset the received or common wisdom, that resist schematization. We are required to keep our eye on the idiosyncratic demands that here and now are made upon us, which in a way demands everything of us, not moderation.

Gifts

That brings us to still another way that the singularity of the wholly other leads us away from the Aristotelian model. Aristotle defended a sensible idea of moderation, of setting out measured or mean states for ethical judgment to aim at, like a target that we do not want to overshoot (excess, hyperbole) or fall short of (defect). For thinking at the end of ethics, that is too tame and moderate, too sensible, middle range, and calculating a way of going about things. In short, it is not *affirmative* enough, for remember that the thinkers at the end of ethics have not come to denounce and deny things, but to affirm them, to affirm the other, the wholly other. Aristotle thought in terms of rules or schemata whose median mark we must somehow hit, like a sensible archer aiming at the center of the target. But this discourse at the end of ethics would rather have us think in terms of the *gift* and *giving*, which would favor the model of excess, of hyperbolic overflow.[11] This is more like an archer shooting arrows at the moon, a slightly mad archer—a divine madness, to be sure, as Plato would say—who would tell us that the point of archery lies not in hitting finite targets but in seeing how far into the air one may send one's shots.

Let us return to our notion of the special sort of "quasi-concepts" this discourse requires, concepts into which the idea of excess, rather than of moderation, has been built, concepts that are defeated by admitting into them the notion of a limit, like Saint Anselm's beautiful idea of God. God's measure is to be without measure. God is the sheer excess of never containable or comprehensible excess, Who is always more than anything we say or think, which is a kind of auto-maximizing idea. Thinkers at the end of ethics want to import this notion of unending excess or maximization into our relationships with one another, while lamenting the limits and measures that ethics is always seeking.

What better example of such a concept than love? Thus, far from letting all hell break loose, the excess that those who think at the end of ethics have in mind has more to do with letting love break out. If someone asks us whether we love them, and, after a long pause, considerable deliberation, and a nervous shuffling of feet, we respond, "well, yes, up to a point, in certain respects," then, whatever it is we feel, it is not love, for love is unqualified, unconditional. The measure of love is love without measure. The condition under which love is possible is that love be given without conditions, unconditionally. Love is that of which we can never have enough. We may ruefully conclude that our love was misguided and misdirected, but there is never too much love. Love is something we "give" and we give it without return, without expectation of a reward. To love someone is to love them for themselves, not for ourselves or for what may come our way as a result of this, for then we would not love them but ourselves. Some people love God, Meister Eckhart said, the way they love their cow: for its milk. Love is not an economic exchange in which I invest my love in someone with the expectation of gain or profit, of being compensated later on, at the point when my love will be rewarded. I was not in it for the reward but for the love, which is "without why," as Meister Eckhart said. Love does not transpire in an "economic" time, in which I think the time now spent loving is well spent because it will come back later on in the form of numerous remunerations.

This notion of giving and loving has the interesting effect of making a certain amount of difficulty for the idea of "duty," which is the basic stock-in-trade of ethics. My duty is what I ought or should do, what I "have to" do, must do, not with a physical necessity, to be sure, but a "moral" one, so that if I do not do it, I am guilty or in the wrong. That means that if you help me because you are always dutiful in meeting your obligations, you are helping me because you have to, because you must or should or ought to help me, which is better than being guilty or in the wrong, which is most unpleasant. But you do not help me because there is anything about me or my situation in itself that prompts or motivates or calls upon you to help me. Well, frankly, in that case, if it is all that disagreeable to you, I would rather that you not bother. Immanuel Kant thought he could improve the idea of duty by distinguishing (a) doing things that are merely "according to" duty—I might, for example, serve others (do my duty) because I enjoy the sense of dependence upon me that this produces in them—from (b) doing things that are done "for the sake of duty," doing it because I ought to and only for that reason. While that distinction is useful for showing that when it comes to duty we should not be out for self-gratification, and that we should have pure intentions, not selfish ones, it ends up making things worse. For on Kant's telling, it would actually be easier to be ethical, and certainly easier to tell if someone were being dutiful, if they had a positive, physiological dislike for their duty. Once again I would rather you not bother. On this point, the Aristotelian idea of an ethics of virtue, of *arete*, however aristocratic and snooty, has it all over Kant's "deontology," which was however very democratic.

My idea is to make this whole idea of duty tremble. That of course leaves the ethicians gasping for breath, their pupils dilated, their fingers pointed in disbelieving horror at such an unholy suggestion. But I pray you, before the execution is carried out, allow me an explanation.

What is good and salutary about a duty is what I will call its "heteronomic" component, that it comes from without and overtakes me, that it shocks and rocks the circle of the "same" (me) with something coming from without, from the outside, from the other side, so that I am no longer locked up inside the imprisoning walls of the self and am called upon to respond to the other. What I like about the idea of duty is the check it puts upon the "I" and "me" and "mine," those formidable pronouns so much loved and favored by Narcissus. What I like about duty is what is called the "call of duty," for when duty calls, that is the call of the other calling me beyond myself, so that I am no longer confined to the sphere of I and me and mine. (After a while, all that solitude becomes boring and I desire to escape.) But what is not so good, not all that salutary, not all that wonderful about duty is—apart from the fact that duties tend to come as rules that bind us to universals while blinding us to singularity, about which I have already complained long and loudly enough—is the way a duty blocks a *gift*. To "give" someone what is their "due" is to do my duty, and not truly to give a gift. When I pay my loan back to the bank, they send me a letter that says thank you, but everybody understands that if I did not pay my loan back the next letter I would get would be from their lawyers, so there should be no illusions about getting or giving gifts from bankers, especially if we read the fine print on their "offers." Lawyers try to do things *pro bono,* for the good of it, and that is to their credit. Of course, if we give them too much credit, then they get a return, and it turns out to be a prudent thing (good for business) for law firms to encourage their lawyers to do, especially the young junior associates who want to become partners. Then it is not *pro bono,* not really, or *pro deo,* but mostly *pro meo.*

To give a gift (like love) is to do precisely what I do not have to do or to do something for which I do not expect a payback. That, it is turning out, is hard to do. So, far from being a license for an "anything goes" anarchy, the end of ethics is asking for something difficult and rare. To give a gift is to do *more* than duty requires or self-interest permits. The whole idea of a gift is to go beyond what I have or must or ought to do. That means that the idea of a gift is parasitic on the idea of duty, for without duties there would be nothing to exceed. Hence, if ethics is concerned with duties then I am "against ethics." I think that we should put an end to ethics, not in the sense of calling it off and ending it, or of putting an end to the ethicians, but in the sense of de-limiting it, of setting off its limits or ends, and showing that things only start to get interesting when we get past duty. We have to have duties and laws, in order to protect the weak against the strong. Laws and duties have to have force, teeth, a bite, because we cannot run a railroad, or the banks, on gifts alone. We cannot depend upon gifts in a world as violent as ours. We cannot depend upon the love of giving gifts to motivate bankers, stockholders, or the chief executives of tobacco companies. We need the law and we need a salutary fear of the law. We might here invoke an old distinction that Saint Augustine made between a *timor servilis* and *timor castus*. On the one hand, a "servile fear" is the fear of being punished for wrongdoing. In Augustine it is the fear of being banished from God, the fear of going to hell, with which the Jesuits filled young Stephen Dedalus in that unforgettable retreat that Stephen took in *Portrait of an Artist as a Young Man*. The fear of being punished is not all bad (so long as it is not pathological!); it keeps a lot of bankers and lawyers honest. But it is far from the best. A "chaste fear," on the other hand, is the salutary and affirmative fear of offending God. In Levinasian terms, we might say a servile fear is the fear of suffering violence, while a chaste fear is the fear of doing violence, the fear we have of our own violence, the fear of using others for our own ends, of doing everything for our own good and not the good of others, the fear we have that in the end everything will come back to the I and me and mine.

To be sure, there is no way to extinguish the love of self, which would not necessarily be an entirely salutary thing to do in the first place. The idea is, as far as possible, to check the way the self tries to insinuate itself into even our best intentions, to find a way of getting a return out of even the most disinterested gestures. What better way to prove oneself the finest of fellows than to give disinterestedly to the other! Such inner self-congratulation, such silent, heightened self-esteem, is no less a return upon our funds than a testimonial dinner in one's honor, full of fine speeches about our generosity. The best we can do is, as Derrida once said, to concede that there are only degrees of narcissism, ranging from the meanest and most self-interested up to the most open and hospitable, which is where the gift, "if there is one" (*s'il y en a*), is to be found.[12]

Laws and duties, as opposed to gifts, are lower level, structurally blind, coercive structures that we might think of as like training wheels on a bicycle: every cyclist begins with them but they are ludicrous beyond a certain point and every free-wheeling cyclist has long ago thrown them off. Accordingly what I am after is a *non-coercive heteronomy*, a call coming from the other that does not boil down to a rule or a coercion but rather, let us say, a call or invitation, an address—the call coming from the other—to which I respond. Then I can be responsible beyond or without duty, and duties will prove to actually get in the way of genuine responsibility, the ability to respond, to answer, in the form of the gift, without coercion, since an uncoerced response is better than a coerced one. So laws and duties are not enough. I agree that things will not work without laws and duties, but what interests me is how much of an ob-

stacle and blockage laws and duties are to good workings and the free
flow of our lives. Beyond laws and duties we need gifts. Gifts are necessary. So what I am arguing is slightly paradoxical: gifts are necessary, even
though the idea of a gift is the idea of what is not necessitated, of what we
did not need to do. When we receive a gift, one of the things we say is
"you didn't have to do that!" That is true. The gift is what we did not have
to do, but if we do not do them, things will fall apart. The gift obeys the
paradoxical logic of the supplement: the gift is something extra, something you do not have to do, but we need them, and if we do not have
them then something important is missing, something we need. The supplement comes as something extra but all the same we need it.

Let me give two examples: marriage and the schools.

Consider a marriage in which the partners were strictly guided by their
mutual duties to each other. They would each perform their marital duties, dutifully do what each is required to do, nothing less but nothing
more. They would undoubtedly have made a prenuptial agreement (contract) about how to protect their separate interests were they later to
separate and divorce (which in this case we could all have predicted!).
When one could use a little extra help, the other would decline on the
grounds that he or she was not duty bound to do it. The marriage would
turn on a balance of payments, of settling disputes on the basis of whose
rights were being violated. Neither of them would put themselves in the
wrong for the sake of the love. Their lives would not be punctuated by
the multiple acts of loving generosity and gift giving that make marriage
sweet (when it is sweet), that fill the air of the marriage with love. For a
marriage requires what is not required; what it needs is for each to do for
the other what neither needed to do, again and again.

Now one might object that this is a loaded example, for a marriage is a
community of love and not (just) of law, to begin with. We need laws to
protect marriage partners, particularly to protect women in a patriarchal
world, or to protect gay and lesbian partners in a heterosexual world, but
nobody would say that laws are enough to turn the wheels of a marriage.
True enough. But the delimitation of law and duty that I am advocating
goes beyond communities of love, like marriages and families, and applies to institutions, which nobody is likely to confuse with a community
of love.

To see this, I turn to my second example, the schools. When public
school teachers are sufficiently aggravated by their school boards, when
their negotiations for the next contract reach a stalemate, they will sometimes threaten to "work the contract." That means that they will do their
duty, nothing less and nothing more, precisely what is called for in the
contract. The law, the contract, will be all in all, and everything they do
will be contracted to the contract. That means that they will not direct
"*extra*-curricular activities," will not get to school a little bit earlier to help
a student out, or stay a little later, or make a call to a parent that evening,

or make a little *extra* effort with a student who needs a little *extra* attention, or in general do any of the myriad of micro-acts of generosity that lubricate the system and make it work. We cannot have a purely economic order devoid of gifts, or if we do, it will be hell, a nightmare, like a world in which the lawyers run everything, in which nobody does anything without compensation and unless it is mandated by law and under the threat of a lawsuit. So the gift on the part of the teachers is necessary; it is the little extras, the things that teachers do not have or need to do, that we really need and make a difference. The school boards, who represent the taxpayers, are, in contrast, no less bound by the gift, by the need to do what they do not need to do. The schools, the children, represent the future that they will not live to see, so what they are doing cannot be confined to economic time. They cannot exchange the present expenditures for a future return, for they will not live to see the future in which this investment will return a profit. If the schools are an investment in the future, it is not a future they will inhabit. So the taxpayers can either do what they have to do, meeting the requirements to keep the schools open and functioning, while keeping as much money in their pockets as they can get away with, and that is all, or they can give without the expectation of a return to a future that they will not live to see.

What is true of the schools is true of any institution, commercial or governmental, national or international. The workplace, *any* workplace—from factories to universities to law firms—is hell to live and work in precisely to the extent that it is driven entirely by law, contracted to the demands of the contract. The laws are needed, and who would deny this, to get us past the sweatshops and dusty mines which ground the lives and health of workers into the ground. But laws are not enough. When workers will not do anything they are not required to do, when they will not make an extra effort to do something well, when they will not spend an extra moment that is not mandated by the clock, then the work will not be done well and they will be miserable on the job. When employers are not generous with employees, when they will not do anything more than is spelled out in the contract, they will turn the place into a living hell. When a nation's leaders and the electorate that elected them treat the nation's weakest and most defenseless citizens in the most rigorous and parsimonious way, and tell them that the rest of us are not responsible for them, that they are on their own to raise their fatherless children, to get off drugs, to get a job, and to climb out of poverty, they will turn the nation into hell. When nations erect walls of laws around themselves, subjecting refugees and immigrants, legal and illegal, to the most rigorous immigration laws, demanding application fees that such people above all cannot afford, when they offer the others, the *tout autre,* of other nations the minimum of hospitality, the minimum that international law requires, they turn the earth, which on a more generous reading, belongs to us all, into hell.

Conclusion

The end of ethics does not mean that all hell has broken loose. Far from it. It is precisely hell that we seek to avoid by this slightly insolent talk about bringing ethics to an end. It is a question not of leveling the laws but of loosening them up, not of demolishing the rule of law but of opening the law to the singularity of the singular individual, which is all there is, after all. *Sola individua existent.* In raising hell with ethics and with guides to ethical theory, we are not taking sides with hell itself. On the contrary, we make a certain contact with the kingdom of God. Man is not made for the Sabbath, Jesus said, but the Sabbath for man. His attitude toward rules and law bought Jesus a lot of trouble in his day. For Jesus, too, on my telling, belongs to the tradition of those who called for the end of ethics, who thought the individual who strayed (the singular) is more important than the hundred (the universal), who counted every single and singular tear and every hair on our head, who flaunted the Sabbath laws, who dined with sinners, and took the side of the outcast and the stranger. He also had a powerful notion of "forgiveness"—a particularly potent form of "giving"—which is a little shocking and even gives scandal to those who are intent on seeing injustice "compensated," on seeing the debt of "guilt" paid off, who are in general are not inclined to let sinners take a walk, a streak that is not absent from those who claim to follow Jesus. It should be added that Jesus was not picking a fight with the Jews in all this but rather, as himself a Jew, picking up on a Jewish prophetic tradition that took the side of the "widow, the orphan, and the stranger" against the powers that be. This streak surfaces today in the work of Levinas, who has made his way into the forefront of contemporary continental philosophy and into the pen of such writers as Lyotard and Derrida, who are not, by any conventional standard, very "religious," except with that religion without religion that I have defended. But that is as it should be among thinkers who are not impressed with boundaries, limits, and confining definitions, or with contracting contracts. The followers of philosophers such as Derrida and Lyotard love to sing the praises of the "other of philosophy," but they turn pale and grim, and then grow red in the face, if ever it is suggested that religion, too, is the other of philosophy, for when they said "other" all they meant was literature, Friedrich Nietzsche, and the death of God. It never occurred to them that somebody would try to resurrect the dead God on them. They did not see that coming. Had we time enough and space, it would repay our efforts to follow up this biblical streak in what we are saying, for it is not Aristotle or Kant or Nietzsche who can show the way here. In the final section of this book I will take up the question of faith and biblical texts, and we will hear a little more about biblical life.

In sum, the discourse on the end of ethics, which proceeds from the unvarnished honesty of confessing that we do not know who we are, means setting off the ends, limits, and boundaries of ethics. It means to insist upon the provisionalness of ethical rules, upon the inaccessibility of the singular to ethical universals, the unforeseeability of the future to ethical mandates, and the excess of the gift beyond ethical moderation and duty. This discourse proceeds on the belief that ethics ends where singularity begins, which means where existence begins, since singulars are the sole existents. When the seas of singularity get rough, when the winds of existence blow up, ethics generally goes below. When things get difficult and the way is blocked, ethics is nowhere to be found. Just when we need ethics the most, we find that ethics has tipped its hat, politely made its excuses, and quietly slipped out the back door, leaving us poor existing individuals to face the worst.

Part 3

On the Road to Emmaus

In Defense of Devilish Hermeneutics

8

Holy Hermeneutics versus Devilish Hermeneutics

Textuality and the Word of God

In the present and next two chapters, I continue to defend my devilish hypothesis that we do not know who we are, and that we have no access to The Secret, even and especially when it comes to divine revelation, which is precisely where one would think we actually *do* have a Heavenly Hook to bail us out and lift us above the flux of undecidability. What else does "revelation" mean if not that The Secret has been "revealed" to us, has been handed over to us courtesy of a very "Special Delivery?" Here if anywhere, surely something *has* dropped out of the sky, so to speak, the heavens have opened up and given us a Hint that we are on the right track. Certainly, it would be the height of irreligion to deny that with divine revelation, we are admitted into a heavenly secret or two that relieves us of the difficulties with which we have been struggling in the previous two sections of this book. Is not revelation precisely the revelation of a Secret? Surely these difficulties are problems only for the infidels, while the faithful, in virtue of their faith, have a holy hermeneutics at their disposal, having been granted a special hermeneutical leave or exemption from the flux? Not so. I will stick to my guns, even at the risk of making this more radical hermeneutics look a little devilish. The devil after all, in the form of *advocatus diaboli,* serves an honorable ecclesiastical function.

The Road to Emmaus: Revelation and the Secret

As the gospel of Luke draws to a close, the sacred writer recounts the following story (Luke 24:13–35). On the third day after Jesus was crucified, two disciples, one named Cleophas, the other unnamed, were walking to a small village called Emmaus, about seven miles from Jerusalem. Along the way, they are joined by the risen Jesus, whom, Luke says, they were prevented from recognizing. Jesus wants to know what they were talking about, what *logoi* they were exchanging, what *logoi* filled the air as they made their way to Emmaus. The disciples, surprised that this stranger did not know the latest news, said that of course they were talking about the crucifixion of Jesus of Nazareth. Cleophas and his friend were, in particular, astir with a report from "some women from our group" that the tomb in which the body of Jesus was laid had this very morning been found empty and that these women were told by angels that Jesus was alive. The men in the movement had gone to the tomb and checked out this womanly story and had indeed found an empty tomb. Jesus replied that the disciples—these men—were foolish, and slow of heart to believe —their hearts (*kardia*) are slow, tardy (*bradeis*) when it comes to faith and believing (*pistenein*). Slow of heart, and not a little slow of wit and slow to discern—that is how the male disciples are also criticized in the gospel of Mark. They do not know how to read signs, to discern, to make their way among traces. They are sadly lacking in hermeneutic skill. For was it not written in the prophets that it was necessary that the Messiah would go through all these things and only then enter his glory? That, truly, can be shown, Jesus said; it is a matter of *hermeneutics,* of knowing how to read. So Jesus did some hermeneutics for them: "And beginning with Moses and all the prophets he interpreted (*diermeneusen*) to them the things about himself in all the scriptures" (Luke 24:27).

Jesus, of course, was trying to tell these slow-witted disciples two things at once, but he was too fast for them. There was a kind of *double entendre* here, or a double gift. He was telling them that if they could *read* they would know that all these things were necessary in order that the scriptures be fulfilled. What had transpired in Jerusalem should not have dispirited them but should have been viewed as the fulfillment of the scriptures and the confirmation of the coming of the Messiah. But he was also telling them, slow-witted fellows that they were, that here, in this dazzling exhibition of hermeneutic skills they were witnessing, was the risen Messiah, right before their eyes. But they did not get it, not yet; their eyes were not yet opened.

At this crucial point in the formation of the new church, at this crucial juncture for the movement, and precisely in the face of the empty tomb and the failure of these disciples to recognize him, what was *required* was hermeneutics. The skies did not open up, the heavens did not sound forth, the earth did not tremble or the sun go dark. No uninterpreted fact of the matter was lowered on a cloud. Instead, Jesus took Scripture in hand and offered the disciples a *hermeneutic* of how the coming of the Messiah can be found in the Book, if one knows how to read. One has to have a certain amount of patience with the sluggishness of the disciples. These matters are not obvious and it is hard to read a highly complex book, especially when one is looking for figures of something to come, since one is likely to see all sorts of things that are not there, and there are any number of things one may make of an empty tomb.

In any case, the hermeneutic skill that Jesus displayed should have put Cleophas and his friend on the alert. The way Jesus opened up the scriptures for them should have opened their eyes, should have lifted whatever blockage prevented them from recognizing him, that he who was reading to them was the one of whom the text was written. But, Luke says, these two disciples were not too swift.

Having done what he could for them, Jesus seemed about to walk on ahead without these slower disciples, but they prevailed upon him to stay and pass the evening with them in the village. Then, at the evening meal, Jesus "took bread, blessed and broke it, and gave it to them." Then it finally hit them, they who were slow of step and slow of wit. Whatever had blocked their sight before and had retarded their faith was lifted by the sight of Jesus breaking bread. The communal meal, the open commensality: when they remembered Jesus, they remember sharing a meal with him, and they remember that he was not afraid to risk his reputation and share a meal with anyone, no matter how disreputable they were thought to be. Once again, he did not perform a miracle, some supernatural intervention or contravention of the laws of nature. He just broke bread. Then they got it. So the disciples passed through three stages on the way to Emmaus. (1) An initial state of dispiritedness—we thought he would redeem Israel, we were inspired by him, and here he is dead; and blindness—they could not read the scriptures in the right way or recognize the risen Lord, like the men who were checking on the women's story and "saw not" (*ouk eidon*). (2) An intermediate state of hermeneutic understanding of what the written scriptures said, but still without recognizing that the one of whom the scriptures spoke, the fulfillment of the scriptures, was walking along the road with them. (3) A final eye-opener, a decisive hermeneutic breakthrough, and a renewed inspiration, when Jesus broke the bread and it finally it landed on them. "Then their eyes were opened and they recognized him." At long last, after Jesus had connected all the dots for them, they got it.

Just at that moment, at the exact moment of recognition and inspiration, when they finally knew how to view what was transpiring, Jesus disappeared before their very eyes. He became "invisible," a-phantic (*aphantos*), a spirit, divesting himself of every trace of phenomenality, trusting now that the disciples, who had been taught to read and given new hermeneutic skills, would be able to make it in his absence on faith and reading, would know how to read the scriptures and the empty tomb, without his visible presence to sustain them. Now they say, after Jesus disappears, that their hearts, previously slow to believe, were burning within them as he laid open these texts and revealed for them what was written.[1]

So the story associates faith with knowing how to read, and knowing how to read with getting to see and understand, and it emphasizes to the disciples that we are slow of foot, slow of wit, and slow of heart.[2] The seeing depends upon the believing and the believing depends upon reading. We have to know how to take the hermeneutic cue in order to see what is going on, even if it is right before our eyes. The empty tomb makes sense for us but only if we know how to take it, what to make of it. Furthermore, we get to believe by knowing how to read: how to read the scriptures, the written word, in the first place, and then how to read the living word, the life and deeds of Jesus, how to recognize the signs of the Messiah in breaking bread. Faith comes from, comes *as,* a certain hermeneutic, a way of understanding, a way of taking things, of reading signs, of making our way through the play of traces.

All of that we are told in a story, a story about reading, a story we need to know how to read.

The Friends of Cleophas

Christianity is a story that at a crucial point depends upon knowing what to make of an empty tomb. We are all in the shoes of the disciples on the way to Emmaus. Indeed, the *unnamed* friend provides an opening for each of us to write ourselves into the story, to imagine ourselves as the friend of Cleophas making our way along that dusty road, dispirited and bewildered, feeling defeated by the adversities we encounter and confused by the undecidability of the signs we try to discern. We who do not know who we are find ourselves right there in the gospel: we are the unnamed friend of Cleophas. Christianity is a religion of the Book which depends upon knowing how to read, how to read the Jewish scriptures, how to read the signs of the life and death of Jesus, like Cleophas who picked up what was going on when this stranger blessed and broke bread. There is no escaping the textuality, the play of traces, no faith that is not a certain *hermeneia.* That is why there is nothing irreligious, no attack upon religion, God forbid, in this devilish, deeply deconstructive and more radical hermeneutics I advocate. On the contrary, I maintain that textuality, undecidability, and the notorious *différance,* enter into the structure of sacred texts, divine revelation, and religious faith—and that they even make their way into the deepest recesses of mystical life, where all is supposed to be silent and secret—making these events possible just as they make them impossible, which is to say, just as they delimit them.

I wish to enlist the services of this devilish hermeneutics to address three *aporias.* An *aporia* means "Do not Enter. No way out" (and upon seeing such a sign any sensible driver would turn around and head in another direction):

(1) How can we speak of the word of God? How can we speak of God "speaking," and if speaking, then also writing? How could the "words" of God be written down? Does this speech and writing, this sacred *écriture* have a grammar, a vocabulary? Can it be "translated?" How can we interpret and understand the words of God? Do the words of God let us in on The Secret? Do any interpreters of these words enjoy special privileges? (chapter 8)

(2) What are we to make of the empty tomb? How are we to go about interpreting it? What sort of hermeneutic skill do we require to negotiate this emptiness, this silence? (chapter 9)

(3) Is not this concern with words and speaking finally laid aside in mystical prayer, in the silent union of God and the soul, a kind of rapture in which we finally complete the journey to Emmaus and know The Secret? Should we not say that we should say nothing of God? Apart from the fact that this would be an odd result to reach for a religion of the Book, we must also ask why so much is written about the need to say nothing of God. Why are those who counsel silence—like Meister Eckhart, for long my favorite example of this sort of thing—among our most powerful preachers and prolific writers? Why is mystical silence so prolix, so eloquent, so loquacious, such a magnificent part of spiritual "literature"? (chapter 10)

Devilish Hermeneutics and the Hors-Texte

As one of the three great religions of the Book, Christianity has no small investment in what is said about books and writing, about words and *écriture*, about the question of the text and the *hors-texte*. The problem, of course, lies in the paradoxical power of the sign, which resides precisely in its ability to function in the absence of the signified. That power worried Edmund Husserl, who wanted to return the intention to its fulfillment, to fulfill the sign with the intuitive presence of the signified, in order to avoid the "crisis" precipitated by the absence of intuition. But Jacques Derrida pointed out, in a study that is devilishly difficult in its detail, that the whole power of the sign that Husserl had touched upon lay in the opposite direction, in the *emancipation* of the signifier from intuition. For we would move slower than the disciples on the road to Emmaus if we had to pause to fulfill, to intuitively redeem, every signifier every time we used it. Everything—traditions, institutions, theoretical physics, literature, sacred scriptures, and daily newspapers—all depend upon the ability of the signifier to function in the absence of intuition, which vastly extends our reach. The letter, the trace, at once links us to a presence, an Origin, that is no longer present, even as it thereby separates us from it, supplying the substitute or supplement of the Origin, since the Origin cannot always be there and the letter extends its life for those who are too late for the Origin, making up for their tardiness.

So if one day some devilish fellow comes along,[3] yea if the fool says in his heart, *"il n'y a pas de hors-texte,"*[4] that will raise an eyebrow or two among the faithful. For the Christian tradition is a tradition that springs from a Book, from words about the Word Who pitched his tent among us and is not locked inside a text or book, not even the Book. The Divine Word is a word *outside* the text, if ever there was one! So if we are going to insist upon textuality and if we thereby associate ourselves with the fool or the devil, it will be necessary to understand what we are getting ourselves into. What does this denial of the *hors-texte* mean?

According to deconstruction and its famous quasi-transcendental unprinciples, *écriture* and *différance*, which are principles of temporal deferral, the "origin" or "living presence" of which the letter writes, the absolute beginning, is always already "deferred." The letter, accordingly, is marked by an irreducible "undecidability," the written word being, as Plato wrote, an orphan whose father/author is no longer on hand to resolve whatever difficulties the written word may get itself into. As orphans, texts do not interpret themselves. Even if Origins are written in stone, that is still writing, something that Aaron pointed out to Moses in Arnold Schoenberg's opera.[5] Even lapidary inscriptions are still instances of *écriture*. Somebody has to learn the vocabulary and grammar of the lapidary language and put a gloss on it, which is the beginning of hermeneutics. Founding intentions are never unambiguous and cannot be kept absolutely safe. As soon as something is entrusted to the safety of language, is committed to words, an argument breaks out about the right interpretation—about the syntax, the etymology of the words, the usage, the context, the intention of the author, what the original audience would have been assuming, what the common presuppositions of everyone involved were, etc. As soon as something is said or written down, the play of traces is engaged and there is no dodging the difficulties one has bought for oneself. A tradition founded upon a text, whenever it is examined closely enough, never fails to stir with suppressed sub-traditions and counter-traditions that formed around conflicting interpretations of the text. Because a tradition "harbors within it dominant structures, discourses, which silence others, by covering over or destroying the archive, a tradition is certainly not homogeneous."[6] A deconstructive analysis forces a textual tradition back to its founding or originary acts but invariably in such a way as to bring us to see that an absolutely originary act eludes it, that it always recedes behind the trace it leaves behind, and necessitates constant interpretation and reinterpretation. Put more polemically, there never was an absolute Origin.[7] Instead of an Origin we find only a supplement, instead of an absolute beginning, a series of slightly undecidable substitutions. We are always like Cleophas and his friend, a little baffled, not sure what is going on. It is necessary, as Derrida reminds us in one of his most recent works, to avoid confusing the *arche* with the "archive," the pure beginning in its absolute start, if there is one, with the record left behind, the store of memory, the historical memory.[8] The Origin—this is the strongest version of this hypothesis—turns out to be a beginning at which no one was or even could in principle be present (like creation itself) and as such is something of a derivative of our memories and desires.

The point, however, is that the deferral and undecidability surrounding the Origin does not have the effect of destroying or undermining the tradition or the traditional faith, of proving that it is a fraud or sleight of hand. Rather, it *produces it,* by necessitating a constant rereading and reinterpretation of the founders and their founding acts, which never were quite foundational, never quite what they are made out to be by those who invoke the authority of the Origin, usually for their own ends. Deferral and undecidability do not destroy the tradition or the common faith but make us *responsible* for them in a way that is not otherwise possible. "Undecidability" does not spell chaos and confusion, but the non-programmability of an under-determined situation that requires judgment and human determination. When Jesus tried to open the eyes of the disciples, he turned to a hermeneutic of the scriptures. That is because the coming of the Messiah is not outside the text; it is not what it is if it does not occur as the *pleroma,* the fulfillment, of what is written (*ta gegrammena*) (Luke 24:44), and we will not get it if we cannot read. We have to know how to read signs, to interpret, to cope with the play of traces, even if he is standing right of front of us: "Who do men say I am?" The Messiah is never *given, even when he is present.* Jesus did not command the sun to grow dark or lift the town of Emmaus from its foundations and set it at the feet of the disciples to show them who he was. He taught them how to read signs, which is the human lot, the hermeneutical dice we have been cast, and how they were going to have to get along after he left for good.

If the glory of Jesus simply glowed from every gesture he made or word he spoke while he lived in ancient Galilee, if he continued to show himself with unmistakable glory in every age ever after, if everything in the tradition of the Book simply dropped into our laps, ready-made and self-interpreting, unambiguous and authoritative, we would have no decisions to make, no need to rethink or to think at all, no need to read or interpret. Everything would have been done for us, signed for and delivered, pre-processed, pre-paid, and pre-packaged. There would be no advantage in that, because the tradition would then be as dead as a doornail. That is something we have all learned from Hans-Georg Gadamer and his notion of hermeneutic distance,[9] and we cannot be grateful enough to Gadamer in this regard. So the devilishness of the deconstruction of a tradition or a text, of the insistence that we have always to do with the interpretation of signs, is not the devil itself, and is not to be conceived as a way of destroying faith or tradition, but rather of exhibiting their contingency in an effort to preserve them and keep them open-ended. That is why Derrida can say, with only a certain amount of irony, "I am a very conservative person."[10] Deconstruction does not demolish authority and the "force of law," but divests the authority of the law of the trappings of absoluteness, thereby making the bearers of the tradition responsible for the forms the tradition assumes and the formulae in which the faith is cast. Deconstruction has the salutary effect of preventing the configurations that have come to figure in the faith and form the tradition from acquiring absolute and unquestionable prestige. We cannot merely invoke the story that the originary charter has been handed to us on tablets of stone or by divine appointment, for that, like every story, is a story, and as such it stands in need of reading and interpretation, commentary and exegesis. Stories are stories, not uninterpreted facts of the matter. They are transmitted, and have to be translated, interpreted, kept in good editions, and are permanently susceptible to the crisis of interpretation.

A deconstruction of a text or an institution, of a discourse or a practice, amounts to the claim that all these formations are subject to the sway of *différance*, which is Derrida's way of saying that they are subject to the need for constant revisiting and revising, rereading and reworking. Whatever has been formed in the first place can be reformed; whatever has been constructed in the first place is deconstructible. A deconstruction is a demonstration that a decision is a way of coping with the plurivocity and polyvalence, the polymorphism and ambiguity of the formations in which we are steeped. Far from launching an attack, it shows that texts or traditions are rich enough, multilayered and textured enough to "deserve" deconstructing, that deconstruction is what they deserve, which means both merit and need. A deconstruction is an exhibition of complexity and hidden tensions which demonstrates that beneath the calm surface of unity a thing puts forth there lies a multiplicity of competing elements, that beneath the reassuring look of certitude and knowledge there is restlessness and undecidability. Underneath the look of seamless continuity there are ruptures and interruptions and disruptive discontinuities. As Derrida says so well of the fiction of the homogeneous *identity* of the tradition (which is not to oppose everything traditional):

> . . . it is the idea itself of an identity or a self-interiority of every tradition (*the one* metaphysics, *the one* Christian revelation, *the one* history itself, *the one* history of being, *the one* epoch, *the one* tradition, self-identity in general, the one, etc.) that finds itself contested at its root. (ON, 71)

Things are never as simple as they seem, never as easy as they look, never as settled as they appear, never as finished as they make themselves out. This is not to say that there is no truth or tradition, but rather that truth and tradition and continuity are not what they say they are, that they always bear closer analysis. Deconstruction is an analytic and interpretive style that inhabits such structures as religion or science, or literature or politics, exposing in a painfully close and scrupulous way the complex and unsettled character of these discourses and of the communities and traditions that grow up around them.

The willingness to read under these disconcerting conditions is what I have been calling a more radical hermeneutics, and what I am calling here, in this theological setting, a devilish hermeneutics which I am pitting against a holy hermeneutics. For after all, the devil of deconstruction is in the details.

But such devilishness has nothing to do with a philosophical *Schadenfreude* that rejoices in chaos and confusion, because deconstruction is affirmation: the affirmation of the possibility of the coming of the other that stirs within the plurivocity and multiplicity of our traditions, which is all too easily suppressed when a single assured and reassuring style holds sway. Deconstruction is the affirmation—not the simple toleration or grudging admission—of discontinuity in the name of the coming of something unforeseeable. For the discontinuity is an opening, and the coming of the other is like a flower growing in a crack. Deconstruction is the advocate of the devil of discontinuity, of the little break or tear, not out of a mean-spirited or spiteful devilishness, but because it construes the tears (sounds like cheers) and the tears (sounds like prayers) as so many openings, so many chances for something new. The first word of deconstruction is "yes," indeed its first two words: *"Oui, oui,"* or three, *"Viens, oui, oui."*[11]

Eucharistic Hermeneutics versus Devilish Hermeneutics: Too Good to Be True

On the devilish hypothesis that I am pursuing throughout this book, the claim is that we get the best results from facing up to the worst, the inverse of which is that we should be suspicious of things that look too good. So when Jean-Luc Marion—an author to whom we are deeply grateful for his many gifts—speaks of "Eucharistic hermeneutics," that is so beautiful, so edifying, that it looks too good to be true and it raises our suspicions, poor devils that we are.[12]

Deconstruction has its doubts about the absolute beginning, that point in the past where heaven and earth intersect and some moment in time gets charged with eternity and absolutely foundational value. The Origin has always already retreated; there is always already mediation and interpretation. The Christian tradition(s) ought not in principle to be disconcerted by mediation, for Christianity has unceasingly been a religion of the Mediator, of God's icon, and hence of God's sign and supplement, of mediating, mediations and vicars, all of which concedes in principle the need to address the gap or bridge the discontinuity, between God and humankind. Johannes Climacus, who was very much interested in the absolute difference between God and us, between the Teacher and the Disciple, pointed out that there were only two ways this distance could be crossed, two solutions whose imaginative possibilities he invited his "poet" to explore in *Philosophical Fragments:* Either (a) by way of the elevation of the Disciple to the level of the God, which would deceive no one, human or divine; or (b) the descent of the God to the lowly level of the human, which in its historical garb is called Christianity.[13] Christianity turns on the accommodation that God makes to us by taking human form, the concessions God makes to the limits of our intelligence, which, slow of heart and slow of step, does the best it can by piecing things together, reading signs, deciphering symbols, and generally trying to cope with the dismaying degree of ambiguity by which we friends of Cleophas are beset. Christianity is one of the religions of the *Book*, of Jewish and Christian testaments, of signs and symbols, full of sounds and significations and sacraments, and not of absolute, divinizing silence.

Now it is my preference for hypothesis b that causes me concern with the hermeneutical approach that Marion has taken.[14] Marion has performed the admirable service of showing us in a theologically sensitive way that any truly *theo*logical theology will always include a deconstruction of the *logos* of theo*logy*, of the idols of metaphysical conceptuality. Nevertheless, while I love Marion's critique of idols, I am wary of dispensing with "screens" and "conditions," which sounds to me like dispensing with mediations, signs, and supplements of every sort, like a dream of presence—or givenness—without *différance*. When Marion speaks of adopting a standpoint *à partir de Dieu*, that makes sense to me, if it means abiding by the categories of the Scripture and not trying to translate them into the categories of Plato and Aristotle, but as it stands it sounds to me too much like hypothesis a, like trying to reattach us to an absolute Origin in an absolute way, which is, while beautiful, a little too good, a little too much.[15] *God without Being* is an exquisite and powerful book that has been important for English-speaking philosophers and theologians. In it, Marion enjoins us to think of God as G×d, where that cross is all at once a Heideggerian crossing out (*Durchkreuzung*), the Hebraic crossing out of G-d, the crossing out proceeding from a negative theology, and the Cross of Christ.[16] This culminates in what Marion calls "Eucharistic hermeneutics," which is the part that worries me. This beautiful hermeneutic does not leave room enough for the little gaps and discontinuities that deconstruction advocates in its own devilish way, which also—remember our principle—gives a tradition and its participants room to breathe.

The New Testament, we all agree, is a text, an historical text, which indicates both a text with a history and a text about an historical event, written in a natural language with a social, historical, political setting, with an inherited vocabulary, a certain syntax. As a text, there is something dangerous about the New Testament. On the one hand, it poses a danger to philosophers by positing a completely different way of thinking about things. But it also presents a danger to the faithful, for a text by definition can operate in the absence of its referent. It is a supplement and a substitute, a system of signifiers—perhaps even a screen separating us from the Origin—that can be devilishly difficult to read, especially if the story ends with an empty tomb and everyone fleeing, as Mark did (once). As such it is constantly bedeviled by the problems that beset other texts: there is always a certain uncertainty surrounding a text, about its authenticity, its sense, and above all its reference, its *hors-texte*. For the unique power of a text lies in its ability to function in the absence of the intuitive or firsthand presence of the signified, so that a text draws its life as a supplement from a dangerous gap, for it represents a presence that has since disappeared. The texts of a tradition are situated between the founding act, the absolutely authorizing Origin, and everyone who depends upon the Origin, which is the setting of the "religions of the Book." The referent of the New Testament is no longer present, and even when it was present it was not *given as the Founder.* But this text, the New Testament, as a sacred text is different, Marion contends, because its referent is not past, but present, made present again and again, every day, in the Eucharist. So the reading of this text has a context—the Eucharistic celebration—which prevents it from going astray, which attaches this text daily to its referent, which allows us to "go beyond the text to the Word, interpreting it from the point of view of the Word" (GWB, 149). That keeps the reading straight and protects the text from the fate of all other texts, insulating it from the danger that clings to any other text, from any risk incurred by crossing the abyss between the text and the *hors-texte.*

I believe that what Marion says is on one level deeply true, if he means to associate reading the scriptures with prayer, *ratio et oratio,* but I am nervous about what Marion means. Marion bases his Eucharistic hermeneutics upon the story of the disciples on the road to Emmaus which he, as did we, takes to be a story of the hermeneutic situation of us all. But for him the moral of the story is what he calls an "absolute hermeneutic" (GWB, 150), which sounds a lot to me like unlocking The Secret, getting back to an absolute Origin. But for us devilish hermeneuts an absolute hermeneutic is incoherent, for it implies an absolute perspective, a perspective that was not a perspective at all, but the end of perspectives, a view from nowhere. When there is only one, absolute interpretation there are no more "interpretations," but only the special delivery of The Secret courtesy of God, or Being, or the Absolute Spirit, or even G.O.D. (Guaranteed Overnight Delivery). An absolute hermeneutic is the end of hermeneutics, which is why it is too good to be true. So where we read in the story of the road to Emmaus the inescapable necessity of interpretation, Marion reads the One Final Inescapable Interpretation, which means the end of interpretation. But in addition to incoherence as a theory of hermeneutics, Marion's interpretation is a worrisome idea, representing, as Graham Ward argues, an "evasion of the hermeneutic question."[17] For Marion this story is a text about the text. It is a kind of self-instruction that the text leaves behind, an auto-hermeneutics inscribed in the text, something like the stage instructions that a playwright inscribes in his text, by means of which the text instructs us about how it is to be read. Marion understands this story to mean that reading must always be left in the hands of the one whose hands break the bread, which is preeminently the hands of the bishop, or the hands of the ones whom the bishop consecrates, lest the gap between the text and the *hors-texte* grow too wide or even become an unbridgeable abyss. The one who has the sacramental power to let the Word become flesh in the Eucharist is likewise the one with absolute hermeneutical power, who is empowered to give interpretive words to the Word and speak from the vantage point of the Word:

> And just as a priest who breaks his communion with the bishop can no longer enter into ecclesiastical communion, so a teacher who speaks without, even against, the Symbol of the apostles, without, even against, his bishop, absolutely can no longer carry on his discourse in an authentically *theo*logical site. (GWB, 153, 152–158)

For Marion, if one has the ecclesiastic authority to consecrate the bread, then one has the authority to interpret. That seems to me the contrary of the point of the story, which appears to say that unless one has the ability to interpret, one would not see a thing or belong to the assembly (*ekklesia*). On my telling, the story tells us of the necessity of interpretation, that we are all committed to the flux and must learn to make our way by reading signs. On Marion's telling, it tells of the rigorous delimitation of interpretation which stills the conflict of interpretations, which arrests the flux. That, of course, is Derrida's objection to hermeneutics and why he will not use the word, for hermeneutics seems to him to mean the "mistake" of trying to "arrest the text in a certain position, thus settling on a thesis, meaning, or truth."[18] Marion's interpretation of the story seems to me a little too arresting, slightly too close to silence for a religion of the Book, not mystical silence, the silence of *theologia mystica* or of the *pati divina*, to be sure, which he and I love, but just plain silence, the kind the police of The Secret like to enforce, the kind that produces what Jean-François Lyotard calls *le différend*, the silenced dissenter who has been deprived of an idiom in which to state his dissent or his injury.[19] Certainly, Marion is not recommending silencing anybody, but his powerful hermeneutics deprives the dissenter of the *authority* to dissent, of the right both to offer a different interpretation and to speak on behalf of the community or the tradition. Marion does not explicitly advocate the devilishness of outright, institutional silencing, which would be violent, but a sort of moral silencing, depriving the words of the dissident of any moral or spiritual authority, a sort of moral de-situating, a destituting of the theologian—which leaves the dissident out in the cold, without a *mandatum*. On my more devilish account of hermeneutics, "the" tradition—which is a fictitious unity, an identity without identity, there being many voices and traditions in the tradition, male and female, Jew and Greek, orthodox and heterodox—sputters and clanks along nicely, thank you very much, driven precisely by the polyphony of its voices and the polymorphic forms which contend with one another for a hearing.

In *Truth in Painting*, Derrida warns us to beware of those who promise to give us something unmediated—he would later call it The "Secret"—who would dispense with screens and mediations in order to put us in direct contact with the Origin, for we will later on find ourselves visited with the most massive mediations, with bishops and long robes and police all over the place.[20] Marion, I think, wants to minimize the undecidability, to narrow the gap between the text and the *hors-texte,* to smooth out all the discontinuities, to build a bridge, a supremely secure *pons* that swings across the abyss, perhaps even calling up a supreme *pontifex.* Such a *pontifex* will arrest the play of the text, stop its trembling (*ébranler*), fix the text within a firm interpretive context so that the river of interpretation will always flow within fixed borders. It is almost as if the story of the disciples on the road to Emmaus was sent into the world to save us all from deconstruction, like a divinely providential preempting of Derrida, which foresees that a devilish fellow would come along some day and say *il n'y a pas de hors-texte.* This story would blunt the tip of deconstruction's stylus a priori, infallibly protecting us from all error—and misspellings. (As we can see, the Society of the Friends of Cleophas has a number of chapters!)

The rub is that Marion's auto-interpreting text is still a text, which means that it too functions in the absence of the intuitive presence of its referent, which means that it is always possible that we might disagree with the interpretation Marion gives to this self-interpreting text. We might always say we have another interpretation of the self-interpretation the text is carrying out. We might follow the reading, say, of Edward Schillebeeckx, according to whom this little story does not actually record an eyewitness event (a commonplace in New Testament studies), does not quite wire us up directly to the Origin, does not exactly make direct contact with a founding, authorizing moment. The truth of the story is not to be measured by the standards of the *adequatio rei et intellectus.* For Schillebeeckx says that this story comes after the Origin, that the Origin has already passed by and is meant to give expression to the faith of a community that Jesus is Emmanuel, that the power of God was in Jesus, that God was with us in Jesus, and, now that Jesus is dead, that Jesus is with God. It is a way of saying that in this time of deferral, while we wait for the Lord to come *again* ("Christianity" being the religion that arises precisely in the time of the deferral), the faith of the community is that the power of God is with Jesus. On this devilish reading, which is the sort of thing that is always liable to happen when we are dealing with texts, a certain reversal sets in according to which the Easter faith is not based on the post-Easter appearances, but rather, conversely, the post-Easter appearance stories express the Easter faith. "The presence of the present is derived from repetition and not the reverse," Derrida says, to the dismay of some.[21] So it turns out that the story comes later than the faith. The story then does not establish episcopal authority on the basis of a direct report from the Origin or the Secret, but expresses our faith in the Origin, which means that the Origin is always already absent, which is why faith is required, viz., a faith that the power of God was felt in the words and the deeds, the life and the death, of Jesus. The story does not establish the power and the authority of the bishop to enforce consensus, but rather brings us back to the faith through a glass darkly (through a *glas*), which refers to the little gap and discontinuity between the Origin and us.[22]

To be sure, no bishop gave his *imprimatur* to Schillebeeckx's book, but that is an argument that chases its own tail, for it gives the bishop the authority to decide the meaning of the text upon which the authority of the bishop to rule on the meaning of texts is founded. That ground turns out to lack a ground, to stand in need of a ground, to be a little ground-less. The auto-hermeneutical operation of the story is clogged by the textuality of the text, which prevents it from being self-interpreting, from leaving behind its own reading instructions. The idea of a self-interpreting text makes no sense, since texts are texts only because they operate in the absence of their authors. Marion gives us an interesting reading, in a beautiful book which I have purchased twice, in English and in French, but whose argument—despite my expenditure without reserve—I do not quite buy, although, as I said, I think what he says is on one level deeply true. I fully endorse the inseparability of *ratio* and *oratio,* of praying and predicating or interpreting, so that for the readers of the New Testament Jesus *lives,* but that does not give us a footing *outside the text* in Derrida's sense. For praying, too, is a textual operation for Derrida, which is why it can decline into rote repetition and become not only formulaic but highly hypocritical. Indeed, the more one is steeped in textuality, the harder one has to pray for help, a law of writing which is written all over Saint Augustine's *Confessions,* the West's weepiest author. We must confess our limits and come to grips with the *différance* and *écriture* that engulf us, all of us, both holy eucharistic hermeneuts and us plain as day devilish hermeneuts who are just trying to make it to payday.

The discontinuity with the Origin is not simply a bit of bad luck that has befallen us latecomers who had the misfortune to be born too late, but something always already in place, structurally in place. Even if we walked along the dusty road to Emmaus, we would be as slow of wit, slow of heart, slow of step as Cleophas. Even if we belonged to the first generation, walking the dusty roads of Galilee with Jesus, Johannes Climacus argued, we would still have needed the "condition," faith, to recognize him, so that even when Jesus was *present* the God with or within him was not "unconditionally *given.*" The idea that we would catch a glimpse of the *tout autre* in the gleam of his penetrating eyes is paganism, Climacus said. A tradition takes place in the discontinuity with its Origin, which is an opening in which we must assume responsibility for our *interpretation* of the Origin. The Christian tradition(s) is a certain form of *différance* and textuality—how could a religion of the Book be outside textuality?—occurring precisely in the space opened up by the deferral of the Origin, in the impossibility of making contact with the first coming, on the one hand, and of the Lord's increasingly delayed return, on the other hand. Christians are always already latecomers, always already the latter-day disciples, always arriving too late for the Origin, after a crowd (*ecclesia*) has already gathered at the scene. We are the *ecclesia* of those who come too late for the Origin and too early for the *parousia*. *Différance*, which is not a bad word, is the space of *ecclesia*.

Radical Translation

That is why it is always a question of starting from below, *in medias res*, in the midst of the tumult, amidst supplements and signs, mediations and substitutes, without a heavenly hook to bail us out, doing the best we can. It is a question of beginning where one is, as Derrida tells us[23]—not where God is, we may add. That is an old Aristotelian idea much honored by medieval masters and saints. "It is certain and evident to the senses that in the world some things are in motion," Thomas Aquinas said at the beginning of a famous book.[24] Thomas begins with the senses, and he was the *angelic* doctor (which means, does it not, someone learned about messages and messengers?). "None is good but God," the scriptures say. From this it follows that we who are not God should be wary of things too good to be true and content ourselves with a more devilish beginning, more earth-bound and in need of mediations and messengers (*angeli*), wary of trying to start *à partir de Dieu*, or of reaching to God *sans l'être = sans lettre*, a pure *hors-texte* without the literality of the letter.[25]

Where do I begin? How do I start? That is the question that G. W. F. Hegel posed and thought he had resolved by starting the Logic with the dialectic of being and nothing. Johannes Climacus made notable fun of that and showed us—in what is a seminal postmodern gesture—how it is not possible to make an absolute beginning, how one can never be sure one has gotten back to the start. There is always something we have forgotten or left out, some fragment and detail we will have missed that will clog the absolute beginning, which is why Johannes de Silentio described himself not as a systematizer but as an *Extraskriver*, a supplementary clerk, a freelance writer of supplementary and occasional pieces.[26] So Derrida belongs to an honorable tradition when he advises us to begin where we are, in the midst of a text, of a sentence, of a tradition, and not to imagine that we can somehow escape the condition of textuality by means of some kind of Archimedean *hors-texte* which, *mirabile dictu*, stabilizes the trembling of the text and arrests its play.

Here I am (*me voici*), in the midst of a complex of events and structures, discourses and institutions, histories and traditions, in the plural, which I must sort out and sort through. Here I am in the mist of *différance*, with the misspelling, surrounded by the difficulties and discontinuities of life. The word of God, the mind of God, what God wants, what God has said, that is a matter to be settled in fear and trembling, with *timor castus*, Augustine said, a chaste and healthy fear. The word of God, as a word, is marked by *différance* and wavers in undecidability, as a mark or trace I can never hope perfectly to retrace, as if it were a code I could decode.

What then, to be precise, are the words of God? Here—this book, the New Testament, let us say (there are other examples). But this is English, a translation. Are we to understand that God speaks English? Is it American English or the Queen's? What sort of accent does God have? Then let us go back to the original, to the Greek. But is that not also a translation? For Jesus did not likely speak Greek but Aramaic, and, according to John Dominic Crossan, another devilish hermeneut, very likely could not even read.[27] Then is Aramaic the original, the divine tongue? Divine tongue? Should that phrase not stick in one's throat? How can there be a divine tongue, not a *lingua franca* but a *lingua divina*? After all, God does not actually, literally, strictly speaking, "speak." God has no vocal cords, lungs, or tongue; has no recourse to grammar; uses no writing instruments. In God's own being, God's being without being, *sans l'être, à partir de soi, kath'auto,* God is without "letter" (*sans lettre*), is not subject to the scrambling, disseminating, Babelian condition of *différance,* which makes speaking and writing possible (and impossible) by its differential play. What then, we repeat, are the "words" of God?

Here we must recall the principle we have borrowed from the second poetic hypothesis of Climacus. If the god and humankind are absolutely different, the union cannot be brought about by an *elevation,* by making the human into something divine, for no one will find that credible, there being only so much one can do with human materials. Instead, the poet adopts the hypothesis of a *descent,* in which the god agrees to accommodate himself to the frailty of our condition, to cross over and assume our limits, to meet our need for a translation into some humanly readable form, not by a jest (*docet*) but in earnest, even unto assuming the lowliest, the humblest form of a "servant." And if the form of a servant, then also subject to the humble constraints of *différance* and *écriture.* The god freely takes the form of a man who speaks in human terms, who descends into the play of traces, and risks being misunderstood, misremembered, misquoted, misused by people with intentions quite the opposite of his, risks having his (or her) sayings corrupted by corrupt manuscripts or by copyists in Irish monasteries having a bad day. The god, according to the second poetic hypothesis (whose historical realization is only thinly disguised, although one could always read the sequel, the postscript to the *Philosophical Fragments,* if it eludes a reader), has freely submitted his message to the mess of textuality and *différance.* The good news willingly takes the form of *écriture,* which however *saint* is still *écriture.* That means that we are not lifted up by a divine hook above the play of differences (hypothesis a), but that the god has chosen to enter the fray, to submit to the conflict of interpretations (hypothesis b). Even the god seems to prefer devilish hermeneutics to holy hermeneutics, which is a little too good to be true.

So even if we could get back to some text which would be what Jesus said in Aramaic, which Paul or John actually wrote in their own hand, to some autographed manuscript, in fact signed by Paul, or even by Jesus—what would Sotheby's or Christie's give for that!—we would still be dealing with a *translation*. The very idea of the *word of God* is implicated in translation, in *meta-phorein, trans-ferre, trans-latio*, a radical translation, not from one natural language into another, but a translation by which the god has agreed to transfer himself *into language itself*, to become something *linguistic* at all. For, *à partir de soi, kath'auto*, the god has no need of language, and the decision freely to submit to language, to the conflict of interpretations, is to decide to submit to the most radical sort of translation one might imagine. So we ought not to imagine revelation as if it were a matter of taking dictation from a divine speaker, for that is already to make use of an *intra-linguistic* relation, as if the god were already speaking some divine language before making his descent. Indeed, that is the hypothesis of elevation, that we have been lifted up to within divine earshot, enabled to overhear a divine monologue. But on the hypothesis of descent the god agrees to enter *into language*, to *descend* into the play of differences, and both the god and humankind must be willing to abide by the terms of this agreement, to cope with the difficulties this imposes, without attempting to bail out of this textual fix by means of some extra-textual, holy hermeneutical hook, which would be a kind of double dealing that would nullify the agreement.[28]

I am reminded of what Husserl said about God and perception. So sure was Husserl of the "eidetic" law of adumbrations (*Abschattungen*) that he said that even God would need to perceive a spatial object one side at a time. If God perceived at all—instead of knowing in some higher way, *eminentiore modo*, which is the way Thomas Aquinas extricated God from such a fix—God would be bound by the laws of perception. That means, God would freely choose to take the humble form of a servant, of a perceiving servant. The same thing is true of language. The word of God would be part of the humility of the god who freely chooses to submit to the differential play of traces.

It is with that being said, with that little proviso being stated, that we can say that, for the religions of the Book, the words of God are the words of the scriptures, which are the traces of the god who has descended into the play, who has assumed the form of the play, not as a jest but in earnest. In the religions of the Book, faith proceeds by way of a certain hermeneutics, a particular reading and hearing, lending an ear to these words, which being real words, natural words in a natural language, need to be "read" and rendered, interpreted and translated, and that requires good manuscript traditions and copyists, and a good deal else besides.

Faith is assigned the task of reading traces which cannot be absolutely tracked down, deciphered, decoded, of reading without the hope of a heavenly hook to lift it up, to elevate it, above the fray. That means too that the original authorship of ancient manuscripts gets fuzzy, so that it is not entirely clear who is saying what to whom, whether the biblical figures are speaking in their own name or are being supplied lines by a redactor, say, from a saying that caught on in the community and could be heard in the prayers or rituals or old stories of the community, and by repeating it, modifying it. How are we not sure that the whole thing is not being carried along by "a mistake on the part of a copyist or specialist in hermeneutics,"[29] like the mistake that Augustine made with the Latin Vulgate which introduced Original Sin into the world?[30] Can we be sure there is no mistake on the part of a copyist or specialist in hermeneutics? No philological sidetracking? That is what Derrida means by the weavings, the *texere,* of textuality, and nothing could be clearer than that there is nothing about the ancient origins of the religions of the Book that escapes those menacing questions. *Il n'y a pas de hors-texte.* The god, by his freedom, who freely took the form of a servant, and the faithful, by necessity, are both marked, traced, inscribed within systems of signifiers or traces from which there is no escape, until death we do part. The alternative is to advocate a kind of textual docetism, which only halfheartedly admits that these words are really words, and with the other half of its heart insists that they are transparently marked by a heavenly or eucharistic *hors-texte.* On my devilishly difficult hermeneutics, the very idea of escape from the textuality of the text into a holy hermeneutics is, in addition to lacking heart, a transcendental illusion, the illusion of the perfectly unconditioned and unmediated, like the illusion Immanuel Kant described of the dove that thinks it could fly all the more swiftly were it not for the air which offers it such resistance, the air being just what holds it up. For what would words be, what would they have to say, how swiftly would they not fall, without the winds of textuality to sustain their meaning-making work?

We thus are forced by the humility of our circumstances to wrestle through the night with ambiguous traces. The sacred text, Hebrew, Christian, or Islamic, is inhabited and disturbed by a transcendence, an alterity. That is why we say it is sacred, *saint,* "holy," and marked by transcendence. A good reading does not reduce a text—any text, sacred or secular—to something entirely immanent and mundane, something familiar and devoid of an Other. Unless it is just out to get religion, to deface and smear it, reading does not divest the sacred text of the shock of divine transcendence, of an intervention from without, of the trauma of alterity. The point of "reading," its stylus tip, is to cope with the *undecidability* of the text, which is the condition of its readability, to maintain the ambient difference between the divine and the human in all the undecidability of this difference. For, now that the divine has assumed the humble form of the servant, the speaking servant, in truth and in earnest, and not merely in appearance, the task is to discern the difference between the divine and the human, with all the undecidability that accompanies that assumption.

Undecidability is not a way of mistreating the text, of casting doubt on it, of handling it with disrespect. On the contrary, it is the condition of possibility for respecting the distance that structures the text and makes it readable, which means both able to be read and *in need of reading,* of deciding its undecidability, however tentatively and temporarily, however subject to revision and rereading our reading may be. Undecidability prevents the text from settling into stability and familiarity, protects us from settling into mastery and authoritativeness, domination and certitude toward it. That would undo the transcendence of the text, the way it disturbs us, and that disturbance is required if the text is to provide an occasion of the coming of the other. Far from destroying anything, undecidability saves the text from destruction—this text, the New Testament, or any text worthy of the name. Deconstruction is a way to prevent the text from becoming an idol, which like a deep well (or a shallow one) simply sends back to us our own image. Undecidability shelters the "iconic" quality, which is to send us soaring toward transcendence only to discover that we have it backwards: transcendence is not our doing, our crossing-over, but the crossing over or coming of the other, the other's descent, Climacus would say, and undecidability provides an opening for that coming. The devilishness of deconstruction is to make it always a matter of undecidable wonder, of wondering out loud, when we have to do with the divine trauma, with the shock of revelation, and when we are just being beaten over the head by something human all too human.

Two Pointed Examples

(1) One pointed example of the need for the undecidability of sacred texts these days, an example that would seem amusing were it not so serious, has to do with the place of women in the religions of the Book. On our hypothesis, the Origin in its utter originariness, its utter alterity, is always already withdrawn or deferred, and has accordingly transferred itself into a humbler, derivative form, the form of a servant, a sign and a supplement. That means we are constantly forced to discriminate between the original and the copy and, given our limits, we friends of Cleophas who are slow of foot, slow of wit, and slow of heart, we are constantly exposed to mistaking the original for its substitutes. The reader will, I trust, pardon the following imaginary exchange for its lack of proper ecclesiastical solemnity:

"CONVERSATION ON A SEMINARY PATH"

HOLY HERMENEUT: The vicar must be in the likeness of Christ, the *imago Christi.*

ADVOCATUS DIABOLI: *Oui, oui.*

HOLY HERMENEUT: But Jesus and the apostles were all males.

ADVOCATUS: *Concedo, non dato.*[31]

HOLY HERMENEUT: It follows, therefore, that the essence of the redemptive act which God effects in Jesus is tied up with the maleness of Jesus, with masculine sexuality.

ADVOCATUS: *Mais, non.*

Are we, following this holy hermeneutics, to believe that God's redemptive power, the divinity of the fact that God has redeemed us all—Greek and Jew, male and female, black and white, bondsmen and slave (Gal. 3:28)—is somehow constrained by or confined to, or even is in any way connected with—I am trying to be precise, I do not mean to be rude—male genitalia? Is this what the blood of the martyrs has come down to? Do we not at this point fall down before an idol, a classical one, indeed one with roots in our subconscious? The idea behind the beautiful distinction between an idol and an icon is that, with an idol, our look (*regard*) is arrested by something visible, trapped and fascinated by the visibility of some graven image. The result is that instead of proceeding on to the infinite beyond it, instead of being overtaken by the otherwise than being, the look is trapped in immanence, sent back to us so that we find ourselves regarding our own reflections, ourselves, not God. Something is wrong on our hermeneutic telling when we look into this book, any book, and see only ourselves. But if our look is arrested by the masculinity of Jesus, then is it God and God's transcendence we have in view, the God who is Otherwise than Being? Cannot the God Who is Otherwise than Being, the God without Being, *epekeina tes ousias*, be otherwise than masculine? If we insist upon the masculinity of Jesus, or of God, is that to get back to the original or is it to stop with an idol and a substitute—something human, something obviously, conspicuously male, and a human all too human, masculine all too masculine, socio-politico-sexual power structure, an historical contingency? Do we honor the saving power of Jesus or a patriarchal model borrowed from the Greco-Roman household? Do we make contact with the original or do we fall down before the oldest, most phallocentric idol one can imagine? Is this not precisely to fail to preserve the distance of the ever deferred Origin, to fail to proceed on to God and respect the divine self-deferral, as befits an icon, in which one does not so much see as one is envisaged by the Divine, and this specifically with the aid of God's icon, God's *imago*, God's Mediator? Is the loyalty of the biblical religions to a male clergy loyalty to the Original or simply loyalty to itself, the loyalty of men to themselves?

If, to the confinement of the power to break the bread to men, we add the additional hypothesis of a eucharistic hermeneutics, that the authoritative reading of sacred texts is left in the hands of those who break the break, we quickly see that women are confined to *baking* and *serving* the bread and excluded from authoritative reading. These hermeneutical issues clearly pack a political punch.

So one can see why I am an advocate of the devil, of a devilish hermeneutics, and why I think that deconstruction—which warns us about the loss of the Origin—is one of the better angels of our nature. We see the good undecidability does for the religions of the Book, for whom deconstruction is, I would say, a good fit and a good gift. This devilish business is not as far removed from the truly divine God[32] as those who think they speak with the tongues of angels would like to think. It is in virtue of undecidability that the distinction between the human and the divine, between the derivative and the Origin, between devils and angels, is unsettled, which makes it necessary for us to assume some responsibility for this distinction and to proceed with all due *timor castus* in making it. Far from scuttling the project or discouraging us from reading further, this undecidability forces us to assume responsibility for the reading of this book and to put at risk the comforting assumptions with which we surround ourselves. The advocates of this devilish hermeneutics, these *advocati diaboli,* are a loyal opposition, for the advocatus is an old and venerable ecclesiastical function, whose work is to save us from the worship of idols and false pretenders to sanctity. The beautiful distinction between idol and icon does not take the worry out of reading, but, like all distinctions, is itself something to worry about, to be bedeviled by. We cannot be reassured by this distinction, for it only shifts the problems of faith and theological reflection to another level, viz., that of determining what is iconic and what is idolatrous, what is divine and what is manmade [*sic!*], what is transcendent and what is mundane, what is original and what is a copy, what is part and parcel of the calming reassurance and continuity of the same or immanence, and what belongs to the shock of the divine, the jolt and trauma of something different, of something—*grâce à Dieu*—divine and discontinuous.[33]

We all know the famous cover of *La carte postale,*[34] which portrays the utter perversity of Socrates—who never wrote—seated at a writing table while Plato—who condemned writing but wrote a great deal—whispers in his ear, dictating to Socrates what he should write. Derrida loves this postcard, which he found in the bookstore of the Bodleian Library in Oxford, for many reasons, among which is the way that it scrambles the wires of the West's most venerable communication system, its oldest hermeneutic code. We like to think that Socrates taught and asked questions and that Plato, his disciple, taking pen in hand, wrote the intellectual biography of Socrates, and that the history of Platonism, which is the history of us, is to have been on the receiving end of these messages ever since. But this postcard suggests that these wires have been crossed, that when we read Plato quoting Socrates, it is Plato dictating to Socrates, Plato putting words in Socrates' mouth, Plato speaking through the mouthpiece of Socrates. That is to say, the relationship between Plato and Socrates is an undecidable, which does not mean something completely chaotic, but rather that this is a distinction to be held in fear and trembling. Are we to understand that in the *Dialogues* Plato speaks with the authority of Socrates, or rather, contrariwise, that Socrates speaks with the authority of Plato? Are we sure who is saying what to whom in the Platonic dialogues? Who is the original and who the follower? Must we not proceed here with care?

Let us imagine now the reversal of another scene, this time with Jesus seated at the writing table while the evangelists whisper in his ear and Jesus takes dictation. Imagine the reversal of the painting by Raphael in which the evangelist Mark sits with his ear cocked to the heavens, waiting for the next inspired word; imagine that it is Jesus seated at a writing table and that it is Jesus whose ear is cocked to the wind. That is to say, let us put the distinction between the original sayings and the ones we have supplied, between what Jesus says and what we have portrayed Jesus saying, into undecidability, so that we are not quite sure which is which, so that the margins around the text are blurred just a bit. Is that unimaginable, unthinkable, perhaps even blasphemous? Would that destroy the transcendence, the shock of alterity, or would it preserve it? Is this not what we know, what we learn when we study New Testament exegesis and we learn about "later theological reflections," about "theologoumena?"[35] These theologoumena do not represent callous falsifications but certain dialogues that the community imagined and then recited or prayed in liturgy and attributed to Jesus in a kind of prayerful theatrics. They are not transcriptions of Jesus' original and actual words, which constitute an *hors-texte* almost impossible to access, but a way we have found to imagine an Origin that is always already out of view. Such undecidability comes along with the territory of saying that the god has entered, has *descended,* into the condition of textuality, of history, writing, and memory.

(2) I single out—and this is my second pointed example—a particular saying of Jesus, which contains a celebrated, one is tempted to say, an inspired pun, which illustrates what Derrida calls the violence of the Origin or of the foundation. There is a logion in Matthew in which Jesus says to Simon, "Thou art Peter and upon this rock I will build my church" (Matt. 16:18). This is a linchpin, a foundational stone, a *fundamentum inconcussum,* engraved in stone around the rotunda in the Vatican. But suppose we let a bit of undecidability, which is meant to be a protective cover and shelter of transcendence, settle upon this saying? There is every reason to think that Jesus did not intend to found a "Christian Church" or to have a beautiful cathedral built in Rome in Peter's name, let alone to establish the Vatican library and museum, and hence that these are not actually *ipsissima verba*. We can imagine Jesus at the writing table and the

early church, which had begun to coalesce around Simon/Peter, whispering in his ear, giving him, giving itself, a few crucial lines.[36] Is there not a fragment of discontinuity between the Founder and Simon/Peter which the church has filled in, a little missing supplement that the church has supplied? Could it be that the small slash in Simon/Peter has a deconstructive edge on it, that it represents a little gap or discontinuity? Could it be that the Founder, Jesus, is founded, that he has been made or constituted a Founder by those who followed him, so that the Founder is founded by the church which he founded (or did not quite found)? Could it be, once again, that the Origin, the originary foundation, has been deferred and the repetition precedes the presence? Could it be that we have founded ourselves, that the church has founded itself, that we must assume responsibility for this foundation?

This reversal goes to the heart of Christian tradition(s). It is the reversal in which the Proclaimer becomes the Proclaimed, in which the Proclaimer is proclaimed by those to whom he meant only to proclaim something else. The idea behind Jesus' ministry, the exegetes think, was not Jesus but the father, *abba* (which I think a devilish hermeneut would recommend we translate as "mother"). If he came to give glory to the father who was greater than he, then the followers of Jesus may well have ignored what Jesus had in mind. The birth of Christian tradition(s) depended upon the death of its author, not because he died for our sins and to establish his church, but because while he lived he was preaching something else. Christian tradition(s) is a living example of the need for the hermeneutics of the death of the author and of ignoring the Founder's intentions.

That puts us friends of Cleophas back on the road to Emmaus, back in the hermeneutic situation, with texts and empty tombs, wondering whether to believe the women, trying to resolve the multiple forms of undecidability that beset us. The whole idea of interpreting the text on the basis of the authority of the authorized interpreter is made to tremble when it turns out that this interpretive authority is partly the authorized interpreter's own idea, that the enabling or authorizing legislation was actually written by the interpreter. The founding act turns out to be a little supplement, derived by prompting the Founder, supplying him with an extra word or two, that covers up the slight gap that separates the Founder from the Founded.

One is reminded of the analysis that Derrida makes of the American Declaration of Independence, or that Lyotard makes of the French Declaration of the Rights of Man.[37] There is always the question of who authorized the delegates assembled in Philadelphia to speak on behalf of the "people," or in the "name of God," or in the name of Natural Law. Was this insurrection not a little violent, not only in the sense that it was prepared to use violence against the English monarch, but also in the sense that it was not, strictly speaking, authorized since that in virtue of which it could be authorized, the rule of law and the constitution, did not yet exist? It was a rebellion; it struck out on its own, without enabling legislation. The founding act, the ground, is a bit groundless. That is why we hold in continual undecidability what was done in the name of God and what was not. For example, in the case of the American constitution, we are all free to wonder out loud, without being unpatriotic or facing execution in Texas, whether one could, in the name of God, exclude everyone from the sentence "all men are created equal" except white, male landowners.

If the god freely agrees to descend to the human condition, and if theology is accordingly always being written from below, if things, including theological things, are steeped in *différance* and undecidability, if the difference between the divine and the human, the theological difference, bobs in the waves of *différance*, if the Origin is always deferred, then theology must learn to deal with being bedeviled by deconstruction. I say this despite the preemptive strike mounted by the New Testament against Derrida, or, more precisely, mounted by Marion's interpretation of the story of the disciples on the road to Emmaus, which may be a little too good to be true. For, on our telling, the story tells for Derrida not against him, tells for the necessity of interpretation and faith in order to see and belong to the *ekklesia*. When something begins, when something starts *ab initio*, there is always a slight gap, a bit of discontinuity, a leap, a certain violence, a "mystical force" in virtue of which the foundation of a thing is a bit groundless.[38] Foundations lack enabling legislation because there was not yet, at the founding point, any legislature (this is the act which brings the legislature about). The ground is groundless and the beginning is violent, because the Origin is deferred. The result is that we are forced to assume responsibility for what is founded.

Divine Discontinuity

What, then? What are we to do now, we who are caught up in *différance*, trapped by a misspelling, steeped in *écriture*, following the trace of what has always already withdrawn? Has everything gone to the devil? I would say there is nothing to do but tell and retell old stories and work with our texts. But do not mistake me. I do not take lightly the need to tell stories. It is unceasingly a question of telling stories, good stories, the best ones possible, and it is possible to pit story against story, to see which one wins out, not because of some macho storytelling power of the narratival subject, but because we are struck by the trauma of alterity in a story, by the shock of transcendence, by the blow which is invariably delivered by something divine, which is quite other, wholly Other. So I will tell one of my favorite stories, about the "Deconstructor and the Holy Hermeneut," told by one Magdalena de la Cruz, an old friend from whom I have not heard for a while. But recently she sent me a story about a great Deconstructor who was also, it seems, a rabbi, but definitely not a bishop; he was, I wager, a little too devilish for the bishops. The story is called "Before the Law."[39]

One day a great Deconstructor went up before the Law, and before the Law there were assembled many holy hermeneuts, in long, beautiful robes, stroking their long, fine beards. The work of the holy hermeneuts was to watch over the doors of the Law, to determine who would and who would not be granted admittance to the Law. Now there was a man with a with-ered hand who had been lying there, before the Law, for many years, and the Deconstructor had gone up to see if he could entreat the Law about this man, who was by now quite old and feeble. The man himself had entreated the Law many times before but each time the holy hermeneuts told him that he should wait until later. When the Deconstructor arrived before the Law the holy hermeneuts watched him closely, to see whether he would heal the man, because that day it was the Sabbath and according to the Law it was not permitted to heal on the Sabbath. The Deconstructor looked on the man with the withered hand long and lovingly and then he said to him, "come!" (*viens, oui, oui!*). Then he turned to the holy hermeneuts and asked them, "Is it lawful on the Sabbath to do good or to do harm, to save life or to kill?" The Deconstructor was making a distinction between justice and the law, and he was saying that the Law is deconstructible, but jus-tice in itself, if there is such a thing, is not "deconstructible." The Sabbath you see is the Law, while the man with the withered hand calls for justice. The holy hermeneuts were confounded by this question, which seemed to them very cunning, even very diabolic, and they suspected that the Decon-structor was out to destroy the Law. So they took counsel among them-selves. Huddling together in secret council, they wrapped their long robes about themselves, they stroked their long, thin beards, and they looked down their long, sharp noses at the Deconstructor. But after all this confer-ring among themselves they just looked at the Deconstructor and kept si-lent. That filled the Deconstructor with sadness and anger, and he grieved at their hardness of heart. "Is this man with a withered hand made for the Law," he asked them, "or is the Law made for this man with a withered hand?" Again they kept silent. They wanted to tell him to wait for another day, to defer this justice, that it might be possible to heal the man some other day. But they remained silent. So the Deconstructor bent down low to the man, who was by now too weak to stand, and said, "Stretch out your hand." Thus it was that the Law was deconstructed and justice, which is not deconstructible, was done. After that day, the holy hermeneuts went out and spread the word that the Deconstructor was a danger to the Law, that he meant to destroy the Law and the Prophets and the Church itself.

I commend this story to our reflection on devilish and deconstruc-tionist grounds. It is a little devilish, a little fictitious, a little Derridean, a little Levinasian, a little Kafkaesque, a little Dostoevskian, and a little evangelical, too. But it harbors the shock of alterity, the trauma of tran-scendence, the blow or coup of the divine. It helps us sort through the ambiguous play of traces that fluctuate between the human and the divine in the New Testament. It gives us not a hook but a hint of where the divine alterity is to be found, where it may have left a trace, and of how to go about revising, rereading, reworking the tradition. It and other stories like it have—for me at least, and I commend it to you—the ring (*glas*) of divinity, the echo or the trace of absconded transcendence. The bent limbs of the lame, the withered flesh of the lepers, the deaf and the blind and even the dead: are those not the traces to follow in tracking down the divine retreat (*retrait*)? Does not God take the side of the nobodies, *ta me onta*, the weakest, to confound the great? Does he not accommodate himself to us by assuming the weakest form? Are those not the tracks left in an undecidable text which help steer the risky route of this devilish hermeneutics? It is always a little risky, is it not, but is it not a fine risk?[40] After all, does this man heal by God or by Beelzebub? Who knows? How could we tell?

What is the divine discontinuity, the alterity, the mark of transcendence in the scriptures?

Might it not be found in the contradiction of our freedom, in the appeal for mercy and healing and selflessness? Might it not be uncovered in the astonishing power of God to confound us, to demand that we hold our hand, that we put away our sword, or, contrariwise, that we hold out our hand to help or to heal, that we give what we need for ourselves, to take the bread out of our own mouths? Might not the shock of alterity be discovered in the capacity of the scriptures to contradict our aggression and greed, our violence and power, which is *menschliches allzu menschliches*? When Paul says that God chose what is foolish to shame the wise, what is weak to shame the strong, what is low and despised, the nothings and the nobodies of this world to confound the mighty, does that not have the ring of transcendence (1 Cor. 1:26–29)? Might the trace of the divine be found in the points in the scriptures where our humanity is turned inside out, our human hierarchies inverted, our freedom and self-continuity disrupted by the shock of divine discontinuity? Might not the most divine element of all in the sacred writings be found just at those points where our self-love, self-aggrandizement, and self-importance are jolted by a divine blow, by a contradiction, a *skandalon*, Paul says, in which the foolishness of God confounds our human wisdom, in which the weakness of God stays the violence of our power? It is in that spirit that our devilish hermeneutics seeks to speak when we insist that our identity is to be put at risk by the coming of the other, who bears the mark of God on his or her countenance.

Would not the sacredness of sacred writings lie in traumatizing us with this divine disruption, in the disconcertion, the decentering, the devilish disturbance created by the claim God makes upon us? Would we expect the word of God to reflect the patriarchal structures of the ancient world or their contradiction in the discipleship of equals? Would the word of God not be a function of there being two or three assembled in God's name, instead of being mistaken with the vested interests of a self-authorizing hierarchy and sanctimonious right-wing reactionaries? Does not the word of God resonate in the call to heal the lame and the leper, to respond to the poorest of the poor, to the weakest and the most defenseless? Does not the word of God take the part of *ta me onta,* the nuisances and nobodies of this world?

9

Undecidability and the Empty Tomb
Toward a Hermeneutics of Belief

Let us get back on the road with Cleophas, hoofing it to Emmaus, perplexed by the empty tomb, trying to read the signs of the times, recalling
to ourselves the general principle behind this devilish hermeneutics—
that things are haunted by a quasi-transcendentality, by a principle, or
un-principle, which sees to it that whatever makes something possible
also makes it impossible (that is, delimits it), and that we are better off
dealing with rather than ducking this difficulty. In the case of religious
faith—and this is the *aporia* of faith—this means that faith is faith only
when we are stretched by it, so that the more credible a thing becomes
the less faith is required to believe it, while the more incredible it becomes the more it is worthy of or at least requires faith. That is a point
that Søren Kierkegaard, or his pseudonyms, never tired of visiting upon
full professors of philosophy and others who are full of one thing or another.

For the religious believer (for us more radical hermeneuts, everybody
is *some* kind of a "believer"), faith is inwardly disturbed by what religious
writers going back to John of the Cross called a "dark night," or, in a
haunting phrase, the "silence of God." Even in the religions of the Book,
the words of God break off, silence rules, an unendurable absence, a tor-
menting caesura sets in, just when we need a saving word. "My God,
my God, why have you forsaken me?"—these are famous and beautiful
words spoken by the people of God about God's silence, words taken
from the psalms which belong integrally to any experience of the word of
God. These are words—prayers—from the Cross, when Jesus was tor-
mented by this silence and abandonment, and also words from the psalms
that the Jews recited daily throughout the darkest days of this century.
How could God permit this? How could God be God and allow such undeserved suffering? The question goes unanswered, is met with silence,
and faith is faith in and through and against this silence.

The premise of this chapter is that God's address to us is always ac-
companied by silence, that the trace of God is invariably marked by undecidability. We are unsure of the difference between the word and the
silence, between what is God's saying and what is God's silence, what
is God's word and what is ours, what is God's silence and what is ours.
That is the way undecidability hovers over sacred texts. Undecidability is
the condition, the quasi-transcendental condition, of faith, the thing that

makes faith (im)possible, *the* impossible. In the present chapter I pursue the question of undecidability and the silence of God in terms of what has been called the "hermeneutics of belief," which means a reading that believes that something *tout autre* is happening in the text, as opposed to a disbelieving reading, which suspects the text is pulling something over on us. I will undertake this by returning to some of the thorny questions surrounding the "historical Jesus"—questions that have attracted a great deal of public attention through the "Jesus Seminar"—which is in no small part a story about the silence of an empty tomb, and the hermeneutics of that silence. To be sure, this is not just *any* example or line of research. It is fraught not only with formidable scholarly difficulties but also with even more formidable institutional and religious implications, so that someone with more sense would keep his views to himself.

According to the condition of undecidability I have been pursuing in this devilish hermeneutics, the canons of historical "truth" have a good deal more give in them than we would like to think. The theories of interpretation that have emerged in the wake of Martin Heidegger's *Being and Time* are to no small degree a relentless critique of objectivistic conceptions of truth, in particular, of an historical objectivism of the Rankean variety which thinks that history tells it like it was (*wie es eigentlich gewesen ist*). But my idea of hermeneutics is to tell it like it *is,* to make it unmistakably plain that there are no pure facts, only better or worse interpretations, and that interpretations are guided in advance by what Hans-Georg Gadamer does not shrink from calling "prejudices," albeit productive prejudices. That is admittedly unnerving. Just as humanists everywhere are worried that the advent of these theories of interpretation means the relativizing of literary and historical studies, religious conservatives are worried that hermeneutical, genealogical, and deconstructionist accounts of the sacred scriptures will spell the end of faith (and hence the end of the political clout of the religious right!). Although I do agree that undecidability spells trouble for the whitened sepulchers of the religious right, I do not think it endangers faith. I would say that, on the contrary, hermeneutics explains the situation in which faith takes root and springs up. It alerts us to the *silence* of God, which if understood as *God's* silence is the path that hermeneutics takes to faith.

In the pages that follow I will pursue this issue *in concreto* by contrasting the work of philosopher Thomas Sheehan on New Testament research, who published a book back in 1986 that inflamed a lot of passion,[1] with the work of Edward Schillebeeckx, a Dutch Catholic priest and New Testament theologian (who inflamed the Vatican with some regularity).[2] These two authors aptly illustrate John P. Meier's observation, that "[i]n the end there is a hermeneutics of belief and a hermeneutics of unbelief,"[3] a way of approaching this research that stays open to faith and another way that closes faith down.

Philosopher Sheehan, a Heidegger scholar, has a good ear for the trouble that research into the historical Jesus (indeed all historical research) can stir up. As Sheehan puts it, this work takes place within the "inevitability of interpretation":

> . . . the point is to see the *inevitability of interpretation*, that is, to see that what makes us be human is our inexorable finitude, which condemns us to being acts of indirection and mediation, where all is "hints and guesses / Hints followed by guesses." [T. S. Eliot] If . . . living the kingdom means maintaining undecidability (the impossibility of distinguishing the worldly from the divine), then human existence itself, as an act of interpretation, is the *enactment* of undecidability. (FC, 226, cf. 120)

New Testament scholars will readily concede that the New Testament is not to be treated as a simple transcription of the *ipsissima verba* of Jesus, taken down directly from his lips by eyewitnesses. For Sheehan that means that this research is blowing the whistle on the "good news," which is being undone by the historical critical method, and in Sheehan's hands that becomes the basis for taking Christianity sternly to task. The historical critical method has unmasked the cold historical truth about Jesus:

> In Roman Catholic seminaries, for example, it is common teaching that Jesus of Nazareth did not assert any of the divine or messianic claims the Gospels attribute to him and that he died without believing he was Christ or the Son of God, not to mention the founder of a new religion. . . . [T]he Gospel accounts of the claims Jesus supposedly made to be Christ and God did not come from his own mouth but were interpretations his followers created in the decades after his death.[4]

On Sheehan's rendering, the message of Jesus is that God has descended "without remainder" into humanity. Jesus is a case of a messenger trying to get out of the way of the message. The historical Church that issues from his life and death is a misinterpretation that arises from divinizing the messenger whom the Romans killed. The good news, according to Sheehan, is that God disappears into humankind, and that Jesus just plain disappears. The death of Jesus is the end of God and of religion generally and the beginning of a search for a political solution to injustice. Sheehan's conclusions have an air of finality about them, which suggest sometimes that the results of the historical critical method are *not* just an interpretation but an *Erklärung*, even an *Aufklärung*.

Edward Schillebeeckx, a Catholic biblical scholar who also places the hermeneutic method at the center of Christological research, thinks the road to Emmaus leads us down a different path. In Schillebeeckx's hands the hermeneutic method yields the traditional faith (although the Vatican does not quite see it that way)—albeit without what he sometimes refers to as all the "hocus-pocus" (J, 649). In Schillebeeckx's view, if the historical critical method has removed the magic, hermeneutics retains the mystery, and his "experiment in Christology" is a call to a considerable, indeed I would say a fairly classical, faith (although Kierkegaard might have objected that Schillebeeckx has removed some of the "scandal"). At the heart of Schillebeeckx's approach to Christology lies the disciples', particularly Simon/Peter's, "conversion experience": Simon's realization that God stood by Jesus to the end, which is what they meant when they said that God had raised him up, and that the disciples were forgiven for abandoning him. In Schillebeeckx's approach, a great deal depends upon what we think happened to Peter in the days and weeks immediately following the crucifixion. Indeed there is almost existential ardor in Schillebeeckx's attempt to put us in the disciples' shoes, urging us to make a decision much like the one the disciples faced. For in the days and weeks and months following the crucifixion Simon experienced the silence of God for himself, the undecidability of what had taken place in the life and death of Jesus. Jesus was dead, his words were no longer to be heard, and they had abandoned him, even as Jesus lamented abandonment by God. Everywhere death and defeat, silence and abandonment. What now?

On my telling, faith will founder if, when faced with the silence of God, of the *tout autre,* one closes down the undecidability and lets God disappear into humankind in a gesture, not of undecidability, but "reductionism." Then the "kingdom of God" comes out with a Hegelian twist, even if a left-wing one, which, on the one hand, is what I see happening in Sheehan. Schillebeeckx, on the other hand, is a master of the hermeneutics of belief. He thinks that without the resurrection faith the disciples, and the rest of us, would be driven into the ground by the hopelessness and futility of life, that history would have no purpose. But to Sheehan, that sounds like trying to hope Jesus out of the grave (FC, 162); it is just a complaint about the meanness of the cosmos, not a way around it. So if Sheehan has closed down undecidability in the direction of suspicion and atheistic humanism, the question for my devilish hermeneutics is whether Schillebeeckx makes faith too safe, basing it on a trust in things for which hermeneutics gives no warrant (an objection that would amuse the Vatican, which does not think the problem with Schillebeeckx is that he is too safe). I will also draw attention to another feature of this contrast which is central: the common commitment of Schillebeeckx and Sheehan to an ethics of mercy, a politics of peace and justice, of *shalom,* which for Emmanuel Levinas should be the bottom line of any reading of the Scriptures.

So in what follows I will do three things. (1) I will lay out Sheehan's and Schillebeeckx's conflicting hermeneutics of the disciples' experience of Jesus. (2) I will then offer a criticism, first, of Sheehan, who closes off the historical Jesus from religious faith, and then of the way Schillebeeckx attempts to link them. (3) Finally, I offer a "more radical hermeneutical" rendering of the disciples' experience of the silence of God, a silence to which we are all exposed, and hence of what religious faith would look like in a hermeneutics more radically conceived.

Sheehan, Schillebeeckx, and the Kingdom of God

Sheehan and Schillebeeckx are drawing on the results of the "new questers," the post-Bultmannian quest for the historical Jesus launched after World War II, which unlike the first quest does not reduce Jesus to a humanitarian liberal, and unlike Rudolph Bultmann does not reduce the "Jesus of history" to an unknown X separated by an abyss from the "Christ of faith." The new questers concede the gap—Jesus probably did not call himself the Son of Man, did not take himself to be the coming Messiah, the Son of God, or God the Son. But they do find a basis, a *fundamentum in re,* in the historical Jesus for the later claims of faith, viz., the extraordinary authority with which Jesus conducted himself (he was not a mild-mannered liberal) and the great freedom he felt with respect to the Law, thus suggesting an exceptional, unprecedented, even mystical (J, 657) intimacy with the one he called his father (*Abba*). While Schillebeeckx is painfully scrupulous in maintaining the continuity, the *fundamentum in re,* Sheehan thinks the best work of the new questers is to no avail, that a leak has been sprung for which there is no plugging.

According to most of the new questers, Jesus was born of Joseph and Mary, in Nazareth not Bethlehem—the virgin birth and the Bethlehem nativity stories are a later "theological reflection" (J, 554)—into a politically beleaguered Jewish world with rising "eschatological" expectations of the end of the world. In the midst of confusing, competing expectations of a messiah king or messiah prophet, there also arose the idea of an "eschatological prophet," sometimes taken to be a new Elijah, who would come on the scene at the beginning of the end and announce that the rule of God was at hand; that was the context for Jesus' preaching. Jesus may well have started out as a disciple of John the Baptist. The synoptic version of his baptism—with the voice from heaven—that he let himself be baptized as a show of humility is what Schillebeeckx names a later "updating" or "secondary reflection." Sheehan describes such differences as putting words into Jesus' mouth, colored memories, inventions, etc. Jesus starts out under the spell of John's grim version of the eschatological message which calls for a conversion, change of heart—*metanoia*—Schillebeeckx translates this as "about turn" (J, 174), avoiding the usual translation as "repentance," which Hannah Arendt has criticized in a superb discussion,[5] because the day of God's judgment is at hand. But John's is an eschatology—the end is at hand—without apocalypse, no wild vision of cosmic fireworks; it is an existential, not a cosmic reckoning, which asked people to change their lives. John was a renegade religious figure. He leveled his critique at Israel, not her enemies; and he told Israel it would not be saved by a casuistic adherence to the law, but by a change of heart (FC, 54). "Jesus," Sheehan says, "was pierced to the heart. He repented and was baptized" (FC, 53; cf. J, 136–139). Maybe Jesus became an intimate of John's inner circle and was delegated by John to carry on the work of baptizing.

In any case, the message that Jesus delivered was clearly a variant, a revision and an extension of John's, and after John's beheading John's enemies became Jesus' enemies. In the place of John's grim dirge, Jesus put a lyric which "preached the joy of God's immediate and liberating presence" (FC, 57). He replaced John's mercilessly judging God with a loving father. "Change your heart. God's reign is at hand!" (Mark 1:15)— the loving forgiveness of the father is at hand, and it begins right here and now, in Jesus. Instead of a life in the desert and meals of locust and honey, Jesus scandalized the establishment by his indiscriminate companionability and his taste for a good meal. The powers that be were nonplused at the way Jesus put the kingdom into practice: dining with sinners and tax collectors, befriending a prostitute, violating the multiple prescriptions that had turned human beings into the slave of the Sabbath, instead of letting the Sabbath serve us (as a time of rest and revivification). As Schillebeeckx points out again and again, the God of Jesus stands solidly on the side of the human. He espouses the cause of the outcast and the excluded, the sinner and the despised, the poor and the disenfranchised, the "crippled and the lame, all who are cold-shouldered" (J, 145). John Dominic Crossan, the leading maverick New Testament scholar of the day and a former priest, has developed this image into a radical figure whose "kingdom of God" is a non-hierarchical, revolutionary community of equals, of nuisances and nobodies.[6] Jesus came to say that this coming kingdom was already under way, in him and in the easy familiarity he felt with the Father. The future is up ahead, but it is also now. The kingdom of God is at hand, starting with Jesus.

Sheehan, however, thinks that the "kingdom of God" of which Jesus speaks means that God has dissolved into man:

> . . . it meant God's act of reigning, and this meant—here lay the revolutionary force of Jesus' message—that God, as God, had *identified himself without remainder with his people.* The reign of God meant the *incarnation* of God. (FC, 60)

We will be pardoned if we are reminded of Ludwig Feuerbach's *Essence of Christianity* (or maybe even Karl Marx's *Theses on Feuerbach*). There is a parallel text in Schillebeeckx, but with a fundamentally different import:

> What we have here cannot be other than a message and style of conduct that proclaim God's universal love, the true God's lordship, *without reservation or without remainder.* (J, 145; my emphasis)

The kingdom of God means that something happens "without remainder," viz., that the father *loves us* without remainder, unconditionally. The measure of the father's love is love without measure. There is no stopping it, and there is no one who is excluded from it, so that Jesus makes a special point of shocking the establishment by keeping company with the very people from whom they wish to keep themselves separate. But for Sheehan the kingdom of God means God just *disappears into humankind* without remainder, in a kind of ontological hominization, although it is not clear how one would know that, for that sounds like a bit of unlocking The Secret. The kingdom of God then is an ontological declaration that God *an sich, kath'auto,* is dead, but Emmanuel, the God-with-us, or God-for-us, the God who *is* us, is alive and well in good works and orthopraxis, peace and justice. For Sheehan, Jesus is the eschatological prophet, announcing the beginning of the end—not of the world, but of Old Testament religion, of religion generally insofar as it is centered on a transcendent God. For Schillebeeckx the father commits himself to the human cause, without remainder; for Sheehan the father just slips into human shoes, without remainder.

Now that means that for Sheehan the post-Easter period represents a peculiarly perverse turn of events. The new questers agree that Jesus is a case of a messenger who was trying to get out of the way of his message. He was trying to remain invisible so that the father's forgiveness would be visible to all. He did not speak of himself, but of his father. He came proclaiming not himself, but his father's loving rule. The one time he spoke of the coming Son of Man he likely did not have himself in mind. But what happened is that after the Romans killed the messenger, the disciples divinized him. In a matter of a few decades the message that Jesus had delivered was displaced by the person of Jesus. The preaching of the kingdom gave way to the preaching of the preacher; the proclaimer became the proclaimed.

Like Schillebeeckx, Sheehan attaches a lot of importance to the fact that Jesus' message was rejected, not just by the establishment, who had everything to fear from him, but by the people themselves, whose side he was taking. Jesus' fatal journey into Jerusalem appears to be a last-ditch stand to put the movement back on its feet. Now as Schillebeeckx points out, Jesus would have been a fool not to know that by going down to Jerusalem, to the center of power of the religious orthodoxy of the day, he was putting his life in mortal peril. He had held no punches, calling the powers that be "hypocrites" and a "generation of vipers." A cloud of lurking danger, of impending doom, hung over his final meal with the disciples—"I shall not drink again of the fruit of the vine" (Mark 14:25)—in which he enjoyed for the last time his fellowship with the disciples.

The point is that Jesus had taken his stand on the kingdom of God absolutely, and he was willing to see it through to the bitter end. They could kill him, but they could not refute him. Even if they killed him they could not silence his father. The father would be with him, and he would trust the father, even if the worst happened. The father's loving hand is everywhere, even in the killing of his messenger, even if that messenger be a son, that is, someone with a special intimacy with him.

This was lost on the disciples. They were devastated by the crucifixion—the story of the disciples on the road to Emmaus picks up on their confusion—and they scattered to the four winds when it happened. But Schillebeeckx, following Rudolph Pesch—and this goes to the heart of the hermeneutic issue—imagines Simon/Peter back in Galilee, back at his fishing trade, mulling these matters over, fishing and thinking, and crushed by his own desertion of the master. And then it hit him: God did not abandon Jesus.[7] As Sheehan puts it, everything, even Jesus' merciless death, is in the hands of the loving Father. Jesus trusted God, but the disciples fled; they abandoned him after he shared with them "the cup of a fellowship that was supposed to be stronger than death" (FC, 103). If the disciples had expected that Jesus' faith in the father's loving care would be validated by his being safeguarded from the sword of his enemies, that was a misunderstanding on their part that painted the kingdom of God in too earthly a tone. The point of Jesus' unfathomable confidence in his father was to trust the father no matter what, no matter even if they put the messenger to death, no matter even if the disciples themselves abandon him. The father's loving care was with Jesus up to the end, even in letting him fall victim to his enemies, and it is here, with them now, extended to them in Jesus' *forgiveness of them, even now,* after they deserted him and fled as he was put to death. Jesus is the suffering servant, the martyred prophet, who trusted God up to his last breath of life and he will come again on the last day, and his father is a God of forgiveness. His faith in Jesus thus restored, Simon set about reassembling the disciples.

So Simon's "conversion experience," his "Easter experience" is the pivot around which the disciples regroup shortly after the crucifixion. Simon is the *cephas,* the hard rock, of the regrouping and that is the basis of the nickname he got—*cephas, petrus,* Peter ("Rocky"). The synoptics later on put this nickname into the mouth of Jesus and have him founding a new church. A later "theological reflection"? Or just plain revisionary history? It depends upon whether one uses a hermeneutics of belief or a hermeneutics of unbelief.

On the one hand Schillebeeckx has incurred a good deal of official ecclesiastical wrath because of his confidence in the historical critical method at this point. The disciples' retreat to the upper room awaiting the Spirit, Jesus' appearance to them—coming right through a bolted door —doubting Thomas sticking his hand in Jesus' side, eating food in the risen body, his appearances to the disciples on the road to Emmaus and elsewhere, the angel at the empty tomb with the rock rolled back: in short, all the miraculous Easter and post-Easter stories, everything that the mainstream faithful has taken to be the Gospel truth, is taken nowadays by most new questers to be later updating, secondary reflection, added on at a later date by the synoptics. Even the Gospel of Mark, the earliest, shortest, simplest, and above all the starkest of the synoptics, had been altered. Mark starts with Jesus' baptism, skipping all the nativity stories (of which he seems to know nothing) and ends with the women fleeing from an empty tomb on Easter morning—afraid, with no visions, and consigned to silence (Mark 16:1–8). Later on a new and more reassuring ending is tacked on (Mark 16:9–20).

But for Schillebeeckx the historical critical method has removed the magic but not the mystery. It replaces a certain simplistic belief in the scriptures as providing eyewitness reports of supernatural interventions in the natural order to clear the way for the essential faith and for reading them as effects and expressions of faith, not as apologetical proofs and historical documentation. The stories of the appearances and the empty tomb are an historically conditioned way of "expressing" in terms that made sense to themselves and others the profound "experience" the first members of the "Jesus movement" had undergone and the faith that they already had. Here is where Edmund Husserl's phenomenology can help us out. Schillebeeckx thinks in effect that to understand the "appearances," we have to bracket *natural* reality—nothing happened that a videotape would have picked up—in favor of the *experienced* reality. We cannot get the point of these stories without a religious version of the phenomenological *epoche*. Faith in the resurrection is not *based* on the appearance stories but *presupposed* by them. These stories do not serve the apologetic purpose of justifying or legitmating belief in the resurrection, which antedates and does not depend upon stories of the appearances. Rather they give a hermeneutic rendering or expression to an experience which transpired (J, 329–397). The "visual" element in these post-Easter "appearances," according to Schillebeeckx, is that the faithful are those who come to "see" what Jesus is about, as when, upon coming around to a new point of view (*metanoia*), someone will say "I see."

But Schillebeeckx thinks these experiences, to continue our Husserlian trope, are "motivated" by something that is taking place on the "noematic side," viz., by the movement of Jesus' spirit, which is also the father's spirit. He thinks these experiences have an "intentional correlate," that they are not just an arbitrary flow of *Erlebnisse*, even if they do not have a "natural object" for their correlate. The appearances are not perceptual "objects" (*Gegenstand*) but they do have their own special form of phenomenological *Sachlichkeit*. Schillebeeckx believes that Jesus has somehow been lifted up into the father's power, and that he exerts his influence upon the reassembling disciples. "Where two or three are gathered together in his name, Jesus is in the midst of them." "This New Testament text," Schillebeeckx comments, "is in my view perhaps the purest, most adequate reflection of the Easter experience" (J, 646).

Sheehan on the other hand thinks that this research lets the historical critical cat out of the bag. For Sheehan, whatever "experience" Peter underwent after the death of Jesus is available neither to us, *nor to Simon,* since all experience is mediated by the available language one has to articulate it. Whatever happened, it is *merely Simon's interpretation* that Jesus has been taken into God's eschatological future, has been vindicated by God, and will come again on the last day. Thus back at the founding moment of Christianity we find not a fact but a hermeneutics, not rock-hard historical evidence but Simon's (Rocky's) hermeneutics. That leads Sheehan into an interesting rereading of Simon's "denial" which lay not in abandoning Jesus—that under the circumstances was only prudent, or the whole movement would have gone under—but in following him. At the point Simon began attaching importance to Jesus personally, he betrayed Jesus, who had always taught that the father was all in all and had tried to get out of the way of his own message. But Simon turned him into "a hero and an idol, an obstacle to God-with-man" (FC, 124). Thus Simon's interpretation of his Easter experience perpetuated the denial of Jesus, in the sense of what Jesus was "really" getting at, institutionalized that denial, and makes of the standing church, vis-à-vis Jesus' own intentions, a heresy (FC, 223–224).

Starting out with Simon's misinterpretation of Jesus, and his self-interpretation of his Easter experience, a series of progressively more divinizing interpretations evolves that culminates in the formulae that the councils attempt to write in stone, and thus as it were to pluck out of the flow of history and hence of interpretation, just at the point that the "established" church finds convenient and agreeable. The councils reduce the plurality of interpretations to be found among the early Christians to a single, established, enforced, normative, canonical version, which is the end of hermeneutics, or so they hope. After a while that produces the illusion of an uninterpreted fact of the matter, an objective event, which finally reduces or erases the hermeneutics (FC, 160). The origin of Christianity starts looking like the origin of geometry according to Jacques Derrida: they both come down to erasing the trace. But by retracing the "genealogy" of the orthodox belief, which is supplied by Schillebeeckx and other new questers, Sheehan thinks that the contingency, not to say capriciousness of the orthodox view has been exposed. Presumably, the longevity of orthodoxy is in no small part due to the institutional power which backed it up and closed off alternative readings, which is a good example of what Michel Foucault means by power/knowledge. But the historical critical method has put an end to that cover-up. The truth is out.

According to Schillebeeckx and Pesch, Peter's "Easter experience" in Galilee transpired without his knowing anything about the empty tomb stories that were beginning to form among the Jerusalem community. The earliest disciples, starting out with Simon Peter, became convinced that God had vindicated Jesus and had taken him into his heavenly power, so that Jesus still lives—in heaven, with the father, and will come again, probably soon, as the appointed Son of Man to act as God's judge. And they put all that simply by saying "God has raised him from the dead" (1 Thess. 1:10). It was within the context of a preexisting belief that the father had stood by Jesus and (somehow) raised him up to be with him that the stories of the appearances and the empty tomb, that the whole Easter chronology regularly celebrated in the liturgy and spelled out in the New Testament, were to evolve.

But philosopher Sheehan disagrees. Sheehan accepts the notion of the empty tomb and that the body of Jesus just disappeared, but he attaches a different significance to it, which is that we have to learn how to live with the "absence of Jesus." The women's fruitless journey to the empty tomb that the disciples on the road to Emmaus were discussing is emblematic of humankind's futile search for transcendence, its longing for what it cannot have. (Derrida might give it another reading: the Messiah must always be *to come*.) At the other end of the finite human being's aspiration for infinity lies nothing at all. Human being is a projection upon nothing, upon absolute absence. The silence is just that, just silence. The human condition is absurd, and so the point of the story is being missed. We should do what the women do in the unaltered Marcan ending: leave the scene and lay off the search. The point is to get on with establishing the rule of earthly justice and stop malingering over the person of Jesus (FC, 163–173). Under Sheehan's hands, the stone rolled back from the tomb looks a lot like Sisyphus's rock, and the angelic messenger sounds like a 1950s French existentialist. But, we are forced to ask, if we are committed to the inescapability of interpretation, to the hermeneutics of undecidability, how can we be so sure there is nothing on the other end? How, if we are committed to the hermeneutics of undecidability, which throws all presence/absence systems into confusion, can we let "absolute absence" slip from our lips? At this point, I think, Sheehan is offering us, not undecidability, but The Secret, which turns out to be a decisive, well-centered atheistic humanism. But more about that later.

There is a parallel text on the absence of Jesus theme in Schillebeeckx, which he also locates in Mark (J, 417–423). In the original version—already an updating, composed around 70 A.D., and probably drawn from the liturgy that was celebrated around Jesus' tomb on the anniversary of his death (FC, 138)—the women find the empty tomb, are told by an angel that Jesus is raised and is not there, and finally that they should tell the disciples, especially Peter, that Jesus will meet them ahead in Galilee. Instead, the frightened women flee and say nothing to anyone. The Gospel ends with this mute fear: no appearances of Jesus, no ascension—just silence and fear. Later on, this disconcerting ending is updated, that is, brought into conformity with the more reassuring accounts in the still later gospels of Matthew and Luke (85 A.D.) and John (90 A.D.). But for Schillebeeckx, the "absence of Jesus" theme in Mark evolved from a pre-Marcan oral tradition and gives us an insight into the earliest version of

belief in Jesus, which is located among the Aramaic-speaking Jewish converts and the family of Jesus in the Jerusalem church. The story was
meant to enjoin the point that Jesus lives with his father in heaven and
so it is fruitless to come to his tomb in search of him. In its earliest version
it did not include a reference to a future appearance in Galilee; and its
"angel" (*angelos*, messenger) is a standard narrative vehicle of the day to
communicate a message, a biblical message-bearing Hermes.

Mark thinks that Jesus died and that was the last that was seen of him.
He thinks that Jesus lives with his father in heaven but, for the present at
least, in a kind of suspension or epoche, "absent in the brief period of the
eschatological community" but "soon to come" (J, 417). Marcan theology moves entirely between the memory of the earthly Jesus and the
hope in the second coming, so that ". . . Mark does not see the celestial
Jesus as presently operative, but affirms the complete absence of Jesus
from his sorrowing and suffering Church . . ." (J, 418). For the present,
Jesus is dead—between the two comings of Jesus there is only the empty
tomb—and we are summoned to faith that he will come again. The silence is broken only by prayer, "Come, lord Jesus! *Maran atha.*" Mark's is
a maranatha Christology, a *Christologia negativa*, where Jesus is presently
absent but coming in the future. The Church is an orphan, and Jesus is
the Lord of the future, so that Mark is wary of present pneumatic experiences of the risen Lord. As to Paul's theology of the church as the mystical
body of Jesus in which the celestial Jesus is continuously effective, Schillebeeckx says that "in the Marcan Gospel there is not the slightest opening for it" (J, 422). In Mark the emphasis falls on the parousia, not on the
resurrection or presently reigning, risen Jesus. Mark is not a skeptic; he is
just faithful to the earthly Jesus' preaching. The kingdom of God is near;
it has begun in Jesus' first coming, and the death of Jesus is the beginning
of the eschatological woes. Now we await in "a drab but necessary interim period" (J, 422) the second coming, the fulfillment of Jesus' prayer
that his father's kingdom may come, when Jesus will return.

But with the *delay* of the parousia—the Christological deferral of presence—a supplement is required (J, 542–543). Thus over and beyond maranatha Christology a divine miracle man Christology (*theios aner*) evolved
among Greek-speaking Jews, which demonstrates Jesus' divine character
by telling tales of marvelous miracles and acts of power and stories of the
risen Jesus (J, 424–429; FC, 192–205). Now the disciples claim that, far
from having to wait for the parousia (which is starting to look far off),
believers have *already* received salvation. Jesus is exalted as reigning Lord,
called in Greek the *christos;* his personal status is enhanced, the futural,
eschatological dimension begins to weaken. Lastly, Greek-speaking Gen-
tile converts, who were steeped in wisdom literature, identify Jesus with
an hypostasized wisdom who cooperates with God in the creation of the
world, of which the Johannine prologue is the best example (J, 431). The
wisdom Christologies pave the way for the now normative Christologies
of John and Paul in which God's Eternal Son became man, died for our

sins, and rose again to reign with God from whence he shall come to judge the living and the dead.

Thus the earthly Jesus undergoes a series of "theological reflections" (Schillebeeckx) or "enhancements" (Sheehan): from eschatological prophet (the historical Jesus), to the coming Son of Man (maranatha Christologies), to the reigning Lord (divine man Christology), to the Eternal Son of God. Only in the last version does Jesus acquire flat-out divinity, which gives the councils the opening to "define" the status of Jesus unequivocally as God the Son and to work out the doctrine of the Trinity of persons.

The Hermeneutics of Belief and of Unbelief

On the one hand, in Sheehan's hermeneutics of unbelief, the historical critical method has irreparably severed the Jesus of history from the Christ of faith and exposed the kingdom of God as the death of God. Schillebeeckx, on the other hand, deploys a hermeneutical move which will bridge the gap and preserve the continuity; his faith unshaken, he is willing to let the historical critical chips fall where they may, as Meier says.[8] My own view, however, is that there is something more to undecidability than either Schillebeeckx or Sheehan allow, as I will attempt to show in the present section. Then, in the next section, I will address the question as to where this all leads us.

Let us return to the status of the resurrection for the new questers. Both Schillebeeckx and Sheehan identify three ways of interpreting the resurrection, which I will follow Sheehan in calling the traditional, the moderate, and the liberal views (J, 644–646; FC, 164–165).

(1) The traditional version takes the Gospel at its face value, as the *literal Gospel truth*, which records a series of miraculous contraventions of natural law. The resurrection is conceived in physicalistic terms, as an empirical, perceptual event that would have been picked up by a video camera, were one available. Resurrection means resuscitation. Now it is this traditional view—which really is the mainstream belief and the one commonly preached to the faithful—that has been washed out by the historical critical method and reduced to the status of biblical fundamentalism. Neither Sheehan nor Schillebeeckx, nor any higher criticism, accepts this.

(2) In the moderate view, the resurrection is conceived as an ontological event, *ex parte objecti,* but not a physical one, in which God has somehow assumed Jesus into his power. It is not literally but ontologically true. That is the prevailing view among informed Catholic and mainstream Protestant New Testament scholars. In Schillebeeckx's version in particular, the resurrection stories are taken as "expressions" of a "faith-experience" which actually antedate the stories, but they nonetheless have a real, though not perceptual, correlate.

(3) Finally, there is the liberal view, found in such authors as Bultmann

and Willi Marxsen, which treats "Easter" as a *symbolic truth*, inasmuch as it signifies something which took place, *ex parte subjecti*, strictly in the subjective life of the disciples. If in the traditional version the body of Jesus is physically risen, and in the moderate view, his living spirit continues to guide us, in the liberal view it is but his "meaning" or "cause" which lives on.

Sheehan seems to be to the left of everybody, because he thinks all three interpretations are a misinterpretation which cover up the fact that God makes a Feuerbachian descent into humanity never to surface or ascend again. The disciples rescued just what should have gone under and they ended up divinizing Jesus. But that is anachronistic. If Sheehan wants to play historical critical hardball and to work Christianity over for not abiding by Jesus' own historically limited self-interpretation, then to put in the mouth of this devout Jew of first-century Galilee the main argument of left-wing Hegelianism is to dwarf any of the later "updatings" in the synoptics which he is so fond of criticizing.

The historical critical picture of Jesus which is emerging does not portray Jesus as a death of God theologian, but a devoutly monotheistic, slightly mystical Jew. Contra Sheehan, the *Abba* experience does not mean that the father has just disappeared *into* his children, but that he stands unequivocally *with* them, takes their side in thick and thin, like a faithful and loving father. The whole point of this is *religious* in just the sense that Sheehan denies, viz., to give every assurance to the poor and despised, the outcast and excluded, that they have infinite resources to draw upon, that they are sustained by a higher power, that they are in a special way the ones whom the father supports. Even if from a strictly worldly point of view they have drawn the short straw, Jesus assures them that the father is with them no matter what. Jesus was not just trying to boost their morale. He was telling them there was something on their side which the philosophers would name "ontological." So Jesus' special calling, the reason he came into the world, was to deliver this message—he was carrying out a prophetic role—that they had an infinite support behind them and that the kingdom was theirs for the seeking.

Now it is true that Jesus spoke with shocking authority and freedom, but this arises not from his *own* authority, but from his scandalous sense of intimacy with the father. His authority was delegated; he was a special emissary empowered to speak on his father's behalf. He does not speak in his own proper name, but in the name of his father. In the historical critical picture Jesus always defers to the father, speaks on behalf of the father. He is always delivering the message of the one who sent him and for his own part tries constantly to get out of the way of the message. According to the historical critical view Jesus attached no importance to himself, and that is why he walked right into the teeth of death: he had an unfathomable confidence in the father and a sense that the father would prevail even if he personally was erased. Jesus called Simon a Satan when Simon suggested to him that he should look for a way around this mortal peril, for it is only the father that matters and he, Jesus, has come only to spread his word. He is not himself the word, but the one who has come to deliver the word; he is not the message but the messenger; not the proclaimed but the proclaimer. There is little in the historical critical picture to sustain Sheehan's hypothesis that God has *dissolved* into human solidarity, nothing to suggest a proleptic version of left-wing Hegelianism. What it does suggest is a profoundly Jewish monotheism, and a sense of human solidarity rooted in the fatherhood of God.

I do not think Sheehan can cut Christianity off by arguing that Jesus taught the death of God. Still, as a devout Jew who does not speak in his own name but in the name of the father, who does not mean to be the message but the messenger, it can hardly be thought that he had anything like Christianity in mind, which is the sense of the "betrayal" of Jesus by Christianity that Sheehan remarks. Christianity looks like a mistake, like the child who looks at the finger instead of what the finger is pointing toward, not because, as Sheehan makes out, Jesus was an atheist but because he was so devoted to the true spirit of the Torah. On the new questers' account Christianity is not what Jesus had in mind. He did not mean to displace Judaism but to say that its eschaton was at hand, here and now, that what it was about had come about. He intended to be the end of Judaism, not in the sense of its demise, but of its fulfillment. He meant to announce the beginning of the end, that the father's loving rule had begun. He thus recalls Judaism to its most profound intuitions, revivifies its deepest insight into God's loving care for Israel, and blows the whistle on the legalism and hierarchical hypocrisy among the Temple authorities which was obscuring the genuine meaning of the Torah, and that cost him his life.

If the new questers are right about this, the claim of the traditionalists that the New Testament is an historically faithful account of what really and truly happened back in the first century, *wie es eigentlich gewesen ist,* is hopelessly discredited. As Crossan says, the gospels are "gospels," *good* news: they have *already* built a positive hermeneutic spin into their stories; they do not even pretend to be disinterested historical chroniclers.[9] The moderates are, hermeneutically speaking, more swift of foot. They see the traditionalist difficulty coming and they are ready with a hermeneutical comeback, viz., that they are not governed by the intentions of the author. Schillebeeckx writes:

> Unintentionally, therefore, though Jesus preached not himself but the rule and lordship of God, it was "himself" that he had proclaimed: the Proclaimer is the One proclaimed. (J, 543)

That is, at this point Schillebeeckx and the moderates invoke the hermeneutics of Gadamer and Paul Ricoeur, which is descended from Heidegger's *Being and Time.* They claim that the meaning of a text, an event or

—in this case—a life, is not governed by the author's or the agent's self-understanding, that a text or an event has a sense and significance, repercussions and implications, that "exceed" the original intention and that continuously unfold in, through, and as a "tradition." The ability of a tradition to "appropriate" its founding act is what keeps it afloat; that enables the moderates to establish the much needed link or continuity, and to justify the talk about updating and secondary theological reflections. So it is not necessary for the historical Jesus of Nazareth to have understood all that much about the "Christ of faith." In an ironic turn of events, then, the moderates could throw Heidegger and Gadamer up against Sheehan, the Heidegger commentator. The problem of Christian faith lies in the gap between Jesus and the course taken by the Jesus movement after his death, and the only way to bridge that gap is with a hermeneutic theory that delimits the author's authority and allows things really to get rolling only after the death of the author.

Now while this is a classical hermeneutic gesture, and while Gadamer's theory works nicely with William Shakespeare and the American constitution, there are rather special complications involved in the claims that the moderates make that at least make it an odd version of this theory. I see three such complications. (a) To begin with, the moderates have an inverted version of the argument. The argument against privileging the intentions of the author says we should ignore the person of the author and pay heed to the intentional content, the *Sache,* of his message. But the moderates are doing exactly the opposite, viz. overriding the message of the author and exalting his person. On the one hand, Jesus seems clearly to disavow his own importance as an author and to make himself a vehicle of the message. He attaches no importance to his empirical reality—that he is willing to offer up in the name of the father—and every importance to the message, the *intentum,* the intentional object of his utterances and actions. Christianity, on the other hand, absolutizes Jesus personally, makes something out of the personal life and death of the author of the message, while altering the message. Now, from the point of view of the "death of the author" schema, that is like making a cult out of the person of Shakespeare or Thomas Jefferson and ignoring what they said or wrote.

(b) Mainstream Christianity is in the delicate position of holding to a view that seems to be inconsistent with and opposed to Jesus' self-interpretation. If Jesus was thoroughly turned toward the father, he may well have objected to these later developments. If—as a purely counterfactual conditional—someone had projected the subsequent course of events in Christian theology after the crucifixion and submitted it to Jesus' consideration while he was alive, we may well imagine that he would have been scandalized by it and have regarded it as the suggestion come of Satan (particularly had he foreseen the fate his Jewish people would suffer at the hands of Christianity).[10] Would the moderates still persist, even if the historical Jesus would have rejected the later interpretation that was put on him? How far can we go in disregarding the intention of the author if we also claim the author was divine?

(c) Finally, suppose Jesus' message was roundly accepted by everyone, that he lived a long life, and died as an honored prophet who had revivified Judaism with his *Abba* spirituality, having sensitized everybody to the problems of legalism. Then Christianity would have never gotten off the ground because everybody would have believed Jesus, and not the Jesus movement, that the father was all and Jesus was nothing. Jesus' message would have prevailed and he would have cut off in advance the idea that he was personally important. His message would have been clear and it would have been obvious that he had no interest in transcending Judaism or in attaching a divine status to himself. In other words, Christianity could not get going unless Jesus is rejected and killed and is no longer around to explain himself. If he succeeded in doing what he wanted to do, there would be no Christianity.

The recourse the moderates have to a death of the author hermeneutics is not contradictory, by any means, but it is unusual.

Undecidability and the Silence of God

What now? Where does this leave us?

We recall our guiding principle, that we get the best results from facing up to the worst. We more radical hermeneuts are all agreed that we are always already interpreting, always hoofing it down the road to Emmaus, that nothing escapes a hermeneutic fashioning. There is nothing outside textuality, no uninterpreted facts of the matter lying outside the interpretive web, no way around language and history, no secret passage which gives us access to a privileged, unreformable insight into what is happening. The secret is, there is no Secret. Having the heart to see that concession through to the end is what I have been calling throughout these pages a "more radical hermeneutics." Religious faith is a kind of hermeneutics, a way we have of reading the traces in the sand of human existence. That hermeneutic feature is not only true of faith, but a good many philosophers today are agreed that it is true of reason, too, which is also, I would add, similarly shot through with faith. It is true in general, I think, that, as Gadamer says, understanding is interpreting, a way of getting an angle on things, a way of approaching. Both faith and reason are ways of reading and construing, and both have no other recourse than to invoke the historically conditioned models and linguistic artifacts that are at their disposal. Faith is a read we have on the human condition; it is not a supervening miracle that lifts us up out of our boots (FC, 6). That explains the difficulties believers of all sorts get into with the rest of the human race. They seem to think, and everybody else thinks they think, that they have gotten privileged access to a "truth," to The Secret, that the rest of humankind has not. So one of the effects of pressing the claims of a radical hermeneutics is to blur the clean line between believer and infidel. We proceed from the vivid, disturbing sense of the historicality and linguisticality of what phenomenologists once too naively called "experience." There is nothing called experience, or perception, or the things themselves, outside the textuality of language and history. So the radical hermeneutic situation leaves us without firm footing.

It is important to observe that both Sheehan and Schillebeeckx have recourse to an ethics and politics of mercy, as indeed does Levinas, to whom I will return shortly. But if we have a heart for hermeneutics then must we not concede that ethics, too, is an interpretation?

Let us return to Simon Peter's experience, only this time with a hermeneutic more radically conceived in mind, which means keeping the undecidability and the slippage, the "through a glass darkly" in mind. Fishing and thinking, Simon is trying to bring to words what had *happened* to him in the short space of a year or two. Simon was trying to unfold, explicate, lay out (*aus-legen*) the implicit horizons and content of his experience, to reach an *Auslegung,* an interpretation, we hermeneuts might say. This man, he thought, had knocked him off his pins. What to make of that? Who was he? Where did he come from? "Rabbi, where do you dwell?" (John 1:38–39), he remembered asking Jesus. "Who do you, Simon, say that I am?" Jesus had asked him. What Simon came up with and then began to run by the other disciples was that Jesus *was* the coming Son of Man, not just the forecaster of him, and that God had vindicated his death. But that formulation which took root in the early church did not drop from the sky; it was the fruit of a man working within an inherited tradition and its handed-down vocabulary. It is unlikely that he would have used that formulation today, where we would be more likely to say the Force was with him. So it came from a history, a language, a tradition. Moreover, as everybody admits, it also had a subsequent history and vocabulary that was to lead all the way up to the Nicene Creed.

From Sheehan's point of view, that subsequent history is a scandal which makes a mockery of the historical critical method. From Schillebeeckx's point of view, which is much closer to the hermeneutic mark, it means that Simon hit on something which captured the imagination of its hearers, formulated their experience for them, and generally gave them an *Auslegung* to hang on to.

What it means from my point of view is that Simon had a brush with the deep undecidability in things, with the wavering instability in things, with what we have been calling the silence of God that we cannot avoid even as it elicits a choice from us. Undecidability is a condition of choice, not an excuse for staying on the sidelines. Simon had a chance not afforded to everyone to meet someone who just brought him up short and left an unforgettable impression on him, who just would not go away even after they killed him. But what does that mean? Let us bracket Sheehan's death of God atheology, and bracket, too, Schillebeeckx's doctrinal concerns, and undertake a particular phenomenology or at least a quasi-phenomenology of Simon's situation. For this, I trust I will be permitted to have recourse to the aid of a Jewish phenomenologist, or quasi-phenomenologist, Emmanuel Levinas, all this being a profoundly Jewish matter and a matter of fateful importance to the Jews. What happened to Simon, and to the other disciples, I believe, is beautifully captured in what Levinas calls "the impossibility of murder."[11] Levinas is not denying that it is possible to physically kill somebody; that is a well-known and tragically banal fact which is actually his point of departure. It was his own experience of the Holocaust that provoked the great ethical outburst that today goes under the name "Levinas." But even if one murders someone, one cannot, to use the discourse of the gangster movies, "erase" them. Levinas explains this by attributing a certain "infinity" and hence inextinguishability to the other person. The arm of the murderer is not long enough to reach the other, not in the other's true otherness, which is infinite, which exceeds everything empirical, and is thus an invisible excess, an irreducible transcendence. In Levinas this analysis is focused on the *murderer* who is always haunted by the deed, by the "ghost" of the victim. Levinas was trying to keep the ghosts of the Holocaust before the mind of "Christian Europe."

But let us here shift this focus to the impact of the murder on the *survivors,* the intimates, the friends of the victim. They too experience the ghost of the victim, his *Geist, spiritus,* especially when they assemble together. By deploying this Levinasian theme we can say that Simon and the other disciples had a remarkably profound experience of the stamp of infinity upon Jesus, of the transcendence, the invisible depths, the mysterious sources and resources of Jesus. "Rabbi, where do you dwell?" Where do you come from? What landed on Simon one day was the inextinguishability and inexhaustibility of Jesus, and the best way Simon could find of expressing that inextinguishability was to use the best language at his disposal—the coming Son of Man. (The Force was with him.)

We can imagine that Simon had been penetrated by the look of Jesus, pierced by those eyes, that he was sometimes just paralyzed by the face of Jesus. When Jesus "turned and looked straight at Simon" the night of his arrest, Simon ran out and wept bitterly (Luke 22:61–62). Sheehan does a remarkable analysis of that look (FC, 121–122). "Face to face," Jesus had power. When he would talk to people who were described in those days as "possessed by devils," he could calm them down. (We would not describe them that way anymore, and instead of talking to Jesus we would prescribe Prozac.) Sometimes Jesus would simply enter a room, Simon might have remembered, sit down with a disturbed man, perhaps take the man's hand in his, look him straight in the eye, and the poor fellow would calm down. Jesus could do things like that.

Now let us push this Levinasian analysis one step further, while recalling the related warning of Johannes Climacus, that it is paganism to think that the divinity of Jesus was visible, and that it would require the "condition" to get further than Jesus' "penetrating eyes." Once again, the Jewishness of Levinas is not an obstacle but crucially significant, given the Jewishness of Jesus. Levinas helps us see how Jesus would be turned so essentially to the "father." But more important, Levinas has this strong Jewish sense that we cannot see the face of God, that no one can see the face of God—even Moses only caught his back—except in the face of our fellow human beings, that the father withdraws behind the face of the little ones. So what Simon experienced when he experienced the infinity of Jesus, the invisible depths of that extraordinary man, was a glimpse of the face of God. Not directly, unambiguously, in a naked experience outside of history and unaffected by language. Not without textuality. But with such authenticity and liveliness that when Simon ran this by the other disciples they agreed and it caught on. Had Simon come up with something that made no sense, it would not have caught on, and that would have been that. Something extraordinary had just happened to them and Simon had found a way to formulate it.

So one side of Simon's undecidable experience is coming into view. This is not meant to be a phenomenological proof for the divinity of Jesus, but a Levinasian "explication" (*Auslegung*) of one side of Simon's experience, viz., of the kind of power that came crashing in upon the disciples, and which can come crashing in upon all of us, the kind of "infinity" that a deep encounter with another person harbors. Now for Levinas the experiential contact we make with the life of God in this experience of the face of the other is strictly *ethical;* it consists in justice, in a life of service to others. That deeply Jewish spirituality goes to the heart of Jesus' message about the father's loving care for humankind. That is why Schillebeeckx cites Levinas to make a meaningful point about Jesus:

> Even when dying, Jesus has no desperate concern with his own identity, . . . but is taken up with the matter of God's rule. . . . God has man's interest at heart, but in a world which itself does not always appear to do so. . . . It says something that it was a Jewish thinker and philosopher, E. Levinas, who could speak of the irresistible power of the "defenseless other one" who goes on trusting. (J, 638)

It is always the "widow and the orphan," that is, the innocent and the defenseless one, who evokes our responsibility according to Levinas. Now Jesus' life was given over to the message that the father loves us and has already forgiven us, and he kept that faith in the face of death. For that he was brutally punished and murdered. What lies at the basis of Simon's experience, I submit, is this experience of the *impossibility of murder,* of the inextinguishability of innocence, of the triumph of love over death, which early Christianity expressed by saying Jesus lives, God has raised him up. The impossibility of murder is the phenomenological counterpart to the theology of resurrection.

Levinas is describing an ethical, hermeneutical, and phenomenological experience that is in principle available anywhere, and is not localized in Jesus of Nazareth, a universal claim that exceeds what one does or does not think of Jesus, that is not localized in Christianity or even, for Levinas, in Judaism. "Every other is wholly other" (*tout autre est tout autre*), as Derrida says.[12] We are *all* the chosen people, according to Levinas, all chosen to serve the neighbor and the stranger. So what comes undone in this gloss upon Simon's experience is Schillebeeckx's claim that there is something *exclusive* about Jesus. On this account, Jesus would be a unique, but not an exclusive site for the event of the infinite. This is a more philosophical, universal account, more like Derrida's talk of a pure messianic apart from the concrete messianisms,[13] or like Heidegger's reference to the manifestations of the divine "in the world of the Greeks, in prophetic Judaism, in the preaching of Jesus," that is, the multiple historical occasions of this manifestation.[14] Otherwise, we would have to think that God plays favorites with chosen people, who are in some special way that is unique to themselves the "people of God." We would have to think that God preferred Christians or Jews to inhabitants of the deepest recesses of the most remote places, who have not heard of Jesus or the Jews.

From a hermeneutical point of view, the infinity that Levinas describes is present in us all. These innocents are everywhere, from Jerusalem to Auschwitz, from Bangladesh to Cambodia, and beyond. Every man—and every woman, too (although this is not Levinas's strong suit)—reveals the face of God. There is an infinity which inhabits every other—*tout autre est tout autre*. Every other, and each for the other, is a site for the divine, a point of entry for what Derrida calls the coming of the other. That means that the extraordinariness of Jesus, his uniqueness, would lie in being an extraordinarily good example of a universal human possibility, an exemplary "event" of transcendence. In Jesus something would happen with an explosiveness and white-hot intensity that in principle can happen elsewhere. In Jesus we would hear the rush of God as God withdraws from the world, catch a shadowy sight of God in the face of Jesus, catch a glimpse of the back of God as he passes us by in Jesus. Jesus would be a particular place of the divine event or advent, of God's coming, of the coming of the *tout autre*, maybe the best case a lot of Greco-Europeans can remember. But not the only possible one.

The Jesus described in the historical critical method, well, *one* of them, for there is no such thing as *the* Jesus here—is the friend of the outcast and the enemy of hierarchy and of hypocrisy, with a faith in the father stronger than death. Of that Jesus we have offered, in the spirit of Levinas, a hermeneutical rendering. But Sheehan would close off the undecidability of what happened in Jesus of Nazareth and provide us with a definitive hermeneutic key, a perfectly transparent *Erklärung* of it, a religiously insensitive reduction of it, in short, an offer of an atheistic version of The Secret. But Derrida, who knows a thing or two about undecidability, has made all such definitive hermeneutic keys questionable. He calls that sort of hermeneutics "onto-hermeneutics." Derrida criticizes such identifying reductionism wherever it shows its head—for example, when Heidegger tried to *identify* the *es gibt* as *Ereignis* as if that were some unique "meaning of Being," or when Freud undertook to reduce the unconscious to male sexuality, or when Marx attempted to reduce historical profusion to "historical materialism," etc.[15] So when Sheehan describes what he does as "deconstruction" (FC, 142) and speaks of "undecidability" (FC, 225), I would say beware of those who wear long hermeneutic robes. He is *not* serving up deconstruction but a reductionist hermeneutics of suspicion with a strongly left-wing Hegelian twist. But deconstruction is neither reductionistic nor hermeneutical key-making. If Jesus is an undecidable, then he is a place where the bottom drops out and we are called upon to assume responsibility for what we make of him.

The whole idea behind the more radical hermeneutic style I am pursuing here is that we ought to adhere rigorously to the element of undecidability, that we not break off too quickly and reach a resolution of the hermeneutic conflict. That means there is another side to Simon's experience that needs to be discussed. According to both Sheehan and Schillebeeckx, the kingdom of God means universal *shalom* (J, 594), the rule of peace and justice (and Levinas would agree). For Sheehan, the kingdom of God *reduces* to peace and justice without remainder, so that Marxism would do just as well, and for Schillebeeckx the kingdom of God gives a transcendent *warranty* or backup for the human order of peace and justice. Schillebeeckx thinks that Jesus gives us a promise that history has a meaning, that suffering has an opponent (J, 615–616), while Sheehan thinks that promise should be translated "without remainder" into orthopraxis. In the face of innocent suffering, Schillebeeckx says, philosophy and theology are bereft of counsel. History has a demonic strain; evil eludes our explanatory devices (J, 620), and the only answer is given in Jesus' message of faith and trust that the father is with us, no matter what:

> Despite the historical failure of this message, Jesus bore witness to the indestructible certainty he felt regarding the salvation given by God, to a certainty which in his case was grounded in an exceptional *Abba* experience. For us it entails a promise from God that the salvation and "making whole" of man is possible and there is ultimately a point, a meaning to human life. (J, 625)

It is through Jesus that "limitation and alienation, impotence and even death, are finally overcome: the finite itself—for that is what we are—is redeemed" (J, 666). For Schillebeeckx everything turns on the notion that death and suffering must be overcome, defeated. The world must be redeemed. Sheehan thinks that if "Jesus" moves one in that direction, that is fine, but one does not need Jesus, and that an ethics of mercy *sans* Jesus will do just as well (FC, 222–223). For Sheehan, the name of God is to be demythologized, reduced to ethico-political justice; he is not serving up the end of religion but its flip side, the secularized version of universal *shalom*. His notion of social justice retains all the theological momentum of religion, but with this difference, that God has melted down into humanity. This is the end of religion in the sense of its completion and translation into an ortho-praxis which is out to redeem a fallen world but in a way that is bereft (*kenosis*) of the divine, transcendent backup.

I am closer to Schillebeeckx, but I would add a hermeneutic qualifier to what he says. We must resist the tempting illusion to still the hermeneutic flux, to arrest the play that is set in motion once we have conceded the inescapable undecidability in things. For the ethics of mercy, peace and justice, *shalom*, is *also* a perspective. The implication, the terrible and terrifying implication, of the "undecidability" of it all, of the radical hermeneutical fix we are in, just might be that the world is innocent and does not need saving, whether by Jesus (Schillebeeckx) or Marx (Sheehan). Suppose with Friedrich Nietzsche we simply insisted that the world was never guilty, that nothing needs to be redeemed, that everything is innocent, suffering included. When Nietzsche spoke of the "innocence of becoming" he meant that transiency and history, change and travail, are not a fall from *ousia*, not depraved, evil, unjust, or sinful. The world just plays itself out, the quanta of energy just discharge, and it—the world, *das Spiel, das "es"*—just does not know we are here. Now it is no objection to this point of view to say that if that were so history would have no goal, life would have no meaning, and we would have nothing to hope for or in. That is a complaint, not an objection, and the cosmos is under no obligation to answer our complaints. Put another way, the ability of an idea to answer our complaints, to give us meaning and comfort, is little guarantee of its truth. I say this not with the idea of refuting faith or driving it back into hiding but with the idea of *situating* it within undecidability, for faith is a decision, an interpretation, made in the midst of just such undecidability, just when such undecidability has sunk its teeth in our hide. Otherwise faith is a convenience or a way of getting elected to public office.

Nietzsche was making a case for what I called in the last chapter of *Radical Hermeneutics* a tragic, ir-religious view of life. I know that there are strongly religious and prophetic streaks in Nietzsche, but on this point I take him to be deeply irreligious. Nietzsche had a "merciless" way of viewing things which saw the cosmos, not in the religious terms of universal *shalom*, of an ethics of mercy, but in a presocratic vision of war where the only justice is the sort one finds in Anaximander and Heraclitus, where the endless strife of things, the incessant going over and going under, strikes an overall balance. Now that is a hard saying. Nietzsche had a merciless view of truth, a truth without mercy.[16]

> How much truth can a spirit *endure*, how much truth does a spirit *dare?*
> . . . this does not mean that [his philosophy] must halt at a negation, a No, a will to negation. It wants to cross over to the opposite of this—to a Dionysian affirmation of the world as it is, *without subtraction, exception, or selection. . . .*

In another place Nietzsche says that "his" philosophers do not want the truth sweetened, softened, blunted, attenuated. All things are caught up in an eternal wheel which binds happiness with suffering, birth with death, pleasure with pain, joy with sorrow. There is no suppressing of one side in favor of the other, no subtraction of one part from the whole to which it belongs. All things are wedded to each other so that to affirm life is to affirm the whole wheel of becoming, the going over and the going under. We cannot accept life with mental reservations, for better but not for worse, like a bridegroom with his fingers crossed when he makes his vows. Nietzsche replaces "redemption"—whether by God or by revolutionary social movements; for Nietzsche it is a matter of indifference how we prop up "morals"—with *amor fati,* love of the earth as it is, without allowance for line-item vetoes. It is not the Lord Jesus that he prays come again, but the eternal circulation of life, with its endless wheel of joy and sorrow.

Now we can see the full dimension of facing up to the inescapability of hermeneutics and the radical concept of undecidability with which we are faced. A radically hermeneutic reading of Simon's experience has to concede the possibility of this reading of it. The powerful portrait of Jesus Schillebeeckx draws in *Jesus* must be situated against the horizon, indeed the specter that perhaps history has no point at all, that undeserved suffering has no meaning, that the cosmos does not know we are here. Faith is faith, not a convenience or a version of privileged access, only if we confess this possibility, which is what I mean when I say that we get the best results by confessing the worst elements of the fix we are in.

Undecidability is a way of describing a point where the abyss opens out on us. Derrida has been recently calling this the *khôra,* using a text from the *Timaeus,* which he interprets as the counterpart to the *agathon,* viz., to the attempt to put the best face on the flux.[17] Schillebeeckx recognizes the structural undecidability upon which I am insisting and indeed makes occasional references to "God's silence" (J, 651). That *silence,* I have been arguing, is intrinsic to any talk about God's saving "*word.*" The prototypical case of the silence of God in the Christian tradition is his silence at the crucifixion. The historical critical method paints a different picture of it: no heavens opening up at the crack of 3:00 P.M., no centurion confessing that this was the Son of God in truth. Just abandonment, death, and maybe even no empty tomb at all, just burial in a common grave, maybe even, as Crossan imagines, no burial at all, just exposure to the dogs.[18] "My God, my God, why have you forsaken me?" The seven last words may be a later adornment, but they have a ring of truth, of Nietzsche's cold, merciless truth. Many of the results of the historical critical portrait are sobering and are often as filled with religious import as the later "up-datings." Maybe more. In the Jewish tradition the Holocaust is the most painful evidence of the silence of God, and about that I have no right to say anything more than has already been said, by Elie Wiesel and by countless others who have heard this silence and have lived to tell it. Where is the father's loving care then? How does one continue to push an *Abba* spirituality then? Who can imagine a human father like that? Here is where we need negative theology lest we throw the whole thing over. That silence is the scream of undecidability in any faith and it takes raw courage to weather it out.

In this spirit, let me add a final rendering of Simon back at the Sea of Galilee, this time with all this *undecidability* and the silence of God in mind. Who is this man, Simon asks himself, and where does he dwell? Who do you say I am? Jesus asked Simon. I would let a radical herme-neutical thought cross Simon's mind, that Jesus' cruel murder was just part of the way the cosmos discharges its energy, that the universe knows no mercy, that the cosmos does not know or care about Jesus, and that the taking of Jesus' life belonged as much to the cosmic economy as does Simon's own work as a fisherman, which spelled death for the fish but life for Simon. Simon would have to have shuddered with that thought, too, before he started to round up the disciples, and even after he had gotten the whole thing going and they started to call him the rock, he would continue to worry about that.

I must confess this rendering is shamelessly lifted from a bit of e-mail I received not long ago, from an old friend, one Johanna de Silentio,[19] from whom I had not heard for a while, which she entitled "The Parable of the Fish." I am happy to reproduce it here for you as an "appendix" and I am grateful to Johanna for remembering me.

The Parable of the Fish

Simon had been fishing all night. Fishing and thinking. He would look up at the vast blue black emptiness of the night sky as he waited for his net to fill, watching the stars flicker and flirt with the clouds, now disappearing behind a cloud only to emerge again a few moments later twinkling all the more brightly. The vast sky seemed so ominous and mysterious to Simon. Sometimes it filled him with the most sublime thoughts and lifted his spirit so mightily that he thought he could get out of his boat and walk across the waters. At other times the same night sky made him feel immeasurably alone, abandoned, insignificant, utterly forgotten and forgettable. If his boat capsized and he were drowned in the middle of that dark night, what notice would the stars take? Would they not continue their nightly dance without him?

It had always been like this, ever since he started fishing at night, but now it was much worse. For he was sick at heart and had been for quite a few weeks. He had behaved despicably, like an utter coward, denying the best friend he ever had, the one man who had made a difference in his life, who cared for him, who actually loved him. First he let them arrest Yeshua without a struggle. Then he kept a safe distance between himself and the soldiers, and tried to disappear into the mob that was following the scene. And when someone singled him out as a friend of Yeshua he denied it up and down. Friend? Why I don't even know the man, he said over and over.

"Friend": that word had now come back to haunt him under the stars. Friend. When Yeshua used to tell them to love their neighbors, and that was what the Father really wanted of them, Simon would ask him who their neighbor was. Then Yeshua would tell them some strange story about how their neighbor was some very remote people with whom the rest of them felt no fellowship at all, people from Samaria, tax collectors, all sorts of strange people. Yeshua had the oddest idea of a neighbor; he did not seem to define it in terms of someone near, the nearby herdsman down the road a piece, but someone far. The farther and stranger the more Yeshua seemed to be drawn to them. He was always telling them stories like that which had a way of sticking in their memories.

Simon and Yeshua really were friends, as close as possible. So much the worse then for Simon. After the night trial, they led him out the next day and executed him. The best man he ever knew and the best friend he ever had. They just executed him. The powers that be were frightened by Yeshua, and you could see why. Yeshua had a sharp tongue, a low tolerance for hypocrisy, and a merciless way of exposing it. But he had no power, at least he had no soldiers. Mostly they were afraid of what he said. Yeshua's words had a way of hitting their target. He could be immensely gentle and loving. But Simon could never forget the way Yeshua would take on the authorities at the Temple, telling them that the very ones who were going around collecting money to build tombs to the prophets were the same ones whose fathers had killed the prophets in the first place. That was hard talk and Yeshua's words rang like a mighty bell that you could not block out. The thing that made this talk so tough was that everybody knew it was true. You couldn't help but love Yeshua at that moment. There he was standing up to people who had the power to kill him, his eyes afire, leveling a blistering attack on them. He was so eloquent, so fearless, and all on behalf of the ones who had no power, of the ones who were being ground up by power. You could hear a pin drop when Yeshua talked like this, and the authorities seethed with anger at him. They did not take him on in public but they made him pay for it.

In less than twenty-four hours it was all over. And Simon had done nothing to save him: on the contrary, he fled in order to save himself. As fearless as Yeshua was in life, that's just how cowardly Simon had been. He wasn't even around at the end. He just kept himself under cover in Jerusalem long enough to hear that Yeshua was actually dead, and then he took to his heels and never looked back. He ran for his life, back to the obscure safety of his life as a fisherman, miles removed from the Romans and Temple politics.

God, it was unfair, he thought, as the boat rocked in the gentle evening sea and the stars darted in and out behind the clouds in their never ending dance. Yeshua was a man of justice; he wanted nothing more than to let justice flow through the land like these waters upon which his boat rested. So they killed him. That was really it, really why they killed him. He kept taking the side of all those strange and offbeat people, and in a way that made the "best" people look bad. He actually seemed to prefer sinners to the upright and he had a special place in his heart for lepers. And people are so afraid of lepers. The very word throws cold fear into your heart. It made Simon sick even to think about those people and he shivered in the coldness of the night air.

Some of those people really smelled bad, Simon thought to himself, and now he could not help smiling to himself. The worse they smelled, the more Yeshua seemed to like them.

Yeshua would do the most outrageous things. He thought nothing of breaking the letter of the Law if one of his "little ones" as he called them needed help. The Father made the Law for us, he used to say, not us for the Law. That used to make the Temple authorities sputter with anger. But the funniest thing of all, Simon thought—it really was funny to see —was the utter astonishment on the faces of those self-righteous author- ities when Yeshua would stop and talk to a prostitute and let her give him an embrace. That just left the authorities speechless and wide-eyed. But they never dared say anything to his face, because they knew Yeshua would expose them, or tell them one of his odd little stories which would cause them a lot of embarrassment because everybody in earshot would know what Yeshua was saying. They really were afraid of him.

By now the net had swollen and Simon could feel its weight as he tugged on it. So he strained and strained until he had succeeded in pulling the net into the boat. He was glad to see that the net was full and that his night's labor was not in vain. He could feel the life he had captured as the net trembled in his hands from fish flipping violently about, twisting and turning, gasping for oxygen, although there was air all around them, in one final, futile fight to save their short, narrow little lives. It was a good catch and Simon watched with some satisfaction as the commotion of his catch subsided; soon all you could hear was the gentle lapping of the sea against the side of the boat.

"Abba": Yeshua actually used to call God *abba*, father, not a distant, forbidding "father," but a loving, familiar "dad." *Abba* loves you, he used to say, especially the least ones, the ones that smelled bad, Simon thought. Love is the *abba* of all. He loves you no matter what, no matter whether you are from Galilee or Samaria, a tax collector or a prostitute, poor or lame, a sinner or a leper. He loves you no matter what you do, even if you are as ungrateful as that ungrateful son who took all his inheritance, wasted it, and then came back to his father looking for mercy. Especially then. That was one of Yeshua's favorite stories, and he told it many times so that Simon would have no trouble repeating it. He still remembers the smile on Yeshua's face when he got to the end of the story, the part where the father has to explain to the faithful son that what he really had to give his son was love, not a portion of his estate. That's what a father is, one who loves and who forgives his children. No matter what. He does not measure his love out in portions, half for each, so that one could actually use up the measure of love the father had to give. There is nothing that unfaithful son could have done that would have exceeded the father's love and capacity to forgive.

The boat rocked gently in the sea. Simon could see the faintest traces of red over the eastern shore and he knew it would soon be light and his night's work would be over.

Then the strangest feeling came over Simon, like a mighty breeze blowing over the sea, even though he could plainly see that the waters were calm and the boat was bobbing safely up and down. There was nothing the unfaithful son could do that the father could not forgive. Yeshua must have told that story a hundred times. How could Simon be so dense! The whole time that Simon had known Yeshua he did little else but tell Simon and Mary and the others, everybody he met, that the kingdom was here, that the father loved them and stood by them and forgave them. No matter what. Simon could hear Yeshua telling people that. Only this time it seemed that Yeshua was telling that story to Simon, just to Simon, as he sat all alone under the outstretched night sky under the play of the stars. He could see Yeshua's piercing eyes, hear the eloquent rhythms of his voice, see him smile as he reached the end of the story.

Simon could see Yeshua smile and he knew he was forgiven. Yeshua was dead. But for a moment, for the briefest twinkle of an eye, Simon thought he was not alone in the boat.

The sun was getting higher now and the night's work was over. So Simon pulled the anchor and began rowing slowly toward the shore. With every pull of the oars, the conviction grew in him that he should go round up the others and talk some of this over with them. Maybe they could go fishing together. Maybe if they could spend an evening under the stars, if they could hear what Simon had to say, maybe they too would agree that Yeshua wasn't gone, that he was still offering them the father's loving forgiveness, that his strangely beautiful stories could still be heard floating softly above the waters of an evening sea.

Still, there was one thing in all this that bothered Simon and he would never be able to get it out of his mind, even long after he had gotten Yeshua's followers together again, long after they started calling him "Rocky." That was a kind of joke, because he was the rock they always fell back on when they started to meet resistance. But the name stuck. Simon kept thinking of the fish, struggling and twisting, fighting to get free from his net. He remembered how he looked on at their struggles, all the while remaining quite impassive to their fate, for it was their ap-pointed role to be food for Simon and his wife and his family. He won-dered whether—and this was just a passing thought, but he couldn't quite get it out of his mind—life was not like this, a chain of stronger and weaker, and whether life simply played itself out, without justice or injustice, but with a kind of vast stupidity. He wondered whether the death of Yeshua was like that of the fish; it had nothing to do with guilt or innocence; it is simply the way life plays itself out, like the game the stars played overhead. Maybe the stars do not care about Yeshua or Simon or anyone else.

The only thing that helped Simon cope with that abysmal thought was the memory of Yeshua's smile.

Johanna de Silentio

10

The Prayers and Tears of Devilish Hermeneutics

Derrida and Meister Eckhart

Therefore I pray God that he may make me free of God.

—Meister Eckhart

What do I love when I love my God?

—Rabbi Augustinus Judaeus

In the end, as they say, is silence. So I will conclude this study by saying something about silence. Silence is a particular problem to me because the most difficult and invulnerable form The Secret can assume is that of silence. We all run around the circle and suppose, the poet says, while The Secret sits silently in the middle and knows. Silence, especially mystical silence, lays claims to know The Secret but to be, alas, unable to say it. We are not up to saying The Secret at the moment, it being above our powers today (Plato, *Republic,* 506d–e), but perhaps later on in the week, when we are feeling better. Or so it says. Fortunately, silence, especially mystical silence, being surprisingly verbose, has had a great deal to say about the Unsayable, about The Secret that exceeds all saying, which gives us something to talk about.

Mystical silence, I will argue, is one of our most beautiful forms of *prayer,* of praying and weeping for the coming of the *tout autre,* for something that eye hath not seen nor ear heard, something beyond, *au-delà,* "outta sight," as the students say. So I will conclude this study by reassuring everyone that we more radical hermeneuts, we practitioners of this devilish hermeneutics, also have our *prie-Dieu.* We too love to pray and weep, and our eyes are blinded by tears for the coming of I do not know what. We are not praying for The Secret, but praying and weeping all the more because we are *in the secret,* deprived of secret access, which is the occasion of more and more prayers. The absolute secret does not leave us disconsolate and without a prayer, but, on the contrary, it leaves us on our knees, praying like mad, praying like hell, praying like the devil.

Language without Language

With God, silence is the highest praise. *Silentium laus.* That is the ancient insistence of mystical theology and the unbroken testimony of mystical prayer. The only fit way to speak of God is not to say a thing, or to say that whatever we say of God is not true whereas what is true is what we do not say. I agree, and I love this silence, a point that I would argue long into the night. Mystical life is mystical prayer and praise, singing to God in the highest, praising God to the heights, pushing language to its very limits, to the breaking point, which is silence. For silence is the fine tip of language, the *Seelenfünklein* of language, its little spark and finest tip. Silence is language, but it is language *without* language, which according to the logic of the *sans* means that it is something of which beings without *language* altogether are altogether incapable. However much we wish they could speak, rocks cannot keep silent.

The reason Jacques Derrida loves mystical discourse so much is that it represents such an extraordinary case of the attempt of language to efface its own trace and this in the name of an ineffaceable desire. Silence is that point in language where language grows white hot, where driven to an extreme it finally can stand no more and turns on itself, consumes its own substance and effaces itself, and all this in order to be true to itself, as language. Mystical language is the best example of this self-effacing, self-wounding language, for mystical language is language without language about a God without God. For what else could it mean to say and to pray, as Meister Eckhart does, "Therefore I pray God that he may make me free of God" (CM, 202)?[1] Mystical prayer is marked by the most moving prayers and tears, by a deep desire for something surpassingly *tout autre*. Like deconstruction itself. What unites deconstruction and mysticism—an alliance calculated to unnerve both mystics and deconstructionists—I will argue here in my devilish hermeneutics, is their common structure as *prayer*, a prayer for something unimaginable, inconceivable, *impossible*.

This brings us back once again, for the third time, to the road to Emmaus, to the scene that Eugène Delacroix has conjured up of the story in a famous painting. Delacroix portrays the disciples not on the road, still *in via*, heatedly debating competing interpretations of the empty tomb, but at the end of the day, after their journey is over, sitting around the table in the inn, looking on in rapture while Jesus, all aglow, breaks bread. The painter's eye is on the end of the day, the end of the road, the culmination of all that hermeneutical give and take, the joy of rapture and mystical union. Beautiful, indeed. But let us not forget that rapturous silence of the disciple is *praise* and *prayer*, and hence an exquisite twist language takes. Let us not forget that we see this painting by reading its name (otherwise we might misinterpret it), which refers us to a story, a text in the New Testament, which supplies its context. This painting, and the rapture it depicts, are situated within language. Silence, we insist, is not to be taken as a simple or absolute silence, an escape from language into the Mystical Secret, a mystical *hors-texte*, but rather as a linguistic operation transpiring in the inner chambers and most secret resources of textuality and *écriture*. When Meister Eckhart prays God to rid him of God, is that not—and here is the mystical aporia that I love so much—the most remarkable way to *speak* of God, the most felicitous way to speak of not speaking of God? And is not "God" here the name of what we desire beyond desire? Far from contradicting (speaking against) our insistence upon *écriture* and *différance,* upon textuality and hermeneutical readings, and upon our lack of a Secret Access, this aporia speaks on their behalf. We call upon all the discursive resources of *différance* in order to pray and weep for the God beyond God, the God whom we can neither imagine nor conceive, who is not cut to fit human proportions, a God beyond every human idol, *tout autre.*

The *language* of mysticism—a language of prayer and preaching, of praise and poetry, of predication and theology—the *language* in which we insist on silence, is not the language spoken by The Secret having found in us a human tongue, but the language of our *desire* for, our affirmation of, the *tout autre.* The prayers, the sermons, the poems, the treatises of the mystics are among the most beautiful and powerful discourses in all literature, among the most powerful discourses of desire we can know. That is why this prayer is not far removed from eroticism, a point that makes Emmanuel Levinas nervous, who wants the relation to God to be very ethical *and non-erotic* par excellence,[2] a point he shares with a good many Irish priests. The desire for mystical silence, like *eros* itself, issues in a prolific and fecund language—of liturgy, literature, and theology. Far from standing simply outside or exterior to language, mystical silence occurs in and as a mystical caesura *within* language, like a pregnant pause, or like a pause in a musical movement. It is a work of language, part of its repertoire, an artful way that language has of pushing itself to its limits, to a point where language reaches out to what it cannot have and hence desires all the more, in a language without language. The language of desire is a desire for something that language longs for but cannot quite reach, before which it grows silent, which is what constitutes the *tout autre.* For the *tout autre* would not be *tout autre* were the arrows of language to reach that far; the *tout autre* must always be to come, unheard of and unthought. The silence of this language is a language of silence, a space opened up by language and within language, a wordlessness, a being lost for words, a groping for words that only a verbal being can undergo. The silence of mystical life issues in a self-tormenting, self-wounding, self-effacing language of prayers and tears, which attempts to erase its own trace in the name of something impossible. Silence is the language of desire, of the deepest desire of language.

The silence does not, therefore, constitute a prelinguistic or nonlinguistic contact with The Secret, with unmediated being, *kath'auto,* but, on the contrary, a sublime work of language which calls for, which prays and weeps for, the other of language, for the incoming of the other, *l'invention de l'autre.* Mystical discourse is a sublime poetics, a *logos* of a different sort, one more *logos* to enter into the conversation *on the way* to Emmaus, re-membering that Jesus did not advocate silence to Cleophas and his friend but good Jewish reading and hermeneutics. The way of silence remains a *way*, an eloquent and prolific way, a condition of the *homo viator*, of the slow of foot and wit on the way to Emmaus, one more way among other ways, traced across the *terra difficultatis* of everyday life. The practitioner of mystical prayer has not been hoisted aloft by some Extraterrestial Se-cret and absolved from the human condition; she has not been relieved of the difficulties of factical life. Mystics who fall to their knees before the living God in praise and prayer develop calluses on their knees and in any case pull their pants on one leg at a time. They are, like the rest of us, doing the best they can in an impossible situation, all along praying for *the* impossible. They have not been secreted away from the human condi-tion and given privileged access to The Secret. They remain caught up in the hermeneutic situation, in which they turn and twist with exquisite and memorable ingenuity.

I shall document these claims in terms of Meister Eckhart, the great Rhineland mystic and preacher, one of the veritable founders of the Ger-man language, whom I shall discuss in the light of the devilishness of *différance*. I shall try to show, once again playing the devil's advocate, first of all, that mystical life is inscribed within *différance*, which does not mean that mysticism can go to the devil, but rather that mystical discourse is one of the most resourceful ways desire has found to express itself. For mystical life, too, like everything else, passes through the trace and needs to make interpretive sense of itself. In keeping with our general thesis, this is not bad news but helps to keep us all safe.

In what ensues I argue as follows: (1) I identify a devilish phase in Meister Eckhart, in which he calls upon a certain deconstructive practice in order to make medieval onto-theo-logic tremble. (2) Then I take up Eckhart's affirmative side, the great "disseminative" energy at work in both the German and Latin sermons aimed at promoting and enhancing the life of the spirit, a grammatological exuberance and joyful wisdom whose political subversiveness did not go unnoticed by the guardians of onto-theo-logic. Far from escaping beyond the limits of textuality and *différance*, Meister Eckhart, a great preacher and a bit of a spiritual prank-ster, made a living off them (although the powers that be made him pay for his sallies), in order to revitalize spiritual and everyday life! (3) Fi-nally, in a concluding section, I come back to the language of desire and my contention that mysticism and my more devilish, deconstructivist hermeneutics are united by a common prayer for the impossible, a long-ing for the other. The difference between them is that in Derrida this prayer is left in a more indeterminate form and we are left as it were hanging by a prayer, which is altogether befitting our more radical her-meneutical fix. We are not abandoned without a prayer but, on the contrary, hoping against hope and praying like the devil, which is where my more radical hermeneutics ends up, on its knees.

Bedeviling Ontotheologic in Meister Eckhart

In *The Prayers and Tears of Jacques Derrida*, §1, I endorsed Derrida's warnings not to confuse what he says about *différance* with a form of mystical theology, on the grounds that mystical theology, however sublimely negative it may be, is always oriented toward the *hyperousios*, the God beyond God, whereas, however highly we may think of it, *différance* is not God. Accordingly, the mystical theologian invariably knows without knowing to whom she prays, while we more radical hermeneuts more easily get lost. I argued there for a kind of "armed neutrality" (borrowing an expression from Søren Kierkegaard) when it comes to *différance*. Neutrality: it neither implies nor excludes the existence or non-existence of anything—God, for example, or the commonplace furnishings of daily life—but remains existentially neutral. Armed: it pleads with us to proceed with caution in making existential claims, remembering the "presumptive unity," as Edmund Husserl puts it, of what we affirm, the contingency of the nominal unities that we constitute; it keeps a wary, watchful eye on existence claims. Biblically speaking, it may be regarded as being on the watch for the many idols of presence that tempt our worship, or for the many false Messiahs commanding our faith. *Différance* does not wipe out the real world, steal it right from under our nose, threaten us with the prospect that when we awake in the morning we will find it gone, or lock us in a prison house of signifiers. It simply attaches a coefficient of contingency to existential claims that ought to inspire a certain amount of referential humility. But all of this, I argued at some length, has an affirmative aim, for this devilish, deconstructive hermeneutics is, at the end of the day, deeply affirmative and dreams of an evening dinner at the inn with Jesus, or Elijah, or somebody.[3]

When it comes to mystical theology, Meister Eckhart is my case in point, the one I know and love the best. The Meister is a salient example of the recognition that language is caught up in an enterprise that is significantly self-defeating, that the terms we employ to assert something are caught up in complicity with their opposites, so that language keeps unsaying what it says, undoing what it does, and in general failing again and again to make good on its claims in a definitive way. That, I might mention, without being too smug, is exactly what someone with the notion, or quasi-notion, of *différance* up his sleeve, would predict. To be sure, Eckhart did all of this is the name of a super-essential being. His confession of the failure of language had a hyperousiological agenda, viz., to establish the super-existence of God beyond the frailties of language.[4]

That is why I think there is a difference between mystical theology and deconstruction. When the theologians of the Curia swept down upon

Eckhart with charges of heresy, he hastened to assure them that he spoke with "brother Thomas" (Aquinas), that he believed in the living God, and that his more extreme formulations were spoken *emphatice,* intended mostly to show the existential clout of the truths of the Christian faith.[5] The Christian religion, he insisted, is filled with teachings which should swell our hearts and stir our passions, instead of sitting helplessly on the shelves of the friary library. Eckhart had a faith, a commitment, to the God of Abraham and Moses and to the God Whom Jesus dared call *abba,* "father." (Nowadays, the dare is to call God "mother.") Furthermore, Eckhart thought, in the spirit of the Neoplatonism that he also loved, that the point of unity between God and the soul, the point where the *Gottesgrund* and *Seelengrund* touch, is a point of absolutely silent union, outside and above language, prior not only to human words but even to the Trinitarian Word, a notion that depends upon a classic theory of language as an external sign of the inner words of the soul. I do not deny that that is what he *taught and thought,* and that consequently Eckhart, like many mystical writers, took themselves to be admitted to The Secret, to be speaking from the heart of Truth. What I am arguing is that what he *did* in practice is not what he said about what he did. My devilish insistence is that whatever it is that overtakes the mystics and leaves them "speechless," which *never* seems to happen, is still in need of interpretation.

Deconstruction is first of all a practice—it is what it does—not a body of theories, and what it does depends upon what is on the table. If there is anything to it, it is not the work of Derrida or his enthusiasts, but would be at work in any text worthy of the name, especially in texts where we are worried about the wobbliness of words. In its more devilish phases, deconstructive practice needles its way—but not without a point—into the details of the discourse of others and shows them how much trouble they have brought upon themselves. Deconstruction is devilish, I do not deny that. The devil is in its eye for details. But it is not out to deny that something exists, but only to show the difficulty we have getting that claim nailed down in a definitive way. That is what it means to say that nothing exists outside the text—viz., that existence claims cannot be disentangled from the web of discourse that makes them possible to begin with. Existential assertions cannot break out into the open with atomistic independence, seize upon the things themselves, and then vaporize, leaving us sighing and heaving in naked contact with *die Sache selbst,* after which we both feel the need for a cigarette. Deconstruction does not try to scatter existential claims to the four winds, but to heighten our appreciation for their difficulty.

That is why I find in Meister Eckhart a great late medieval deconstructive practice, one keenly appreciative of all the trouble that medieval onto-theo-logic has brought down on its head. He understands quite well that the terms "Being" and "Nothing" are functions of each other, that each is inscribed in the other, marked and traced by the other, and that neither gets the job done, alone or together. Neither alone seizes upon the living God, nor do both together carry it off in a Hegelian synthesis. The idea, he would show, is not to seize God at all but, if anything, to let oneself be seized by God. As a professional theologian at Paris, Eckhart presented to his colleagues the complicity in which such binary schemes as Being/Nothing or creator/creature are caught up. He argued, on the one hand, that if we start out affirming being of creatures, then that means that God is a "nullity," not even a "little bit." On the other hand, if we concede the nullity of creatures, then we have perforce admitted, not only that God has being, or is being, but more strongly still that being is God (*esse est deus*). And he did not just make these claims off the cuff, in vernacular sermons to an uneducated audience that could not give him an argument, but Eckhart made them in Latin at Paris, to the most so-phisticated audience of the day, and he used the most refined arguments of medieval onto-theo-logic to back them up.[6]

Eckhart, I maintain, had an acute sense of the "textuality," the interde-pendence and differential structure of the terms of scholastic discourse. That is why he had no high confidence in any particular name we sent God's way, like an arrow aimed at God's heart. He argued emphatically that to call God "creator" was just to mark Him off in terms of "creatures"; to call God "cause" was to draw God into relation with "effects"; to call God "good" was to name God in reference to the will; and to call God "true" was to give God a name relative to the intellect (CM, 200–203). Every one of these "absolute" attributes was "relative" to something else in the discursive chain. Every time the intentional arrow was aimed at God, it came up with "God," which sends us skidding back to something else in the chain of signifiers. That is why Derrida says in *Sauf le nom* that if the names of God are arrows directed at the divine being, then they keep God safe (*sauf*) precisely by falling short, God being everything ex-cept (*sauf*) what is named.[7] The reason for this is that divine names keep referring back to other names in the chain, without seizing upon some absolute *hors-texte*, grasping it in its eagle claws. We never get a name which is really God's own name, which really seizes upon God, and then, having done its duty, having delivered us into the inner chambers of the Godhead, quietly dissipates into thin air or rides off into the distance on a great white horse. Eckhart kept warning his fellow theologians about the contingency of the signifiers we deploy. This warning reached its shrill-est and most startling moment when, faced with the difficulty of getting something said about God, he openly preached one day to what must have been a startled congregation, "Therefore I pray God that he may make me free of God" (CM, 202). Little wonder that the apparatchiks in the Inquisition came gunning for him.

Now we may hear in the prayer to God to rid us of God a prayer for presence, for the transcendental signified which puts the play of signifiers to rest and makes us one with the One. I do not deny that there is a wide streak of this in Eckhart, a streak of Neoplatonic, henological metaphysics, in which everything gets centered on the "Godhead" beyond "God," on the One beyond multiplicity, on the silent unity of soul with God beyond time and place. There is always a *hyperousios* at the bottom of mystical theology. This notion of mystical unity does not contradict onto-theo-logic but crowns and perfects it. It fulfills the metaphysical desire for presence in a way of which metaphysics itself was incapable, with a surge of intuitive unity which surpasses the wildest dreams of conceptual reason, surpassing conceptual presence with super-presence. God's givenness in mystical life "saturates" our intention with overflowing plenitude, as Jean-Luc Marion says, which is the heart of the difference between him and Derrida on the "gift."[8] I would say that something has saturated Eckhart's intentions but whatever it is requires interpretation, which drags it kicking and screaming back into the play of signifiers. Having discovered the complicity and play of terms in medieval onto-theo-logic, Eckhart was not above trying to arrest that play and calm the storm he had stirred up, by bringing the onto-theo-logical system which he had disturbed into a higher, mystical closure, into union with The Secret. He was after all a priest and a friar.

But I am asserting that to reduce everything in Eckhart to such a gesture is to cut him off at the knees, to repress everything *else* that is astir in his text, and to miss the good that deconstruction does for religious thinkers, which I argue Eckhart was putting into *practice*. For if Eckhart was not above pushing for a silent mystical closure he was at the same time acutely aware of the impossibility of closure, of the wide-open uncompletability and unstabilizability of conceptual discourse, which instability issued in a continuous outpouring of mystical discourse. When Eckhart prayed aloud for God to rid him of God he was blowing the whistle on metaphysical theology, even though he was a professional theologian.

Now it is my claim that if he thought (as he certainly did) that there was a higher, unitative way, a silent mystical way *beyond* language, he was in practice at the same time—whether he liked it or not, whatever his *vouloir dire*—putting such a way into question. For once *he* has recourse to the stabilizing discourse of the Neoplatonic One beyond multiplicity, to the Godhead beyond God, to the timeless unity of the soul's ground with God's ground, we today recognize that that *too* is just another creature, another signifier which belongs to an historical-Neoplatonic vocabulary. Neoplatonism did not drop from the sky, did not emanate from the One; it is not, as far as we know, God's favorite philosophy. "Godhead" too is another effect of *différance,* a differential effect achieved by a discourse which deploys a God/Godhead binary distinction. "Godhead" sends us skidding back to "God" from which (by being differentiated from which) "Godhead" derives its sense and impact. To reach out for the "Godhead" beyond God is to name God relative to "God," to remain within the differential chain of mundane predicates. Like old Marley in *A Christmas Carol,* "Godhead" too drags a chain of signifiers behind it. The Godhead beyond God is also a creature, what a religious person would call an idol, what Derrida would call an effect of *différance.*

We do not get anywhere if we let our frustration and impatience with the play of signifiers lure us into invoking another domain of signifiers in which the reigning truth is that we have here to do with the transcendental signified beyond all signifiers. The only headway to be made is to confess that we never escape the chain of signifiers, to concede that the trouble we are in is permanent, and to press ahead anyway, praying and weeping like mad. The prayer to rid us of "God" has to be kept permanently in place. It demands a constant vigil, watching and praying all through the night that we do not fall down to graven images, including that most alluring image of all, the image that we are beyond images. The prayer to God to rid us of God is a prayer to keep the play of images in play, to give ourselves no rest, to be unattached to any creature, no matter how sublime and fine, even if it be the mystical Godhead itself, or the *Seelenfünklein,* even if it be the most exquisite reaches of Eckhart's dazzling mystical speculations.

The only headway is to "awaken" to the fix we are in, we who believe in something—and who does not?—to raise our level of vigilance, to watch and pray, to be permanently on the alert against mistaking graven images for the living God, mistaking the effects of *différance* for the things themselves (be they perceptual, scientific, or theological). "I pray God that he may make me free of God" is an ongoing prayer which keeps the discourse open. It has in fact a felicitous generalizability: I pray God (read: science, religion, economics, art, ethics, psychoanalysis, etc.) to rid me of these gods. That is the prayer that sets this entire more radical hermeneutics in motion. This is a prayer against closure, against turning the latest and best creations of our discourse into idols. It arises from an ongoing distrust of our ineradicable desire for presence, of our insidious tendency to arrest the play and build an altar to a produced effect, a nominal unity, the golden calf of a presumptive unity. I pray God—that is, He Who is everything and none of the things that this signifier names, *nomen omninominabile et nomen innominabile*—to rid me of "God," that is, all of those nominal effects which try to cow us into submission, all of those historico-cultural-linguistic effects which are collected together by the word "God" (or any other sacred cow).

I am arguing that if we pressed these considerations upon Eckhart it would show clearly that, in the end, he had very little invested in the metaphysics of presence, in Neoplatonic henology, and that everything he had to say revolved around seeing the failure of signifiers to catch God in their net.[9] I am maintaining that it belongs to the innermost tendencies of his thought to let go of the Godhead too, of the henology, of the *Seelengrund* and *Gottesgrund,* for they too are "nominal effects." The dynamics of his own teachings are to rid us of all idols, of every "God," of every signifier which gets too important and asserts its authority, even if that be "Godhead" itself. I pray God to rid me of "Godhead," that is, to keep me free of attachment to any signifier.

None of that is meant to gainsay what we learn from "Circumfession,"[10] that the name of God has a special way of functioning as the name of what we love and desire. The beautiful question Saint Augustine raises in Book Ten of the *Confessions,* "what do I love when I love you," my God, is the question of all questions. For, the name of God is the name of whatever it is, beyond name and God, beyond language and silence, that I desire. The name of God is the name, not of some transcendental signified beyond language, but the name of what language most deeply loves and affirms, dreams and desires. The name of God is the name of yes, the name of the yes, yes, not a determinate yes but the archi-yes that accompanies every name. That is why, in order to hear what Meister Eckhart says, listen to his yes.

Eckhart's Joyful Wisdom

By resisting any closure of Eckhart's discourse, I am not turning it into a despairing and faithless agnosticism, a dispirited silence about an infinitely deferred God. Far from it. I am defending its open-endedness and enormous affirmative energy, which explodes with all the affirmation of Derrida's *oui, oui,* a notion that is developed in commentary on a saying of Angelus Silesius—a seventeenth-century mystical poet who versified a lot of Eckhartian spirituality—*"Gott spricht immer nur 'Ja.'"*[11] God, *Jah*weh, always means just *"Ja."* Eckhart's sermons say yes to God's enveloping action in the world and his own life. His writing explodes in an extravaganza of images, in a play of mystical signifiers, in a profusion of discourses that aim at keeping the life of the soul with God alive. There is no better example, to my knowledge, of a certain mystical dissemination and a religiously joyful wisdom than the brilliant, playful virtuosity of Eckhart's German sermons and Latin treatises. He rewrites the words of Scripture, turns and twists the most familiar sacred stories, reinterprets the oldest teachings in the most innovative and shocking ways. Eckhart crosses the wires of Derrida's dichotomy between rabbinic and poetic hermeneutics[12] for Eckhart's mystical hermeneutics, his mystical commentaries on the Scriptures, are astir with a poetic energy which exploits all the associative and rhythmic power of his Latin and Middle High German tongues, in a veritable fourteenth-century version of James Joyce, producing an effect not at all unlike Derrida's *Glas.*

Meister Eckhart speaks always with the same effect: to prod the life of the spirit, to promote its vitality, to raise its pitch, to enhance its energy. Like a religious answer to Nietzsche six centuries earlier, Eckhart engages with Dionysian productivity in a multiplication of religious fictions that serve the interests of a "life" that lives out of its own superabundance, without why or wherefore, for the sake of life itself:

> If anyone went on for a thousand years asking of life: "Why are you liv-
> ing?" life, if it could answer, would only say: "I live so that I may live." That
> is because life lives out of its own ground and springs from its own source,
> and so it lives without asking why it is itself living. If anyone asked a truth-
> ful man who works out of his own ground: "Why are you performing your
> works"? and if he were to give a straight answer, he would only say, "I
> work so that I may work." (Q, 180, 23–31; CM, 184)

Life is like the gift, an expenditure without return, an exercise not for the
sake of something, for some why, for some return, but for itself. There is
a grammatological exuberance, a transgressive energy, in Eckhart which
suggests a kind of medieval analogate of Stéphane Mallarmé and Joyce.
Eckhart had a way about him of making the whole tremble, of soliciting
the foundations of onto-theo-logic. The papal bull condemning him said
that even when his sayings were not in error they were still dangerous
(CM, 80). On this point, at least, the Pope was right. The powers that be,
the guardians of orthodoxy, always have a fine ear for disruptive discourse. For the life of him, Eckhart could not see what they were exercised about. That is because Eckhart was concerned with the dynamics
of the soul's life with the living God, not with defending the political
power base of the magisterium. The Inquisitors understood that texts
outlive good intentions, that they would retain their disruptive power
long after the reassuring voice of this humble Dominican friar was silenced—by everyone's account, the Pope's included (CM, 81), a loyal son
of the Church.

This master of silence and the silent unity of the soul with God was
an eloquent preacher—by profession and vocation—and a prolific writer
who produced a massive corpus, only a fragment of which has come
down to us today. His defense of silence was carried out by a multiplication of discourses. He is a master of life (*Lebemeister*) *and* a master of the
letter (*Lesemeister*) who plays with the syntax and semantics of the scriptural texts and the texts of the masters before him in order to tease out of
them ever new senses. He is a master of repetition who knew well that
his *commentarium* was not to be a simple reproduction but a new production, a fresh rendering that made the old text speak anew and say what
had not been heard.

He was constantly altering the syntax of a text, re-writing it so that
it said something new. He would fuss with trivial features of texts to
which no attention at all had been paid and make everything turn on
them, even to the point of reversing their traditional meaning. He would
also play with the letters in a word. When he was defending his notion
that *esse est deus*, he said that *esse* is the tetragrammaton, that *ESSE* and
YHWH constitute the same sacred four-letter word, the four-letter word
of the Sacred itself.[13] His grammatology included a tetragrammatology.
He would invert sayings to see what fruit they would yield. When brother
Thomas soberly taught, in a carefully nuanced way, that *deus est suum esse*

(God is his own being), Eckhart boldly announced that *esse est deus* (being is God) and creatures are a pure nothing. His Thomism did not block his Neoplatonism, did not prevent him from also teaching that God is above being and being is the first of all creatures. Nor was he afraid to tamper with the literal meaning of scriptural stories. When Jesus said that Mary had chosen the better part (traditionally taken to be the *vita contemplativa*), Eckhart explained that Martha had chosen the better part, which he said is what Jesus really meant by invoking Martha's name twice ("Martha, Martha, you worry and fret about so many things . . ."). Eckhart said that the repetition of Martha's name meant that she had two gifts (the *vita contemplativa* and the *vita activa*) and hence that Martha had chosen the better part! (Q, 280–289).

Frank Tobin's study offers an interesting catalogue of the ways Eckhart played with the phonic and graphic substance of the two languages he spoke.[14] Eckhart reads *mutuo* (reciprocal) as *meo tuo et tuo meo* (mine is yours and yours is mine). He asks us to hear in the angel's *ave* to Mary the Middle High German *ane we* (without pain) which is what Mary experienced once she consented to God's demands. (*Ave* is the reversed anagram of *Eva*, the first woman who brought sin into the world, while Mary is *immacula*, the only human being born free of this first sin.) He toys with the proper name of his own religious order (*ordo praedicatorum,* order of preachers) which he said meant order of praisers, those who offer divine predicates. Eckhart even tinkered with the word "eagle," hearing in the Middle High German *adeler* (eagle) not Hegel, to be sure—that would have been quite something!—but *edeler,* the noble man. He said that true thankfulness (*dankbaerkeit*) is, not thoughtfulness, but fruitfulness (*vruht-baerkeit*), that is, to be made fruitful by the gift one receives, and that means to give birth (*gebern*) from it in return (*in der widerbernden dank-baerkeit*). In the Vulgate version of Rom. 6:22, *Nun vero liberati a peccato* ("Now, however, you have been liberated from sin"), Eckhart finds eight grammatical functions in *vero,* including: "truly" (*vere*) delivered from sin; "delivered from sin by truth" (*vero,* the dative of *verum,* "by truth"), and so on. In the opening line of John's Gospel, *"In principio erat verbum"* ("In the beginning was the Word"), the words *"principium," "erat,"* and *"verbum"* are submitted to similar multiple readings, disseminating and multiplying their senses. He even changes the opening lines of the *Pater Noster,* according to Christian belief the only prayer to come from the lips of Jesus himself, so that "thy will be done" becomes "will, become thine (= God's)," because he taught that willing to do God's will is not as high as getting beyond willing altogether.

The only test to which Eckhart seems to put his innovations is their ability to generate new spiritual vitality, to keep the life of the soul with God in motion. He is a pragmatist of the spiritual life with a taste for multiplying and inventing discourses aimed at promoting and enhancing spiritual life. He is a *Lesemeister* (master of readings, of letters) because he is a *Lebemeister* (master of life, spiritual master).

Moreover, his bold and emancipatory discourse put the powers that be on the spot and tended to break open the rigid hierarchy and exclusionary order of the political system which accompanies onto-theo-logic. He produced a significant deconstructive effect upon the prevailing onto-theo-logical power structure, upon, let us say, the onto-theo-politic of his day—for which he was made to pay personally.[15] In Eckhart everything turns on *Gelassenheit* (a mainstay of Heidegger's vocabulary), which means letting-be and includes everything which liberates and sets free. *Gelassenheit* means letting God be God, letting God be—in oneself, in others, in everything, which is obviously a non-exclusionary idea. *Gelassenheit* is a principle of love (*caritas*) with some teeth in it, a *caritas* put forward by a Christian which had a deconstructive kick to it.[16]

> Eckhart saw the life and love of God to be ubiquitous, not confined to just a few privileged souls, not just to priests, e.g., which made the *church*men of his day uneasy, or to males (he preached to women and told them that they all had the divine spark, the *Seelenfünklein*), which made these same church*men* uneasy, or even just to Christians, which made nearly all Christendom uneasy. Furthermore, he did not think that the presence of God was confined to *churches* at all, or that God necessarily prefers the Latin language, but that the German vernacular in which he preached would do just fine. And that is why the Reformation took a liking to him and why the Papal Inquisitors gave him a hard time. Although a high-level Dominican administrator himself, Eckhart set about disseminating power-clusters in medieval Christendom, disrupting the political power of onto-theo-logic, and for that he earned the wrath of the Curia and felt the blows of its institutional power.

We can write Eckhart's writing off as a closet metaphysics of presence, or we can let it be what it is. My claim is that if we press Eckhart about his Neoplatonic henology, his metaphysics of the one, he has to give *that* up too as so much idolatry, so much onto-theo-logic. At the end of the day, what Eckhart was doing and saying, preaching and teaching, did not have to do with onto-theo-logic or henology but with the celebration of the life of the soul with God, with piping, not mourning, as Jesus said. Nothing turns for Eckhart on calling God Being or presence, even a super-essential Being, a super-essential presence. That is just a way of making the prevailing onto-theo-logic tremble.

At the end of the sermon on poverty Eckhart says, "Whoever does not understand what I have said, let him not burden his heart with it" (CM, 203). This discourse on mystical poverty does not defend some onto-theo-logical theory about God or the soul. And it can be well understood without understanding any of the subtleties in which the sermon engages. The sermon means only to lead us to the point where we will try to be indeed and in truth the poverty of which it speaks. It is a question, as Augustine said, not of a truth to know but of a truth to do, *facere veritatem*. We cannot "understand" his sermons, Eckhart says, unless we make ourselves like what he is talking about. And if we are like this poverty, then we do not need to burden ourselves with this talk about God and Godhead.

What Eckhart taught ultimately had little to do with a Neoplatonic One or a super-essential presence. Rather he taught with irrepressible exuberance the joyful wisdom of a life graced by God and in the process shattered with loving joy the most prized graven images of onto-theologic. Nothing is more typical of Eckhart than the argument the Meister pursues with mystical perversity that the better part belongs not to Mary, languishing dreamily at the feet of Jesus, trying to be one with the One, but to Martha, who rushed about making the preparations for Jesus's visit, with all of the energy and robustness of life. Mary was a little more Husserlian, a little more in love with *Anschauung*, while Martha, on Eckhart's telling, had taken the turn to factical life.

Conclusion: The Prayer of Devilish Hermeneutics
(or, Hoping and Praying Like the Devil)

Différance, we have said, is not God. But neither is it the devil, a mean-spirited attempt to short-circuit mystical life, to demythologize it and unmask it as a fraud that can be reduced to the play of signifiers, class conflict, the cunning will to power of priestly tarantulas, or a desire for our mommy. On the contrary, *différance, écriture*, undecidability, the whole repertoire of deconstructive quasi-transcendentals, go hand in hand with desire, with the desire of language, the language of desire, with what Derrida in one place calls the "promise" inscribed in language.[17] For language is an archi-"yes" to the coming of the other. The first word we utter when we speak or pray is yes.[18] Yes is not so much a single word in the language but the yes of language itself, language as a saying yes to what calls upon us to speak. But *without knowing* what calls upon us to speak, responding without being able to identify what addresses us. So that primordial yes is second, coming as it does as the yes which answers yes to the first yes, the first affirmation, the prior calling of what is to come, which solicits us. What is calling? What is coming? What is happening? Who knows, if we do not know who we are? Is it God or justice? God's kingdom to come or a democracy to come? Are they the same? Or is it no more than cosmic noise, the rumble of the great cosmic stupidity? The characteristic trait of such undecidability is to say that our lives are marked by a radical, structural inability to settle such archi-questions, even as it insists on keeping them alive, which is what the name of God means for Derrida. While Heidegger thinks that the name of God puts questioning to sleep, Derrida, like Augustine, regards the name of God as the name of what throws everything into bottomless questionability, and beyond questioning, the name of what we desire and love without question, *sans voir, sans avoir, sans savoir*.[19]

What the critics of deconstruction, slower of step and duller than Cleophas and his companion, have never quite been able to see or make out about deconstruction is the *viens, oui, oui,* the sighing and dreaming, the "prayers and tears" of deconstruction for the coming of something that surpasses expectation. That is why mystical prayer and preaching, mystical praise and poetry, are so important to Derrida. For nowhere else in our language is there a more fervent language of desire and dream, of hope and prayer, of longing for something *tout autre,* something *impossible*. A passionate understanding really desires, according to Johannes Climacus, what it cannot understand, what surpasses understanding, otherwise it is a mediocre and passionless fellow. The understanding desires to run up against something that surpasses understanding. Go where you cannot go, Angelus Silesius says, to the *impossible. The* impossible is not the simple logical contradiction of the possible, but the terminus of a hope beyond hope, of a hope against hope, of a faith in what we cannot imagine or in any way foresee, a *tout autre,* beyond any present horizon of expectation. That is the common coin of deconstruction and mystical prayer, the common aspiration of what I dare call deconstructive prayer and mystical prayer, and the common reason that they drive language to its limits. "I am praying all the time," Derrida says. Praying and weeping for the coming of what he cannot see coming, hanging on by a prayer, *oui, oui, amen*. What deconstruction and mystical life have in common is not some secret access to the Secret outside the play of signifiers, to some *hyperousios* that stills our tongue, but desire, dreaming, hoping, and praying.

That desire for the impossible, the desire of language to live without language, is language's own desire. It is the desire of the mystical preacher and poet whose heart has been touched by desire for the impossible. The *viens, oui, oui* of deconstruction is as close to that desire as possible, in the service of which it holds everything deconstructible, while the *tout autre* itself, if there is one, is not deconstructible. The difference between Derrida and Eckhart, the difference that makes a difference, is that, in keeping with what I called above the armed neutrality of *différance,* Derrida regards this undeconstructible something to come, this nameless *tout autre* as subject to an endless translatability, whereas in Eckhart's Christian Neoplatonism there is no doubt about what he was referring to, a point which exposes the pointlessness and mean-spiritedness of the Inquisition conducted against him. Eckhart's unknowing was a *docta ignorantia*. But when Derrida takes up Augustine's question, "what do I love when I love, you," my God, it is because he really is a little lost, really does not know the answer to this question of all questions. What do I desire and love when I love and desire God? That loving desire is linked in a radical way with the claim that we do not know who we are, that the secret is there is no Secret. Derrida asks that question without knowing the answer, earnestly. Derrida's prayer is more indeterminate, more determinable, and he is not quite sure whether his prayers to heaven rise. His is an ankhoral prayer, the prayer of an anchorite, out in the desert/*khôra*, because he does not know who we are.

Conclusion without Conclusion

I dream of finding one day, perhaps in the Bodleian library, a postcard of Derrida and Meister Eckhart weeping and praying side by side, *sans voir, sans avoir, sans savoir,* each on their *prie-Dieu,* perhaps, or maybe standing together before the weeping wall, their eyes blinded by tears. Derrida will be dressed like a friar (*frère Jacques*), in the beautiful flowing white habit of a Dominican, while Eckhart will be draped in a tallith. Between their tears they will be chanting a psalm to *sans,* to the blessedness of life without this or that. They are singing, love is without why, *sine ratione, ohne warum.* Like life. Like the rose. Like the gift. They sing to *sine/sans* (more Christian Latin French). *Beati pauperes spiritu,* happy are they who live without, who live without why. The poverty of the *sans* structures the prayers and tears of Eckhart and of Derrida, of mystical prayer and deconstruction's more ankhoral prayer. They chant long into the night of truth, *facere veritatem,* unless you *are* this poverty of which I speak, unless you give testimony to it, you need not bother with this prayer. Their prayers rise up like soft circles of smoke, drifting far above the earth, floating off who knows where, to heaven perhaps, or dissipating in a distant cosmic night. *Je ne sais pas. Il faut croire.*

That is what happens when you do not know who you are, when your conclusion is unscientific and without conclusion, when you are hanging on by a prayer, when the best you can do is to pray like mad.

To pray like the devil.

Notes

Introduction

1. Epigraphs: these four texts are from Jacques Derrida, *Cinders,* trans. Ned Lukacher (Lincoln: University of Nebraska Press, 1991), p. 75; *Points . . . Interviews, 1974–94,* ed. Elisabeth Weber, trans. Peggy Kamuf (Stanford: Stanford University Press, 1995), p. 201; *The Gift of Death,* trans. David Wills (Chicago: University of Chicago Press, 1995), p. 92; *On the Name,* ed. Thomas Dutoit (Stanford: Stanford University Press, 1995), pp. 131–132 n. 1.

2. On Derrida's conception of the secret, see Derrida, *On the Name,* pp. 22–31.

3. Edmund Husserl, *Ideas Pertaining to a Pure Phenomenology and to a Phenomenological Philosophy,* bk. 1, trans. Fred Kersten (The Hague: M. Nijhoff, 1983), §145, p. 345.

4. Derrida, *On the Name,* p. 30.

5. John D. Caputo, *Radical Hermeneutics: Repetition, Deconstruction, and the Hermeneutic Project* (Bloomington: Indiana University Press, 1987), hereafter cited as RH. For an excellent and stimulating collection of essays that responds to various claims in *Radical Hermeneutics,* see Roy Martinez, ed., *The Very Idea of Radical Hermeneutics* (Atlantic Highlands, N.J.: Humanities Press, 1997).

6. Derrida, *Points,* 96.

7. Jacques Derrida, *Given Time, I: Counterfeit Money,* trans. Peggy Kamuf (Chicago: University of Chicago Press, 1991), p. 152.

8. Edmund Husserl, *Cartesian Meditations,* trans. Dorion Cairns (The Hague: M. Nijhoff, 1960), §39, p. 81.

9. As Johannes Climacus writes, "In the language of abstraction, that which is the difficulty of existence and of the existing person never actually appears; even less is the difficulty explained. . . . If abstract thinking is assumed to be the highest, it follows that scientific scholarship and thinkers proudly abandon existence and leave the rest of us to put up with the worst." Søren Kierkegaard, *Kierkegaard's Writings,* XII.1, *Concluding Unscientific Postscript to Philosophical Fragments,* trans. and ed. Howard Hong and Edna H. Hong (Princeton: Princeton University Press, 1992), p. 301.

10. John D. Caputo, *The Prayers and Tears of Jacques Derrida: Religion without Religion* (Bloomington: Indiana University Press, 1997), pp. 41–57.

11. Jacques Derrida, "Psyche: Inventions of the Other," trans. Catherine Porter, in *Reading De Man Reading,* ed. Lindsay Waters and Wlad Godzich (Minneapolis: University of Minnesota Press, 1989), pp. 25–65.

12. Jacques Derrida, *Parages* (Paris: Galilée, 1986), p. 25.

13. Jacques Derrida, *Politics of Friendship,* trans. George Collins (London: Verso, 1997), p. 232, hereafter cited as PF.

14. Alan Sokal and Jean Bricmont, *Fashionable Nonsense: Postmodern Intellectuals' Abuse of Science* (New York: Picador, 1998).

15. Friedrich Nietzsche, *Beyond Good and Evil,* trans. R. J. Hollingdale (Baltimore: Penguin, 1972), no. 39, p. 50, no. 270, pp. 189–190. See my discussion of these texts of Nietzsche in Caputo, RH, p. 189.

16. Søren Kierkegaard, *"Fear and Trembling" and "Repetition,"* trans. and ed.

Howard Hong and Edna H. Hong (Princeton: Princeton University Press, 1983), pp. 200–201.

1. On Not Knowing Who We Are

1. See chapter 4 for a discussion of Derrida, Rorty, and politics.

2. Hubert Dreyfus and Paul Rabinow, *Michel Foucault: Beyond Structuralism and Hermeneutics*, with an afterword by Michel Foucault, 2d ed. (Chicago: University of Chicago Press, 1983), hereafter cited as BSH.

3. See the discussion of "cold hermeneutics" in John D. Caputo, *Radical Hermeneutics: Repetition, Deconstruction, and the Hermeneutic Project* (Bloomington: Indiana University Press, 1987), chap. 7, hereafter cited as RH.

4. Michel Foucault, *Mental Illness and Psychology*, trans. Alan Sheridan, with a foreword by Hubert Dreyfus (Berkeley: University of California Press, 1987), p. 74, hereafter cited as MIP. This is a translation of the 1962 French edition, *Maladie mentale et Psychologie*, which is an extensive revision of the 1954 edition, *Maladie mentale et personalité*. The important difference between these editions is examined carefully in James Bernauer, *Michel Foucault's Force of Flight: Toward an Ethics for Thought* (Atlantic Highlands, N.J.: Humanities Press International, 1990), pp. 24–36 and app. 1.

5. Dreyfus discusses Foucault's interest in Heidegger in his instructive foreword to MIP, pp. ix, xviii–xix, xxviii ff. Martin Heidegger, *Being and Time*, trans. E. Macquarrie and J. Robinson (New York: Harper & Row, 1962).

6. Friedrich Nietzsche, *Beyond Good and Evil*, trans. R. J. Hollingdale (Baltimore: Penguin, 1972), no. 39, p. 50, no. 270, pp. 189–190. See my discussion of these texts of Nietzsche in Caputo, RH, p. 189.

7. Michel Foucault, *Madness and Civilization: A History of Insanity in the Age of Reason*, trans. Richard Howard (New York: Pantheon, 1965), hereafter cited as MC. This is an abridgment of *Histoire de la folie à l'âge classique* (Paris: Gallimard, 1972).

8. Jean-François Lyotard, *The Differend: Phrases in Dispute*, trans. G. Van Den Abbeele (Minneapolis: University of Minnesota Press, 1988), p. xi.

9. "Untruth" is an expression used by the later Heidegger in such a way as to say that there is always a radical core of untruth within truth; truth is not truth "all the way through," concealment is the hidden ground of unconcealment, a wresting of unconcealment from a prior concealment. See Martin Heidegger, "On the Essence of Truth," trans. John Sallis, in *Martin Heidegger: Basic Writings*, ed. David Krell (New York: Harper & Row, 1977), pp. 132–135. Foucault seems to think of unreason as a prior untruth and concealment embedded in the core of reason.

10. Edmund Husserl, *Ideas Pertaining to a Pure Phenomenology and to a Phenomenological Philosophy*, bk. 1, trans. Fred Kersten (The Hague: M. Nijhoff, 1983), §§47–49.

11. See Michel Foucault, "Madness, the Absence of Work," trans. Peter Stastny and Deniz Sengel, in *Foucault and His Interlocutors*, ed. Arnold Davidson (Chicago: University of Chicago Press, 1997), pp. 97–104.

12. Husserl, *Ideas Pertaining to a Pure Phenomenology*, §§124–127. "The attempt to write the history of the decision, division, difference runs the risk of construing the division as an event or a structure subsequent to the unity of an original presence, thereby confirming metaphysics in its fundamental operation."

Jacques Derrida, *Writing and Difference,* trans. Alan Bass (Chicago: University of Chicago Press, 1978), p. 140; see Foucault's hostile response in Michel Foucault, "My Body, This Fire," trans. Geoffrey Bennington, *Oxford Literary Review* 4, no. 1 (1979): 5–28. For a good account of the acrimonious character of this exchange between Foucault and Derrida and for a sensible appraisal of the convergence of their thought around the themes of power and ethics, which I am also suggesting here, see Roy Boyne, *Foucault and Derrida: The Other Side of Reason* (London: Unwin Hyman, 1990). For Derrida's most recent statement on Foucault, see Jacques Derrida, "'To Do Justice to Freud': The History of Madness in the Age of Psychoanalysis," trans. Pascale-Anne Brault and Michael Naas, in *Foucault and His Interlocutors,* pp. 57–96.

13. Michel Foucault, *Power/Knowledge: Selected Interviews and Other Writings, 1972–1977,* ed. Colin Gordon, trans. Colin Gordon et al. (New York: Pantheon, 1980), pp. 118–119, hereafter cited as P/K.

14. See Søren Kierkegaard, *Two Ages: The Age of Revolution and the Present Age,* trans. Howard Hong and Edna H. Hong (Princeton: Princeton University Press, 1978), pp. 68ff., esp. pp. 92–102.

15. Søren Kierkegaard, *"Fear and Trembling" and "Repetition,"* trans. Howard Hong and Edna H. Hong (Princeton: Princeton University Press, 1983), p. 36.

16. Michel Foucault, *The Birth of the Clinic: An Archaeology of Medical Perception,* trans. A. M. Sheridan Smith (New York: Pantheon, 1973), pp. xvi–xvii.

17. Michel Foucault, *The Order of Things: An Archaeology of the Human Sciences,* trans. Alan Sheridan (New York: Pantheon, 1970), p. 373. Dreyfus and Rabinow use this text to set the terms of their own understanding of hermeneutics.

18. Michel Foucault, *The Archaeology of Knowledge and the Discourse on Language,* trans. A. M. Sheridan Smith (New York: Pantheon, 1972), p. 32.

19. "Judiciousness in Dispute, or Kant after Marx," in *The Lyotard Reader,* ed. Andrew Benjamin (Oxford: Basil Blackwell, 1990), pp. 328, passim.

20. Jacques Derrida, "Circumfession: Fifty-nine Periods and Periphrases," in Geoffrey Bennington and Jacques Derrida, *Jacques Derrida* (Chicago: University of Chicago Press, 1993), p. 122.

21. I have found James Bernauer's work (see endnote 4) to be singularly insightful in its approach to Foucault and congenial to my notion of "radical hermeneutics," a notion I developed in connection with Derrida, not Foucault. For more on Bernauer's notion of Foucault's negative theology, see James Bernauer, "The Prisons of Man: An Introduction to Foucault's Negative Theology," *International Philosophical Quarterly* 27 (December 1987): 365–381, and his excellent conclusion of *Michel Foucault's Force of Flight,* pp. 175–184, on "ecstatic thinking." For more on the long-range consonance between Foucault and Derrida, which focuses on the question of reason and unreason, see Boyne, *Foucault and Derrida.*

22. *Meister Eckhart: An Introduction to the Study of His Works with an Anthology of His Sermons,* ed. James M. Clark (London: Thomas Nelson and Sons, 1957), p. 159.

23. The motif of the irreducible residue, the unassimilable fragment, the remains, the leftover that cannot be *relevé,* is central likewise to Jacques Derrida, *Glas,* trans. John P. Leavey and Richard Rand (Lincoln: University of Nebraska Press, 1986), which like so much of recent French philosophy is on the lookout for something that cannot be consumed and incorporated into the Hegelian "dialectic." Cf. MC, p. 285.

24. There are late Heideggerian tones in late Foucault: where Heidegger has analyzed the *Gestell* that is the "essence of technology," in its application to nature, Foucault discusses the *Gestell* that is applied to us in the various "technologies of the self," or technologies of behavior. Michel Foucault, *Discipline and Punish: The Birth of the Prison,* trans. Alan Sheridan (New York: Vintage, 1977, 1979), pp. 135–169.

25. "This . . . force of resistance, this Foucaultian spirituality, bears witness to the capacity for an ecstatic transcendence of any history that asserts its necessity." Bernauer, *Michel Foucault's Force of Flight,* pp. 180–181.

26. Foucault does not have a theory of pure or radical freedom, of the sort he suggested in his early work on Ludwig Binswanger, but of a circumscribed, circumstantial (circumcisional!) freedom, a capacity for contextual alteration, for modification of the circumstances one finds oneself by way of refusal. It is also a theory of local revolt as opposed to total revolution. See John Rajchman, *Michel Foucault: The Freedom of Philosophy* (New York: Columbia University Press, 1985), chap. 1, "The Politics of Revolt."

27. Jacques Derrida, *The Other Heading: Reflections on Today's Europe,* trans. Pascale-Anne Brault and Michael Naas (Bloomington: Indiana University Press, 1992), p. 9.

28. I have expanded on the notion of a hermeneutics that gives up on the idea of a hermeneutic secret, of uncovering the master name, and that finds itself in an abyss in Caputo, RH, chaps. 6–7.

29. Foucault, *The Order of Things,* p. 373.

30. That is fundamentally the argument in Søren Kierkegaard, *The Concept of Anxiety,* trans. Reidar Thomte (Princeton: Princeton University Press, 1980), which is the reason that Heidegger had a fairly easy time of rewriting this concept in a secularized or, as he said, "formalized" way in Heidegger, *Being and Time.*

31. Hannah Arendt, *The Human Condition* (Chicago: University of Chicago Press, 1958), pp. 236–243. "Trespassing is an everyday occurrence which is in the very nature of action's constant establishment of new relationships within a web of relations, and it needs forgiving, dismissing, in order to make it possible for life to go on by constantly releasing men from what they have done unknowingly" (p. 240). Forgiving is releasing, forgetting, and moving on.

32. Julia Kristeva, *"Qui tollis peccata mundi,"* in *Powers of Horror: An Essay on Abjection,* trans. Leon S. Roudiez (New York: Columbia University Press, 1982), pp. 131–132. Duns Scotus located the essence of the sacrament in the word of the confessor, not in doing penance. Hannah Arendt says that *metanoein* (Luke 17:3–4) is better understood as "change of heart," retrace your steps and sin no more, than as "repent" (the usual translation), penance, which means of course to revisit yourself with pain. Cf. Arendt, *The Human Condition,* p. 240 n. 78.

2. How to Prepare for the Coming of the Other

1. Hans-Georg Gadamer, *Wahrheit und Methode,* 4th ed. (Tübingen: Mohr, 1990), 175, hereafter cited as WM; Hans-Georg Gadamer, *Truth and Method,* 2d rev. ed., trans. Joel Weinsheimer and Donald G. Marshall (New York: Crossroad, 1991), hereafter cited as TM.

2. Jacques Derrida, "Psyche: Inventions of the Other," trans. Catherine Porter, in *Reading De Man Reading,* ed. Lindsay Waters and Wlad Godzich (Minneapolis: University of Minnesota Press, 1989), pp. 25–65.

3. For example, see James Risser, *Hermeneutics and the Voice of the Other: Re-Reading Gadamer's Philosophical Hermeneutics* (Albany: SUNY Press, 1997), who thematizes Gadamer's hermeneutics around finitude.

4. Gadamer is not claiming that we are free to hold assertions that are formally contradictory. On the contrary, from a strictly logical point of view, he is invoking the old maxim *ab esse ad posse valet:* if something is actual, it must be possible. If experience is actually limited, it must be possible to account for that without falling victim to a self-referential paradox.

5. See Derrida, *Sauf le nom* (Paris: Galilée, 1993), p. 94; Jacques Derrida, *On the Name*, ed. Thomas Dutoit (Stanford: Stanford University Press, 1995), p. 75.

6. Hans-Georg Gadamer, *Reason in the Age of Science*, trans. Frederick Lawrence (Cambridge, Mass.: MIT Press, 1981), pp. 40, 59.

7. Martin Heidegger, "The Origin of the Work of Art," in *Language, Truth, Poetry*, trans. Albert Hofstadter (New York: Harper & Row, 1971), pp. 31ff.

8. Theology has never been at a loss to reappropriate Heidegger's notion of finitude. It has no trouble reinserting it within a theology of infinity, within a project of transcendence toward infinite Being. That is what Karl Rahner did with Heidegger in *Geist im Welt*. It is also not insignificant that the Gadamer translator Frederick Lawrence is also interested in the Jesuit theologian Bernard Lonergan. Rahner and Lonergan are the preeminent representatives of "transcendental Thomism" which sees inscribed in the finitude of human *intellectus* an intrinsic "dynamism" toward the infinite Being of God.

9. Hans-Georg Gadamer, *The Relevance of the Beautiful and Other Essays*, ed. Robert Bernasconi (Cambridge: Cambridge University Press, 1986), hereafter cited as RB.

10. Jacques Derrida, *Speech and Phenomena*, trans. David Allison (Evanston: Northwestern University Press, 1972).

11. In Jacques Derrida, *The Post Card: From Socrates to Freud and Beyond*, trans. Alan Bass (Chicago: University of Chicago Press, 1987), Derrida criticizes classical theories of meaning which think that meaning can be disengaged from its medium as theories of "message-bearing," and he uses the postal metaphor to do this. This is a problem for hermeneutics which takes its start from Hermes, the first postman. On my accounting Gadamer holds a modified postal theory. See Gadamer, RB, 142.

12. I borrow this expression from Jean-Luc Marion, *God without Being*, trans. Thomas Carlson (Chicago: University of Chicago Press, 1991), p. 149, who uses it in an even stronger and straightforward theological sense: the only interpretation of the Scripture which allows it to yield its gift must be guided by participation in the Eucharist.

13. For Derrida's response to David Tracy, see John D. Caputo and Michael Scanlon, eds., *God, the Gift, and Postmodernism* (Bloomington: Indiana University Press, 1999), pp. 181–184.

14. Jacques Derrida, *Of Grammatology*, corr. ed., trans. Gayatri Chakravorty Spivak (Baltimore: Johns Hopkins University Press, 1997), p. 68

15. Jacques Derrida, *Glas*, trans. John P. Leavey and Richard Rand (Lincoln: University of Nebraska Press, 1986), hereafter cited as G. *Glas* I think is the most utterly unassimilable of Derrida's works from the standpoint of Gadamerian hermeneutics. *Glas* relentlessly disrupts the attempt to give Jean Genet's work a comfortable readability or to let Hegel's work settle into systematic unity. "Why

make a knife pass between two texts? Why, at least write two texts at once? . . . There is a wish to make writing ungraspable, of course." Derrida, *Glas*, 64b.

16. Jacques Derrida, *Dissemination*, trans. Barbara Johnson (Chicago: University of Chicago Press, 1981), p. 253.

17. "There is no name for it (*différance*): a proposition to be read in its *platitude*." Jacques Derrida, *Margins of Philosophy*, trans. Alan Bass (Chicago: University of Chicago Press, 1982), p. 26.

18. I cite here the opening lines of Jacques Derrida, *De l'esprit* (Paris: Galilée, 1987), p. 11; Jacques Derrida, *Of Spirit*, trans. G. Bennington and R. Bowlby (Chicago: University of Chicago Press, 1989), p. 1. Derrida is interested in the recurrence of the *Geist* in Heidegger's writings, how it keeps coming back like a ghost. In Gadamer, I suggest, it is in virtue of the *Geistigkeit* of writing that meaning can keep coming back.

19. This is precisely Derrida's argument against Husserl in Derrida, *Speech and Phenomena*, and it applies *mutatis mutandis* to Gadamer.

20. Contrast the balance between sense and sound which Gadamer seeks in Mallarmé (RB, 134–135) with Derrida's critique of Jean-Pierre Richard's hermeneutic interpretation of Mallarmé in Derrida, *Dissemination*, pp. 246ff.

21. Jacques Derrida, *Truth in Painting*, trans. G. Bennington and I. MacLeod (Chicago: University of Chicago Press, 1987), pp. 371–372.

22. See Heidegger's early Freiburg lectures in Martin Heidegger, *Gesamtausgabe*, vol. 61, *Phænomenologische Interpretationen zu Aristoteles* (Frankfurt: Klostermann, 1985), pp. 108–110; vol. 63, *Ontologie (Hermeneutik der Faktizität)* (Frankfurt: Klostermann, 1988), passim.

23. Derrida, *Of Grammatology*, 162.

24. Emmanuel Levinas, *Totality and Infinity*, trans. Alphonso Lingis (Pittsburgh: Duquesne University Press, 1969).

25. Derrida, *Sauf le nom*, p. 85; *On the Name*, p. 71.

26. See Derrida's concluding remarks in *Deconstruction and Pragmatism: Simon Critchley, Jacques Derrida, Ernesto Laclau, and Richard Rorty*, ed. Chantal Mouffe (London: Routledge, 1996), p. 86.

27. Jacques Derrida, *Points . . . Interviews, 1974–94*, ed. Elisabeth Weber, trans. Peggy Kamuf (Stanford: Stanford University Press, 1995), p. 201.

3. Who Is Derrida's Zarathustra?

1. The following paragraphs are based on Maurice Blanchot, *Friendship*, trans. Elizabeth Rottenberg (Stanford: Stanford University Press, 1997), pp. 291–292. Blanchot is writing a tribute to Georges Bataille on the occasion of the latter's death. For a commentary, see Gerald L. Bruns, *Maurice Blanchot: The Refusal of Philosophy* (Baltimore: Johns Hopkins University Press, 1997), pp. 119–121. It is also the view of Stanley Cavell, *The Claim of Reason* (New York: Oxford University Press, 1979), chap. 4, that it is the irrefutability of skepticism about the other, our un-knowing of the other, that lies at the basis of our respect for others; this is pointed out in Simon Critchley, "Derrida: Private Ironist or Public Liberal," in *Deconstruction and Pragmatism: Simon Critchley, Jacques Derrida, Ernesto Laclau, and Richard Rorty*, ed. Chantal Mouffe (London: Routledge, 1996), p. 32.

2. Jacques Derrida, *Parages* (Paris: Galilée, 1986), p. 25.

3. Jacques Derrida, *Politics of Friendship*, trans. George Collins (London: Verso, 1997), p. 232, hereafter cited as PF.

4. Jacques Derrida, *Specters of Marx: The State of the Debt, the Work of Mourning, and the New International,* trans. Peggy Kamuf (New York: Routledge, 1994), pp. 3ff.

5. I have examined these autobiographical comments in John D. Caputo, *The Prayers and Tears of Jacques Derrida: Religion without Religion* (Bloomington: Indiana University Press, 1997), pp. 281ff.

6. See Jacques Derrida and Anne Dufourmantelle, *De L'hospitalité: Anne Dufourmantelle invite Jacques Derrida à Répondre* (Paris: Calmann-Lévy, 1997); John D. Caputo, ed., *Deconstruction in a Nutshell: A Conversation with Jacques Derrida* (New York: Fordham University Press, 1997), pp. 109–113.

7. Jacques Derrida, *The Gift of Death,* trans. David Wills (Chicago: University of Chicago Press, 1995), p. 49.

8. However, Derrida's frustration with communitarian values is such that he says that the essentials of friendship would not have "the slightest reference to community," unavowable, inoperative, or even a community without community (PF, 298).

9. Diogenes Laertius, *Lives and Opinions of Eminent Philosophers,* trans. R. R. Hicks, 2 vols., Loeb Classical Library (Cambridge, Mass.: Harvard University Press, 1959), 2:464–465. Diogenes Laertius says this text is found "moreover" in the *Nichomachean Ethics,* bk. 7, where, of course, it is not found, although there is evidence to support this rendering in the *Eudemian Ethics,* bk. 7. See Derrida, PF, pp. 208–209.

10. See Diane Michelfelder and Richard Palmer, eds., *Dialogue and Deconstruction: The Derrida-Gadamer Encounter* (Albany: SUNY Press, 1989), pp. 21–57.

11. See Jacques Derrida, "Politics and Friendship: An Interview with Jacques Derrida," trans. Robert Harvey, in *The Althusserian Legacy,* ed. E. Ann Kaplan and Michael Spinker (London: Verso Books, 1993), pp. 18–231, esp. pp. 197, 199, 213. Whence there is the perversity of Mark Lilla's review of *Specters of Marx* in "The Politics of Jacques Derrida," *The New York Review of Books* (25 June 1998). As opposed to being enlightened about the Enlightenment, *The New York Review of Books* is regularly scandalized whenever the dogmas of the Enlightenment are criticized, particularly in and under the name of Derrida.

12. "What's important in 'democracy to come' is not 'democracy,' but 'to come.'" Jacques Derrida, "Politics and Friendship: An Interview with Jacques Derrida," trans. Robert Harvey, in *The Althusserian Legacy,* ed. E. Ann Kaplan and Michael Spinker (London: Verso Books, 1993), p. 216.

13. This makes it hard to understand the decision of the editors of the English translation to exclude the essay on Heidegger found in the original French edition of Jacques Derrida, *Politiques de l'amitié* (Paris: Galilée, 1994).

14. "I'm trying, for example, to think out an equality that would not be homogeneous, that would take heterogeneity, infinite singularity, infinite alterity into account." "Politics and Friendship," p. 213.

15. Friedrich Nietzsche, *Beyond Good and Evil,* trans. R. J. Hollingdale (Baltimore: Penguin, 1972). Derrida, *The Gift of Death,* pp. 114–115.

16. John D. Caputo, *Against Ethics* (Bloomington: Indiana University Press, 1993), pp. 42ff.

17. See John D. Caputo, *Demythologizing Heidegger* (Bloomington: Indiana University Press, 1993), chap. 2, where I argue that Heidegger's work through the 1930s is to be understood as *Kampfsphilosophie.*

18. Laertius, _Lives and Opinions of Eminent Philosophers_, pp. 462–465.

19. Jacques Derrida, _Adieu: à Emmanuel Levinas_ (Paris: Galilée, 1997).

20. Søren Kierkegaard, _Kierkegaard's Writings_, Vol. VII, _Philosophical Fragments_, trans. Howard Hong and Edna H. Hong (Princeton: Princeton University Press, 1985), pp. 31ff.

21. Emmanuel Levinas, "God and Philosophy," in _Emmanuel Levinas: Basic Philosophical Writings_, ed. Adriaan Peperzak et al. (Bloomington: Indiana University Press, 1996), pp. 140–141.

22. Derrida, _Specters of Marx_, pp. 167–168.

23. I first used the term "phainaesthetic," from _phainesthai_, signifying a kind of hyper-aesthetics, turning not on the aesthetic subject's taste and judgment, but on the glow of Being, _das Scheinen und die Schönheit des Seins_, in reference to a critique of Heidegger, in Caputo, _Demythologizing Heidegger_, pp. 142–147. I think this term resonates well with respect to Aristotle's magnanimous man and Nietzsche's _Ubermensch_.

4. Parisian Hermeneutics and Yankee Hermeneutics

1. Richard Rorty, _Philosophical Papers_, vol. 3, _Truth and Progress_ (Cambridge: Cambridge University Press, 1998), hereafter cited as TP.

2. Richard Rorty, _Achieving Our Country: Leftist Thought in Twentieth-Century America_ (Cambridge, Mass.: Harvard University Press, 1998), hereafter cited as AOC. Jacques Derrida, _Politics of Friendship_, trans. George Collins (London: Verso, 1997).

3. This admiration has evolved from a more qualified to a less qualified state. In an earlier piece, John D. Caputo, "The Thought of Being and the Conversation of Mankind: The Case of Heidegger and Rorty," _The Review of Metaphysics_ 36, no. 143 (March 1983): 661–685, whose main merit lies in the way it differentiates Rorty from Martin Heidegger, I was much more worried by Rorty. I am more appreciative now—via Jacques Derrida—of a lot of what Rorty is up to. Although I will voice some criticism of Rorty in this study, I am sympathetic with his nominalism and also with his complaint about my earlier treatment of his work. See Richard Rorty, _Contingency, Irony, and Solidarity_ (New York: Cambridge University Press, 1989), pp. 122–123 n. 4, hereafter cited as CIS.

4. Still, there are curious tendencies in Rorty's work toward a naturalistic reductionism which turns everything over to charged particles migrating through empty space. See Rorty, CIS, 17. He thinks that after the Enlightenment, both naturalism and romanticism should be given full play.

5. Jean-François Lyotard, _The Postmodern Condition: A Report on Knowledge_, trans. G. Bennington and B. Maussumi (Minneapolis: University of Minnesota Press, 1984), pp. xxiii–xxiv.

6. That is also how Rorty reads Donald Davidson. Davidson's critique of the idea of conceptual scheme, on Rorty's view, is not primarily that it would cut off communication between the users of different schemes. That would make Davidson look too much like Karl Apel and Jürgen Habermas, viz., like a defender of transcendental conditions of communication. Rorty takes Davidson to be objecting that the "very idea" is a philosophical one and makes language into some kind of magical mystical something, some sort of unknown somewhat, another Transcendental Object = X. And who needs that? All a pragmatist needs are the physical causes of particular beliefs; everything else is a redundant backup. See

Richard Rorty, "The World Well Lost," in *Consequences of Pragmatism* (Minneapolis: University of Minnesota Press, 1982), pp. 3–18. This talk of physical causes is what I mean by physicalistic reductionism.

7. Rorty's first piece on Derrida was entitled "Philosophy as a Kind of Writing," in *Consequences of Pragmatism*, pp. 90–109.

8. Rorty came to the defense of the "natural attitude" in the discussion which followed a presentation of Richard Rorty, "Two Meanings of 'Logocentrism': A Reply to Norris," at a conference the Greater Philadelphia Philosophy Consortium sponsored in October 1988. I found this defense singularly enlightening about Rorty's views. My commentary on Rorty's and Norris's papers that day was the first draft of the present study. Richard Rorty, "Two Meanings of 'Logocentrism'," was subsequently published in *Redrawing the Lines: Analytic Philosophy, Deconstruction, and Literary Theory*, ed. Reed Way Dasenbrock (Minneapolis: University of Minnesota Press, 1989), pp. 204–216.

9. Edmund Husserl, *Ideas Pertaining to a Pure Phenomenology and to a Phenomenological Philosophy*, bk. 1, trans. Fred Kersten (The Hague: M. Nijhoff, 1983), §30, pp. 55–56. Husserl would never have been able to formulate the principle of the natural attitude in this section without having already implicitly made the *epoche*, which is not announced until §31.

10. Friedrich Nietzsche, *Twilight of the Idols*, trans. R. J. Hollingdale (Baltimore: Penguin Books, 1968), pp. 40–41. Martin Heidegger, *On Time and Being*, trans. Joan Stambaugh (New York: Harper & Row, 1972), p. 24.

11. Simon Critchley, *Deconstruction and Pragmatism: Simon Critchley, Jacques Derrida, Ernesto Laclau, and Richard Rorty*, ed. Chantal Mouffe (London: Routledge, 1996), hereafter cited as DP.

12. "Apart from his incredible, almost Nabokovian, polylingual linguistic facility, he is a great comic writer—perhaps the funniest writer on philosophical topics since Kierkegaard." Rorty, "Two Meanings of 'Logocentrism'," p. 209.

13. Jacques Derrida, *Glas* (Paris: Galilée, 1974); Jacques Derrida, *Glas*, trans. John P. Leavey and Richard Rand (Lincoln: University of Nebraska Press, 1986), hereafter cited as G; *Glassary*, ed. Gregory Ulmer and John P. Leavey (Lincoln: University of Nebraska Press, 1986).

14. Rorty, "Two Meanings of 'Logocentrism'," p. 208.

15. Richard Rorty, "Deconstruction and Circumvention," *Critical Inquiry* 11 (September 1984): 1–23.

16. Rorty, "Two Meanings of 'Logocentrism'," pp. 209ff. See Paul De Man, *The Resistance to Theory* (Minneapolis: University of Minnesota Press, 1986).

17. Norris criticizes Rorty in Christopher Norris, "Philosophy as a Kind of Narrative: Rorty on Postmodern Liberal Culture," in *The Contest of Faculties* (London: Methuen, 1985), pp. 139–166; and Christopher Norris, "Philosophy as Not Just a 'Kind of Writing': Derrida and the Claim of Reason," in *Redrawing the Lines*, pp. 189–203. See also Richard Rorty's review of Rodolphe Gasché, *The Tain of the Mirror* (Cambridge, Mass.: Harvard University Press, 1986), in Richard Rorty, "Is Derrida a Transcendental Philosopher?" *Yale Journal of Criticism* 2 (1988), reprinted in TP, pp. 327ff.

18. Norris, "Philosophy as Not Just a 'Kind of Writing'," p. 193, cf. p. 195.

19. Christopher Norris, *Derrida* (Cambridge, Mass.: Harvard University Press, 1987), pp. 142ff., cf. pp. 150–155.

20. Norris, "Philosophy as Not Just a 'Kind of Writing'," p. 198.

21. See my review of Gasché in John D. Caputo, "Derrida: A Kind of Philosopher," *Research in Phenomenology* 17 (1987): 245–289.

22. See Jacques Derrida, *Of Grammatology,* corr. ed., trans. Gayatri Chakravorty Spivak (Baltimore: Johns Hopkins University Press, 1997), pp. 57–63.

23. See Jacques Derrida, "A Number of Yes" (*Nombre de Oui*), trans. Brian Holmes, *Qui Parle* 2, no. 2 (1988): 118–133.

24. Rorty, "Deconstruction and Circumvention," p. 18.

25. Christopher Norris, *Deconstruction: Theory and Practice* (London: Methuen, 1982).

26. Rorty, "Two Meanings of 'Logocentrism'," p. 212.

27. I have complained about this before, in John D. Caputo, "The Thought of Being and the Conversation of Mankind: The Case of Heidegger and Rorty," *The Review of Metaphysics* 36 (March 1983): 661–685, cf. pp. 672–674, where I argue that the notion of language as freely invented by human subjects for their own use belongs to the most classical metaphysical idea of language. It is not a neutral nonphilosophical idea (CIS, 14–15), but philosophy's most classical gesture, as Heidegger shows (for example, in "Language," in *Poetry, Language, Thought*, trans. A. Hofstadter [New York: Harper & Row, 1971], pp. 187ff.). Rorty is steadfastly stuck in metaphysics when he treats language as a man-made tool, as I hope to illustrate here.

28. See also Rick Roderick, "Reading Derrida Politically (Contra Rorty)," *Praxis International* 6 (1987): 442–449; and John D. Caputo, "Beyond Aestheticism: Derrida's Responsible Anarchy," *Research in Phenomenology* 18 (1988): 59–73.

29. This is a point on which Mark Taylor takes Rorty to task. See "Paralectics," in Mark Taylor, *Tears* (Albany: SUNY Press, 1990), pp. 123ff.

30. Richard Rorty, "Is Derrida a Transcendental Philosopher?" in *Essays on Heidegger and Others* (Cambridge: Cambridge University Press, 1991); Richard Rorty, "Is Derrida a Quasi-Transcendental Philosopher?" reprinted with minor changes under the title "Derrida and the Philosophical Tradition," in TP, pp. 327ff.; Jacques Derrida, "Circumfession: Fifty-nine Periods and Periphrases," in Geoffrey Bennington and Jacques Derrida, *Jacques Derrida* (Chicago: University of Chicago Press, 1993).

31. The notion that language is a tool is, in my view, separable from the theory of autonomy. I think—contra Heidegger—that language is like a tool, but a tool—this is a little more Heideggerian—forged not by autonomous subjects but by communities, slow historical tendencies, erratic and contingent circumstances, collective-impersonal impulses, structural and unconscious forces. Language is filled with inertia, is a culture-wide phenomenon, is not subject to individual volitions or subjective fiats. When Derrida speaks of "prag-grammatoloy," he is also I think trying to appreciate the pragmatic point, which is that language is a way of coping with the world and of getting through the day. But I must say the notion of "tool" leaves a lot out for me.

32. For instance, Derrida defends the linguistic string "green is or" against Husserl, who rejects it on the grounds that it is not only material nonsense but formal nonsense as well. On Husserl's theory, the sentence "the English language is dead" is false but meaningful (*sinnvoll*). "The English language is green" is "countersensical" (*Widersinn*) but in good form, for it is logical form in such that it could, with the proper substitutions, be rendered both meaningful and true. But "green is or" for Husserl is just a plain *Unsinn*, not only semantically but

formally, logico-grammatically incoherent, because one could not substitute a true or meaningful substitution instance for it that would be of the same form. Derrida responded by showing that one can *always recontextualize* "green is or" and make it both meaningful and true—for example, by making it the response to a request for a string of English words, or by color-coding disjunctives, or by changing its inflection, or by a homophonic poetic play, or by a literally indefinite number of other available means. Jacques Derrida, *Margins of Philosophy,* trans. Alan Bass (Chicago: University of Chicago Press, 1982), pp. 319–320; cf. Jacques Derrida, *Speech and Phenomena,* trans. David Allison (Evanston: Northwestern University Press, 1972), pp. 97–99. For a further account of this example, see John D. Caputo, "The Economy of Signs in Husserl and Derrida," in *Deconstruction and Philosophy,* ed. John Sallis (Chicago: University of Chicago Press, 1987), pp. 99–113; and Caputo, *Radical Hermeneutics,* pp. 138–145. Husserl discusses "green is or" in §15 of the *Logical Investigations.* See Edmund Husserl, *Logical Investigations,* trans. J. N. Findlay, Investigation 1, vol. 1 (New York: Humanities Press, 1970).

33. "When Derrida talks about deconstruction as prophetic of 'the democracy to come,' he seems to me to be expressing the same utopian social hope as was felt by these earlier dreamers [Dewey, Mill] . . . When he says that he yearns for a time when man and woman can be friends . . . he seems to me to be expressing the same sort of utopian hope. The interweaving of these two themes in his essay 'Politics and Friendship' makes that very moving text one of my own favorites" (DP, 13–14).

34. I have tried to bring out another side of Foucault in the first chapter, and in the work from which this was excerpted. Mark Yount and I have gathered contributors who tried to show the social use to which Foucault can be put. See John D. Caputo and Mark C. Yount, eds., *Foucault and the Critique of Institutions* (University Park: Pennsylvania State University Press, 1992).

35. "The notion of 'infinite responsibility,' formulated by Emmanuel Levinas and sometimes deployed by Derrida—as well as Derrida's own frequent discoveries of impossibility, unreachability, and unrepresentability—may be useful to some of us in our own individual quests for private perfection. When we take up our public responsibilities, however, the infinite and the unrepresentable are merely nuisances. Thinking of our responsibilities in these terms is as much of a stumbling block to effective political organization as is the sense of sin. Emphasizing the impossibility of meaning, or of justice, as Derrida sometimes does, is a temptation to Gothicize—to view democratic politics as ineffectual, because unable to cope with preternatural forces" (AOC, 97).

36. Jacques Derrida, *Specters of Marx: The State of the Debt, the Work of Mourning, and the New International,* trans. Peggy Kamuf (New York: Routledge, 1994), hereafter cited as SOM. See Rorty's review of *Specters of Marx.* Richard Rorty, "A Spectre Is Haunting the Intellectuals," *The European Journal of Philosophy* 3, no. 3 (December 1995): 289–298.

37. From *Leaves of Grass,* in Walt Whitman, *Complete Poetry and Selected Prose* (New York: Library of America, 1982), p. 16; cited by Rorty in AOC, p. 22.

38. Derrida, *Of Grammatology,* p. 162.

39. Derrida, *Margins of Philosophy,* pp. 6–7.

40. See Caputo, *The Prayers and Tears of Jacques Derrida,* pp. 139–143.

41. Mark Dooley, "Private Irony vs. Social Hope," forthcoming in *Cultural Val-*

ues 3, no. 3 (July 1999) (Oxford: Blackwell, 1999), pp. 263–290. Derrida, "Violence and Metaphysics," in *Writing and Difference,* trans. Alan Bass (Chicago: University of Chicago Press, 1978), pp. 125–126.

42. By justice and injustice, I might add, Derrida means pretty much what Rorty means, protecting the weak against the strong, protecting the poor who are getting poorer against the rich who are getting richer, eliminating the needless suffering and gratuitous cruelty of contemporary life. Like Derrida, Rorty thinks there would be a certain obscenity in demanding a foundational reason for why we should be opposed to cruelty, and he does not think one is forthcoming in any case. In his critique of the cultural left, Rorty distinguishes two kinds of needless suffering: poverty, or economic injustice, and "stigma," the cruelty of discriminating against someone because of race, ethnicity, gender, or sexual orientation. Both forms of evil are evil enough for him, but the cultural left, and the followers of Derrida, are preoccupied with the latter to the neglect of the former. Rorty does not make this charge against Derrida, and rightly so, although the sorts of causes that Derrida has gotten himself involved in—academic reform in the 1960s and 1970s, and more recently immigrant rights, Mandela, Mumia Abujamal, Salmon Rushdie, etc.—might tempt Rorty to do so.

43. Chantal Mouffe speaks of "the dangers of complacency" that his view entails (DP, 6) as does Critchley (DP, 24).

44. See Mouffe, ed., DP, 8.

45. Jacques Derrida, "Politics and Friendship: An Interview with Jacques Derrida," trans. Robert Harvey, in *The Althusserian Legacy,* ed. E. Ann Kaplan and Michael Spinker (London: Verso Books, 1993), p. 216.

46. Rorty, "A Spectre Is Haunting the Intellectuals," p. 290.

47. Someday, maybe a couple of millennia from now, Rorty says we may be able to just walk away from both Jew and Greek, so that the impossibility of avoiding biblical religion and Greek metaphysics will have proven to be a "local, transitory, and empirical impossibility." So why can we not add "democracy" to that list of things that future purposes may find it useful to discard in the name of what now is called democracy? See Richard Rorty, "Derrida and the Philosophical Tradition," in TP, p. 350.

5. Dreaming of the Innumerable

1. Jacques Derrida and Christie V. McDonald, "Choreographies," in *Points . . . Interviews, 1974–94,* ed. Elisabeth Weber, trans. Peggy Kamuf (Stanford: Stanford University Press, 1995), hereafter cited as P.

2. A "quasi-transcendental" is a condition for the possibility—and impossibility—of a thing. As opposed to a straightforward transcendental condition, which sets forth the borders within which a thing may appear, a quasi-transcendental is the condition of a field without closure, for effects that overrun their borders.

3. Jacques Derrida, *Spurs: Nietzsche's Styles,* trans. Barbara Harlow (Chicago: University of Chicago Press, 1979).

4. Since Derrida's position is so anti-essentialist, since he denies that there is an identifiable truth of women (or of men, of course)—most notably in the notoriously difficult *Spurs: Nietzsche's Styles*—he tends to provoke criticism along these lines; see Rosi Braidotti, *Patterns of Dissonance* (New York: Routledge, 1991). For an interesting and appreciative account of Derrida and feminism, see Peggy Kamuf, "Introduction: Reading between the Blinds," in *A Derrida Reader: Between the Blinds,* ed. Peggy Kamuf (New York: Columbia University Press, 1991).

5. Drucilla Cornell, *The Philosophy of the Limit* (New York: Routledge. 1992), hereafter cited as PL; Drucilla Cornell, "Where Love Begins: Sexual Difference and the Limit of the Masculine Imaginary," in *Derrida and Feminism*, ed. Ellen K. Feder et al. (New York: Routledge, 1997), pp. 161–206, hereafter cited as DF; Drucilla Cornell, *The Imaginary Domain: Abortion, Pornography, and Sexual Harassment* (New York: Routledge, 1995), hereafter cited as ID; Drucilla Cornell, *Beyond Accommodation: Ethical Feminism—Deconstruction and the Law* (New York: Routledge: 1991), hereafter cited as BA; Drucilla Cornell, *Transformations: Recollective Imagination and Sexual Difference* (New York: Routledge, 1993), hereafter cited as T.

6. "However—it is woman who will be my subject." Derrida, *Spurs*, p. 37. But then again, some pages later (p. 121), in virtue of his relentless anti-essentialism that there is no single truth of *the* woman, Derrida says: "so woman then will not have been my subject." For a commentary, see Gayatri Chakravorty Spivak, "Displacement and the Discourse of Woman," in *Displacement: Derrida and After*, ed. Mark Krupnick (Bloomington: Indiana University Press, 1983), p. 171.

7. Jacques Derrida speaks of writing like a woman in the discussion following "La Question du style," in *Nietzsche Aujourd'hui*, 2 vols. (Paris: Union Générale d'Editions, 1973), 1:299.

8. That is one of the principal points of Derrida, *Spurs;* see pp. 101–103.

9. On Spivak's interpretation of Derrida's *Spurs*, "woman" is the name, not for being and identity (the transcendental signified), but for dissimulation, style, and artistry, for the play of *différance*, and this because "a man cannot fake an orgasm"; see Spivak, "Displacement," p. 170, passim. But that is all the more reason to deny that "hymen" is the name of an absence. See Cornell's critique of Spivak in T, p. 85. On Cornell's use of *mère/mehr*, see T, pp. 2, 84, 94.

10. Having originated in a 1994 American Philosophical Association, Central Division, panel on *The Philosophy of the Limit*, my attention in the present study is largely given to this work. But I have found equally valuable Drucilla Cornell, "The Feminist Alliance with Deconstruction," in PL. While more concerned with Derrida's intervention on Jacques Lacan than on Emmanuel Levinas, in *Beyond Accommodation* Cornell makes use of "Choreographies" to much the same ends as do I. See also T, passim.

11. Jacques Derrida, "Force of Law: The 'Mystical Foundations of Authority'," trans. Mary Quaintance, in *Deconstruction and the Possibility of Justice*, ed. Drucilla Cornell et al. (New York: Routledge, 1992), hereafter cited as FL.

12. Cornell is fond of calling the law a "monster."

13. Jacques Derrida, "The Principle of Reason: The University in the Eyes of Its Pupils," *Diacritics* 13 (Fall 1983): 3–20, hereafter cited as PR.

14. Jacques Derrida, *Parages* (Paris: Galilée, 1986), p. 116.

15. Simon Critchley contests Rorty's claim that the other's suffering is something about which we can be ironic, and he wonders whether Derrida's remark about justice in itself constitutes a certain foundationalism; see Simon Critchley, "Deconstruction and Pragmatism—Is Derrida a Private Ironist or a Public Liberal?" in *Deconstruction and Pragmatism*, pp. 19–40.

16. I have attempted to work out an analogous distinction between two postmodernisms, under the names of heteronomism and heteromorphism, in John D. Caputo, *Against Ethics* (Bloomington: Indiana University Press, 1993), pp. 53–68. See also Edith Wyschogrod, *Saints and Postmodernism* (Chicago: University of Chicago Press, 1990), pp. 191, 223, 229.

17. For a theory of obligation that has given up on the Good and turned to a life of evil, see Caputo, *Against Ethics*, chaps. 2–3.

18. Jacques Derrida, *Du droit á la philosophie* (Paris: Galilée, 1990). For a commentary, see John D. Caputo, ed., *Deconstruction in a Nutshell: A Conversation with Jacques Derrida* (New York: Fordham University Press, 1997), chap. 2.

19. See Jacques Derrida, *On the Name*, ed. Thomas Dutoit (Stanford: Stanford University Press, 1995), pp. 87–127.

20. Jacques Derrida, *Given Time, I: Counterfeit Money*, trans. Peggy Kamuf (Chicago: University of Chicago Press, 1992), chap. 1.

21. On George Steiner's term "alternity," as what is "other than the case," see Cornell, PL, p. 111.

22. For the cover quotation, see Cornell, PL, p. 94; and on Arthur Schopenhauer and Theodor Adorno, see Cornell, PL, chap. 1.

23. Emmanuel Levinas, *Totality and Infinity*, trans. Alphonso Lingis (Pittsburgh: Duquesne University Press, 1969), pp. 254–280.

24. Jacques Derrida, *Glas*, trans. John P. Leavey and Richard Rand (Lincoln: University of Nebraska Press, 1986), p. 1a.

25. See the discussion of *parler femme* in "Questions," and the critique of Derrida in "Cosi Fan Tutti," in Luce Irigaray, *This Sex Which Is Not One*, trans. Catherine Porter with Carolyn Burke (Ithaca: Cornell University Press, 1985); cf. Cornell, PL, pp. 101–102.

26. John D. Caputo, *Demythologizing Heidegger* (Bloomington: Indiana University Press, 1993), p. 215 n. 7.

27. Catharine A. MacKinnon, *Feminism Unmodified: Discourses on Life and Law* (Cambridge, Mass.: Harvard University Press, 1987).

28. Jacques Derrida, *Politics of Friendship*, trans. George Collins (New York: Verso, 1997), p. 46 n. 14.

29. Kelley Oliver, *Womanizing Nietzsche: Philosophy's Relation to the Feminine* (New York: Routledge, 1995), pp. 160–162.

30. Kelly Oliver, "Father and the Promise of Ethics," *Diacritics* 27, no. 1 (1997): 45–57.

31. Jacques Derrida, *The Gift of Death*, trans. David Wills (Chicago: University of Chicago Press, 1995), hereafter cited as GD.

32. Oliver, "Father and the Promise of Ethics," p. 56.

33. See Drucilla Cornell, "Civil Disobedience and Deconstruction," in *Feminist Interpretations of Jacques Derrida*, ed. Nancy Holland (University Park: Pennsylvania State University Press, 1997), pp. 149ff.

34. See Jacques Derrida, "A Number of Yes" (*Nombre de Oui*), trans. Brian Holmes, *Qui Parle* 2, no. 2 (1988): 118–133.

35. Jacques Derrida, *Margins of Philosophy*, trans. Alan Bass (Chicago: University of Chicago Press, 1982), p. 27. For an attempt to bring together, to fuse and confuse, these Nietzschean and Levinasian figures, see my discussion of the "Dionysian rabbi" in Caputo, *Against Ethics*, chap. 3.

36. It is for neglecting these struggles that Spivak criticizes Derrida in Gayatri Chakravorty Spivak, "Feminism and Critical Theory," in *In Other Worlds: Essays in Cultural Politics* (New York: Routledge, 1987).

37. Although, for example, Neil Jordan's *The Crying Game* remains shut up within many classical gender stereotypes, it does engage in some interesting "gender-bending" with Fergus (Stephen Rea), who gradually sheds his unambiguous ma-

cho heterosexual identity to enter into a humane and nicely ambiguous relationship with Dil (Jaye Davidson). For an interesting analysis of the "essentializing" limitations of the film, see Kristin Handler, "Sexing *The Crying Game:* Difference, Identity, Ethics," *Film Quarterly* 47 (1994): 31–42.

38. As Hélène Cixous says, "It is impossible to see what will become of sexual difference—in another time. . . . But we must make no mistake: men and women are caught up in a web of age-old cultural determinations that are almost unanalyzable in their complexity. One can no more speak of 'woman' than of 'man' without being trapped within an ideological theater. . . ." Cited in Cornell, BA, p. 110.

6. Hermeneutics and the Natural Sciences

1. Robert P. Crease, "The Hard Case: Hermeneutics and Science," in *The Very Idea of Radical Hermeneutics*, pp. 96–105. See also Robert Serber and Robert P. Crease, *Peace and War: Reminiscences of a Life on the Frontiers of Science*, George B. Pegram Lecture Series (New York: Columbia University Press, 1998); Robert P. Crease and Charles C. Mann, *The Second Creation: Makers of the Revolution in Twentieth-Century Physics* (New Brunswick: Rutgers University Press, 1996); Robert P. Crease, ed., *Hermeneutics and the Natural Sciences* (Dordrecht: Kluwer Academic Publishers, 1997); Robert P. Crease, *The Play of Nature: Experimentation as Performance*, Indiana Series in the Philosophy of Technology (Bloomington: Indiana University Press, 1993).

2. See Steve Adams, "A Theory of Everything," *New Scientist* no. 118 (20 February 1999): 1–4. Edmund Husserl, *Cartesian Meditations*, trans. Dorion Cairns (The Hague: M. Nijhoff, 1960), §2, p. 4.

3. The full story, including the original article that set all this off, is now available in Jean Bricmont and Alan Sokal, *Fashionable Nonsense: Postmodern Intellectuals' Abuse of Science* (New York: Picador USA, 1998). Fortunately, Bricmont and Sokal see that, however fashionable, it is nonsense to implicate Derrida in *Nonsense*, that it would highly unfair to extend the charge of a relativistic view of science to him (8), and so they concentrate on attacking other luminaries on the French scene. Since their goal is to bombard contemporary Paris, they pay no attention to the Freiburg of an earlier time.

4. Steven Weinberg, "The Non-Revolution of T. S. Kuhn," *The New York Review of Books* (8 October 1998): 48–52; and Steven Weinberg, "Sokal's Hoax," *The New York Review of Books* (8 August 1996): 11–15. See Alan Sokal, "Transgressing the Boundaries: Toward a Transformative Hermeneutics of Quantum Gravity," *Social Text* (Spring/Summer 1996): 217–252; and Alan Sokal, "A Physicist Experiments with Cultural Studies," *Lingua Franca* (May/June 1996): 62–64. On the "cultural studies" approach to science that inflamed Sokal, see Andrew Ross, ed., *Science Wars* (Durham, N.C.: Duke University Press, 1996), which is a reprint of an issue of *Social Text* organized as a response to Paul Gross and Norman Levitt, *Higher Superstition* (Baltimore: Johns Hopkins University Press, 1994), which charge the cultural studies approach with science bashing. I discuss some of this in John D. Caputo, ed., *Deconstruction in a Nutshell: A Conversation with Jacques Derrida* (New York: Fordham University Press, 1997), pp. 71–74.

5. For an illuminating account of Martin Heidegger's conception of science, see Trish Glazebrook, *Heidegger's Philosophy of Science*, Perspectives in Continental Philosophy (New York: Fordham University Press, forthcoming).

6. *Wesen* was used as a verb in Middle High German, whence the modern German *west*. The English translators of Heidegger tend to render it as "come to presence."

7. The most thoughtful account of Heidegger's position that I know is Albert Borgman, *Technology and the Character of Contemporary Life* (Chicago: University of Chicago Press, 1987). The best account of its political setting is Michael Zimmerman, *Heidegger's Confrontation with Modernity* (Bloomington: Indiana University Press, 1990).

8. This point is systematically explored in the early work of Theodore Kisiel, who did good work on Heidegger's philosophy of science before he decided to track the young Heidegger's every move. See Theodore Kisiel, "Heidegger and the New Images of Science," *Research in Phenomenology* 7 (1977): 162–181; Theodore Kisiel, "New Philosophies of Science in the USA: A Selective Survey," *Zeitschrift für allgemeine Wissenschaftstheorie* 5 (1974): 138–91. On Martin Heidegger and Michael Polanyi, see Robert Innis, "Heidegger's Model of Subjectivity: A Polanyi Critique," in *Heidegger: The Man and the Thinker*, ed. Thomas Sheehan (Chicago: Precedent Publishing Co., 1981), pp. 117–130.

9. Martin Heidegger, *Sein und Zeit*, 10 vols. (Tübingen: Niemeyer, 1963), hereafter cited as SZ; the page numbers following the slash are from Martin Heidegger, *Being and Time*, trans. E. Macquarrie and J. Robinson (New York: Harper & Row, 1962).

10. Congruent with the discussion of what Karl R. Popper calls the "logic of discovery," Heidegger thinks that the mistake of the philosophy of science up to now has been to concentrate on the finished results of science, on science as a body of established propositions, rather than on the process by which such propositions arise. But the danger entailed by the genealogical approach—which wants to avoid being a pure logic—is psychologism and relativism, as Edmund Husserl pointed out in the first volume of *Logical Investigations*. As an application of phenomenology, Heidegger's hermeneutic genealogy intended to steer a middle course between the two. As a hermeneutic, it is not pure logic, but historical and genetic; as a phenomenological ontology, it is concerned, not with human psychology, but with the ontological structure of understanding (of *Dasein*, not of the "human"). The disagreement between Popper and Kuhn in *Criticism and the Growth of Knowledge*, ed. Imre Lakatos and Alan Musgrave (Cambridge: Cambridge University Press, 1970), is illustrative. Kuhn takes Popper's concerns to be too strongly dictated by an ahistorical logic (21–22) and Popper takes Kuhn's views to be relativistic and psychologistic (55–58). Kuhn would have done better in responding to the charge of psychologism to argue that his work is hermeneutic. To assert, however, that it is "social" and not "individual" psychology does not answer Popper's charge but simply confirms and refines it. Theodore Kisiel makes this important point in Theodore Kisiel, "Scientific Discovery: Logical, Psychological or Hermeneutical?" in *Explorations in Phenomenology*, ed. David Carr and Edward Casey (The Hague: Nijhoff, 1973), pp. 263–284. See also Theodore Kisiel, "The Rationality of Scientific Discovery," in *Rationality Today/La Rationalité Aujourd'hui*, ed. Theodore Geraets (Ottawa: University of Ottawa Press, 1979), pp. 401–411.

11. If the positivists supported a "unity of the sciences" program inasmuch as they wanted to reduce all the sciences to the method of the natural sciences, which was the very thing Wilhelm Dilthey opposed, Heidegger treats all science as a hermeneutic unity, that is, an exercise in projective understanding. That is

not to reduce all science to the method of one privileged science but rather to make all sciences generally conform to the ontological-hermeneutic structure of the understanding, *mutatis mutandis.*

12. Gestalt psychology is a common point of reference for Kuhn, Polanyi, Maurice Merleau-Ponty, Husserl, and Heidegger.

13. This is Joan Stambaugh's rendering of *Vorhandensein* in her translation of Martin Heidegger, *Being and Time* (Albany: SUNY, 1996).

14. It is important for us to observe that Heidegger never questions the legitimacy of the social and human sciences, or that they play a valid role in the work of *Wissenschaft* as a whole.

15. It is not clear to me that Hubert Dreyfus takes this into account in his various treatments of Heidegger's philosophy of science in *Being and Time*. Dreyfus seems to me overly fond of emphasizing the decontextualization of the ready-to-hand without insisting on the concomitant recontextualization or hermeneutic projection without which understanding is impossible for Heidegger.

16. Kuhn's distinction between normal and revolutionary science also evokes the distinctions Lyotard made, between making a new move in an old game, and inventing a new game altogether; and those Derrida put forth, between the invention of the same and the invention of the other. For an account of Kuhn and Derrida, see Caputo, *The Prayers and Tears of Jacques Derrida*, pp. 71–76. For Lyotard, see Jean-François Lyotard and Jean-Loup Thébaud, *Just Gaming*, trans. Wlad Godzich (Minneapolis: University of Minnesota Press, 1985).

17. Heidegger seems to think that such fundamental conceptual breakthroughs would be effected by regional ontologists; this makes sense so long as it is recognized that the revolutionary figures in the disciplines are their own regional ontologists. For Kuhn, they are made by people working at the most advanced and specialized level of puzzle-solving in that discipline. For more on the fulfillment of a predelineated horizonal scheme, see Edmund Husserl, *Logical Investigations*, Investigation 6, §1, chap. 1.

18. Martin Heidegger, *The Question Concerning Technology and Other Essays*, trans. W. Lovitt (New York: Harper & Row, 1977), pp. 117–118.

19. Kuhn seems to have in mind, however, only the Diltheyan sense of hermeneutics as historical empathy. He does not at all intend the Gadamerian view that scientific understanding depends upon *phronesis*. See Thomas S. Kuhn, *The Essential Tension: Selected Studies in Scientific Tradition and Change* (Chicago: University of Chicago Press, 1977), pp. xiii, xv.

20. Imre Lakatos, "Falsification and the Methodology of Scientific Research Programmes," in *Criticism and the Growth of Knowledge*, p. 178. This volume contains, on the one hand, a series of mostly critical responses to Kuhn: the contributions by Popper, Stephen Toulmin, and J. W. N. Watkins. P. K. Feyerabend, on the other hand, "defends" Kuhn by saying that science is indeed at least (and in fact even more) irrational than Kuhn holds, a defense that Kuhn describes as "vaguely obscene" (264) in his instructive "Reflection on my Critics" at the end of the volume.

21. Hans-Georg Gadamer, *Philosophical Hermeneutics*, trans. David Linge (Berkeley: University of California Press, 1976), pp. 201–202. I have learned a great deal about a rapprochement between Kuhn and Gadamer from Richard Bernstein's insightful application of hermeneutics to the problems of the philosophy of science in Richard Bernstein, *Beyond Objectivism and Relativism* (Philadelphia: University of Pennsylvania Press, 1984). In *Plato's Sophist*, trans. Richard Rojce-

wicz and André Schuwer (Bloomington: Indiana University Press, 1997), §§9ff., Martin Heidegger shifts the focus of the analysis of hermeneutic understanding from *phronesis* to *sophia,* but that seems to me more a commentary on the idiosyncratic genius of Heidegger than on Aristotle's text.

22. Hans-Georg Gadamer, *Truth and Method,* 2d rev. ed., trans. Joel Weinsheimer and Donald G. Marshall (New York: Crossroad, 1991), pp. 312–341.

23. The English word which seems to me to cover the range of all the sciences in the manner of the German *Wissenschaft* is "discipline." This word, of course, has a Foucauldian ring which, while foreign to *Being and Time,* would be a welcome nuance in the later Heidegger.

24. Heidegger's *Antrittsrede* at Freiburg in 1915, entitled "The Concept of Time in the Science of History," differentiated the historian's and the physicist's conceptions of time. See Martin Heidegger, *Frühe Schriften* (Frankfurt: Klostermann, 1972), pp. 413ff.; and my review, John D. Caputo, "Logic, Language and Time," *Research in Phenomenology* 3 (1973): 147–156.

25. See the first two essays in Heidegger, *The Question Concerning Technology and Other Essays.*

26. Heidegger, *Poetry, Language, Thought,* trans. A. Hofstadter (New York: Harper & Row, 1971), p. 161. I have discussed this and other related passages in *Demythologizing Heidegger,* chap. 7.

27. Heidegger, *Poetry, Language, Thought,* p. 166; Martin Heidegger, *Discourse on Thinking,* trans. J. Andersen and E. Hans Freund (New York: Harper & Row, 1966), p. 56.

28. For the full German text, see Wolfgang Schirmacher, *Technik und Gelassenheit* (Freiburg: Alber, 1983), p. 25.

29. Steven Weinberg, *The First Three Minutes: A Modern View of the Origin of the Universe* (New York: Basic Books, 1993).

7. The End of Ethics

1. In John D. Caputo, *Against Ethics* (Bloomington: Indiana University Press, 1993), I have developed the views expressed here in book length. To this should be added John D. Caputo, *The Prayers and Tears of Jacques Derrida: Religion without Religion,* in which I have put a more affirmative and slightly (ir)religious spin on these views.

2. The best introduction to Levinas's ethics is a series of interviews published in Emmanuel Levinas, *Ethics and Infinity,* trans. Richard Cohen (Pittsburgh: Duquesne University Press, 1985). The best place to find his ethics of the "absolutely other" is Emmanuel Levinas, *Totality and Infinity,* trans. Alphonso Lingis (Pittsburgh: Duquesne University Press, 1969).

3. I am drawing upon several of Derrida's works here, chief among them Jacques Derrida, "The Force of Law," trans. Mary Quaitance, in *Deconstruction and the Possibility of Justice,* ed. Drucilla Cornell et al. (New York: Routledge, 1992). For an introduction to Derrida relevant to this discussion, see John D. Caputo, ed., *Deconstruction in a Nutshell: A Conversation with Jacques Derrida* (New York: Fordham University Press, 1997).

4. See Jean-François Lyotard and Jean-Loup Thébaud, *Just Gaming,* trans. Wlad Godzich (Minneapolis: University of Minnesota Press, 1985).

5. See Jacques Derrida, "Psyche: Inventions of the Other," trans. Catherine Porter, in *Reading De Man Reading,* ed. Lindsay Waters and Wlad Godzich (Minneapolis: University of Minnesota Press, 1989), pp. 25–65.

6. Jacques Derrida develops this sort of argument against the euphoria of the new world order in Francis Fukuyama in Jacques Derrida, *Specters of Marx: The State of the Debt, the Work of Mourning, and the New International*, trans. Peggy Kamuf (New York: Routledge, 1994).

7. Jacques Derrida, *Politics of Friendship*, trans. George Collins (London: Verso, 1997), p. 46 n. 14. See Walter Benjamin, "Theses on the Philosophy of History," in *Illuminations: Essays and Reflections*, trans. Harry Zohn, ed. Hannah Arendt (New York: Schocken Books, 1969), pp. 253–264.

8. Lyotard and Thébaud, *Just Gaming*, p. 100.

9. See Jacques Derrida, *The Gift of Death*, trans. David Wills (Chicago: University of Chicago Press, 1995), chap. 4.

10. I have elaborated upon the way this Aristotelian ethic makes its way into contemporary ethical thought in Caputo, *Radical Hermeneutics*, chap. 9.

11. For more on the gift, see Derrida, *The Gift of Death*, esp. chaps. 3–4, and Jacques Derrida, *Given Time, I: Counterfeit Money*, trans. Peggy Kamuf (Chicago: University of Chicago Press, 1991). See also Caputo, *Prayers and Tears of Jacques Derrida*, pt. 4; and Caputo, ed., *Deconstruction in a Nutshell: A Conversation with Jacques Derrida*, chap. 5.

12. Jacques Derrida, *Points . . . Interviews, 1974–94*, ed. Elisabeth Weber, trans. Peggy Kamuf (Stanford: Stanford University Press, 1995), p. 199.

8. Holy Hermeneutics versus Devilish Hermeneutics

1. Then (Luke 24:36–49) they returned to Jerusalem, joined the eleven who were in a state of confusion and fear, where they are visited by Jesus again—"they thought they were seeing a ghost" (*pneuma theorein*). This time Jesus ate broiled fish to prove his fleshly reality to those of little faith. This reflected a second tradition, a bread and fish tradition, in addition to the bread and wine tradition, associated with Jesus. Jesus again explains the scriptures to them, opening their understanding (*nous*), explaining how he was the fulfillment of what was written in the law of Moses, in the prophets, in the psalms.

2. For an interpretation of this story similar in spirit to mine, see Nicholas Lash, *Theology on the Way to Emmaus* (London: SCM, 1986).

3. I can document this devilish attribution: Derrida says that he raises the specter of someone who addresses an audience but who does not really wish to be understood; he engages in this devilishness, not to revert to "a diabolic figure of the death instinct or drive to destruction," not because he is the devil himself, but because this bit of devilishness is a possibility of which we must take account, which must enter into the equation when we consider what is going on in communication. See Jacques Derrida, *Politics of Friendship*, trans. George Collins (London: Verso, 1997), p. 246.

4. Jacques Derrida, *De la grammatologie* (Paris: Minuit, 1967), p. 227.

5. See Edith Wyschogrod, "Eating the Text: Defiling the Hands: Specters in Arnold Schoenberg's Opera *Moses and Aron*," in *God, the Gift, and Postmodernism*, ed. John D. Caputo and Michael Scanlon (Bloomington: Indiana University Press, 1999), pp. 245–259.

6. Derrida, *Politics of Friendship*, p. 233.

7. When I capitalize "Origin" it is precisely to signify something out of reach, pre-original, always already deferred.

8. Jacques Derrida, *Archive Fever: A Freudian Impression*, trans. Eric Prenowitz (Chicago: University of Chicago Press: 1996).

9. Hans-Georg Gadamer, *Truth and Method,* 2d rev. ed., trans. Joel Weinsheimer and Donald G. Marshall (New York: Crossroad, 1991), pp. 295–298.

10. See John D. Caputo, ed., *Deconstruction in a Nutshell: A Conversation with Jacques Derrida* (New York: Fordham University Press, 1997), p. 8.

11. Jacques Derrida, "Nombre de Oui," in *Psyché: Inventions de l'autre* (Paris: Galilée, 1987), pp. 639ff. See Jacques Derrida, "A Number of Yes" (*Nombre de Oui*), trans. Brian Holmes, *Qui Parle* 2, no. 2 (1988): 118–133.

12. I refer the reader to the excellent exchange between Jacques Derrida and Jean-Luc Marion on the "gift" in *God, the Gift, and Postmodernism,* pp. 54–78.

13. Søren Kierkegaard, *Kierkegaard's Writings,* vol. VII, *Philosophical Fragments,* trans. Howard Hong and Edna H. Hong (Princeton: Princeton University Press, 1985), pp. 29–32.

14. See James K. A. Smith, "Respect and Donation: A Critique of Marion's Critique of Husserl," *American Catholic Philosophical Quarterly* 71, no. 4 (Autumn 1997): 538 n. 64. Thanks to Jamie Smith for pointing out that hypothesis B is an interesting countering of Marion's Christology.

15. Jean-Luc Marion, *God without Being: Hors-texte,* trans. Thomas Carlson (Chicago: University of Chicago Press, 1991), chaps. 1–2, hereafter cited as GB.

16. Marion, GB, pp. 106ff.

17. Graham Ward, "The Theological Project of Jean-Luc Marion," in *Post-Secular Philosophy: Between Philosophy and Theology,* ed. Phillip Blond (New York: Routledge, 1998), p. 234. My thanks to Tirdad Derakhshani for his critique of Marion and his discussion of the "hermeneutical decision" in an unpublished paper.

18. Jacques Derrida, *Points . . . Interviews, 1974–94,* ed. Elisabeth Weber, trans. Peggy Kamuf (Stanford: Stanford University Press, 1995), 96.

19. Jean-François Lyotard, *Le différend* (Paris: Minuit, 1983), chap. 1.

20. Jacques Derrida, *La verité en peinture* (Paris: Flammarion, 1978), pp. 372–373.

21. Jacques Derrida, *Speech and Phenomena,* trans. David Allison (Evanston: Northwestern University Press, 1972), p. 52.

22. Edward Schillebeeckx, *Jesus: An Experiment in Christology,* trans. Hubert Hoskins (New York: Crossroad, 1985), pt. 2, §3, pp. 320–398; on the road to Emmaus story, see p. 341.

23. Derrida, *De la grammatologie,* p. 233.

24. Thomas Aquinas, *Summa Theologiae,* Ia, Q.2, a.3, c.

25. See Ward, "The Theological Project of Jean-Luc Marion," pp. 229–239.

26. Søren Kierkegaard, *Concluding Unscientific Postscript to the "Philosophical Fragments,"* trans. Howard Hong and Edna H. Hong (Princeton: Princeton University Press, 1992), pp. 111–117.

27. John Dominic Crossan, *Jesus: A Revolutionary Biography* (San Francisco: HarperSanFrancisco, 1994).

28. When he distinguished the way of elevation and the way of descent, Johannes Climacus was speaking of the Incarnation. But I am arguing that revelation is subject to the same law, each being different ways in which God has spoken to us (Heb. 1:1–2).

29. Derrida, *Politics of Friendship,* p. 177.

30. As my colleague Michael Scanlon points out, Augustine, who read Latin a lot better than Greek, took the Vulgate translation of Romans 5:12: "*Propterea sicut per unum hominem peccatum in hunc mundum intravit, et per peccatum mors, et ita in omnes homines mors pertransiit, in quo omnes peccaverunt*" to mean that Paul

taught original sin. As Scanlon says, "From the Latin text *in quo* would mean 'in Adam all sinned' since Adam is the *unum hominem*. However, the Greek text has *eph ho* which could be translated into *in quo*, but the context renders the *eph ho* as an 'adverbial conjunctive'—'since' or 'because.' The New Revised Standard Version has 'Therefore, just as sin came into the world through one man, and death came through sin, and so death spread to all because all have sinned. . . .' Adam sinned, Adam died; we sin, we die. For in Romans 5:12, we 'inherit' death, not sin."

31. Women were certainly among the first and most important disciples, Mary Magdalene evidently being the most important among them. But the place of Magdalene and the other women was erased and displaced by the male disciples who took over the new movement. See Elizabeth Schüssler Fiorenza, *In Memory of Her: A Feminist Theological Reconstruction of Christian Origins* (New York: Crossroad, 1984), esp. pp. 323–334.

32. This is a paraphrase of Martin Heidegger, *Identität und Differenz* (Pfullingen: Neske, 1957), p. 71.

33. The trauma and shock of transcendence—"*[le] traumatisme de la transcendence*"—is of course the language of Emmanuel Levinas, *Autrement qu'être ou au-delà de l'essence* (Nijhoff: La Haye, 1974), p. x, passim.

34. Jacques Derrida, *La carte postale: de Socrate à Freud et au-delà* (Paris: Aubier-Flammarion, 1980); see p. 180.

35. See Schillebeeckx, *Jesus: An Experiment in Christology*, p. 752.

36. See Schillebeeckx, *Jesus: An Experiment in Christology*, p. 388.

37. Jacques Derrida, *Otobiographies: L'enseignement de Nietzsche et la politique du nom propre* (Paris: Galilée, 1984), pp. 13–32; Lyotard, *Le différend*, pp. 209–213.

38. See Jacques Derrida, "Force of Law: The 'Mystical Foundation of Authority,'" trans. Mary Quaintance, in *Deconstruction and the Possibility of Justice*, ed. Drucilla Cornell et al. (New York: Routledge, 1992), pp. 3–67.

39. This Magdalena de la Cruz is a suspicious character. I have heard from her once before, in John D. Caputo, *Against Ethics* (Bloomington: Indiana University Press, 1993), pp. 146–150. This text, I am convinced, is a forgery, forged by running together two famous stories, one from Mark 3:1–6, and the other Franz Kafka's famous parable "*Vor dem Gesetz*" from *Das Urteil*, upon which Derrida has written in "*Prejugés: Devant la loi*," in *La faculté de juger*, ed. Jacques Derrida et al. (Paris: Minuit, 1985), pp. 87–140. I think she has also come upon Derrida's "Force of Law: The 'Mystical Foundation of Authority,'" pp. 14–29. The reader will also detect shades of another story, Fyodor Dostoevsky's "Grand Inquisitor." Magdalena, I would say, has a deconstructionist itch to repeat with a difference.

40. Levinas, *Autrement qu'être ou au-delà de l'essence*, p. 24. In these final pages, I am, like Levinas, looking for the trace of the divine in the trauma of transcendence, in the call of the other. That is also congenial to Schillebeeckx who, after some six hundred pages of historical critical study, concludes that it is Levinas who captures the spirit of Jesus; see Schillebeeckx, *Jesus: An Experiment in Christology*, pp. 614, 638.

9. Undecidability and the Empty Tomb

1. Thomas Sheehan, *The First Coming, or How the Kingdom of God Became Christianity* (New York: Random House, 1986), hereafter cited as FC. Edward Schillebeeckx, *Jesus: An Experiment in Christology*, trans. Hubert Hoskins (New York: Crossroad, 1985; copyright, 1979), hereafter cited as J.

2. Edward Schillebeeckx's approach, which approximates closely that of Rudolph Pesch, has been criticized by Francis Schlüssler Fiorenza because it makes so much turn on this experience. See Francis Schlüssler Fiorenza, *Foundational Theology: Jesus and the Church* (New York: Crossroad Publishing Co., 1984), pp. 18–55. Schillebeeckx has responded to some of his critics in *Interim Report on the Books Jesus and Christ*, trans. John Bowden (New York: Crossroad Publishing Co., 1981). For the political troubles Schillebeeckx incurred, see Leonard Swidler and Piet. F. Fransen, eds., *Authority in the Church and the Schillebeeckx Case* (New York: Crossroad, 1982).

3. John P. Meier, "Jesus among the Historians," *The New York Times Book Review* (21 December 1986), p. 19.

4. Thomas Sheehan, "Revolution in the Church," *The New York Review of Books* 31, no. 10 (14 June 1984), p. 35. This piece provoked a storm of controversy in three issues of *Commonweal*, 10 August 1984, pp. 425–433; 21 September 1984, pp. 490–502; 5 October 1984, pp. 518–534, which drew some notable Catholic scholars into the fray.

5. Hannah Arendt, *The Human Condition* (Chicago: University of Chicago Press, 1958), pp. 236–243.

6. John Dominic Crossan, *The Historical Jesus: The Life of a Jewish Mediterranean Peasant* (San Francisco: HarperSanFrancisco, 1992), pp. 266ff.

7. "May it not be that Simon Peter—and indeed the twelve, arrive via their concrete experience of forgiveness after Jesus's death, . . . at the 'evidence for belief': the Lord is alive? . . . A dead man does not proffer forgiveness. . . . [This experience] thus became the matrix in which faith in Jesus as the risen One was brought to birth. They all of a sudden 'saw' it" (J, 391).

8. Meier, "Jesus among the Historians," p. 16.

9. John Dominic Crossan, "Our Own Faces in Deep Wells," in *God, the Gift, and Postmodernism*, pp. 282–310.

10. A. N. Wilson drives this point home rather mercilessly in A. N. Wilson, *Jesus: A Life* (New York: Fawcett Columbine, 1992), p. 256.

11. Emmanuel Levinas, *Totality and Infinity*, trans. Alphonso Lingis (Pittsburgh: Duquesne University Press, 1969), esp. §3, "Exteriority and the Face."

12. Derrida, *The Gift of Death*, pp. 82ff.

13. Jacques Derrida, *Specters of Marx: The State of the Debt, the Work of Mourning, and the New International*, trans. Peggy Kamuf (New York: Routledge, 1994), pp. 167–169.

14. Martin Heidegger, *Poetry, Language, Thought*, trans. Albert Hofstadter (New York: Harper & Row, 1971), p. 184. See John D. Caputo, "Heidegger's God and the Lord of History," *The New Scholasticism* 57 (Autumn 1983): 439–464.

15. See especially Jacques Derrida, *Spurs: Nietzsche's Styles*, trans. Barbara Harlow (Chicago: University of Chicago Press, 1979).

16. Friedrich Nietzsche, *The Will to Power*, trans. W. Kaufmann and R. J. Hollingdale (New York: Random House Vintage Books, 1968), no. 1041, p. 536, cf. no. 990, p. 517, no. 1052, p. 543.

17. Jacques Derrida, *On the Name*, ed. Thomas Dutoit (Stanford: Stanford University Press, 1995), pp. 89ff.

18. Crossan, *The Historical Jesus*, pp. 391–394.

19. Johanna de Silentio, a name meant to arouse the suspicions of any hermeneut worthy of the name, contributed a number of "lyrical philosophical dis-

courses" recorded in John D. Caputo, *Against Ethics* (Bloomington: Indiana University Press, 1993), pp. 150–174.

10. The Prayers and Tears of Devilish Hermeneutics

1. Meister Eckhart, *Deutsche Predikte und Traktate*, ed. Josef Quint (München: Carl Hanser Verlag, 1963), hereafter cited as Q. Meister Eckhart, *Meister Eckhart: The Essential Sermons, Commentaries, Treatises, and Defense*, trans. Edmund Colledge and Bernard McGinn (New York: Paulist Press, 1981), hereafter cited as CM.

2. Emmanuel Levinas, *Of the God Who Comes to Mind*, trans. Bettina Bergo (Stanford: Stanford University Press, 1998), p. 69.

3. For a fuller version of this argument, see John D. Caputo, *The Prayers and Tears of Jacques Derrida: Religion without Religion* (Bloomington: Indiana University Press, 1997), pp. 1–19. See also Jean-Luc Marion, "In the Name: How to Avoid Speaking of 'Negative Theology,'" Derrida's response, their exchange in the roundtable "On the Gift," and my commentary "Apostles of the Impossible," in *God, the Gift, and Postmodernism*, ed. John D. Caputo and Michael Scanlon (Bloomington: Indiana University Press, 1999).

4. See John D. Caputo, *The Mystical Element in Heidegger's Thought* (New York: Fordham University Press, 1986).

5. The best discussion of this is Bernard McGinn, "Eckhart's Condemnation Reconsidered," *The Thomist* 44 (1980): 390–414.

6. I discussed this point in detail many years ago in John D. Caputo, "The Nothingness of the Intellect in Meister Eckhart's *Parisian Questions*," *The Thomist* 39 (1975): 85–115.

7. Jacques Derrida, *On the Name*, ed. Thomas Dutoit (Stanford: Stanford University Press, 1995), p. 62.

8. See the roundtable "On the Gift," in Caputo and Scanlon, eds., *God, the Gift, and Postmodernism*, pp. 54–78.

9. In Reiner Schürmann, "Neoplatonic Henology as an Overcoming of Metaphysics," *Research in Phenomenology* 13 (1983): 25–42, the late Reiner Schürmann distinguishes Eckhart's "negative theology" (= the doctrine of God as a highest being, the subject matter of onto-theo-logic) from his "henology" (= the Godhead as a process of coming to be, *Wesen, Anwesen*), arguing that the latter, as a non-entitative experience of Being as process, overcomes metaphysics. This point also applies to Plotinus. I will touch upon this dimension of process and overflow in Eckhart in the next section of this chapter.

10. Jacques Derrida, "Circumfession: Fifty-nine Periods and Periphrases," in Geoffrey Bennington and Jacques Derrida, *Jacques Derrida* (Chicago: University of Chicago Press, 1993).

11. Jacques Derrida, "A Number of Yes" (*Nombre de Oui*), trans. Brian Holmes, *Qui Parle* 2, no. 2 (1988): 118–133.

12. Jacques Derrida, *Écriture et la différence* (Paris: Éditions de Seuil, 1967), p. 102; Eng. trans. *Writing and Difference*, trans. Alan Bass (Chicago: University of Chicago Press, 1978), p. 67.

13. Frank Tobin, *Meister Eckhart: Thought and Language* (Philadelphia: University of Pennsylvania Press, 1986), pp. 76–77.

14. Tobin, *Meister Eckhart*, pp. 171–179. See also Michel de Certeau, "Mystic Speech," in Michel de Certeau, *Heterologies: Discourse on the Other*, trans. B. Massumi (Minneapolis: University of Minnesota Press, 1986), pp. 80–100.

15. There is thus even a Marxist interest in Eckhart; see A. Hans, "Maître Eckhart dans le miroir de l'idéologie marxiste," *La vie spirituelle* 124 (1971): 62–79.

16. John D. Caputo, *Radical Hermeneutics: Repetition, Deconstruction, and the Hermeneutic Project* (Bloomington: Indiana University Press, 1987), pp. 265–266. See also John D. Caputo, *The Mystical Element in Heidegger's Thought* (New York: Fordham University Press, 1986), pp. 118–127, 173–183, for a comparison of *Gelassenheit* in Heidegger and Eckhart.

17. Jacques Derrida, "How to Avoid Speaking," trans. Ken Friedan, in *Derrida and Negative Theology*, ed. Howard Coward and Toby Foshay (Albany: SUNY Press, 1992), pp. 84–86.

18. See Jacques Derrida, *Ulysse gramophone: Deux Mots pour Joyce* (Paris: Galilée, 1987), p. 122.

19. Jacques Derrida, *Parages* (Paris: Galilée, 1986), p. 25.

Index

JOHN D. CAPUTO is David R. Cook Professor of Philosophy at Villanova University. His most recent works are *God, the Gift, and Postmodernism* (co-edited with Michael Scanlon); *The Prayers and Tears of Jacques Derrida;* and *Deconstruction in a Nutshell: A Conversation with Jacques Derrida.* He is also the author of *Against Ethics; Demythologizing Heidegger;* and *Radical Hermeneutics.*